MW01090049

WATCH THAT RAT HOLE

And Witness the REIT Revolution

KENNETH D. CAMPBELL

ARCHWAY
PUBLISHING

Archway Publishing books may be ordered through booksellers or by contacting:

Archway Publishing
1663 Liberty Drive
Bloomington, IN 47403
www.archwaypublishing.com
1 (888) 242-5904

Because of the dynamic nature of the Internet, any web addresses or links contained in this book may have changed since publication and may no longer be valid. The views expressed in this work are solely those of the author and do not necessarily reflect the views of the publisher, and the publisher hereby disclaims any responsibility for them.

Any people depicted in stock imagery provided by Thinkstock are models, and such images are being used for illustrative purposes only.
Certain stock imagery © Thinkstock.

ISBN: 978-1-4808-2316-7 (sc)
ISBN: 978-1-4808-2314-3 (hc)
ISBN: 978-1-4808-2315-0 (e)

Library of Congress Control Number: 2015919541

Print information available on the last page.

Archway Publishing rev. date: 1/8/2016

To Irene
My shining bride, whose
inspiration, indomitable spirit,
moral compass, and
sharp eyes made this work possible

CONTENTS

LIST OF EXHIBITS

LIST OF TABLES

APPENDICES

ACKNOWLEDGMENTS

So many persons helped bring this memoir to your hands that inevitably some will be omitted from this page. My apologies to all those overlooked.

First and foremost, thanks to my wife, Irene Campbell, the queen of the red pen, who has read every word at least six times and offered invaluable assistance on punctuation, grammar, tense and sense, and everything beyond. She frets that some undetected gaffe will make it into print, but I assure her that she is blameless and all errors trace to my fallibility.

Next to Irene stands my employer, CBRE Clarion Securities; my longtime partners, Ritson Ferguson and Jarrett Kling; and the firm's willingness to provide resources to complete this work. Maria Lucci used her artistic talents to develop the photo pages herein and helped overcome technical troubles on the computer and many other difficult obstacles. Administrative Assistants Kaitlyn Claas and Michele Laub typed and retyped spreadsheets, created graphs, and helped when needed most.

I relied upon a number of family and friends to give of their valuable time to read the manuscript and offer suggestions from their unique viewpoints. Five detailed critiques were invaluable from: my son Rick and his wife, Lois Campbell; my friend Ray Hoffman; and my colleagues Ritson Ferguson, Steve Burton, and Diane Wade. Other readers combed the draft and provided a helpful overview: my daughter Dr. Carla Campbell and her husband, Dr. Ron Ross; my son Douglas Campbell and his wife, Janie Bingham; and my granddaughters Katie Ross and

Grace Campbell. My colleagues Ritson Ferguson, Jarrett Kling, Dan Foley, Jon Miniman, Joe Smith, Chris Stephan, and Ken Weinberg added useful insights. Personal friends Bob Herion and Anna Wilkins also took valuable time to read the draft, and Ray Hoffman discovered that he and I both attended the same two games of the 1960 World Series. Small world.

Professional and business acquaintances who joined this valuable review process are widely respected real estate guru Peter Linneman of Wharton School at the University of Pennsylvania and Kimco Corporation founder Milton Cooper. REIT executives Leland Speed of EastGroup Properties, John McCann of United Dominion (now UDR), and Sam Zell of Equity Residential and Equity Office Properties provided invaluable detail on their roles in events. Bill King, longtime REIT expert at Goodwin Proctor in Boston, NAREIT General Counsel Tony Edwards, and NAREIT accounting expert George Yungmann added technical aid.

Longtime friend Frank Lalli was an early inspiration. To all, my deepest gratitude and thanks for your help. Yours is the honor from this work. Again, many, many thanks.

Ken Campbell
November 30, 2015

PREFACE

Why?

Throughout the writing of *Watch That Rat Hole*, that one question persisted.

Why dig through those old files moldering in storage? Why read and reread those long-forgotten *Realty Stock Review* issues? Why poke into nagging questions locked into the deep recesses of my brain? Why chronicle your actions in a ringside seat witnessing the REIT Revolution?

Writing this memoir was sometimes personally painful, forcing me to fess up to mistaken judgments and spreading on the public record events and experiences previously known by only a few family members or friends.

Let sleeping dogs lie, right?

This work began in 2009 as a letter to my children to answer a comment from one of son Doug's friends: "If I can figure out what Doug's father does, I'm going to do it too."

Perhaps that comment reflects the eternal divide between the parents' occupations and their children's perception of what parents do to put food on the table. Biographies and obituaries routinely refer to the subject's parents as shopkeepers, businessmen, or teachers, a shorthand way to explain the home environment and life station into which the subject was born. Often these references serve to indicate how the individual being profiled rose from humble beginnings to achieve some exalted station in life.

Take it as fact that great literature can be born from the desire to explain, or justify as the case may be, an individual's personal route from point A, his or her origins, to point B, his or her present station. In this context, that 2009 beginning was solidly within the normal desire of those of advanced years to communicate to subsequent generations roads taken or abandoned, risks assumed, and choices made, all with the unstated motive of helping those who may follow similar paths.

My effort moved from a simple letter to children when the late Bob Elfers, a longtime friend with whom it was impossible to have a brief or inconsequential conversation, wrote me a challenging note quoting Socrates' immortal dictum, "A life unexamined is not worth living." Somehow those words resonated and impelled me to analyze more deeply my work chronicling the REIT Revolution by editing and publishing *Realty Trust Review* and later *Realty Stock Review*, during the 1970s and 1980s. But by what standards?

I could obviously view *RTR/RSR* through the lens of its time or more rigorously through contemporary standards of heightened transparency to serve investors. I could use rubbery standards producing an inevitable whitewash, or I could measure my work against the eternal benchmark of innate honesty and integrity for investors.

Ultimately I reverted to my reporter's instinct to report what I wrote or said without editorial comment. It is what it is, without embellishment. The result may feel lumpy, like a sack of potatoes, to some readers. But I believe the result is also unvarnished Ken Campbell, and I hope reveals insights into my thinking and decisions as situations unfolded.

"Who would be interested in reading about the REITs, or real estate investment trusts, during their unhappy decades of the 1970s and 1980s?" asked one colleague, more attuned to the vagaries of the vastly different REITs and stock market of 2015. I reply that I hope to enlighten without preaching, to pass on to a new generation of professional strivers a few insights learned on stock market and business topics that never go out of style. My paradigms are my grandchildren and colleagues at CBRE Clarion Securities, mostly twenty- and thirty-somethings with long lives of knotty options and choices ahead. They constitute my eclectic sample of one hundred, future leaders and potential readers. It's my hope that retelling decades-ago events in the dawn of a new and vibrant REIT industry may offer guideposts to those facing today's challenges and opportunities in whatever setting and may inspire them to take paths less trodden, to try the new and unique, the unproven and unpredictable, and even the wildcard every so often. Let serendipity reign! Some "wisdom" acquired along the way:

PICKING PARTNERS

How does one choose partners and structure partnerships? My life is enormously enriched by three partnerships: with my wife, Irene, now sixty-four years in duration and counting; with Bob Dillmeier during the 1980s, embodied in the investment banking combo Campbell & Dillmeier and described in chapters 22 and 23; and with Ritson Ferguson and Jarrett "Jerry" Kling, my current partners in CBRE Clarion Securities, a relationship now nearing a quarter century in duration and covered briefly in chapter 25. Those chapters elaborate my principles for selecting partners and structuring these intimate relationships. I will not repeat them here.

HUNTING JOBS

My most successful job campaign was the quest for the one open spot at *House & Home* magazine in 1960–61. My initial turndown deeply disappointed me because I knew I had the right credentials and experience for the post. So while life was comfortable in Columbus, Ohio, I knew I was ready to move on to Manhattan and write for a national publication. My second call to the man who'd turned me down, Gurney Breckenfeld, was perhaps a desperate Hail Mary—but it turned up the fact he'd rejected me for an illogical reason. Six years later, I took a chance of getting fired by pursuing a slot at Standard & Poor's because I knew deep down my training and experience fit the opening. I got the job. Chapter 5, "The March" and chapter 7, "The Gestation," are my best advice to job seekers. Keep at it, and don't take a casual "No" for an answer.

PLANNING RETIREMENT

I've always considered the concept of retirement a snare and delusion, a social planning concept adopted from Europe's desire to create job openings for younger citizens. This goal of getting oldsters out of the workforce still prevails in the United States. Doubtless retirement is attractive to thousands, even millions, locked into unexciting and repetitive jobs. I did many scut jobs working my way through college, and I was determined to seek a better path in occupations presenting new challenges every day. That led to newspaper reporting, which led ultimately to the infinitely riskier decision to start our own investment publishing business and later to migrate into money management.

That mind-set begat the decision to pull up stakes from a comfortable niche in northern New Jersey and relocate to Philadelphia in 1994 in hopes that our start-up money management business could catch fire in serving investors. I was sixty-four, and Irene was sixty-two.

That decision produced a company managing over twenty-two billion dollars today, created jobs for my professional family now nearing one hundred persons, all younger than I, and generated more excitement than most persons experience in a lifetime. See chapter 25 for that story.

The business keeps changing, and while I no longer work in daily operations, the job evolves and I keep on working, arriving at the office before 10:00 a.m. five days weekly after thirty to forty minutes treadmill time and generally leaving about 5:30 p.m. I cheerfully acknowledge that my lifestyle is crazy, but it keeps me in contact with colleagues less than half my eighty-five years. Their new ideas and insights renew me daily and keep me young and fresh, and the paycheck helps. I cannot imagine myself settling into the inactivity of retirement, really.

GIVING BACK

I saw a license plate one morning that says it all: "GIV BACK." Irene and I have been blessed with economic success, and we seek to give back a portion of our modest achievements with intense involvement in service to others. We choose activity in two churches, the 304-year-old Baptist Church in the Great Valley in Devon, Pennsylvania, and Emmanuel Baptist Church in Ridgewood, New Jersey, because both are socially active and outgoing congregations seeking to make positive impacts within their local communities.

My interest in housing led to work with INCCA—the Inner City Community Action for Housing—in Paterson, New Jersey, in the 1970s where I shared that organization's pride in sponsoring about 240 new moderate housing units in that congested city. In the last fifteen years, Irene and I both have worked with BCS-YES—the acronym stands for Baptist Children's Services: Youth Empowered to Succeed—a nonprofit owning homes sheltering at-risk youth of all races and religions 24/7 in the Delaware Valley. We try to give these youth, many from fractured homes and with limited reading and math skills, a respite and boost, but resources are never enough.

These are not "give money to feel good" activities because both Irene and I were and are involved members and the many hours contributed far outweigh the dollars.

My lifetime in investments leaves me with these thoughts and insights:

ASSESSING CEOS

Understanding the strategic vision and personal risk/reward tolerance of the chief executive officer, or CEO, is crucial to success for any potential security investment. No investment manual or tutorial in my experience ever stresses that personal dimension enough. My day job has brought me into contact with several hundred company chief executives over the years. Learning the personal risk and reward tolerances of these CEOs, their mix of personal and corporate goals, is an art, not a science. No one individual's judgment is infallible, so I inspect closely what analysts and journalists are saying, all reflected in market trends. If these independent sources differ from my perception, experience teaches me to dig deeper. Looking backward, I see that I failed to appreciate fully the concentrated risks of Gene Phillips and his Southmark Corporation or the fact that Tony Gumbiner's rescue strategies with Hallwood Group took many years to mature (see chapter 19, "The Reit Catchers"). I am not perfect, but I am certain that every investor must always focus on this aspect, always.

The Internet and social media revolution now give individuals unparalleled access to CEOs' personalities and thinking via webcasts of quarterly earnings conference calls and other interactive encounters with analysts and investors. Serious investors will tune in both before and after making an investment in any company to pick up nuances in Q&A sessions not apparent in the written record. Use these opportunities profusely.

JUDGING MARKETS

The experience of four-plus decades teaches me that if a market trend looks too good to be true, it probably is. In retrospect, I overstayed the 1970–73 mortgage REIT bull market by two to four months and should have issued my sell signal earlier. Signs of deteriorating mortgage lending were all there in the market tea leaves—more frequent dividend cuts, earnings declines, builder bankruptcies, and rising nonearnings assets—but my optimistic nature excused the unfolding imperfections (see chapter 13, "The Sell"). Today, I look most carefully at market trends over five and seven years, compare company valuations to historic averages, worry about every unexpected event, and above all, try to estimate future actions by the Federal Reserve and other central banks. The advent of REITs with their accent on low debt leverage has greatly reduced cyclical swings for REIT investors, making REITs a moderately leveraged proxy for the economy. Their hardy track record of beating the S&P 500 by 1.6 percent annually over the past forty-three years and by 1.5 percent annually over the last twenty-five years makes them go-to stocks for the ages.

FISHING MARKET BOTTOMS

Picking values after major market sell-offs is *not* like shooting fish in a barrel. The most common mistake is entering the market too early. Chapters 18 through 20 attest that sharp-eyed bottom-fishers did not enter the market for fallen REIT angels until summer 1978, fully three and one-half years after the December 1974 bottom, and their activity continued for another five and one-half years. Bottom fishing is not for traders but for very patient stockholders. Most individual investors will profit from rereading chapter 18, "The Reit Chasers," to see how the Warren Buffetts of the world profited from that recovery.

SELECTING INVESTMENTS

I began investing in the 1960s as a typical in-and-out investor, picking stocks from random news reports and getting jerked around by short-term market swings. At first, this produced short-term losses, as told in chapter 7, "The Gestation," and detailed in Appendix II, which hurt even though I was experimenting with small amounts. As I gained experience, my stock selection got better and I learned to let my winners run while chopping losers quickly. Eventually, this strategy produced over $10,700 in gains or nearly 200 percent, enough to satisfy Irene's desire to have one year's income in the bank before venturing into the chancy business of starting a new business of writing investment newsletters.

Our 1969 investment in that venture proved very rewarding over the next quarter century, although we faced many stressful moments along the way. At root, we were investing in ourselves. Our later investments in Regency Investors and Central Realty turned up disappointing results, as detailed in chapter 23, "The Surprises." Over the years, we've also lost significant investments in private companies on three occasions, not detailed here, with the result that we no longer consider investing in any entity not publicly traded. Liquidity, thou art golden.

Individual stocks have lost their allure for us. We favor investing in carefully selected portfolios, generally mutual funds or other funds managed by our firm. Nonprofessional investors should survey the huge menu of fund products available to find something that meets their goals. Focus, please, on asset allocation to specific economic sectors, not individual stocks.

As to a holding period, we measure that in years, not days, weeks, or months. We review every holding quarterly, draw a personal balance sheet, and make decisions at that time. Hip-hop trading seldom wins and doesn't cut it in our household. One note: as an investment professional, I am required to report holdings and stock activity quarterly, which brakes frequent trading.

THAT REIT REVOLUTION

My rat hole slice of the 1970s and 1980s REIT Revolution emerges as a riches-to-rags-to-riches unscripted gothic saga writ large upon a sprawling canvass, with one ambitious memorable character after another entering and exiting, some achieving lifetime acclaim and riches while others depart in frustration, fatigue and even ignominy. Each play their roles against a backdrop of historic and sometimes cataclysmic events: the shedding of the gold standard in 1971 and soaring inflation and interest rates later that decade; the OPEC oil embargo in October 1973 and its unsettling ripples through real estate; the historic stock market flash crash of October 1987 and its seismic shocks; and even the first-ever resignation of a US president in August 1974.

The success of the REIT Revolution demonstrates that legal and financial innovations can equal the impact of the most dazzling technological innovations. To me, REITs prove that *Hello, Dolly!* Levi got it right when she said, "Money … is like manure. It's not worth a thing unless it's spread around, encouraging young things to grow." The underlying REIT principle of paying most earnings to shareholders without federal income taxes spreads money to shareholders, making REITs a powerful growth force in the economy. That principle is reflected in the success of mutual funds, master limited partnerships, and other pass-through entities. REITs took thirty years of churn, turmoil, disappointment, and experimentation, all detailed in these pages, to win recognition for their successes, which bespeaks the truth of this foundational concept of returning investment income to the people. REITs, primarily those owning commercial income properties, use this revolutionary idea to earn the trust of individual and institutional investors by minimizing risk through prudent debt leverage while providing investors with growing earnings and dividends.

Beyond the growth stimulus of boosting shareholder purchasing power, the REIT Revolution brings two other benefits. First, the revolution removes some sting from the real estate cycle by reducing overall real estate debt leverage. Supply and demand remain brute forces in our economy, as Sam Zell reminds us in chapter 20. But lower leverage keeps more people working by reducing the number of real estate bankruptcies in down cycles.

Second, the REIT Revolution broadens the amount of data available to real estate professionals and investors, and this enhanced transparency helps those supply and demand stallions race in better match. Public investors, who ultimately provide most of the money behind new structures, now have a better handle on the market risks they are assuming, thanks to a mountain of timely information available via the Internet. The REIT Revolution does not automatically give us perfect pairing of supply and demand in all instances, but today's commercial real estate world is certainly superior to, and much less riskier than, the one from the good old days.

DISTANT REPLAYS

My lot and joy is to witness how several hundred of the ablest and most ambitious REIT and company executives of the 1970s and 1980s deliver for their companies, mapping strategies and managing people, raising money and spending resources, ultimately accounting to their shareholder owners for their stewardship. I always try to call results as I see them, and my distant replays of events twenty-five years or more in the past provide mini–case studies and personal observations of nearly two dozen individuals. All are intended to highlight dos and don'ts for future executives and managers.

Chapter 18 profiles the disparate investment styles of the late Richard Rainwater, Carl Lindner, David Murdoch, Ivan Boesky, Warren Buffett, and a future president.

Chapter 19 looks closely at the 1980s and Carl Icahn's management of Bayswater Realty, the Belzberg brothers' conversion of State Mutual into First City Properties, George Mann's amalgamation of sickly equity REITs into Unicorp American Corp., Tony Gumbiner's creation of Hallwood Group, and Gene E. Phillips's helmsmanship of Southmark Corp.

Chapter 20 explores strategies that Leland Speed used in creating EastGroup Properties, Sam Zell employed in building upon the ruins of Great American M&I, Jim Harper found effective running both a short-term mortgage and an equity REIT, and Martin Bucksbaum deployed in a long and outstanding career with General Growth Properties.

Chapter 22 describes the mixed results investment banker Campbell & Dillmeier experienced with Clyde W. Engle and mergers creating Sunstates Corp.; mergers involving British Land of America and its successor, Medical Management of America; John McCann's sterling run building United Dominion Realty; and John Lie-Nielsen's unhappy stand with Johnstown-American Corp.

Chapter 23 takes you inside my two disappointing stints chairing two tiny public realty companies, Heitman Mortgage/Regency Investors and Central Realty Investors.

And chapter 25 tells the largely untold story of the controversial birth and lucrative death of Hallwood Realty Group.

Enjoy.

THAT NAGGING QUESTION

But back to the question of why.

Every writer writes to be read, and my writing of *Watch That Rat Hole* is no exception. It's my fervent desire that you will see this work not as rehashing long-dead events of years ago but as a living record intended to inspire, elucidate, and empower a younger generation facing today's challenges and typified by my aspiring colleagues at CBRE Clarion Securities.

To that end, I've cast the book's action in the present tense, hoping to recreate all the uncertainty and tentativeness prevailing when events were unfolding, often with unclear results. Events are treated in relatively short sections, generally running five hundred to two thousand words, all intended to make it easy to read short portions, lay the book aside, and return later for another dip into the action. Each chapter similarly covers a defined topic or period, again intended to facilitate easy reading or reference.

Five words for life stand out to me for everyone, especially aspiring professionals:

Learn—Nothing happens unless you learn from those who have gone before. Cutting class doesn't make it in a world demanding higher skills. So much is said nowadays about the wealthiest 1 percent that we as a society basically ignore the 1 percenters of academic achievement. Politicians have sold the top-down idea that education will improve if we just throw more money at it, again ignoring the bottom-up fact that true learning starts with a willing and motivated learner. The example of Abe Lincoln poring over books by firelight is lost. Yes, supportive parents, inspired teachers and well-kept schools help, to a point. I lucked out by having nurturing parents dedicated to learning. But at root, education is the responsibility of the student, not the teacher. See chapter 2, "The Prep"; chapter 3, "The Drill"; and chapter 7, "The Gestation," for my old-school approach.

Labor—I hoed corn, stocked grocery shelves, bottled laundry bleach, pumped gasoline, dug ditches, washed dishes, steered metal coils through steel mills, and delivered newspapers—all before graduating from college. Such jobs helped me understand how the world works and appreciate those doing unglamorous tasks on my behalf. I have been continuously employed since the age of twelve, except for my freshman year in college. Don't bypass labor, physically demanding or otherwise, because the psychological rewards far surpass the perspiration.

Lead—Prepare yourself to lead. Don't duck when it comes time to select the chair of some board or committee. You can accomplish more from the head of the table. And—foolish notion—you might just write a book about your life one day.

Love—Love whatever you do to earn your daily bread. If you can't summon up fire in the belly every day, you need to consider changing whatever you're doing. If you understand the merits of menial labor (above), you'll know that love for your fellow man and woman follows and pays big personal dividends. Love "the least of these, my brethren," as in Jesus's ringing call for social action echoing through the ages. Find a helpful spot, and fill it.

Live—Live life to the fullest. Try everything once. That's why I've eaten rattlesnake and other wild game—once. Find out what you are good at, and hone those skills. My life journey is equaled or surpassed by millions of Americans.

Don't duck or hedge in sharing your honest opinions with others. Hence a reminder: The views and opinions expressed herein are solely mine and not those of my employer, CBRE Clarion Securities, or any other entity.

Invest in yourself, whether in business, your family, or your passion.

Find *your* rat hole, and watch it eagerly, diligently, and, above all, happily.

You will never regret it. Blessings and peace.

Ken Campbell
November 30, 2015

Chapter 1
THE ASSIGNMENT

"Watch that rat hole."

The speaker is my new boss, Gurney Breckenfeld. As assistant managing editor of *House & Home* magazine (*H&H*), Gurney runs the best news operation in the housing business. The date is Friday, February 3, 1961—two weeks after John F. Kennedy's inauguration as the thirty-fifth president of the United States brings Camelot to Washington. It is my first full day in *H&H*'s Rockefeller Center offices in Manhattan.

Gurney's "rat hole" is journalese shorthand for a beat, a topic to be covered intensively and mined for future stories. Just as city hall and police headquarters were, in earlier times, my beats—my rat holes—Gurney is now giving me a new one.

I pay attention!

The rat hole in question that February day refers to real estate investment trusts, entities then freshly minted in the halls of Congress. Gurney's instruction does not imply that REITs are "rats" but makes REITs the prize actors on the stage on which I must concentrate my attention, my beat, my *rat hole*. And by extension that Rat Hole can be any imaginable topic that you, dear reader, choose as the focus for your life.

My boss and I contemplate for a few minutes the import of this legislation, signed into law by President Dwight Eisenhower the previous September 14 as a rider to a bill extending, of all things, a cigar tax. True then and now, the Feds get their money anywhere they can find it. Such are the bizarre workings of the sausage factory we call Congress.

The question before us is whether these new REITs would or could bring new mortgage money to merchant homebuilders and materials suppliers across the land, because they, our loyal subscribers and advertisers, are always on the lookout for fresh flush lenders. At that moment, the only real news is that pronunciation of the "REIT" acronym is already diverging into two camps—the one-syllable "Reeeeets" is already favored while the phonetically pure two-syllable "Ree-its" wins highbrow adherents. "Reeeeets" wins!

Gurney's command to "watch that rat hole" is accompanied by a whimsical smile and slight uplift of the pen in his right hand, as if cueing the tenors in a choir, a purely involuntary gesture reflecting Gurney's long tenure in an amateur Gilbert and Sullivan troupe. Gurney strikes an imposing presence, standing perhaps six feet or more, neither heavy nor thin, his hair already lightly speckled with gray, although he is only ten years older than I, and blessed with a wry, boyish smile that fascinates women and lifts the curse from any tart comment.

Thus it transpires that, on that day and forevermore in my mind, REITs become, in journalese, a rat hole—a potential news source on which a reporter, editor, or writer camps, like a ravenous cat, until from the rat hole emerges a "rat"—i.e., a story idea, often depending upon the writer's contacts, creativity, or chutzpah. That day, I understand my assignment is to keep a lookout for any news relating to REITs and bring any specific story idea back to Gurney. The entire discussion lasts a scant two minutes.

Gurney's assignment lasts a lifetime.

The rat hole watch becomes an animating force in my life, signifying the elusive pot of gold at the rainbow's end, the search for personal perfection that drives any and all of us to continual discovery and self-improvement, to deeper understanding of personal motives, and ultimately to our highest possible achievement. Watching that rat hole is why Columbus sailed the ocean blue, why Cortez sought El Dorado, why John Glenn became America's first astronaut, why Neil Armstrong took that "one small step for man, one giant leap for mankind," why authors dream of writing the great American novel, and why most of us strive for perfection in whatever pursuit turns us on. Watching the rat hole becomes the eternal thirst for adventure and personal achievement and recognition keeping us from taking life too easy.

For out of my rat hole marches a new industry, the real estate investment trusts, or REITs. Over the years and decades to come, the REITs overturn old notions of how commercial real estate is owned and financed, capture the attention of investors in the United States and around the globe, and bring new modes of real estate investing to Wall Street. They incite, from my vantage point, the REIT revolution, both in real estate and the stock market—and all from one innocuous rat hole.

At this point, I should introduce myself and detail how I arrived at this propitious moment. My name is Ken Campbell—Kenneth Dale Campbell on my birth certificate, if you must know—but I prefer the punchier version. I arrive at that brief moment in Gurney Breckenfeld's office at the intersection of two turning points in my personal and professional life.

On a personal level on that February Friday in 1961, I am a thirty-one-year-old father struggling to put food on my family's table. Professionally, I am a Manhattan newcomer freshly arrived from the hinterlands, and that Manhattan office encounter with Gurney Breckenfeld marks a personal pinnacle, given a pedigree of hard-scrabble beginnings.

Within days of that first encounter, I learn that Gurney is an editor not easily pleased or impressed. "The trade press is the soft underbelly of journalism," Gurney is fond of saying, making clear that his mission at trade publication *H&H* is to disprove his own pejorative and make its reporting quality the equal of any general circulation publication, period.

I like his dedication to no-nonsense journalism in ferreting out and reporting the news of housing and real estate, although, as I later learn, Gurney, like all of us, holds certain prejudices that sometimes creep into his selection of news topics.

He definitely favors small government, so stories pointing out any excesses in the federal bureaucracy find a sympathetic editor in Gurney.

He buys into Henry George's belief that only land should be taxed, so local property tax horror stories are guaranteed a big play.

Then, as now and for all time and for all media, the definition of *news* depends upon the selective eye, enthusiasms, prejudices, and sensibilities of the editor. News is what your editor says it is. Period.

Gurney can indulge his pursuit of quality news thanks to unstinting support from *H&H*'s owner, Time Inc., and its legendary founder and alter ego, Henry Luce. Luce and his Yale classmate and partner Briton Hadden start *Time* magazine in 1923 as the nation's first weekly news magazine to demonstrate their vision for innovative reporting of both news and cultural changes across a broad range of topics. In effect, they stick their thumbs into the collective eyes of every daily newspaper publisher across the land.

But Luce also loves architecture and building so much that the first magazine he starts, after the wildly popular *Time* magazine survives its dangerous toddler stage, is *Architectural Forum* in 1927, a vehicle that becomes an influential arbiter of good taste and quality in commercial building. When the postwar housing boom ignites, *House & Home* is spun out of *Architectural Forum,* with separate staff, readers, and advertisers.

Once I learn, some months earlier, of Luce's soft spot for architecture and Breckenfeld's cachet as a no-prisoners newsman, I set out to land a job with either *Architectural Forum* or *H&H*, above all other journals. After many false starts and painful rejections, this coveted job offer arrives (chapter 5, "The March").

My first assignment for *H&H* is to join Gurney and the *H&H* staff in covering the sprawling homebuilder's convention in Chicago's McCormick Place. That done and now back in our Manhattan offices, it is time to sit in Gurney's office for our initial news conference, a time to learn more about each other, a time to dole out assignments and set deadlines for a rookie writer (me), with me pretending this was just another ordinary day at the office. Gurney's nineteenth-floor office in the Time-Life Building in Rockefeller Center in Manhattan commands a sweeping view westward over the Hudson River and onward to New Jersey, where the George Washington Bridge peeks into view at the right. Gurney's office is unadorned and tiny, perhaps no more than eight or ten feet wide and fifteen feet deep, not at all what one might expect.

Worse, Gurney's filing system leaves precious little space for even a side chair for an outsider (me). Gurney's filing system can only be described as a gravity-defying architectural marvel—multiple piles of press releases, cables, query replies from correspondents, newspapers, notebooks, and unedited proof sheets, all stacked three or four feet high, some piles teetering precariously askew, spilling from the desk onto an extra-small table. In Gurney, the "file pile" mode of desk management finds its champion of champions. I learn in subsequent weeks that Gurney, and only Gurney, can retrieve any piece of paper he desires, at any time, from this unruly paper warehouse. For him, and for him alone, the *system* works.

For me, all this clutter matters not one whit. For me, this meeting signals heady career advancement, my first day in the rarefied atmosphere high in a Manhattan skyscraper in the editorial offices of a magazine published by Time Inc., the feared but envied publishing house created by Henry Luce. It makes scant difference to me that the magazine for which I toil this day is *House & Home*, a low-watt monthly trade publication with barely over a hundred thousand readers instead of glamorous million-circulation titles like the breezily iconoclastic weekly *Time* or the stuffily academic monthly *Fortune*. This is New York, New York, the center of the publishing universe, the big time, compared with Columbus, Ohio, where I polished my skills for nearly ten years.

I have arrived.

Watch out, world!

Chapter 2
THE PREP

My prep for the rat hole assignment starts with my birth on the second day of January of 1930, little more than two months after the October 29, 1929, stock market meltdown ushers in the Great Depression. I am delivered at home by a retired woman missionary doctor who happens to live across the street from the small white frame house rented by my parents in Grove City, Pennsylvania, about fifty miles north of Pittsburgh. My dad and mother, Ira Pressley Campbell and Madge Fausta Miller, set up housekeeping only seven and one-half months after their marriage in May 1929, when jobs are starting to disappear.

Dad is the fifth generation of Campbells to farm the rolling hills and sometimes balky soil of Concord Township in Butler County. John Campbell, born either in 1742 or 1746, according to family genealogies, emigrates from Argyleshire on Scotland's western coast sometime in the late 1760s or early 1770s and, after a sojourn in southwestern Pennsylvania, makes his way to Butler County, Pennsylvania, about 1796, the year Pennsylvania is opened to settlement. John takes residence in the hamlet of Hooker, then part of Slippery Rock Township but later subdivided into Concord Township. Along his way to the New World, young John meets and weds Ann Christy, a daughter of Ulster, Northern Ireland, and the couple welcomes their first son, Robert Campbell, in

May 1777 (the triple-seven date can be read as imparting good fortune to family offspring).

There follow seven other sons and one daughter. First son Robert marries Jane Cumberland, daughter of a nearby landowner, and Robert's only sister and one brother also marry Cumberland offspring, explaining why the Concord Township Cemetery displays an unusually high proportion of Campbell and Cumberland tombstones.

THE HOMESTEAD

The Campbell offspring stake out reasonably prosperous farms on the gently sloping hillsides and fields of Concord Township. Here, in about 1888, Isaac Pressley Campbell, grandson of Robert and great-grandson of John, pays two thousand dollars for eighty-five acres of farmland on both sides of a gentle stream and sets to farming with his new bride, Melissa Jane Gould. The farm, then regarded as one of Concord Township's finest, is graced by a handsome brick farmhouse. This sturdy dwelling—the walls are eighteen inches thick, providing surcease from summer's heat—becomes the homestead for eleven children, enlarging the number of hands to keep the farm running but adding to the number of mouths to feed.

Farming a small family plot in the last quarter of the nineteenth century is a precarious hand-to-mouth enterprise, subject to all the vagaries of weather and commodity prices, and with a growing number of mouths to feed, family lore avers that Isaac Campbell is falling further behind in his mortgage payments by the time the twentieth century rolls around. But, as in the ageless tale of the poor widow escaping the clutches of the greedy banker, help arrives at the last minute in the person of Emmet Queen. Seeking an outlet for bituminous coal underlying twenty-eight thousand nearby acres, Queen sends rail agents from his Great Lakes Coal Company to buy rights-of-way for a new Western Allegheny Railroad (WARR) to carry coal to New Castle (literally) in adjoining Lawrence County. The Campbell homestead stands directly in Queen's path to progress, and the WARR pays $1,125 in July 1903 for a swath of land—just enough to repay the mortgage, held by a local schoolteacher.

Thus by the time my father arrives in February 1907, the last of eleven children and twenty-one years younger than the firstborn, the Campbell farm is running on reasonably sound financial footing. Three boys go on to become farmers; two, including my dad, find work with nearby railroads, and one dies of appendicitis before he turns forty. Four of the five daughters find husbands, two of whom farm nearby tracts and two who move out of state. One daughter never marries and lives her life on the farm of an unmarried brother.

Father is in fact also named Isaac Pressley Campbell, making him a junior, but his elder sisters, charged with most child-rearing duties, hate the first name and begin calling him "Ira." The name sticks, and Dad goes through life as "Ira" until the error comes to light in a record search over sixty years later when he applies for retirement benefits. He must go to court to truly become "Ira."

THE MEETING

In his teens, Dad, now called Press by everyone, attends West Sunbury Vocational School, less than two miles from that stately brick homestead. At West Sunbury, he cuts a handsome figure playing basketball for WSVS and catches the eye of Madge Fausta Miller, a winsome brunette who walks three miles to school every day from the nearby hamlet of Euclid. Madge "finds religion" as they say and worries about her beau's wilder streak.

"He was not really the 'church type,' was rather wild, and this did not please my mother," Madge writes in a "letter" to her children many years later. "Nevertheless our romance grew."

Press graduates from WSVS in 1925 and finds work in the oil fields of Bradford, Pennsylvania, about a hundred miles to the northeast, but returns after six months "because of me," Madge writes. During their courtship, Madge recalls one instance when Press walked sixteen miles to be with her.

"Was this true love?" she asks. "I believe it was."

Madge, two years younger than Press, wins her diploma in 1927. Her brother Chester Miller, called Ched by everyone, and family head after their father dies in 1916, provides a comfortable home, stocked with books by Shakespeare, Longfellow, and Emerson. A railroad telegrapher who never marries because he is the family breadwinner, Ched turns misty-eyed when playing Beethoven and Fritz Kreisler on his beloved violin.

After her graduation, Ched sends Madge to business college in Butler, requiring a twelve-mile daily commute via the Bessemer and Lake Erie Railroad. After graduating, Madge wins an administrative job at Slippery Rock State Teachers College, about ten miles north of West Sunbury and newly purchased by the State of Pennsylvania after thirty-seven years as a private teacher training school.

THE UNION

During this time, Press asks my grandmother, Abbie McNees Miller, a tough, pragmatic single mother, whose husband died when Madge was eight, for permission to marry Madge, as required by state law.

She refuses.

On her own for the first time in her life, Madge dates Press a lot, and "when I had worked in Slippery Rock for about a year, I discovered that marriage was a 'must' for us," Madge later writes.

Press, who's been driving Chevy autos from Detroit to Pittsburgh, takes a job with the Bessemer Railroad, just before the couple set out in a Model T Ford, requiring frequent stops to tighten the brakes on the intervening mountains (no interstate highways then) for Cumberland,

Maryland. There, Madge waits in the car while Press buys a marriage license—"It was so easy at that time"—and they are united by a Methodist minister on a rainy Monday afternoon.

The date is May 20, 1929, five months before Wall Street crashes.

"My baby left me and got married," Grandmother Abbie Miller laments to her diary. "My heart nearly broke. I don't think I'll ever feel happy again."

When I enter the picture seven months later, Grandmother Miller writes: "Went to Grove City to see Madge Dec. 30. On Jan. 2 a baby boy [me] was born. I staid [sic] with Madge until her baby was 2 wk. & 1 day old."

It happens that Grove City is located in adjoining Mercer County, making me the first Campbell heir in six generations to see the light of day outside the confines of Butler County. Did this foretell my wanderlust? We shall see!

Before my third birthday, two more mouths are added to the new Campbell family, sister Lois Jane, born March, 1931, and sister Sue Joann, born October, 1932. Thus our family numbers five by the time Franklin Delano Roosevelt is elected president in November 1932 as Americans seek to break the Great Depression then ravishing the land and blighting the lives of young families. The growing Campbell family moves frequently as Dad seeks work, most often piece jobs whose erratic pay doesn't provide stability.

For a time, Dad snaps rock on two-lane macadam farm-to-market roads then being built. No job is more unglamorous and inglorious than snapping rock. At the worksite, unskilled laborers armed with sledgehammers reduce truckloads of stone—sub-boulder-size cold, hard stone—to pebble size for the road bed. Dad calls these highways *Pinchot* (pronounced *pin-shot*) roads in honor of Pennsylvania's then governor Gifford Pinchot (who pronounces his name *peen-show*). In truth, these blacktop roads likely are funded by the ubiquitous WPA (Works Progress Administration), a New Deal agency set up in 1935 to provide jobs for millions of out-of-work Americans. Dad also works for a time in the Wildwood, Pennsylvania, coal mines, but the black dust clogs his lungs and he moves on before the coal dust kills him. I still remember his coughing ugly black mucus for years afterward.

DEATH COMES CALLING

About 1934, our family moves into a white rented home on Route 8 in Unionville, a crossroads town about eight miles north of Butler, where the family expands once again with the birth of my third sister, Marjorie Ruth, in November 1934. Marjorie is born suffering from a severe form of spina bifida known as "water on the brain," or hydrocephalus, causing her head to grow monstrously large and robbing her legs of any mobility or feeling. Mother sees Marjorie's deformity as punishment for conceiving me out of wedlock, and this notion haunts her the rest of her days. If true, why not me? Why afflict Marjorie with such horrible disability? For me, the cause and supposed effect do not then, and do not now, compute. *Post hoc* is not always *ergo propter hoc*.

In February 1936, a month after my sixth birthday, I discover that Marjorie has stopped breathing during one of the many checks that became routine, everyday life in our home. Marjorie lived fifteen months to the day.

Marjorie's death—the euphemism *passing* is not yet then in vogue—marks my first close-range encounter with death. I still remember the hushed silence that descended upon our house the day "Marjorie went to be with the angels," as Mother explained. Something had clearly happened, for Marjorie was absent from our family. But six-year-old boys aren't given to metaphysical ponderings, and Marjorie is soon out of my immediate thoughts. Today, she lives as a "what might have been" memory.

A few months later, in late spring 1936, we move to an outbuilding at the Campbell family farm near West Sunbury, Pennsylvania. Now here is a real place for kids. My sisters and I spend the summer on extended "vacation," exploring the fields and orchards on this eighty-five-acre paradise and getting to know the resident horses—an aged workhorse named Prince is my favorite—cows, pigs, chickens, and other farm animals.

Politics is in season that summer as Kansas governor Alf Landon tries to unseat Franklin Roosevelt from the White House. Determinedly Democratic, my parents and paternal grandmother (my grandfather died in 1934) warn of horrible punishment if I misbehave:

"If you aren't good, we'll pin a Landon button on you."

But moving back in with one's parents is a bleak commentary on Dad's inability to find steady work during those hard times, although this certainly happened frequently. The togetherness likely weighs heavily upon the young couple's relations with Dad's mother, although we children never hear a complaint. The code of that era's farm life called on everyone to make do with whatever adversity life threw at you.

THE BIG CITY

All that changes dramatically in October 1936 when Dad is called to a yard switchman's job with the Bessemer and Lake Erie Railroad, an ore and coal-hauling subsidiary of United States Steel Corporation. To be close to Dad's new job, my parents determine to move the family to the "big city" of Butler, an aging western Pennsylvania steel town whose population peaks just shy of twenty-five thousand in 1940. The steel industry's decline does not deal kindly with Butler, and today Butler counts slightly more than half this number of souls.

Dad and Mother find our new home in Butler's workaday West End at Number 312 on an ash-covered street running straight up one of the city's many hills and appropriately named Ridge Avenue. On moving day in October 1936, three months short of my seventh birthday, I am entrusted with guiding the moving truck to our new home while Dad and Mother follow by car with my two younger sisters. We make it even though I have been there only once before.

The incident displays my innate sense of direction, which never deserts me, and an ability to handle jobs well beyond my years. Mother always said I was born as an adult, and maybe she had it right.

Ridge Avenue's name tells the whole story: we are about two-thirds up the hill and as close to heaven as any working family could expect in those parlous times. But the front porch affords a sweeping panoramic view of the city of Butler and its wondrous sights:

- the Butler County Court House high on the next hill, flanked by the stores and office buildings along Main Street
- the Pullman-Standard railcar plant, Butler's second largest job source, where workers turn out railroad cars before switching to American Bantam autos during the Depression and developing the prototype Jeep in 1940; the plant closes in 1982, throwing 2,800 persons onto relief rolls
- best of all, the local baseball park, snuggled close to the Pullman plant and home to the Butler Yankees, a farm club of the mighty New York Yankees, perennial champions of baseball. It matters not to me that the Butler Yankees play in the Pennsylvania State Association, a class D league, the lowest in baseball's hierarchy, or that they began play only that year and face a less-than-certain future. From our new front porch, the Yankee ball park spreads out right at my feet!

As I grow older, I learn that the Yankees grant admission to any urchin who returns a foul ball to the main gate. The park is small enough that most foul balls wind up on neighboring streets. Soon I become one of those urchins and spend many summer evenings racing for foul balls to see a free baseball game.

When the Oil City Oilers come to town, admission is all but assured because Al Gionfriddo, a wicked left-handed batter, is certain to foul several balls my way. Gionfriddo finally makes the big leagues in 1944 with the Pittsburgh Pirates and, after being traded to the Brooklyn Dodgers in 1947, is remembered for a spectacular catch of Joe DiMaggio's fly ball deep in Yankee Stadium's center field in game six of the 1947 World Series. DiMaggio kicks second base in a rare display of displeasure, but Gionfriddo never again plays in the bigs.

The Butler Yankees win league championships for three years running, 1940 to 1942, during the peak of my love affair with them, and breed a lifelong love of baseball that continues to this day.

The rented house on Ridge Avenue, then over fifty years old, is steel-town plain: basic kitchen, dining room, and living room on the first floor; four smallish bedrooms on the second floor; one bath; and a basement with a hard-packed earthen floor. Since money remains tight, the girls double up in one bedroom and Mother rents one upstairs bedroom for a time to provide extra cash. The house at 312 Ridge Avenue—or Poverty's Peak, as we dub it, half in jest, half in truth—becomes "home" to our family for the ensuing fifty-six years.

In that home, three more children are born. All six siblings attend grade and high school in Butler, all graduate, all go forth to their weddings, and all establish new homes of their own. From it, Dad ultimately begins his final trip to the hospital in 1991, and a year later, Mother, now a widow, moves from it to a new home in a retirement community. The house at 312 Ridge is stripped of its contents and becomes a cheap rental property under a new owner. Today, it looks unloved.

When we arrive in 1936, 312 Ridge is heated by a monstrous coal stove installed in one corner of the dining room. The stove requires constant feeding with coal (Butler lies in coal country), necessitating someone strong (usually me) to fetch coal once or twice daily from the basement's coal cellar in a large coal bucket. Every so often (every week, it seems to me), the stove belches and blows the stovepipes askew, requiring Mother to don heavy canvas men's gloves and reassemble the pipes so smoke can once again follow its appointed path up the chimney. All this travail vanishes a few years later when a brand-new furnace, still fueled by coal shoveled into an adjoining coal bin, is installed in the basement.

But the new house has running water (no need to fill buckets at an outdoor pump), electricity (no more oil lamps), and an indoor bathroom (no more trips to a too-often-cold and evil-smelling outhouse). For all its plainness, 312 Ridge represents ultimate modernity compared to life on the Campbell farm.

As the new man on the railroad's roster, Dad works the night shift, leaving for work about 10:00 p.m. and arriving back home in the early morning hours. We often find him eating breakfast when we arise for school.

"Be quiet. Daddy's sleeping," becomes Mother's constant mandate to me and my sisters. This routine never varies because railroaders work seven days a week without vacation in those prewar and World War II years.

Dad's night shifts continue until I am in high school, when his seniority finally earns him a normal second evening shift—but still seven days a week. The railroad brotherhoods finally negotiate a one-week vacation in 1947, the year I leave for college. But railroading is steady work and paychecks are always on time, so Dad sticks with the B&LERR until retiring in January 1969.

Mother thus becomes *de facto* head of household for all questions relating to school, conduct, and living. Big items go to Dad for approval.

One result is that I interact with my father infrequently. When I am very young, Dad cuts my hair with a pair of hand clippers that tend to pull hair more often than cut. He is making do with what we have because barbershops are expensive—a quarter for a haircut at one of the shops uptown in Butler. Today, Dad's hand clippers are among my most prized possessions, a reminder that all of us can make do with less when forced by circumstance.

As Depression babies of the 1930s, we learn to make do with what is available. Hand-me-down clothes are common, especially for my two sisters. That practice accelerates when three other siblings arrive: Jim Campbell, born in January 1939; Betty Campbell, arriving February 1941, and Press Campbell, born November 1945. Shoestrings are made to last as long as possible, and the last sliver of soap is squeezed onto one side of a new bar. All were little things then, all big things now in my memory.

Individuals and organizations—schools, clubs, churches—can easily succumb to making do with less than 100 percent of resources when finances become pinched, practices that can become habitual and pernicious and may persist for years. Breaking a make-do mind-set requires some person or event to sound an alarm for change, to lead members to a new promised land. Making do can be ennobling for a time, and everyone should survive a stint of making do to challenge and build character. But I struggle mightily to leave this pinched state. Departing make-do land becomes the path toward upward mobility that, for me, ultimately leads to my encounter with Gurney Breckenfeld and his assignment for a lifetime.

FIRST JOBS

Money is always tight in the Campbell household, and so in the summer after my twelfth birthday, I begin working as a farmhand on the McCullough farm near Chicora, with my cousin Lyle Campbell, my "twin" since we share the same birthdate. We hoe endless rows of corn, mow hay, and thrill at being "man" enough to be asked to help with threshing, a time when able males from nearby farms come to bring sheaves of wheat from the field to feed through a roaring threshing machine.

In the fall of 1942, I find work as a stock boy at the New Castle Street Fruit Market, a small store with sagging floors on heavily trafficked New Castle Street about three blocks from home. Proprietors Jack Isadore "Izzy" and Mary Mintz extend credit to Dad and Mom when they first move to Butler at the tail end of the Depression, and my job seems to enhance this family closeness. One or another member of the Mintz family guards the cash register with relentless zeal, mimicking my dad's relentless work schedule.

Izzy possesses dazzling mathematical prowess and can add the prices of a counter full of groceries faster than anyone can ring them up on that register. I always believe his numerical skills all but assured profitable weekly trips to poker games in nearby Youngstown, Ohio.

In my junior year of high school in 1945, I switch to helping George Varnum, a cheerful man always humming a tune, make and peddle Mon-D-Aid laundry bleach door-to-door. Varnum creates Mon-D-Aid from his own fertile imagination and is invariably called "the Mon-D-Aid Man." My job is to siphon hydrochloric acid from large glass vats in his basement into gallon jugs, add a prescribed amount of water, affix labels, and carry the completed bleach bottles upstairs to his garage for loading into the trunk of Varnum's black coupe. The pay beats the fruit market, and the Varnum house is only a few short blocks from high school. There, after an evening's work on April 12, 1945, George Varnum tells me that President Franklin Roosevelt—the only president I had ever known until that time—is dead.

After getting my driver's license in 1946, I work extra on Saturdays at

Mintz's, delivering the store's Saturday grocery orders all over town in the market's new International pickup truck. That weekly contact with public customers of varying temperaments and ethnic backgrounds—Butler's steel mill attracts immigrants from Italy, Hungary, Romania, Poland, and nearly every other European country on the map—bolsters my ability to deal with all manner of situations and instills a gritty work ethic. The exploits of Stan "the Man" Musial, a product of nearby Donora, are staples of conversation in those days because he is setting records almost daily with the St. Louis Cardinals, and his widely touted "play every day" motto seems a good example to emulate.

The onset of World War II changes everyone's daily lives, palpably. Izzy Mintz is drafted into the army and loses over fifty pounds during basic training; the Butler Yankees suspend play after 1942, and their young players march off to war; and schools sell war bonds and stamps and become depots for used toothpaste tubes, tin cans, and other metals needed for the war effort.

Less perceptibly, Dad, then thirty-five years old, is deferred from the draft and continues railroading, deemed an essential industry. Gasoline rationing limits pleasure trips in our family's 1936 Ford, although Dad is able to get some extra gasoline stamps from his farmer brother Frank, who qualifies for more generous gas allowances.

CASEY AT THE BAT

In 1944 and 1945, Butler organizes summer baseball youth leagues, and I sign up for a West End team, aspiring to be a catcher. The position appeals because I am short—five feet six inches—and the catcher is the field general, calling every pitch, positioning outfielders depending upon hitters' tendencies, and making things happen. Alas, my throw to second base is weak and erratic and my batting only so-so. From my baseball effort, I carry only one lasting legacy: the nickname "Casey" bestowed by a pitcher named Paul "Goon" Hiack. Goon never said whether he was sounding out my initials or referring to the famed poem, "Casey at the Bat," and I never asked. The sobriquet sticks with my family and is part of my e-mail address nearly seven decades later.

Butler contains ample opportunities for a young boy to get into trouble. Several other neighborhood boys and I roam a boyhood turf, extending about three blocks from 312 Ridge Avenue—from Sixth to Thirteenth Avenues to the east and west and between New Castle Street and Cleveland Avenue in the other directions. This turf is only partially built up with older, nondescript homes, but the good news for me is there are enough open lots that I never feel hemmed in. No one is rich, but we aren't poor either.

Pickup baseball games become a favored way of passing free time when leagues aren't going. The games are mostly played on the unforgiving red-brick playground of West End School. Wally White, the only African American in the crowd, possesses one of the wickedest curve balls I've ever seen and laughs in glee whenever he strikes out a batter. Others in this group include Bob Lehair, slim and muscular, and Ivan Dandois, just the opposite. Willie, whose last name is lost from my memory, is a wiry youth always pushing to bend the boundaries of conduct. One weekend, Willie and a buddy try to burglarize a grocery store but get trapped in the basement. We hear they are sent to a detention home in nearby Grove City. Willie never returns to our group.

As the eldest child, I follow the trail of a self-contained, somewhat introspective, and even nerdy boy who generally pulls the highest marks in the class. I love the intellectual challenge of schoolwork, of learning, of thinking, and even of composing poetry and fiction that turn out to be limp and turn my interest toward nonfiction. Above all, I learn how to work alone, a necessary trait for someone who's spent countless hours before a typewriter or computer keyboard staring at that infernal blank sheet of paper.

THE JOYS OF DEBATE

During high school, I come under the spell of Allene "Monty" Montgomery, a charismatic speech and drama coach ceaselessly pushing to elevate the skills and career aspirations of her students. First she teaches me how to stifle my innate fear of speaking before an audience and then how to make that speech persuasive and convincing. She casts me as U-boat captain Von Stumm in the school production of *Incognito* and then urges me to try debating. Monty becomes my first mentor, aside from my parents.

Debating turns out to be my pure cup of tea. I plunge into the research needed to build an opening speech defending my assigned side of the proposition in question. But the to-and-fro of rebuttal captures my full attention. During rebuttal, debaters must command both facts and speaking delivery in ad lib virtuoso arguments to win a nod from judges. I aspire to excel as a winning rebuttal debater.

Thrust and parry, parry and thrust.

Push and shove, shove and push.

I decide my persona best fits the role of Mr. Parry, Mr. Shove, the guy always pronouncing the last word.

Checkmate!

In my senior year, Butler debaters place second in the state championships, a good showing but a comedown from the state championship of the previous year. Both members of our negative team, Rod Norris and Armand Cingolani, go on to successful legal careers; my affirmative partner Bill McClung becomes an executive for Cleveland Electric Illuminating.

Debating teaches skills that virtually anyone can use to advantage in nearly all walks of life, and ever since, I have recommended the virtues of debate and public speaking without hesitation, whether asked or not.

When graduation day arrives at Butler High School, I am picked as one of seven valedictorian commencement speakers, even though I navigate the normal four-year curriculum in three and one-half years. About three of every five of my fellow male high school graduates go into the town's Armco steel mill, hoping for a lifetime paycheck. I too go into the steel mill, but only for the summer of 1947, to earn money for college, my consuming goal.

Most of my mill time is spent as a strip-guider on a stainless-steel annealing unit making sure long strips of steel coils remain centered on rubber rollers during processing—hot, smelly, and b-o-o-o-ring!

I follow the shift schedule standard for all mill laborers—a seven-day second-trick stretch beginning on Monday afternoon, followed by seven days on day shift, and then rotating to seven days of night shift, before emerging on Thursday mornings to enjoy a long four-day weekend. Come Monday afternoon, you dive back into the mill to repeat this pattern

My gross pay that summer of 1947 totals over seven hundred dollars for about 560 hours in the Armco mill, or about $1.25 an hour. Deductions are small and leave me in a good cash position.

OFF TO COLLEGE

During my senior year in 1946–47, my dad and I prospect for prewar cars stored during the war in barns and outbuildings on many farms because they are useless without gasoline. It marks my first real interaction with my dad as an adult. We find a 1929 Ford Model A coupe, apply a coat of black paint, and sell it at a good profit. A 1929 Buick sedan likewise needs only burnishing before turning another good profit. Our car trading nets close to two hundred dollars—good money for a young man still short of his eighteenth birthday.

In September 1947, four months shy of my eighteenth birthday, I hitchhike to Upland, Indiana, a speck of a town set amid flat farmlands, to enroll at Taylor University.

Except for three months following my freshman year, I never again live in my parents' house.

Chapter 3
THE DRILL

Those car-dealing profits help pay for about half the cost of my first college year, and I am awarded two hundred dollars in scholarships. My dad chips in with two hundred dollars, a surprise because by then I have five younger siblings and my reality is that railroad pay, although steady, leaves little room for college tuition in the family budget.

That two hundred dollars is the only financial help I ever receive from my parents with the exception of free room and board when I return home to work after my freshman year.

My freshman year at Taylor University turns out to be a mistake; the school's rigid moral code—no dancing, for instance—curbs my adventurous spirit, and the only work available is digging endless drainage ditches in Indiana's flat farm fields. The year stands out as one dreary detour.

In June 1948, the big money to be earned at Armco is too compelling to pass up and brings me back to Butler in summer 1948 for a second stint in Armco's mill. Again I am making do.

Higher ambitions drive me, and since becoming the first in my family to attend college, I want more. College is always on my radar, thanks to a Mother who tirelessly believes that education is the pathway to a better life. Always ready to read to her children, always ready with a brain-teaser question or puzzle, always ready with encouragement when bad news arrives, Mother is the eternal coach, egging me on toward the college goal. Being an upwardly striving male, I am eager.

Sadly, my father, perhaps mired in a backward look at how his own sisters handle their lives, refuses to countenance any suggestion that my younger sisters follow my college path.

Searching for both a better college education *and* job opportunities, I migrate, again courtesy of my thumb, in fall 1948 to Capital University, a small Lutheran-sponsored liberal arts college in the Columbus, Ohio, suburb of Bexley. One big incentive for switching to Cap is that Monty Montgomery, now Professor Montgomery, has also moved to Cap from Butler High School. At Cap, I find dedicated and skilled professors willing to go one-on-one with students.

Dean Reuben Smith faithfully lugs a briefcase nearly as large as his frail eighty-plus-year-old body to 8:00 a.m. Latin class without fail, whatever the weather, lingering over the lines of Cicero's *De Senectute (On Old Age)* as if reading a personal letter. Professor Paul Schacht labors so lovingly over the beauty of Shakespeare's plays that I become hooked for a lifetime. "To be or not to be?" Ah, that is always the question.

But George Dell and his English lit and creative writing courses steal my heart. Dell writes Cap's *Alma Mater* and is revered for his willingness to adjourn late-afternoon classes to his office where any student is welcome to free-wheeling bull sessions on any topic, no holds barred. I attend whenever my work schedule permits, and while not a single sentence of those sessions surfaces today, that access to a seasoned thinker and writer remains the most prized recollections of my days at Cap.

Late in Dell's life, his family finds a manuscript, written when Dell was thirty-seven, of a novel titled *The Earth Abideth*. The book is subsequently published in 1986 by the Ohio State University Press and made into a TV drama. Yes, George Dell is an outstanding mentor for a young aspiring writer, and he can write a pretty fair yarn after all.

Better, the Columbus metro presents a cornucopia of job opportunities. Within a week of landing on campus, I sign on as part-time service station attendant at the Sohio station scrunched onto one corner of campus, satisfying my need for tuition and spending money.

Three years later, in June 1951, Cap grants me a sheepskin "with honors"—a serviceable Midwestern degree but hardly the academic dossier you'd expect to catch on at the Yalie-elitist Time Inc. The words "With Honors" are sandwiched below my name because Cap's administrators didn't expect me to make the honors list. My late rush fools them.

And best of all at Cap, in June 1949, I serendipitously meet Irene Applegate, a prospective student, who finds me playing bridge with her sister Louise Applegate while checking out the campus. I like her instantly. She is pert and good-looking, with an air of holding very definite goals for her life. She wants to be a teacher and plans on enrolling at Capital in the fall. Better, she catches her bus homeward most evenings right in front of my Sohio station, so we can chat while she waits.

After a sometimes on-again, off-again courtship, she agrees to postpone her dreams of becoming a teacher in favor of becoming my lifelong partner. The commitment to marriage is a life choice not made lightly, advertising to the world that you will go forward on the family-first side of the street. At that time, we carry the invincibility that love bestows, an all-knowing belief that we can handle any adversity the world may throw at us.

We marry in March 1951, about three months before my graduation, and live in designated rooms in a spacious house about two blocks from campus. In 1951, the early marriage route is widely expected. Irene, however, is determined to shun marriage in favor of her career goals but ultimately decides to accept my proposal.

We make our choice without regret to this day, although Irene's pregnancy with our first son, Kenrick or Rick Campbell, four months after our wedding, initially brings remorse because it means Irene must put her career on hold. By the time I arrive in Gurney Breckenfeld's office a decade later, Irene and I have produced three children: Rick Campbell, born April 1952; Carla Cay Campbell, born February 1955; and Doug Campbell, born June 1959. Their births complete our family circle for then and all time. By the time I receive Gurney's mandate, our offspring range in age from nine to one and one-half years.

At a professional level, I am an aspiring writer whose cheese is making a mark as a writer in Manhattan, to my eyes the center of the publishing universe. Many, if not most, of my college classmates go on to careers in teaching or the ministry. But my goals diverge because my mother, a staunch advocate of reading and learning as the path to advancement, instills a love for the written word and admiration for those who inscribe words on paper. Her encouragement makes it no surprise that I become the first in my family to aspire to newspaper reporting and writing as a profession. But how to maneuver into that first reporting job?

Serendipity steps in, as it has on numerous occasions in my life! The importance of serendipity extends well beyond luck or good fortune or chance or happenstance, all implying that pure chance dictates the outcome of an event or a life. In contrast, the word *serendipity* traces to a Persian tale *The Three Princes of Serendip*, in which three princes survive life-threatening perils by using their powers of observation and deduction. Thus, *serendipity* implies that the ability to control life's events lies within our preparation and conduct and is not dictated by a role of the dice by some grand croupier. Webster defines serendipity as "the gift of finding valuable or agreeable things not sought for," but this definition skips the preparation part. And by leaning heavily on self-reliance, serendipity stands apart from the belief that providential intervention by a higher power shapes our lives.

FIRST REAL JOB

Serendipity plays its part in that first job search in this fashion: "Part-time" means anything less than a forty-eight-hour week to my employer Sohio, so I am able to put in many forty-seven-hour weeks pumping gas at that Sohio service station, at the corner of Main and Pleasant Ridge Avenues on the superblock then encompassing the Capital campus. Taking out student loans to pay for college is an idea whose time had not yet arrived, and working this part-time job, steady and close to campus, becomes an easy option that doesn't interfere with classwork and reinforces the notion, now sadly quaint, that if one wants something hard enough, one has to work and plan for it.

Serendipitously, one Sohio customer who fills his big bulky Buick regularly at my pumps is Don Weaver, the placid, pipe-smoking editor of the *Columbus Citizen*, a Scripps Howard afternoon daily newspaper of about one hundred thousand circulation. I plot to find the perfect time to hit him up for a job, and as graduation nears, one evening in early May 1951, I pop the jackpot question in my best no-big-deal manner:

"What can I do to land a job at the *Citizen*?"

"Come on down and talk to Don Easter, our city editor. He may have a summer job for you filling in for reporters on vacation."

Within a day or two, I find the *Citizen* doing business from a non-descript three-story building scrunched between two taller towers on North Third Street in downtown Columbus. An achingly slow self-service elevator carries me to the third floor where I am ushered without fanfare down a row of mismatched wooden and steel desks to the city desk, a semicircular corral of desks. The man in the middle is City Editor Don Easter, a pleasant, round-faced man of about thirty-five, tie loose and seemingly always harried.

"Show me what you can do," is his noncommittal answer to my job inquiry. The fact that I know Don Weaver, the editor, and am about to graduate from Capital matters not one whit. "Turn in a story so I can see what you can do."

"On what topic?"

"Pick anything you like."

"When?"

"The sooner the better. Make sure it gets to me in person."

How to fulfill this open-end assignment?

Presciently, I am drawn to a troubled real estate project for my first published story.

Serendipity again. The answer turns out to be in plain sight, an ugly unfinished building site directly across Main Street from the Cap campus. On that site, the city of Bexley seeks to build a new Bexley City Hall, a delayed job that to Cap students seems to stretch on endlessly.

I decide to find out what is going on. The receptionist at a tumble-down structure housing city offices at the time—"Bexley really needs a new building," I note—puts me in touch with the mayor, William Schneider, who turns out to be well connected in county Republican circles. He fills me in with a few facts—why the building is delayed (weather), how much it will cost ($250,000), latest anticipated completion date (September 1951).

He then puts me in touch with the general contractor, who describes a spiffy finished structure with mahogany paneling, terrazzo floor, and the city jail in the basement. I carefully turn these fact snippets into a page or so of copy and send it off to Easter.

Within a couple of days, on May 26, 1951, a five-paragraph story headlined "Bexley City Hall Behind Schedule," appears in the pages of the *Citizen*, and Easter calls to ask when I can start work as a summer fill-in.

Thus on the morning of Tuesday, June 5, 1951, with a diploma from the previous evening's graduation ceremonies safely sequestered in our apartment, a green-as-grass college grad signs on as a summer fill-in cub reporter at the *Columbus Citizen*, earning the grand sum of forty dollars a week—less than my Armco pay three years earlier.

That summer, I scramble as never before covering an unending stream of general assignment feature ideas handed out by the city editor, a process not unlike a fraternity hazing, testing my speed, observation prowess, versatility, judgment, and accuracy.

Within days, I am assigned to interview the national enforcement officer for the Office of Price Stabilization—the Korean War began a year earlier, remember. "Price control is one of the vital factors of freedom," my story quotes the tough-cop enforcer. "The price control program is so essential to the survival of freedom that we shall have no compunction about invoking every sanction and every instrumentality which Congress and the law have given us."

My twelve-paragraph story, with photo, appeals enough to the city editor that he awards a byline and the story sees print on June 8 under the headline "Price Chislers (c.q.) Face Fight, Official Says." The copy desk, and not reporters, writes headlines and is responsible for spelling. Four days into the job and already a byline, I flatter myself, even though the story is buried on page 22.

Within a week, that byline hits the front page for an interview with Lt. Col. Dean Hess, an Ohio ordained minister who logs 250 combat missions during a year's action in Korea. Col. Hess is outspoken in declaring that America's fighting men prefer total victory to a truce at the thirty-eighth parallel, a compromise being discussed at the time and later agreed upon. The story runs June 12 under the headline "Flying Parson Back from Korea," along with an engaging photo of Col. Hess showing his medals to his two young sons.

"I was so proud of this," wife Irene writes in a scrapbook she begins.

I too swell with pride because the sight of one's name atop a written work is, and remains, an author's adrenalin high and greatest validation of a job well done. In my pride, I never once question whether the article's appealing photo is responsible for the page 1 placement.

In July, the paper arranges for me to ride in a police cruiser with two Columbus policemen during their all-night tour of duty in a rough precinct bordering downtown. The prospect presents both challenge and danger. Because the Columbus police department almost never lets reporters get this closely "inside" its operations, the challenge is to take full advantage of this rare opportunity and not screw it up. The risk is that the cops might run into real trouble and someone might start throwing lead that cannot be ducked. The cops are Jim Maze and Chuck Barleycorn, not much older than I but obviously trained to handle a wide range of emergencies. During the night, they pick up a somewhat inebriated elderly man who claims he has been robbed of $125 while drinking with a man he remembered only as "Bill"; referee a standoff between a husband and a young wife who'd fled to her parents because "there's no food in the house … and he [husband] won't work"; and investigate routine fender-benders. The lengthy bylined piece runs July 15, 1951, under a feature headline, "They Meet the Unknown."

By summer's end, I am reliable enough to cover the Ohio State Fair, a big test because the fair reporter is charged with finding *three* separate lead stories—one each for edition at 10:00 a.m., 11:30 a.m., and 2:30 p.m.—so newsboys can hawk three separate headlines throughout the day. Only one example of these exercises in journalistic ingenuity survives, an August 25, 1951, piece under the unexciting headline "Half-Hourly Contests [at a fish pond] Popular."

By summer's end, City Editor Easter decides my skills measure up enough that my job can continue into the fall and beyond as a full-time reporter.

The end of my summer stint gives me time to push back and take stock of where I now stand professionally and competitively and assess what might lie ahead. The *Citizen*, I now knew, is a distant second to our afternoon rival, the *Columbus Dispatch*. I am told the two papers battled neck-and-neck in circulation until about 1931 when, during a bitter editorial feud over coverage of a banking crisis, the *Dispatch* cut its home delivery price to one cent per copy. Economic exigencies did not permit the *Citizen* to follow, and within a few months, the *Dispatch* opens a wide circulation gap, never again to be closed.

The *Dispatch*, with whom we go to war every day, has been owned since 1905 by the Wolfe family, which also owns other key outposts: the city's third daily paper, the morning *Ohio State Journal*, plus CBS-affiliated radio and TV stations; Ohio National Bank, then the region's largest bank; and the Ohio Company, then central Ohio's largest stock-brokerage and investment banking firm. Those key holdings bestow enormous economic clout on the *Dispatch* and the perception of that day holds that nothing major can get done in central Ohio without Wolfe family support.

The two papers battle over ad revenues—with the *Dispatch* holding an enormous edge—and exclusive news stories. The reality is that the web of Wolfe business interests and a network of politicians beholden to Wolfe support creates dozens of eager *Dispatch* tipsters. We at the *Citizen* must hustle to come up with unique stories for our readers.

A deep political chasm also demarcates the two. The *Dispatch* does not support a Democratic presidential candidate since Woodrow Wilson in 1916, while *The Citizen*, whose editorial, advertising and circulation employees are unionized by the Newspaper Guild, is far more likely to come down on the Democratic side.

As it turns out, the *Citizen* is in its final glide path into history by the time I leave the paper in April 1957. Two years afterward, the *Citizen's* aging and balky presses force it into a joint printing arrangement with the *Dispatch* that in turn requires the *Citizen* to merge with the *Ohio State Journal* to create a new afternoon paper masthead, the *Columbus Citizen-Journal*. The *Dispatch* switches to morning publication to circumvent mushrooming traffic congestion that effectively strangles home delivery for afternoon papers. The *C-J*, as it is called, folds in 1985.

To this young reporter in 1951, the two-paper rivalry is a daunting uphill challenge, but I thrill at the prospect of testing my skills against competition.

THE MENTORS

One personal benefit of continued *Citizen* employment, not lightly discounted, is the intangibles I stand to learn from working with an eclectic blend of experienced newsmen and women. Within shouting distance of Don Easter's city desk chair sit seasoned reporters, all at open desks and all plying unique tools of the journalist's trade. If serendipity equals preparation, then preparation must also include access to willing mentors. Inhabiting that newsroom are the following:

Ralph "Rip" Manning was a well-traveled journeyman and assistant city editor (the ACE), who sits opposite Easter. Dyspeptic by nature, Rip strives to upgrade writing quality by ferreting out cliches and hackneyed phases. "Let's declare a moratorium on 'Dreams come true,'" he scowls many times at any reporter guilty of leading a story with that hoary chestnut. Dozens of times, his vigilance squelches the offending phrase, and his repugnance spreads to the copy desk, which bans the phrase from headlines.

From him, I learn how to spot and highlight the drama inherent in news stories. At his urging, I am able to capture the drama inside the cockpit of an Air Force KB-29 refueling plane that encounters trouble one August afternoon in 1954 in the skies east of Columbus. My story, "Pilot Protected Lives on Ground," tells how the pilot directed his navigator to head the plane toward the least-populated areas before ordering his men to ditch the plane.

Rip insists each story have "an ass to boot," meaning the reporter must come up with some unexpected angle, some twist, some snapper to leave readers saying, "I didn't know that," or "Isn't that [fill in the superlative—beautiful, funny, ironic, horrific, tragic]," to give readers some sense of why the writer is moved to tell a story important enough for the editor to devote precious space to it and most of all, why they should care. There are more elegant ways of expressing the idea, but over the years, Rip's earthy phrase resonates in my mind because it tells it all. Rip later moves on to San Diego, where he dies about ten years later in his sixties.

Maurice "Maury" Portman, the *Citizen's* smooth-as-silk political reporter, can smell political intrigue intuitively. Maury teaches that every politician shapes his or her public persona to win votes and that the reporter must be ever alert for any nuanced change in a politician's public statements. When a politician's story changes, the reporter pounces to find out what's going on behind the curtain, fast. Maury leaves the paper in 1956 to become an aide to Mayor Jack Sensenbrenner. Still later, he runs for city council and ends his political career as council president. He dies in 2003.

Katherine Sullivan, who covers the "welfare beat," daily cajoles social workers and welfare officials for story ideas from their world of welfare privacy. From Katie, I learn the art of playing "dumb reporter" to unsuspecting contacts until the contact, seeking to brandish his or her superior insider knowledge, lets slip some nugget of information. Katie then pounces on this fresh meat and generally turns the contact's gaffe into an exclusive. More than once, I emulate Katie's masterful art when I need to penetrate an insider's defenses.

And **Perry Morison**, last but certainly not least, the "Old Sarge" to one and all, was then a thirty-year veteran at the *Citizen* and, at about fifty-six, easily the oldest reporter on the floor. Perry worked briefly for a railroad before enlisting in the army in World War I and serving as an infantry sergeant in France. He turned to newspapering in 1921 and survived the Great Depression at the *Citizen*.

"We took two 10 percent pay cuts which we handled with great difficulty. But that last 5 percent cut was a killer," he recalls. Pay cuts notwithstanding, Perry persevered and became the paper's expert on railroad, military, and union matters.

In action, Perry shouts into a stand-up phone as if its wires were nonexistent and pounds a typewriter with two fingers like a manic black-smith striking his anvil. But Perry also possesses an elephantine memory for names, places, and events, in effect becoming a living morgue [i.e., files of old articles] with total recall of long-ago news stories. His memory is so legendary that Perry is assigned to read the daily list of deaths, gar-nered by the obit writer from a canvass of hospitals, for his recollections about the names. I strive to make my memory the equal of Perry's. Perry retires from the *Citizen* for health reasons less than two years after I move on and dies in1962 at age sixty-seven.

From these role models, this reporter in this mid-twentieth-century American heartland is trained to be the true, honest, and impartial observer of human endeavors and events as they unfold, the one whose often unpleasant task is to strip masks from pretenders and the self-de-luded, see through the shams and scams of society, and arrive at the hard reality of truth. Just get the facts straight, no personal opinions, no personal involvement, no gushiness. Talk to as many sources as possible to glean the widest possible range of comment and opinion on the topic at hand. Like courtroom cross-examination, the ensuing thrust-and-parry commentary is likely to produce something approximating "truth." Transparency and truth are the Holy Grail, eternal verities the gospel of the journalist.

Gradually I learn the reporter's 1950s bag of tricks: how to find drama in a dishwater-dull press release; how to pick an attention-grabbing lead from a pedestrian interview; how to peer through the drabness of a city council meeting to latch on to some headline-grabbing action or event. The reporter's job is to tell a story in the most interesting and compelling way possible!

The reporter's overarching job is to ensure fairness and objectivity in the pursuit of truth. But as Pilate asked many centuries ago, "What is truth?" The reporter must know almost instinctively whether a source at hand is telling the "truth" or providing a slanted version to further some obvious or hidden motive. After a while, this "truth" screen becomes automatic and self-actuating; the reporter in you knows instinctively whether any given source is reliable. Some statements are invariably slanted, such as press releases and utterances put out by political parties and cause groups. Statements by parties involved in accidents, strikes, demonstrations, or other contentious events likely to become involved in litigation are also suspect but should be reported *if* the reporter gets or seeks comment from others who may have a contrary view. The reporter's job then is not to judge truth but to gather as much information as possible to let the public decide. In covering the annexation beat as detailed in the following chapter, I always carefully talk to all sides of any given annexation fight and never form an opinion of who is right. The reporter should not judge truth but facilitate airing of as many opinions as possible so full disclosure may illuminate ultimate truth.

Sadly, this objective standard of truth is antiquated in today's journalistic world, where reporters are encouraged to put themselves into a story so readers or viewers may empathize with their feelings. Such insertions flourish under the banner of "news analysis" or "context." However done, the reporter's job today is to infuse readers or viewers subtly with his or her own human perceptions of events. Thus the objective journalism of the 1950s warps into the subjective journalism of the 2000s.

The story of three umpires shop-talking their play-calling techniques is relevant here:

"I calls 'em as I sees 'em," avers the first ump, an existentialist.

"I calls 'em as they are," rejoins the second ump, an objectivist.

"They ain't until I calls 'em," vows the third, a subjectivist.

Until, of course, the call is overturned upon video review.

Thrust and parry, parry and thrust.

Push and shove, shove and push.

Listen and see, smell and observe, and then turn what the reporter sees and hears into instant history with fidelity, without bias, and damn the consequences. The reporter's dispatch stands as an on-the-spot, contemporary account of events. Commentators, columnists, talking heads, blowhards, and historians may later impart their spin to the events, but if the reporter does an honest job, the substance of what happens will stand for the ages.

Relative journalism has today morphed into advocacy journalism, featuring the hawkers and gawkers of convicted news media—think MSNBC and Fox—hurling carefully selected factoids at the populace in hopes of convincing them of the rightness and righteousness of their positions. Truth, thus unmoored from objective fact, falls victim to these dueling ideologies. Perhaps, just perhaps, back-to-basics journalism could improve the low estate of the fourth estate.

Thrust and Parry. Checkmate!

Not long into my newsman's tour, our newsroom is instructed to honor the precepts of Rudolf Flesch, whose *The Art of Readable Writing*, preaches the virtue of lowering the "fog index" in writing. That translates into reducing the number of words in a sentence—thirteen words is a good average to shoot for—and limit polysyllabic words that might not be understood by some readers. Literature it is not. Then again, today's newspaper will, its purpose fulfilled, wrap tomorrow's garbage.

THE EXECUTION

Late in 1951, Rip Manning talks me into volunteering to witness an execution at the Ohio State Penitentiary, hulking like a medieval fortress on the edge of downtown. Hence on the evening of November 15, 1951, at 8:01 p.m., along with a dozen other reporters, I watch as the State of Ohio straps twenty-eight-year-old Max Amerman of Medina into the electric chair and surges 1,950 volts of electricity through his body. He is dead by 8:10 p.m.

Amerman is convicted of talking mentally-slow eighteen-year-old Gerald Killinger into killing Harold Mast with a twelve-gauge shotgun blast so Amerman could continue his affair with Mast's Norwegian war bride Randi, even though Amerman is six hundred miles away in a New Jersey motel en route to the World Series when the murder occurs.

"He died like a man," my story in the *Citizen* quotes the prison chaplain.

"He died secure in his faith in Christ," says a Seventh-Day Adventist minister who baptizes Amerman.

But Amerman's death does not end the story. Accomplice Killinger is scheduled to ride the lightning bolt at the same hour the next evening. I labor into the wee hours crafting my story, partly because of the emotional impact and partly because Killinger's fate is unknown. As expected by many, Governor Frank Lausche commutes Killinger's death sentence the next day.

Much changes after that 1951 evening. The Ohio Penitentiary ceases executions in 1963, the prison is closed in 1984, and its massive stone walls and grim cellblocks are finally leveled in 1998 to make way for new downtown developments. Today, the Nationwide Arena, home to the Columbus Yellow Jackets National Hockey League team, stands near that long-ago prison yard.

Ohio, in common with many states, executes fewer prisoners now because of protracted legal appeals, while its death row population mushrooms. Did Max Amerman's death, or those of the other 314 men and women electrocuted at Ohio Pen, deter any future killings? Probably not.

Those early years are also filled with many softball, innocuous features in the *Citizen*.

Just before Christmas 1951, I interview the wife of entertainer Rudy Vallee, who brings twenty-eight pieces of luggage and two pet dogs on her Columbus stopover. In August 1952, I catch up with Indian prince Aly Khan when he stops to inspect racing horses on John W. Galbreath's Darby Dan Farm west of Columbus.

"I don't discuss that," the prince sniffs to questions on whether he hopes to patch up his rift with wife Rita Hayworth. He did not, and they divorce a year later.

In November 1952, the country elects General Dwight Eisenhower, on the Republican ticket, as president. The election means an all-nighter in the trenches at the Franklin County Election Board following local races. Momentously for me, 1952 marks the first year I can vote for president, and I believe I voted for Democrat Adlai E. Stevenson, whose famous photo displaying a hole in his shoe probably clinches my choice.

The year 1953 brings more varied fare: World War I flying ace Captain Eddie Rickenbacker, founder of Eastern Air Lines, cuts short his October visit to Columbus because of an EAL crash, and I tell how a thirteen-year-old Worthington lad wins the *Citizen*-sponsored Soap Box Derby in a repaired racer in July.

In 1954, I try, unsuccessfully, to find some truth in the story of death row inmate Russell Muskus's claim that he is innocent of a "badger game" killing in Canton, Ohio. I cannot find truth in Muskus's claims of innocence and he is executed the following July.

STOP THE PRESSES!

Only once during the *Citizen* years does someone actually shout that staple of fiction.

One Saturday evening, about 8:00 p.m., when everyone on duty is reading the first edition of the Sunday paper for errors, someone on the copy desk screams without warning: "Stop the presses!"

There, in the preprinted Society section, is a three-column headline remembered as: "*Welcome Back Charlie, Glad You Enjoyed Your San Quentin Quail.*"

A local theater manager returns from visiting a Florida restaurant with a trick menu that definitely is not family fare. Among the listed offerings, the manager says he enjoyed his "San Quentin Quail."

Every sentient male knows that "San Quentin quail" is a common term for jailbait: girls under the age of consent whose sweet favors could lead to a stretch in San Quentin, California's maximum-security prison.

Our society writer, an innocent fresh out of Vassar, obviously is unfamiliar with the phrase and falls for the joke. Hence that headline, of which no copies survive.

That Saturday night, the society section is replated with a new and unoffending headline.

Monday morning, the managing editor decrees that one male must read all society copy in the future.

The gulled society writer is Charlotte Curtis, who goes on to elevate society reporting at the *New York Times* with gritty, penetrating coverage during a twenty-five-year career, becoming the first woman to grace the *Times* masthead, according to *Wikipedia*. She dies in 1987 at fifty-eight years of age.

SHOTS IN THE NIGHT

And only once do I come under gunfire and then by accident.

One Saturday evening, responding to police squawk box chatter of police chasing a stolen auto in downtown, fellow reporter Harry Franken and I jump into a car and head to the scene near Grant Hospital in downtown. Alighting in a side street, we run toward Grant Avenue when we hear an ominous hiss in the air. One hiss. A second hiss.

The chased auto turns and is coming our way, and the chasers—the cops—are throwing lead at it from their .38-caliber service revolvers.

We duck into a doorway and press ourselves close to the wall. Perhaps we should have fallen to the ground, but that option didn't occur to us in the milliseconds we had to react.

Bullets hiss. Ssssssssssssss. All crime novels say they "whiz," but I can only testify to an ominous hissing sound as these slugs split the air.

Harry remembers three bullets; I recall only two.

But it only takes one.

Thankfully, none have our names written on them that Saturday evening.

THE QUESTION

In 1955, the *Citizen's* city desk leadership changes dramatically, with me in the middle.

City Editor Don Easter confronts me when I report for work one Saturday afternoon in November with an urgent message: "If anybody asks you, tell them that I called you this morning and asked you to come in to take over the desk."

Since it is now 2:30 in the afternoon, his request seems strange indeed. Saturday is the *Citizen*'s only day for split shifts—a relatively small group coming in very early on Saturday to put out the afternoon paper and a slightly larger corps of reporters arriving midafternoon Saturday to pull a lobster shift preparing the Sunday edition.

Very quickly, I sense tension in the air and am quickly told that City Editor Easter failed to show up about 6:00 a.m. that morning to shepherd the afternoon paper to press. Under intense time pressure, a skeleton force of journalists produces a slim paper.

Easter's absence is not unexpected to me, since he recently begins drinking more heavily. About a year before, Easter calls me in the wee hours to bail him out of the clink, where police have locked him after answering a late-night call about a man relieving himself at the rear of a closed drive-in restaurant. At that time, I rescue Easter from the law's clutches but say nothing to anyone at the paper.

But this Saturday is different. Shortly after my arrival, Managing Editor Jack Keller calls me to his desk—no closed office—and puts the blunt question to me. Did Easter indeed call me to fill in for him that Saturday morning?

Checkmate! I am trapped between that proverbial rock (Easter's job) and a hard place (my journalist's job).

If I support Easter's alibi, I am history.

If I tell the truth, Easter is history.

Thrust and parry, parry and thrust.

Push and shove, shove and push.

That day, I shove and tell the truth.

By 4:00 p.m., Don Easter, the pleasant but harried city editor who took a chance by hiring a green-as-grass college grad, is packing and heading for the exit.

I later hear that Easter bids good-bye to John Barleycorn, moves to Detroit, and lives a long and productive life. But I never see him again.

Courthouse reporter Pat Phelan replaces Easter as city editor, Rip Manning is promoted, and Ken Campbell becomes assistant city editor, an ACE.

But Easter's departure is still in my future when, in 1953, an event unfolds that reroutes my life's trajectory.

Chapter 4
THE BEAT

In November 1953, Columbus elects Maynard E. "Jack" Sensenbrenner as mayor by a scant 253 votes, the first Democrat to ascend to that office in over two decades. A slender, jaunty, fast-talking self-promoter, underdog Sensenbrenner chases votes ceaselessly in civic clubs, churches, and even funeral parlors, giving eight to ten speeches daily on a slow day.

His favorite word is "*spizzerinctum*," a quality Sensenbrenner defines as "1,000 times greater than enthusiasm," as Betty Garrett Deeds of the *Short North Gazette* writes in an April 2003 profile of Sensenbrenner's life. Webster defines *spizzerinctum* as "the will to succeed," with synonyms of "vim, energy, ambition." For me, the root words, *specie* meaning "money in coin or cash" and *rectus* meaning "right" (think rectitude or rector)—say it all. For me *spizzerinctum* always means simply the "right stuff."

Sensenbrenner carries a grand vision for Columbus into city hall and in his inaugural speech January 1, 1954, declares that suburban growth is choking Columbus's future and freezes water and sewer line extensions outside Columbus city limits.

"Freeze!" That single word evokes a collective yelp from the city's homebuilding and real estate fraternity, because the cozy days of dealing with compliant township zoning officials end with that single word.

From that day onward, homebuilders and real estate developers must annex development sites into Columbus city limits through a gnarly and uncertain legal process called "annexation." In Ohio, annexation requires individual landowners, called freeholders, to petition the three county commissioners to transfer their land from township to city tax rolls. Given that the land involved always bears taxable real property, of great present or future value, the cumbersome mud-wrestle called annexation guarantees that the outcome is anything but certain for developers anymore.

Corporations have no say in the process, ensuring gerrymandering to sweep tax-rich industrial and office properties into annexation tracts.

Annexation thus sets in motion a metro area political firestorm—town versus farm, "greedy" developers versus status quo "purists," big tax dollars in play all around, and the old order suddenly on the table. Today, we call the process urbanization, but in 1954 Columbus, annexation becomes one big guerilla war fought on multiple battlefields, between tax-protective township officers and revenue-hungry city boosters.

ANNEX OR NOT?

The *Citizen* taps me to cover the annexation beat. By then, I had built a franchise as the *Citizen's* go-to writer on all topics urban. The suburban homebuilding boom is in full bloom, and new growing pains pop up daily to vex readers. In August and September 1953, I write a thirty-part series titled "City in Traffic Chains" to spark public action to correct the metro area's most obnoxious traffic bottlenecks. To me, my choice for the annexation assignment is a no-brainer. Cities are growing, and I sit ringside, observing and influencing in some small way the directions in which our built environment unfolds. City Editor Easter concurs.

Serendipity, again.

A new annexation battleground opens every time and every place a developer persuades one or more freeholders to petition to annex his or her wannabe housing tract to Columbus. Covering this sprawling,

unruly annexation beat requires a combination of listening to public officials on both sides of the fight; schmoozing tirelessly with land
developers, homebuilders, and real estate landlords; attending untold
public meetings of all kind at all hours; and on occasion knocking on
homeowners' doors to learn what suburbanites really think.

In March 1954, I report that City Attorney Chalmers Wylie, later
a US congressman, unveils a comparison of home ownership costs in
Columbus and eight adjoining townships, asserting that most residents
will reap dollars-and-cents benefits from annexing to the center city. By
that time—less than three months after the onset of the freeze—petitions seeking to annex 1,760 acres to Columbus are filed with county
commissioners. And the city planning commission says petitions seeking
annexation of another 7,000 acres to the city are being circulated. If all
are approved, Columbus's forty-two-square-mile area would grow by 25
percent. Clearly, Columbus City Hall sees a big upside in winning the
annexation battle.

In late March, over two hundred Truro Township residents, on the
city's east side, line up a dozen township, city, and county officials to face
the music at a town hall debating annexation of 1,200 acres. The county
school superintendent says this is his fifth straight night of meeting with
citizens debating similar questions. Several parents take township school
officers to task for shortened school days.

"Is anyone in Columbus going to school a half day? Does Truro have
classes for handicapped children or for slow learners?"

Eventually this annexation wins a green light and becomes the site of
a major new housing development. Not so incidentally, the annexation
also blocks the suburb of Whitehall from ever expanding to its south.

In mid-April 1954, I follow Mayor Sensenbrenner as he carries
his annexation banner to the west side where over a hundred residents
gather to learn more about a defensive maneuver by township officials

to incorporate the whole of Franklin Township as "Franklin Heights." The twenty-three-square-mile township wraps around Columbus's west side and contains two plum industrial plants owned by General Motors and Westinghouse, a rich source of potential tax dollars.

"Save your township, and save your schools," Clyde Crandall, a township school board member, appeals.

"If the heart of Columbus caves in, you cave in with it, whether you incorporate or not," counters Mayor Sensenbrenner.

But the mayor's comments are ridiculed boisterously and his story falls on largely deaf ears. Township residents subsequently vote to incorporate.

The Franklin Township incorporation eventually fails, shot down by later court rulings. But the fierce opposition to annexation by Crandall and fellow township officers cows most homeowners from seeking union with the city. One revenue-rich plant remains a Franklin Township taxpayer in 2015, while the second is recently demolished to make way for a new-age industry: a casino.

IN THE MIDDLE

County Commissioners are clearly caught in the middle of multiple annexation squabbles and are accused more than once of changing their rules midstream. The law demands "an accurate map or plat" of the territory in question, and commissioners waffle several times by ruling as "inaccurate" maps omitting the first name of corporate property owners. Adherents call these errors trivial; commissioners contend they cannot search county ownership records without accurate names.

The Columbus City Planning Commission is revealed as the source of many of these plats, obtained by tracing over official maps (Xerox does not introduce the first plain paper copier for another five years). Every word is scrutinized.

The number of freeholders residing in many proposed annexations is contested and recontested. Opponents charge that some freeholder signatures are obtained by "fraud or misrepresentation." A rule letting freeholders withdraw their signatures at any time before an annexation becomes final adds bizarre complexities.

Messy, it is, but annexation gradually becomes the force through which the city of Columbus cuts the noose of booming suburbs.

My best single news source during those years is Harrison W. Smith Jr., a recent Princeton and Ohio State University grad who becomes the attorney of choice for annexation-minded landowners. Smith's practice booms, and he ultimately represents such clients as shopping center developer Donald Casto, suburban land developer Pete Edwards and his Edwards Land Company, Continental Realty, and New Albany Company, a real estate company backed by Limited Brands founder Les Wexner to build the wildly successful Easton Town Center and New Albany community northeast of Columbus.

Smith, who dies in 2009 at age eighty-three, probably does more to give concrete form to Columbus's drive for growth than any other individual, using his legal skill and dexterity to maneuver through the maze of Ohio's annexation laws. But Jack Sensenbrenner's native intuition and vision in pushing Columbus to bring the mushrooming suburbs under the city's legal tent makes him a patron saint of city growth.

Today Columbus claims the title as Ohio's largest city by land area, having quintupled its area from 42 square miles in 1954 to 211 square miles at latest count, a five-fold increase keeping Columbus among the ranks of fastest-growing American cities.

And Columbus' 109 percent population growth since 1950 has left its two big in-state rivals gasping for air, as both Cleveland and Cincinnati lose citizens by 57 and 41 percent respectively in those pressurized six decades. The recent bankruptcy by Detroit, loser of 61 percent of its citizens in that same span, along with a recent visit to the ruins of Ephesus in Asia Minor, remind me that no city is guaranteed eternal life.

Columbus's annexation skirmishes bring to the fore all manner of deeper economic and urban questions:

- How are cities to develop in the post-World War II years?
- Do new rings of suburbs make sense financially, aesthetically, and culturally?
- How will people commute to their jobs—car, train or bus—and can metropolitan areas afford to build new commuting arteries?
- What impact will Sensenbrenner's water and sewer ban have upon the price of suburban land and homes, and is it wise to turn farmland wholesale into look-alike housing tracts?

BLACK OR WHITE?

Also pushing to the fore are deeper questions of racial justice and the treatment of black citizens. Once the Supreme Court bans separate but equal schools in its famed May 17, 1954, decision *Brown v. Board of Education,* this burning question leaps to the top of civic agendas.

When I arrive at the *Citizen* in 1951, the newsroom is all-white and nearly all male, save for two women reporters and a few society writers.

The absence of black reporters or editors troubles me because, at the request of Cap's president, I room for one year with Paul Schooler, a talented young black man and delightful companion. We get along famously. Paul becomes a teacher but unfortunately dies at age sixty-three in 1991.

During my time covering the police beat, story suggestions are invariably greeted with one key question: "Black or white?"

If the answer is "black," the almost unvarying answer is, "Two or three 'graphs."

The Brown ruling reshapes the national dialogue on race in dramatic fashion. And this dialogue changes our newsroom, too.

By 1954, I author a lengthy feature on a black couple who become newlyweds at the age of eighty. James Lawson courted Eliza Coles in high school, but his marriage proposal was turned down. Both then marry other spouses who subsequently die, clearing the way for them to finally marry, half a century later. The story is capped by a three-column photo of the happy couple. "Black" is now welcome at the *Citizen*.

The national dialogue on race brings troubling questions to coverage of my annexation beat:

- What are the racial implications of mass suburban housing tracts, which tend to be all or predominantly white?
- Will white flight to burgeoning suburbs leave center cities with only poor and impoverished black residents?
- Are the nascent interstate highway and slum clearance programs inherently unfair to blacks because they promise to turn millions of blacks out of their homes in wide swaths of inner cities?

QUERIES FROM TIME

Both *Architectural Forum* and *House & Home* want answers from the field to these questions. Fortunately, the Columbus correspondent for *Time* publications is a *Citizen* colleague, and he hates everything urban and real estate and begins handing off Time Inc. real estate queries to me. As a result, my work starts to be known in the editorial offices of both magazines, although most requests consist of fairly mundane matters.

In November 1956, the most extensive of these queries asks for voluminous information about center city and suburban real estate prices for both land and completed commercial buildings. I spend countless evenings poring over county records at the courthouse and file two lengthy replies, of fourteen and twelve pages respectively, in November 1956 and January 1957.

"An uncommon political policy has intensified normal economics to jump suburban land prices practically over the moon in the Columbus, O., area," the first reply begins. Since the beginning of Mayor Sensenbrenner's freeze policy, "Columbus has annexed 21.7 square miles of land, a large part of which has been subdivided."

My research finds that raw suburban land prices rise 200 to 300 percent over the most recent decade. The reply cites numerous instances of quantum leaps in raw land prices: One man buys a tract at an estate auction in June 1949 at $127 per acre and then resells most of the acreage about four and one-half years later, at $1,517 per acre, or nearly a 1,200 percent markup. Homebuilder Ernest Fritsche sounds an optimistic note on suburban land price inflation:

"Sewers are the key. You can pump water most anywhere but sewers are a different problem. Once the city gets more trunk lines in, the price of land will level off."

I never know if anyone in New York notices the depth of this work, but I am satisfied that the questions are answered fully.

After covering annexations for nearly two years, in 1956, I am anointed the *Citizen's* city hall beat reporter. That assignment carries a prestigious weekly column on city politics, events, and conflicts. It also brings me in daily contact with Mayor Jack Sensenbrenner, the spizzerinctum man who makes city hall hum or sputter, depending upon your political bent. The legislative battles between Sensenbrenner and a GOP-controlled city council are frequent, across the board, sometimes vehemently bitter, and always newsworthy.

In June 1956, I quit smoking in this fashion: I awaken early Saturday, June 30, slip on some old clothes, and soon am busied with yard work— mowing the lawn, trimming bushes, and the like—at our 392 Yarmouth

Lane home. It is hot, but I keep at it, finally stopping at noon for a blow. While drinking some cool liquid, it hits me.

I have not touched a cigarette that day, which is very unusual for a three-pack-a-day man.

"Can I get through one day without a butt?" I ask myself.

Somehow I do—then the next day and the next.

I have been clean ever since.

Also in June 1956, President Eisenhower succeeds in pushing the Interstate Highway Act through Congress, arguing that the Cold War requires a national defense highway system facilitating rapid deployment of military forces. But the explosion in the amount of the nation's suburbs also requires an instant overhaul of horse-and-buggy highways choking cities. The act creates a twenty-five-billion-dollar program to build forty-one thousand miles of interstate highways, the largest public works program ever enacted until that time.

The prospect of serious federal dollars—the Feds now offer to pay 90 percent of highway project costs—galvanizes city and civic fathers, who've spent years planning an ambitious expressway network (to finally unchain city traffic, we at the *Citizen* proudly aver) but could never find the money to get bulldozers cranking.

THE COMMITTEE

With so much federal money suddenly on the table, Columbus's leading businessmen decide to set aside political divisions and organize a non-partisan group to get as much federal highway boodle as possible for Columbus. Where have we heard this story before?

In January 1957, they coalesce under the mind-numbing but politically correct name of the Development Committee for Greater Columbus (Where, oh, where is Rudy Flesch?).

In early 1957, the Development Committee, as it is becoming known, picks Annapolis grad and former city manager Robert Mott as the group's first executive director. Mott's selection reveals that these city fathers—including Charles Y. Lazarus of Lazarus, the city's largest department store; Preston Wolfe of the *Columbus Dispatch* and Wolfe family enterprises; and Edward F. Wagner of Nationwide Insurance, Columbus's largest employer—are pushing levers behind the scenes and prevail on Columbus to appoint Mott as unpaid but fully official express-way coordinator for both Franklin County and the City of Columbus.

Within a few weeks, in mid-April 1957, the committee picks me to head its public relations—read flack—and research. The official title is director of research and information. By then, I am maxed out on the union's Newspaper Guild pay scale. That means that Perry Morison, now a thirty-six-year journeyman, is making fifty cents more per week than I only because he is "grandfathered" under some long-forgotten guild pact.

This is not the future I envision. So, clunky name notwithstanding, I sign on with the development committee at a good salary bump from a journeyman reporter's scale. More serendipity.

Before long, I become bored with the molasses speed of PR com-pared to the fast pace of newspapering. The PR duties include scheduling ground breakings, ribbon cuttings, and other scintillating news events. But I also must produce an annual report for Development Committee annual meetings in May, an opening for more creative work. Ultimately, three annual reports emerge from my workshop, valued keepsakes today.

Early in my Development Committee public relations stint in Columbus, I return to the *Citizen* one afternoon and in a fit of remorse put this question to managing editor Jack Keller: "Could you find a spot for me?"

"How much are you making now?" he inquires.

"Eight thousand," I reply.

"Not a chance," he says wistfully, looking out over his newsroom jammed with perhaps thirty journalists.

"Kenny, there's not a man in this room making that—including me."

I often ponder what might have happened if his answer had been yes.

But the research half of my job is a ball, giving me free rein to poke into public transportation, parks and recreation, water supply and sewage treatment, city planning, and urban renewal, which was then called slum clearance.

CHRISTMAS CLASH

Slum clearance is just coming into vogue, again courtesy of the Feds. Even though Congress streamlines urban renewal in 1954, its mind-numbing regulations keep slum clearance in the shadows compared to building expressways. Then too politicians are understandably chary about using eminent domain to condemn people's homes and forcing them to move so their land can be sold at a later date to developers of new office towers or apartment buildings.

Columbus's slum clearers seek to combine their plans to uproot hundreds of low-income families on the near north side with expressway building, most notably in the Goodale area just north of downtown, named for a large neighborhood park. The Goodale Expressway, an early part of an inner belt, is planned to slice through the southern half of this area, nearly all occupied by black families and retailers, while slums will be cleared in an adjacent swath of racially mixed homes.

The race issue flares on December 13, 1956, just before I leave the *Citizen*, when sob sister Katie Sullivan breaks a story from her welfare beat headlined "70 Families Face Bleak Christmas."

Thirty-six buildings, "home to 279 men, women and children," may be razed under demolition contracts the state highway department plans to award on December 21, her story reads.

"Few have any place to go." The story explains that the city's Family Relocation Office has a dearth of property listings for suitable relocation housing.

"Most of them are Negro families. Listings for them would be ridiculous if they weren't tragic … White families have much less difficulty in finding places to move. They aren't confronted with unwritten laws prohibiting them from invading certain sections." (Racial deed restrictions are indeed still permitted in those days, and the "African American" designation is years into the future.)

"Columbus is faced either with mass evictions or a slowdown of the expressway," observes city slum clearance director Larry Irwin. "Rental vacancies for these people simply aren't available in size and quantity to meet their needs. The situation will only get worse before it gets better," he observes.

The story points out that highway builders aren't required to find alternate housing for families they evict, while slum clearance officers are mandated under federal law to find suitable decent relocation housing.

Katie's story touches a raw nerve at city hall, still my beat when this brouhaha explodes. No politician likes to be portrayed in the public prints as throwing poor people out of their homes on Christmas Eve, so city hall replies with vigor.

Maury Portman, who by then has shifted to city hall as Mayor Sensenbrenner's administrative assistant, fires a blistering broadside on December 20, reported under my byline in the *Citizen*.

"Reports of a large number of families facing eviction in the path of the Goodale Expressway are 'grossly exaggerated,'" Portman tells his boss in a report.

"No one is going to be evicted before Christmas," he says. "In fact it will be the middle of January at least before a demolition contract for the buildings is awarded."

"My signals are clear," City Attorney Chalmers Wylie chimes in. "My job is to buy land for the expressway, and there will be no delay. If they [Slum Clearance] can't relocate a relatively small number of families, how can they relocate for slum clearance?"

Translation: The bulldozers almost always win, and the people better get out of the way.

CLEARING SLUMS, BUILDING EXPRESSWAYS

But the question of where these displacees will go becomes one of the initial burning issues facing the Development Committee when I change chairs in spring 1957.

Thanks to the patient urgings of Chuck Brooks, Development Committee assistant executive director, and my initial Development Committee research on national relocation housing under Federal Housing Administration (FHA) Section 221, the committee's Slum Clearance and Rehabilitation Committee early on endorses a robust relocation program based on building new housing financed under FHA Sec. 221, providing up to forty-year loans at 90 percent of replacement value. Specifically, the all-white, business-oriented committee backs creating 1,302 new housing units mostly in predominantly white suburban locations. New housing projects include 647-unit Southgate Manor, Columbus's first Section 221 apartments, at a suburban location on Alum Creek Drive southeast of the city; the 180-unit Eastgate Apartments east of downtown on Maryland Avenue; and 307 new homes and purchase of 168 existing homes under Section 221.

All are supported by an all-white committee of businesspeople persuaded by my relentless research to face the plain fact that progress does not come without pain, that if you want to tear down to build, the only fair thing to do is provide a place for displaced men, women, and families to go.

Thus Columbus's white elites take a first painful step on the long road to ending segregated housing.

Those 1,302 homes are open to all comers, but their rents, financing, and cost are tailored to attract families, primarily black, uprooted by the expressway and slum clearance construction.

Bob Mott's expressway coordination soon begins to pay off in ribbon cuttings. Phase I of the Spring-Sandusky Interchange, where two major highways join at the confluence of the Olentangy and Scioto Rivers, opens for traffic August 29, 1956, with Phase II coming on stream September 14, 1957.

Just before Christmas 1957, on December 20, my car is the first to travel the newly built Mound Street Viaduct, a perk earned by arranging the ribbon-cutting ceremony. The viaduct eases a vexatious "traffic in chains" hotspot on the southern edge of downtown. Today the viaduct, along with the Spring-Sandusky Interchange and Goodale Expressway, are indistinguishable links in Columbus's expressway network.

The Goodale Expressway leg finally opens in November 1959, and a month later, the Third Street Viaduct, a traffic planner's dream for over fifty years, finally opens to unclog another long-standing city bottleneck. The Development Committee's May 1960 annual report, last of my PR career, pictures former Mayor Sensenbrenner, whose term has ended, and a longtime viaduct supporter gliding across the span in a 1909 Hupmobile symbolizing the viaduct's half-century gestation.

Meantime, slum clearance director Larry Irwin finally gets Washington's stamp of approval to begin the adjacent Goodale slum clearance project and bulldozers begin razing buildings on September 29, 1958.

"Back, back, cable taut, a shrug which barely stayed the backward track of the bulldozer, the shriek of sundered beams on the crisp autumn air, and bricks, mortar, and timber spewed dust on the tight knot of official and curious onlookers," I describe this event in the committee's May 1959 annual report.

"Demolition day has arrived for the Goodale slums."

By then, my work focus shifts to sewers and sewer bonds. It happens that Columbus has not built a sewage treatment plant in more than a generation, and the postwar housing boom leaves its aged plant seriously overtaxed. Since all major suburban communities depend upon Columbus for this vital service, sewage overloads put metro Columbus in crisis mode.

For decades, the city has depended upon sewer bond issues for money to build new sewer lines and plants, but new heavy construction demands strain this funding source. After poking around for far too long in musty ledgers to understand sewer financing, I write a report that persuades the committee's Water and Sewage Subcommittee to ask the Ohio legislature to extend the maximum term for municipal sewage bonds from twenty-five to forty years.

The legislature approves this change with only two dissenters in each chamber.

My acquired knowledge of bond financing remains invaluable even today.

Chapter 5
THE MARCH

One of my important Development Committee duties is to be the committee's eyes and ears for national trends in city development and planning, expressways and the new interstate highways, and urban renewal. In due course, I conclude that two Time Incorporated monthlies, *Architectural Forum* and *House & Home*, are best in-class news sources and subscriptions are duly entered. Monthly monitoring of their contents soon convinces me they are the New York Yankees of real estate publishing—and this Butler Yankee fan hatches a detailed plan to reach the big league club.

This incipient march on Manhattan requires expanding bridges to decision makers within Time Incorporated, all the while trying to break beyond my experience as a local writer and build a reputation as a freelance writer on national urban and community topics.

On the Time Incorporated front, my March 1958 attempt to win selection as the local *Time* correspondent replacing Ed Reingold, who had been hired for a slot in *Time's* Chicago bureau, is rebuffed politely ("We have tried to avoid public relationers as correspondents, since a clash of interests is almost inevitable," says the rejection letter).

A year later, in early June 1959, I pitch Roy Alexander, *Time* magazine's managing editor, to launch a new section on Urban Affairs. Naturally, I will be a primary candidate to head this coverage. Alexander's putdown is also polite but direct: "A second reading of your letter convinces me no more than the first that while your notion of an Urban Affairs specialty might have a place somewhere, that place would not be *Time*."

Later that same month, Irene and I take a half-vacation, half-prospecting swing through New York City that includes interviews at *Newsday* newspaper on Long Island and at Time Incorporated, where I meet John Titman, *Time's* personnel point man for editorial hiring. Somehow Titman clicks with me and becomes a target of my impassioned letters seeking a slot in the publisher's stable of magazines.

"After speaking with you," I write a year later in June 1960, "I conclude only a practicing writer can merit your serious consideration and pledge my spare time to the pleasure and profit of freelancing … To date the pleasure of again getting my typescript wet in the editorial inkstream has yielded the most productive and satisfying year of my life, albeit a somewhat meager one in profit taking."

The letter recounts several freelance sales to *Kiwanis* magazine and *Suburbia Today*, plus requested assignments by *Nation, True*, and *Suburbia Today*. I begin tackling diverse topics, ranging from traffic to labor relations to humor. "No scintillating success story perhaps, but my acceptance rate indicates I'll match my goal of selling one major article each month during 1960," I write.

"There is nothing in sight just now," Titman responds. "You might let me know if you plan any trips to New York for the future, and you might send along any articles you are doing which you think we might be interested in seeing."

TIME WORDS

Serendipitously, the Development Committee lets me continue moonlighting as real estate reporter for the local Time Inc. correspondent, Charlie Elia, later to preside over the daily *Heard on the Street* column for the *Wall Street Journal*. That gig brings in a few extra dollars sporadically but more importantly gives opportunity to put my wares, in the form of brief query replies, on the desks of key *Time* editors in New York City.

As this planned march to Manhattan dominates my thoughts, I prep for the days I can walk *Time's* golden corridors by extending my vocabulary. Thanks to a long-buried and now rediscovered file, I reremember that I read every issue of *Time* magazine sedulously ("diligent in application or pursuit; steadily industrious") to capture and dissect the nuanced meaning of every unusual word encountered there. The resulting list of Time Words catalogues verbiage favored by *Time's* writers and editors but outside the normal ken of discourse, along with their dictionary definitions. An example from September 8, 1958 is:

"Competence (quoted from Herbert Hoover): 1. Means sufficient for the necessities of life; sufficiency; without excess."

A WORLD SERIES TO REMEMBER

Unbelievably, the real-life New York Yankees play a role in my final march to Manhattan.

My boyhood heroes, the Pittsburgh Pirates, win the National League pennant in 1960 and the right to appear in the World Series for the first time since 1927, three years before I am born. Their opponents: the perennial American League champs and heavily favored New York Yankees. My allegiance is never in doubt: Pirates over the Yankees, despite that boyhood flirtation with the Butler Yankees.

Thanks to special tickets from Dan Galbreath, a Development Committee member and son of Pirates co-owner John W. Galbreath, my dad and I are able to watch the Yankees shellac the Pirates sixteen-to-three in game 2 at Forbes Field in Pittsburgh.

The date is Thursday, October 6, 1960. The following day, copies of my *Kiwanis* magazine article on national zoning arrive at my Columbus home, and I promptly dispatch copies, along with a cover letter detailing other in-process freelance articles, to both John Titman in *Time* Personnel and Joseph Hazen, *Architectural Forum*'s managing editor.

At that juncture, my old friend serendipity comes calling once again.

Early the next week, my Development Committee duties require me to attend the annual meeting of the National Association of Housing and Redevelopment Officials (NAHRO) in Detroit, about a three-hour drive north of Columbus.

There I strike up an acquaintance with Steve Thompson, then an associate editor of *Architectural Forum*, whose work I admire. Steve is regarded as an expert on Webb & Knapp, Bill Zeckendorf Sr.'s deal-a-day development machine. From *Architectural Forum*, I know that Zeckendorf merges his private Webb & Knapp into a tiny utility investment trust then listed on the Curb (American) Stock Exchange in 1952 and transforms W&K into the first headline-grabbing real estate vehicle trying to attract public capital from the New York investing crowd.

Zeckendorf's first major developments—Roosevelt Field Mall on Long Island in 1955 and Denver's Mile High Center in 1956—capture public imagination, unlike the creations of any previous realty titan for their grandiose scale, soaring architectural creativity, and the sheer audacity of their breathtakingly high debt. Thompson dissects many W&K projects and their financing in several *Architectural Forum* articles and maintains, in his talks with me, that if one follows Zeckendorf's projects through to final leasing and sale, all have been profitable ventures for W&K shareholders. But that is history.

Of more personal interest, Thompson tells me that Gurney Breckenfeld, *House & Home*'s assistant managing editor for the news department, arrived at *H&H* several years previously fresh from newspapering in San Francisco and established a reputation as a hardworking, no-nonsense editor. *H&H* and *Architectural Forum* share the nineteenth floor of the Time-Life Building at Fiftieth Street and Avenue of the Americas (formerly Sixth Avenue) and, although *H&H* has been spun out of *Architectural Forum* in 1952, staffs of the two magazines work independently and seldom cross paths.

H&H bills itself as "America's Industry Monthly for America's Biggest Industry"—the merchant homebuilding business that bursts into international prominence when Bill Levitt begins building his seventeen-thousand-home Levittown in a potato field near Hempstead, Long Island, in the summer of 1947. Demand for Levitt's identical 750-square-foot Cape Cod homes astonishes critics and well-wishers alike, and Levitt's highly publicized success is doubtless the midwife assisting the birth of *House & Home.*

From Detroit, I drive late into the night on Wednesday to reach Pittsburgh again, this time to use an improbable ticket to witness an improbable game 7 of the Pirates-Yankees World Series.

My ticket arrives through an unlikely turn of chance. Fellow Pirate baseball nut Ellwood Hill and I both write to seek tickets, chosen by drawing, for one of the final three games of the best-of-seven series, should they be played. Ellwood and I covenant that we would *both* attend if *either* of us got tickets. Amazingly, a few days later, a letter arrives bearing two tickets for game 7, should it ever materialize. Even more amazing, the underdog Pirates manage to carry the series to a deciding game 7, scheduled for Thursday afternoon, October 13, 1960, in Pittsburgh.

The back-and-forth game that played out before our eyes now ranks among the most acclaimed in baseball history for its pulsating drama. The teams battle until the Yankees take a five-to-four lead in the top of the sixth when Yogi Berra parks a three-run homer about four rows in front of our right-field upper deck seats. The Yanks tally two more scores in their eighth turn at bat. *Middle of the eighth inning, Yankees up by three runs, seven-to-four.*

In their next-to-last at-bat, the Pirates answer by scoring five runs in the bottom of the eighth, thanks in part to a pebble that deflects a Bill Virdon grounder just enough to hit Yankee shortstop Tony Kubek in the Adam's apple and thwart a potential double play. *Eight full innings in the book, Pirates up by two runs, nine to seven.*

That lead melts to zero in the top of the ninth inning as legendary Pirate hurler Bob Friend gives up two runs. *Middle of the ninth, score knotted at nine all.*

The disappointed home crowd stirs restively as Pirate second baseman Bill Mazeroski leads off the bottom of the ninth against Ralph Terry, a Yankee starter pressed into a relief role. Nothing on the first pitch. Then lightning strikes. Mazeroski deposits Ralph Terry's second pitch over Forbes Field's towering left field fence into Schenley Park. *Game over, Pirates win, ten-to-nine.*

It marks the first time in baseball history that a bottom-of-the ninth inning homer wins a World Series. For his heroics, Mazeroski ultimately enters Cooperstown's Hall of Fame.

Nineteen runs are scored in each game I witness during that series, with dramatically different outcomes.

Somehow, that victory by the upstart Pirates generates an inexplicable confidence that my march on Manhattan is nearing its end. The feeling doesn't make sense, but it does.

Many years later, one of my partners presents me with a golf hat signed by Bob Friend, the Pirate pitcher who fails to hold that ninth-inning lead. Life must go on.

A JOB OPENS

Back home again in Columbus, the November *House & Home* issue lands on my desk early the following week of October 17, and, wonder of wonders, the name of one associate editor is missing from the masthead. Taking advantage of that brief interview the previous summer with John Titman in *Time's* personnel office, I dispatch a letter saying, "Please forgive my brashness, but I've just learned … of a vacancy on Gurney Breckenfeld's news staff into which my interests, experience and capabilities might fit ideally." A carbon of that letter reaches Breckenfeld, and after I send samples of my work to both, we negotiate a job interview with Breckenfeld in New York City on Friday, November 11, 1960.

With my World Series adrenalin tailwind, I enter my Gurney Breckenfeld interview with sky-high hopes.

But first I must cope with the idiosyncrasies of Breckenfeld's work habits, not foretold by Steve Thompson. Breckenfeld, I soon learn, habitually arrives at his desk about 2:00 or 2:30 p.m.—after a lunch with a contact, he generally explains. After sorting through mail and phone calls, he generally is ready to launch into more serious work about 5:00 p.m.

And that's exactly when my hard-won interview starts, even though my plane lands at LaGuardia Airport at 10:36 a.m. The delay squeezes hard because I am booked on the last plane to Columbus that evening, leaving at 8:00 p.m. The late-afternoon start, when most everyone else is heading for a train or subway, leaves scant time to strut my stuff.

We talk, and Breckenfeld asks me to write a story based on press releases, notes, and other material he has assembled. I recall laboring on this assignment until very late before turning in copy typed on the preprepared three-carbon set used by all *Time* publications. Somehow a cab got me to LaGuardia for the 8:00 p.m. connection.

The time compression causes Breckenfeld to request a second article on Columbus' experience with relocation housing, which I duly send with a brassy cover letter:

"You doubtless can get someone to join your staff cheaper than I. But to me it's like buying tires—the more quality you buy, the safer your ride. At 30 I'm old enough to know precisely what I want, persistent enough to prepare myself for it and young enough to wait patiently for the exact opening. That time is now, *House & Home* is it."

REJECT DEJECTION

Within about three weeks, on December 7, a terse three-paragraph note from Titman awaits when I arrive home from work.

"Regrettably, we must turn you down for the news job," the operative sentence reads.

"The *H&H* possibility is kaput and the real reason is not fully apparent to me," I write in a plaintive letter to Steve Thompson, thanking him for his help in advancing my candidacy.

By some quirk of intuition or serendipity again, I try to call Breckenfeld during business hours the very day his rejection letter arrives but cannot reach him. That evening, I fire off a second note to Breckenfeld, explaining that my phone calls had been to present some new ideas because I did not want our brief acquaintanceship to end on a discordant note.

Five days later, on December 12, the December *H&H* issue hits my desk and sends me into a tizzy. My relocation housing story is butchered by sloppy editing. The final copy says the apartment complex's occupancy falls "to 13%" when my copy said clearly occupancy had fallen "by 13%" from 85 percent to 72 percent. One mistaken tiny two-letter word botches the facts.

"I perceive some erroneous conceptions, which most likely downgraded my sample assignment," I write. "Since the matter concerns me deeply, I'm forced to comment … I've spoken bluntly in hope you will recognize the constructive spirit in which the words are offered."

To me at that moment, defending the integrity of my reporting transcends any job potential.

COMEBACK SPEC

The next week, on December 20, I fire off to Breckenfeld a spec interview with a local mortgage originator arguing that many Columbus home-builders stand to take a financial hit on mortgage commitments because of recent interest rate swings.

"In submitting this copy, I ask no favors, only seek your fair judgment," my only reference to our so-far rocky relationship. "Merry Christmas," the letter closes. I follow this with a second brief bit of spec copy two days later.

Somehow this persistence convinces Breckenfeld and Titman that I am not going to vanish into the dark night, and early in January 1961, I am asked to provide additional supporting data to my job application. I do so with a three-page addendum titled "A Fresh Perspective on the Record." Here I pull out all the stops on the time-tested job-seeker's manual: describe the situation you find, what you did, and what resulted. Sample entry:

"Behind the Development Committee Record: 'When my new information and research position required financial analysis, I enrolled at Public Library U. and pored over accounting books until I could complete my task. In this manner I've completed refresher courses on statistics, graph making, architecture and real estate.'"

"If my work doesn't measure up, I am richer for having met you," the addendum concludes. "If it does stand up, both we and *House & Home* have benefitted."

Breckenfeld calls the following day to fix a follow-up interview date on January 10.

"You don't ask; you don't get," is my motto then and now.

When I arrive in Manhattan on the tenth, Breckenfeld has another assignment with more supporting paperwork, except this time he spends considerable time—perhaps an hour—expounding on the story's background and what the story should say. Needless to say, I follow his bread crumbs carefully in crafting a story that I now recall as only four or five carefully chosen paragraphs. This time, I leave about 11:00 p.m. and bed overnight in a nearby hotel.

JOB OFFER AT LAST

Within a few days, Breckenfeld phones to say he is favorably impressed and wants to go ahead with hiring me. He explains his initial hesitation as fear that if the position doesn't pan out for me, I will be left high and dry without a job after moving my wife and three children to New York. He offers $10,500 a year, about $2,000 more than I am then making with the Development Committee.

On January 18, 1961, Breckenfeld pens the words I ache to read:

"I am delighted you are joining us, and doubly delighted that you can get away to be in Chicago on January 29 for the NAHB (National Association of Home Builders) convention (held in Chicago's McCormick Place)."

On Sunday, January 29, 1961, I board a plane for Chicago and within a matter of hours am introduced to my new *H&H* colleagues at the Blackstone Hotel, where *H&H* staffers were staying. Coverage is fairly routine: lots of meetings to attend, press releases to read and interpret, and many new faces to interview. But it is a blast because once again I am a working journalist.

Was my march on Manhattan serendipity, premonition, luck, or divine intervention? I cannot attest to any of the above, but it probably combines all.

Thrust and parry, parry and thrust.

Check.

Mate!

In Chicago that January, I don my first tux to attend an event styled as the Turn Table Dinner. Ed Birkner, one of my new colleagues, devises the event to dramatize the emergence of merchant builders in the post-war years. Instead of waiting for their suppliers—think lumber, appliance, and wallboard manufacturers—to pick up the tab, these "Young Turk" builders "turn the tables" and invite their contacts from material suppliers to a spiffy black-tie dinner. The concept strikes a responsive chord, and about two hundred builders and their guests jam an upscale banquet room.

My serendipity genie also attends, and I find myself seated at a table with nine builders and their wives. By coincidence, all nine are Jewish.

"Kentilah," wickedly teases one of the builders, Abe Mitchell of Mobile, Alabama, using a familiar Jewish version of my first name.

"It is not right for you, a Gentile, to dine with us. We must first make you Jewish before we can dine properly."

Without warning, Abe and a second builder at the table, Sidney Lassen of New Orleans, rise and walk around my chair several times, all the while chanting incantations in a language I do not understand.

When this mock ceremony ends, Abe intones solemnly, "Kentilah, we now proclaim that you have been bar-mitzvahed. We may now all dine in peace." The bar mitzvah, of course, is the ancient rite by which young Jewish males are welcomed into manhood.

And that's the kosher story of how this Baptist-bred young man from western Pennsylvania came to be bar-mitzvahed in a banquet room-turned-synagogue in a brief ceremony presided over by make-believe rabbis.

For me, the story stands as a high honor indeed, retold many times. During a quarter century of doing business in New York City, I am able to assert with absolute truth and pride that I have indeed been bar-mitzvahed.

Abe Mitchell and his brother Meyer Mitchell, through Mitchell Company, go on to build over 25,000 homes, 20,000 apartments, and

175 shopping centers in Mobile and the Gulf Coast. In 1999, Abe, Meyer, and Meyer's wife, Arlene, endow the Mitchell School of Business at the University of South Alabama with a $36.6 million gift, and Abe additionally endows the Mitchell Scholars Program at USA.

Sidney Lassen forms Sizeler Realty Investors, a REIT named for his father-in-law, in 1986 and becomes an important actor in the growth of the REIT industry until Sizeler is taken over by a Canadian investor in 2005.

Within days of my faux bar mitzvah, I am on a plane to Manhattan and the *Assignment*.

Good-bye, Columbus, good-bye. You are a tenacious, trenchant teacher. Recalling details of those tutorial years—sometimes exhilarating, sometimes excruciating, always enlightening—carries the risk of boring those scanning these pages. But anything less than a full accounting would gloss over events and pressures that shape my actions, expectations, and outlook over the years since. Anything less than blunt honesty would cheat you, dear reader. To paraphrase Walter Cronkite, "And that's the way it was, February 3, 1961."

Viewed from the distance of over five decades, the events and contacts gleaned during the 1950s still tower as foundational prerequisites for carrying out Gurney Breckenfeld's staccato assignment to "Watch that rat hole."

From that rat hole emerges an entirely new industry, a revolutionary mode of owning, developing, and financing commercial real estate totally foreign to the established order of the 1950s, presenting stock market investors with the choice of investing in a previously unknown asset class, real estate. Today the REIT industry joins the transports and industrials, the utilities and the manufacturers, the high-techs and the low-techs, as Wall Street staples. My good fortune is to witness and partake in this REIT revolution from its infancy.

Commercial real estate, once built and financed by cozy country-club klatches and secretive syndicates of risk-takers willing to take a view on projects operating on 100 percent-plus borrowed money, is now dominated by publicly traded real estate investment trusts, whose debt leverage rarely exceeds 50 percent and whose every move is second-guessed by three dozen or more numbers-crunching Wall Street analysts and thousands of investors. This constant oversight and lower leverage convert volatile high-risk commercial real estate into a durable and reliable income-generating asset class suitable for risk-averse Wall Street investors.

But first, over five hundred REITs march forth from that Rat Hole. Thousands of investors lose untold nest-eggs on the test track trials of hundreds of REIT ideas and operators, their losses far outweighed by investors reaping untold millions and billions. In 2015, two dozen REITs have been admitted to that most prestigious index of all, the Standard & Poor's 500 Index, and real estate will become a separate asset class in 2016.

My lot is to witness and record the good and bad of all those pioneers, operators, developers, and sharpies emerging from that rat hole with their models for success.

But components of that dream for tradable real estate—an asset class standing toe to toe with industrials, rails, and techs—mutates importantly over the years.

"Safe" mortgage debt and the income it promises is supplanted by "riskier" real estate equity and the growth it may deliver.

Individual property focus gives way to concentration on large portfolios, generally of one property type, owned by one company.

Income down, growth up.

Parry and thrust, thrust and parry.

In and out, out and in.

Nothing sacred, nothing off limits.

Watch that rat hole, for it is the doorway to the REIT Revolution.

Chapter 6
THE BREAK

In the beginning, Irene isn't sure she wants to make the move to New York for complex reasons: perhaps the newness or unease with the supposed unfriendliness of the East or simple fear of leaving a comfortable life for the unknown. In the end, she teams with me in this new adventure because it means exciting New York.

The moving vans roll in the first week of March 1961, and we take up residence at S-15 Spring Valley Road opposite the Bergen Mall in Paramus, New Jersey, an old rental house I find while bunking temporarily with my cousin Pat Clynes and her husband Dick in nearby River Edge. The house has two floors instead of the single-story home at 392 Yarmouth Lane in Lincoln Village, and there, elder son Rick teaches Doug—then just 21 months old—the mechanics of going up and down stairs.

The house is within yards of Route 4, where I flag a bus each morning and negotiate a steamy trip down Manhattan's West Side on the Eighth Avenue Subway to reach the *H&H* office on the nineteenth floor of 1271 Avenue of the Americas—Sixth Avenue to true New Yorkers—at Fiftieth Street. Since my boss, Gurney Breckenfeld, habitually does not show up until well after noon and then works late into the evening, I am under pressure to work late almost every evening, often not arriving home until 9:00 p.m. or later.

So much for being a big deal writer in Manhattan.

Dragging home after twelve hour days delivers the distinct impression that no one in Manhattan really cares that this Ohio hotshot has arrived. During those years, Irene often asks the children if they want to wait for dinner until their father arrives home. They invariably choose to wait. Many very late and perhaps cold meals result, but I never learn of these daily dinner decisions until years later.

Irene works long hours too, caring for three young children—Rick is just about to turn nine when we move, Carla Cay is six and Doug nearly two—without the usual support system of other relatives. Irene dislikes the New "Joisey" accent with a passion and thinks most of the drivers, especially on Routes 4 and 17, are berserk. And the churches we try are certainly not like the numerous American Baptist Churches we loved in Ohio.

We inspect over 150 houses all over the New York metropolis, meaning most weekends are crammed with house-hunting expeditions. Finally we obtain a list of American Baptist churches and find our way to Emmanuel Baptist in Ridgewood, New Jersey, where Reverend Dee and Thelma Lowen welcome us warmly. This seems like home to us, and after a relatively short search, we buy a split-level at 542 Lynn Street in Ridgewood, New Jersey. We move just before Thanksgiving 1961. Finally we are ensconced in a house and friendly community, with children settled in excellent public schools and the property taxes to prove it.

I arrive at *House & Home* with an insatiable thirst to write for a national publication. Why does a writer write? The reasons transcend the pay, which is important but not dispositive. A writer writes because he or she thinks—knows?—he or she has something important to say to others. Whether one writes for pay as a professional or freelances without predetermined compensation, writing remains the ultimate form of self-expression and communication.

Today the challenge is to write so passionately and personally that others feel compelled to read. Printed books and newspapers are under siege from the electronic world so unceasingly that their very survival seems at stake. Yet the wide availability and easy storage without need of electronic gadgets give printed matter powerful advantages.

In college, I demonstrated enough writing skills to edit the college literary annual. In Columbus, I held my own on a metropolitan daily and honed experience in the nascent field of urban renewal. I freelanced with modest success. This stoked a yen to mount a national stage, to test my skills on a national level, to see my name on the masthead of a publication or to glory in a byline. At root, ambition is the trigger for this move to the unknown East. Hence the chase that lands my name as an associate editor on the *H&H* masthead and Gurney Breckenfeld's injunction to "watch that rat hole" of another nascent field, the REITs.

But at first *H&H* remains a job. A story is a story is a story, and you are not deeply and personally invested in any one story. Do your best with each assignment thrown your way and leave the deep thinking to Breckenfeld and the other editors. Daily routine at *H&H* differs from that of a daily newspaper in two significant ways.

First, the monthly cycle is deadly slow compared to daily newspapering. To compensate, you plot ways to add longer perspective and exclusive context to stories in hope the dailies won't catch up during the sweaty two-week-plus lag between final editing and publication. Stories are bigger and more complex, and you start lugging a briefcase home for the first time. Sometimes you yearn for the daily action and almost instantaneous feedback of a daily newspaper, but you've chosen to strike out on a path followed by few, and you'd better stick to it.

Second, the pay! At *H&H* my starting annual pay as a rookie associate editor is $10,500—about $84,000 in 2015 dollars—but this is New York's wage scale, not Columbus's, as I and my family soon learn. Now I'm earning two thousand more than in Columbus, but it's a stretch for Irene and the children. Commuting even by bus is expensive and consumes over an hour each way.

House & Home is organized like a pair of matched stallions. The news section, where I sit, is run almost independently by Gurney with the title of assistant managing editor, or AME, from the midbook, or feature, section.

News, a late-close set of pages carrying breaking news of the housing industry, covers national and local housing policy and politics, urban redevelopment, and mortgage money availability and pricing.

The homebuilding industry is just beginning its march to raise capital in public markets and the rush to Wall Street becomes a major part of news coverage, and with the team, I begin tracking prices and activities of newly public companies like homebuilders, savings and loans, mortgage bankers, land developers, prefab and shell home builders, and real estate investment trusts, or REITs. The newly-legalized REITs are my "rat hole." It's a steep learning curve because until then Wall Street is *terra incognita*.

The news staff actually consists of two other persons, a blazingly fast researcher named Cecille Steinberg and a second associate editor, John Gerfin. The gulf between Breckenfeld and Gerfin becomes clear almost immediately when, during our interviews, Breckenfeld complains that he has to put out the news section single-handedly with no help. Imagine my surprise when I arrive to find Gerfin ensconced in a cubicle next to mine. He is news in name only. Breckenfeld rarely if ever refers to him, makes no story assignments during editorial sessions, and effectively treats Gerfin as a nonperson. Breckenfeld seems to lack the will or authority to fire Gerfin, playing a waiting game. Gerfin finally tires of the game and leaves. Strange place, this *H&H*.

The *H&H* news section counts some distinguished alumni, I learn. Art Watkins leaves not long before I arrive to freelance books. Since then, Art turns out numerous books on finance, housing, real estate, and mutual funds during a distinguished run. Pierre Salinger's name briefly adorns the masthead before President Kennedy picks him as his press secretary. Someday my name might stand with these successful alums, I dream.

Midbook, directed by AMEs Walt Wagner and John Goldsmith, focuses on topics of interest to merchant builders who've reinvented homebuilding after World War II. Before the war, the vast majority of new homes were built by families who bought a lot and hired a contractor to build their dream home. Pent-up demand following the war impelled Bill Levitt and many other emulators to buy large swatches of land on which they built tracts of homes with little design variation for sale to unknown buyers. Ample government financing guaranteed by the Veterans Administration (VA) and Federal Housing Administration (FHA) facilitated growth of these merchant builders. *H&H* caters to these new merchant builders. Midbook's job is to take the "cookie" out of cookie-cutter houses! Hence midbook editors focus on house design and layout, subdivision and land planning, marketing and nitty-gritty topics essential to successful merchant building.

Midbook associate editors include Jonathan Aley, Max Huntoon, Bob Murray, Dick O'Neill, and Jim Gallagher. Aley is a whiz on construction details and tools, but I never get to know Max Huntoon well. Murray is an elfin and ofttimes impish character who loves a martini or two for lunch and is a prodigious writer on deadline. On deadline, he mopes about the office claiming not to understand the essence of a feature until the evening before due date. Then in a caffeine-fueled burst of all-night writing, he turns out perfect copy and layout by the following morning. My take is that he needs mulling time to put all the ribbons in place around his story's maypole.

Big Jim Gallagher is Murray's opposite: Irish friendly, outgoing, and a great conversationalist who knows merchant building from the vantage point of a Levitt homeowner on Long Island. Dick O'Neill, the technical editor, is a strapping Irishman with unruly curly hair, a disarming smile, and a ready opinion on any topic. Later, he authors the book *High Steel, Hard Rock and Deep Water: The Exciting World of Construction.*

Making Midbook an eye-catching read is art director Jan V. White, who later finds a flourishing career as a magazine design consultant and author.

Keeping these two stallions in tandem is a publisher and managing editor (no editor under *Time's* scheme). Bob Chasteney, a *Time* veteran, holds the managing editor's hot spot, balancing the egos of news and midbook AMEs. Pierrepont Isham Prentice, a Yale classmate of Luce known professionally as P.I. and as Perry to close friends, keeps everything in balance as publisher. A relatively small man, Prentice is an engaging conversationalist in private who becomes a glaring stutterer when speaking in public. The defect does not inhibit his *H&H* leadership. On pretext that he has a conflict, Prentice later delegates me to deliver a speech he has written to a builder group in Columbus, Ohio.

TRACKING ZECKENDORF

Steve Thompson, the *Architectural Forum* writer who gave me valuable prehiring advice on *H&H* and Breckenfeld, confides during a brief corridor talk a few weeks after I arrive that he has signed on as Bill Zeckendorf's publicist at Webb & Knapp. A strange turnabout: Steve wants to leave journalism for the life of a flack, while I risk mightily to leave public relations for journalism.

Hence I track W&K's fortunes, even though it is not a REIT and thus outside my rat hole. Zeckendorf lives a life of leverage ("I'd rather be alive at 18 percent than be dead at the prime rate [then 6 percent]," he is famously quoted). Big Zeck also dreams of becoming king of the then-new urban renewal hill, but his grand intentions strangle in red tape and cash shortages. It is a sad story, but one I never write for housing-centric *H&H*.

Zeckendorf's real estate genius is ultimately felled by his penchant for undertaking champagne projects on the beer budget that undercapitalized W&K cannot afford. Early in the 1950s, he signs on to redevelop 240 acres in Southwest Washington, one of the nation's earliest clearance projects. W&K develops the concept for the L'Enfant Plaza office center and its approach mall in 1953, but a tortuous approval process delays completion until 1966, by which time W&K is in bankruptcy and facing liquidation.

"Southwest Washington was the most long, drawn-out, and frustrating of all of our projects," he writes in his autobiography *Zeckendorf*. "Had we had a true idea of what it is really like to get a great, invigorating project under way in Washington, we would never have tackled the job" (Zeckendorf, 1970, 205) He continues,

Washington's trouble was that too many forces kept tugging it in separate directions—and, as regards civic government, it was a headless monster … At one time Webb & Knapp was dealing with no fewer that twenty-seven separate Washington agencies, departments, or sub-departments … There were moments … when I felt we were part of some mad surrealist's real-life Monopoly set: every time we were about to acquire a key property or pass "Go," the "Chance" card turned up reading, "Go back three paces …(Zeckendorf 1970, 214-15). . [When] the first units of the Town Center were completed … almost six years had somehow vanished down the drain, and we were still prisoners of the wonderful Washington time machine (Zeckendorf, 1970, 205)… but from 1960 on, Webb & Knapp was so pressed for funds that I could not find the long-term cash to enable us to force the situation at L'Enfant Plaza.

Zeckendorf's legacy remains his single-handed gambit that brought the United Nations to New York City in 1946. Zeckendorf designed a dazzling project called "X City" for an East River land assemblage and then persuaded New York City powers to offer the site to the UN; it accepted within a week. An engraving of the UN graces his stock certificates, which today are worth far more to collectors than W&K's highest-ever $3.13 stock price. One certificate adorns my office wall, a strikingly unique reminder of Zeckendorf's creative flair.

But the Webb & Knapp story is merely one thread in a rush by homebuilding, real estate, and savings and loan companies to come public in the first wave of public offerings. I learn about IPOs (initial public offerings) and the intricacies of reading a prospectus. *H&H* is already printing a monthly listing of homebuilding, savings and loan, and real estate stocks when I arrive, and ultimately the intersection of housing and Wall Street becomes a major story source.

News, as in daily newspapering, is what your boss says it is, period. In those early days of 1961, I am sent to Washington several times for specific stories covering housing conferences and interviewing officials at the National Association of Home Builders. In that spring of 1961, there's new freshness in the Washington air—or so it seems to me—since Camelot has come to the nation's capital in the form of John F. Kennedy's Democratic administration. Cabbies seem more upbeat, and conference-goers seem to expect bigger things than they got from Eisenhower's Republican regime. Never mind that the Eisenhower years produced the nation's first workable urban renewal law, the interstate highway system as the nation's biggest public works program ever, and also the law creating REITs, whose future impact is then still very much unknown.

THE COLOR OF THE CABINET

In March 1961, little more than a month after my Manhattan arrival, President Kennedy sends major proposals to Congress to "remold our cities, improve our pattern of community development and provide for the housing needs of all segments of our population," according to the *New York Times*.

What catches our eyes at *H&H* is Kennedy's proposal to create a new cabinet-level Department of Housing and Urban Development (HUD); Dr. Robert C. Weaver, then administrator of the Housing and Home Finance Agency, is widely expected to become secretary.

Dr. Weaver is an African American and would thus become the first black to serve in any president's cabinet.

That puts race front and center on Washington's housing griddle. Dr. Weaver, a respected housing economist and academic with three Harvard degrees, has just ended a term as national chairman of the National Association for the Advancement of Colored People (NAACP). Southerners in Congress oppose the idea, and President Kennedy is forced to withdraw his plan under accusations that Dr. Weaver's views are "extremist."

Instead, Dr. Weaver remains head of the smaller Housing and Home Finance Agency (HHFA) until 1965 when Congress approves the idea. By then, public opinion turns favorable, partly the result of Dr. Martin Luther King Jr.'s August 1963 "I Have a Dream" speech on Washington's National Mall, which Irene hears in person, and partly because President Johnson wins passage of the Civil Rights Act of 1964. Dr. Weaver finally becomes the first African American to sit at the cabinet table.

I interview Dr. Weaver numerous times during my six-plus years at *H&H* and always find him erudite, well-informed, and a reliable source of information. *H&H* does not regularly editorialize on policy matters, but Breckenfeld almost automatically opposes HUD's creation, not on racial grounds but because it shackles housing with another layer of regulation, as stated by "The Many-Fingered Federal Puppeteer," a later Breckenfeld article in *Fortune*.

I am supposed to be neutral in political matters and register as an

Independent for the 1952 presidential election. That registration is never changed. But I vote twice for Adlai Stevenson, a Democrat, in the 1950s and support Kennedy in 1960, based on my impression of the man during an impassioned October speech at a Cleveland urban-renewal gathering. Hence I am somewhat simpatico with Washington's wider reach over the economy in those early 1961 days—a position that puts me at odds with my new boss, Gurney Breckenfeld, who views any federal intrusion upon laissez faire housing as something akin to mortal sin.

In November 1962, *H&H* focus shifts abruptly to integrated housing, thanks to a November 20 executive order by President Kennedy prohibiting racial bias in any homes financed with federal insurance or guarantees. That raises the question of whether the order will shrink FHA and VA housing starts, hurting the economy.

HHFA Administrator Dr. Robert Weaver has an answer, I report in the April 1963 *H&H*. "Homes with conventional financing not subject to the antibias order dropped 14% from December to January, he [Weaver] argued in a press release, while FHA and VA starts dropped only 12% and 4% respectively," my copy reads. "On this evidence he [Weaver] continued to insist the order will have minimum impact on housing.

"But regional figures, released later, raise questions about his interpretation … conventional starts are up 8% and FHA and VA starts down 20% from January 1962 to January 1963." The story goes on to quote two parties on opposite sides of the equal opportunity housing debate, the NAHB and President Kennedy's housing committee, as agreeing it is too early for any definitive conclusion. Thus does *H&H* provide even-handed coverage to an intensely debated issue.

My rat hole comes alive almost immediately after my arrival at *H&H*. Events transpired before my entrance that are important to an understanding of how REITs came about in the first place, hence the following brief detour.

MUTUAL FUNDS FOR REAL ESTATE.

Mutual funds for real estate start in the early 1950s when a group of real estate men active in Boston set out to convince Congress to approve "mutual funds for real estate." Like stock and bond mutual funds, the real estate entities they envision would pay only a single level entity tax by distributing substantially all their earnings tax free to shareholders. All the mission's backers are real estate owners and borrowers, not lenders.

The drive starts when Joseph W. Lund, an executive of Boston real estate firm R. M. Bradley & Co., is elected president of the National Association of Real Estate Boards (now National Association of Realtors) in November 1951 and from this seat embarks on an aggressive "Build America Better" program. While BAB focuses on improving urban mass transit and revitalizing rundown neighborhoods via urban redevelopment, Lund plants seeds of support for "real estate mutual funds" within the powerful realtors' national lobby.

By summer 1956, the group, now including Philip Theopold and John H. Gardiner of 174-year-old Boston investment counseling firm Minot DeBlois & Maddison Incorporated (now Minot DeBlois Advisors), which manages several Massachusetts business trusts that own real estate, prevails on Congress to approve letting real estate business trusts forego entity-level federal taxes to the extent earnings are distributed to shareholders. The bill lands on President Eisenhower's desk the last day of July 1956.

The Minot firm is so sure that business-friendly Eisenhower will sign the bill that in 1956 it merges three smaller managed business trusts, including one formed in 1886, to create Real Estate Investment Trust of America (REITA), thereby creating the first truly national equity real estate business trust. Phil Theopold becomes REITA's first chairman.

To everybody's dismay, President Eisenhower vetoes the bill on August 10, 1956.

He opposes special taxation "that might well become available to many real estate companies which were originally organized and have always carried on their activities as fully taxable corporations," Eisenhower tells Congress. "Though intended to be applicable to a small number of trusts … it is by no means certain how far a new provision of this sort may be applied … The effect would be to exclude from the corporate tax all but a small margin of retained earnings of real estate trusts."

Scuttlebutt of the day blames the defeat on opposition from Treasury Secretary George M. Humphrey, a staunch opponent of deficit spending.

Undaunted, the Boston REIT backers soldier ahead, sure their idea for pass-through taxation of collective real estate vehicles will benefit the economy by broadening and stabilizing ownership of real properties. They also argue that REITs will give smaller individual investors access to real estate investments previously available only to wealthy professional investors. Support is broadened to key real estate operatives in Washington, Philadelphia, New York, Chicago, Cleveland, and other cities.

Real Estate Investment Trust of America (REITA) also pushes ahead with its growth plans and lists on the American Stock Exchange on September 28, 1959, becoming America's first listed real estate trust.

Mortgage bankers and brokers around the country are also enrolled by defining real estate assets as "interests in real property and interests in mortgages on real property." It is believed the first-time mortgages are defined as real estate assets.

To meet Eisenhower's objection that realty corporations might reap windfall tax benefits, legislation limits REIT benefits to an "unincorporated trust or unincorporated association," language letting business trusts in Massachusetts and a few other states qualify easily.

Significantly and perhaps unintentionally, the new language gives the new REITs one powerful word—*trust*—with which to woo investors. In a Wall Street world where trust seems too often subordinate to profit, the word resonates, especially with older investors all too eager to reach for the higher dividend yields putatively offered by REITs.

Limiting pass-through taxation to trusts and including mortgage lenders persuades Congress, and the REIT legislation is melded into a bill extending cigar taxes and passes Congress September 14, 1960, one day before Congress adjourns to let members take part in the heated campaign that ultimately elevates Massachusetts Senator John F. Kennedy to the presidency.

Eisenhower signs this time, since Humphrey has moved on, and pass-through tax treatment for REITs becomes the law of the land on January 1, 1961.

The REIT revolution is about to begin—or so its backers hope.

In November 1960, the real estate men found the National Association of Real Estate Investment Funds, or NAREIF, predecessor to the National Association of REITs, or NAREIT, as a national trade association to represent REITs.

The Boston realty men dominate the fledgling group's officer lineup: Joseph Lund is elected president, John H. Gardiner is secretary, and Philip Theopold, REITA's chairman, joins the board.

REITS GO LIVE

Lund's R. M. Bradley & Co. is ready for the law to take effect and, in January 1961, merges three corporations and six managed trusts into Bradley Real Estate Trust, owner of property in Boston, Minneapolis, St. Paul, Duluth, and Seattle. But realty operatives in many other cities are eager to answer the call.

In Washington, DC, up-and-coming realty man B. Franklin Kahn visits local stockbroker Ferris & Company to inquire about underwriting a new REIT. The next day, attorney Arthur Birney, after reading a Kiplinger's article on REIT legislation and enlisting a small group interested in forming a REIT, calls on George Ferris, an old schoolmate, with the same question.

"It's funny, but just yesterday another group came to see me with the same question," Birney recalls Ferris responding. "I think they know a lot about real estate, but I'm not sure how much they know about running a public company. If you combine these groups, I'll give you an underwriting."

Soon the two groups consolidate, and on June 7, 1961, Washington Real Estate Investment Trust (WRIT) raises three million dollars by selling six hundred thousand shares at five dollars per share. Frank Kahn becomes president, and Birney is one of five trustees.

Kahn proves a marketing genius, penning provocative and attention-getting annual reports and passing out souvenir green turtles at WRIT annual meetings to demonstrate his belief that the real estate tortoise almost always beats the technology hare.

WRIT grows cash flow steadily, and dividends rise by 8.9 percent annually over the three decades before Kahn retires in 1993. "We were very astute and careful," recalls Birney. WRIT's string of yearly dividend boosts ends at fifty years when payout is cut in 2012.

Variations of WRIT's story unfold in a half-dozen local brokerage firms around the country during 1961's early months, when I am testing my *House & Home* sea legs.

By mid-1961, a half-dozen small equity REITs backed by local real estate operators break the ice and raise over $40.6 million for new REITs.

Greenfield REIT, backed by Philadelphia realty interests, sells ten million dollars of new stock March 28 through a Philadelphia-based broker.

Denver REIA follows with an eight-million-dollar sale on May 9, underwritten by two local brokers.

US Realty Investments, backed by Sheldon Guren and based in Cleveland, raises $6.6 million on May 24 via Hornblower & Weeks-Hemphill, Noyes, the first New York City firm to back a REIT.

Pennsylvania REIT, headquartered in Philadelphia and sparked by Sylvan Cohen, markets two million dollars on June 9 in a self-under-writing, and Real Estate Investment Trust of America (REITA), the Boston-based REIT headed by Philip Theopold and John H. Gardiner, caps the first half of 1961 by selling eleven million dollars of stock on June 13 via three New York City firms.

The new entrants are all property-owning equity REITs created to own commercial properties, so we at *H&H* pass on covering them. Notably, two of these early arrivals still operate today: Pennsylvania and Washington REITs.

THE TURN TO MORTGAGES

The first mortgage REIT to poke a nose out my rat hole is First Mortgage Investors (FMI), raising the biggest money yet through New York broker Shearson, Hammill & Co. with a September 22, 1961, offering of one million shares at fifteen dollars a share. FMI becomes the first mortgage REIT to reach market following an IRS finding that mortgages are indeed "interests in real estate." FMI is formed by two Miami brothers, Jack R. and Arthur H. Courshon, whom I did not meet at that time.

At *H&H*, we are intensely interested in the mortgage REITs since homebuilders are eternally on the lookout for mortgage money and FMI says it intends to put the fifteen million dollars raised entirely into first mortgages. FMI is expected to borrow up to twice its new fifteen million dollars in capital, adding a potential forty-five million dollars of fresh money for mortgages. At *H&H*, we like this number.

The REIT concept is simple. If a REIT invests most of its assets in real estate and pays 90 percent of REIT income to shareholders as dividends, it will not pay corporate income taxes on the income it distributes. This single-entity tax treatment virtually ensures that REITs will pay above-average dividends, a compelling proposition for individual investors. And no more than five persons may own over 50 percent of a REIT's shares, ensuring that no single group or small clique can control a REIT.

Three more equity REITs spring to life in the second half of 1961, including the twenty-five-million-dollar offer by New York–based First National Real Estate Trust, proving REIT attractiveness in the Big Apple. REITs raise fifty-eight million dollars overall in the back half of 1961 for total proceeds of $98.9 million in this maiden year.

By then, I am writing the monthly mortgage market story built around a survey of about twenty local mortgage bankers compiling their prices for FHA-insured single-family and apartment mortgages, whose interest rates are fixed and thus trade in the market like fixed-rate bonds. The survey also covers rates for conventional and single-family construction loans. At that time, no national market for mortgages exists, and hence our monthly update becomes a must-read for builders on cost and availability of mortgage money. For me, presiding over this monthly staple imparts new insights into the financial side of housing and real estate.

In November 1961, I write the obituary of Robert A. Futterman, one of three prominent New York publicly owned syndicators who chokes to death on a piece of beef while dining with friends at his Westchester home. He is only thirty-three. Reputedly able to remember almost anything he read, Futterman began investing in New York City properties at age twenty-seven and was so successful that he founded a one-hundred-million-dollar publicly traded real estate syndication empire, Robert A. Futterman Corporation, before his death. Futterman, the corporation, survives its founder's demise, but unhappily, my Futterman obit does not survive.

By March 1962, my rat hole disgorges a second mortgage REIT. Continental Mortgage Investors (CMI) pulls off the largest REIT offering to date by raising $22.5 million with a 1.7 million share offering via two New York City brokers. Backed by Boston lawyer brothers Monte J. and Neil W. Wallace, CMI barely makes it out of the IPO scrum because the soggy market is off about 4 percent from a December 1, 1961, Dow-Jones Industrials high of 728.80. CMI puts on a good run and in June 1965 becomes the first REIT to qualify for listing on the New York Stock Exchange.

Six other equity REIT offerings join CMI by raising $39.3 million in those early months of 1962, all completed before April 6. Two are based in Philadelphia, making the City of Brotherly Love the favorite home of REIT sponsors.

THE MARKET BREAKS

In April 1962, President Kennedy engages in a brief but highly charged public spat with the president of US Steel Corporation when Big Steel raises steel prices. President Kennedy insists that prices and wages must serve the national interest, while US Steel chairman Roger Blough counters that "each individual company in our competitive society has a responsibilioty…to do the things that are necessary price wise, however unpopular that may be at times, to keep in the competitive race," according to a *New York Times* transcript of his press conference.

Blough capitulates within three days, leaving investors to contemplate these new economic marching orders. Whether by coincidence or design, the market breaks in May, falling about 20 percent over six gut-wrenching days running.

On Monday, May 28, the market cracks under an avalanche of 9.35 million shares traded, fifth highest turnover until then in New York

Stock Exchange history. The next day coincides with a dinner trip Irene and I have planned to the city, and after dinner, at 9:30 in the evening, the NYSE tape at Merrill Lynch's office in the Time-Life Building in Rockefeller Center is still grinding out trades. Harried brokers are checking prices happily, for the market rallies smartly and the 14.75 million share volume, the highest since the Great Depression, is good news.

REIT of America, the only exchange-listed REIT on that day, sinks 13 percent to a new annual low of $17.50 on Monday on only eight hundred shares traded. REITA recovers one dollar or 5.7 percent to rebound Tuesday on 3,800 shares.

The market drifts lower to 535.76 on the Dow by June 25, down 26.5 percent from the December peak for its largest post-World War II decline. From there, the market rallies, recovering most lost ground by September and touching new highs within a year.

REVOLUTION POSTPONED

The 1962 flash crash ends the early-1960s bull market run by REITs. Its aftermath kills twenty-six REITs hoping to sell nearly $165 million in stock. My favorite never-was name is Manna REIT, dead before arrival. A Securities and Exchange Commission examination of the break finds that initial public offerings (IPOs) dropped nearly two-thirds between 1962's first and fourth quarters. The SEC report omits mention of the Kennedy-US Steel brouhaha however.

The REIT revolution is on hold.

My rat hole goes dark as new REIT formations hibernate for five and one-half years, until 1968, after the little-remembered May 1962 market break. Realty trusts raise only $75.6 million in that half-decade, less than half the $163.7 million capital offerings in just over a year before the break. Only ten new REITs form during these silent years, but they are tiny, averaging less than four million dollars in size. None survive to 2015.

While REITs recover after 1968, the break spells the final curtain for New York syndicators. The syndicators are large limited partnerships and some corporations, primarily based in New York City, that own office towers and other large commercial buildings. In the early 1960s, they come to represent real estate to investors. Increasing competition and rising supply kills the market for anything real estate after the break.

Robert Futterman's two main competitors in the public market, Kratter Corporation, listed on the American Stock Exchange, and Glickman Corporation, traded over the counter, come under pressure. The trio owns over 110 properties combined, mostly in New York City, and cynics insist they make money by swapping properties among themselves. "Kratter-to-Glickman-to-Futterman" becomes the derisive mantra, echoing baseball's famed Tinker-to-Evers-to-Chance double-play combination. Merited or not, investor cynicism kills the syndicators, with a modest push from realty trusts.

By November 1963, Lawrence A. Wein, a whip-smart tax attorney acknowledged as "king of the syndicators" for siring over one hundred public and private syndications—including the granddaddy of all syndications, which bought the Empire State Building in 1961 for a then-record $65 million—quits the syndication field. Investors in real estate investment trusts are willing to accept lower rates of return, he says, because their shares are sold by securities dealers "who think in terms of a different set of returns than we [real estate professionals] do," he tells the *New York Times*.

"Although in their early stages of development, realty trusts will eventually absorb the majority of realty investment groups," he predicts. My rat hole is expanding.

GOODBYE, TIME INC.

On May 27, 1964, *H&H* staffers are ordered to assemble at midmorning in Time's sixth-floor auditorium for an all-ears announcement.

Hedley Donovan, who's recently replaced the retiring Henry Luce as editor-in-chief and no lover of trade magazines, wastes no time. *Architectural Forum* is being folded into *Fortune* (emphasis on "folded") immediately, and *House & Home* has been sold to McGraw-Hill. Despite a circulation rise to 138,000, *H&H* ad pages drop over 30 percent from its peak, and the magazine is losing money. Thus Time Incorporated exits trade magazine publishing.

Prentice is out; a new publisher is in. For my *H&H* colleagues and me, there is a severance package based on seniority whether or not McGraw-Hill chooses to employ us, along with a whiff that McGraw-Hill hopes to employ most of us. But there's no guarantee of a future job.

Thus ends my coveted career at Time Inc.

And thus ends my rat hole assignment—for the time being.

Irene's family is visiting from Ohio, and we decide to enjoy the rest of the day at the New York World's Fair, just opened in Flushing Meadows.

Sans job, sans paycheck, sans worries, I take a break from rat hole watching.

Chapter 7
THE GESTATION

In May 1964, I am cut adrift by Time Inc. and looking for a job.

But an entrepreneurial seed is planted.

By the end of the 1960s, the seed is gestated to full flower, and I launch my own tiny but ambitious investment advisory publishing company.

How that seed matures and flourishes remains something of a mystery even today, but gestate it did. Here is how and why it took place, as precisely as I can recall and reconstruct.

My days within the carefree jobless class are precious few. After that devil-may-care day luxuriating at the World's Fair, reality quickly asserts itself. I remain responsible for provisioning a wife, three young children, and all the food, shelter, and essentials they require.

My colleagues and I still show up at the *House & Home* offices, still in our Time Inc. digs, and nothing changes at first except the focus shifts to résumés and contacts for possible job openings. We are told we may apply for any openings inside Time Inc. and so everyone updates résumés, builds dossiers of published works, and scrambles for contacts. Ed Reingold, a Columbus friend now thriving inside the Time-Life correspondent network, suggests having a go at Dick Clurman, then chief of correspondents, who agrees to take a look. But when I meet him, it quickly becomes apparent that he's in no mood to hire a refugee from a trade magazine and that trail goes cold. A few days later, he makes the rejection official, citing budgetary pressures.

Gene Weyeneth, *H&H*'s new managing editor and a McGraw Hill vet, calls to interview me and my colleagues within a few days. He quickly proffers a new job: news editor, in effect letting me replace my previous boss Gurney Breckenfeld—he of the rat hole assignment—at a 10 percent salary bump. It is an honor, and since my hasty efforts to land a spot at *Time* magazine come to naught, I accept.

Breckenfeld eventually shuttles to *Fortune* magazine, technically truncating my rat hole watch at *H&H*. But my rat hole watch does not end there.

On July 1, 1964, I join fifteen colleagues in reporting to work at the McGraw-Hill Building at 330 West Forty-Second Street in Manhattan. The move shaves a half hour from my daily commute because the building's back door opens on the Port Authority Bus Terminal where my daily bus from Ridgewood lands me every morning.

The McGraw-Hill Building is only a brisk fifteen-minute walk from the Time-Life Building, but the only similarity is that both bear hyphenated names.

At Time-Life, we worked across from the entertainment crossroads of Radio City Music Hall and could feast at dozens of world-class restaurants nestled in Rockefeller Center and environs. The digs were classy, upscale, and culturally bracing.

At McGraw-Hill, we sit on the fringes of a tenderloin district spilling over from Times Square; Radio City is replaced by all-night X-rated movie houses, and luncheon choices boil down to either bars-cum-eateries or ethnic restaurants near the Ninth Avenue produce markets.

We are assigned one corner of the lowly fourth floor because there's no room at the inn elsewhere, a comedown from our previous nineteenth-floor perch. Nicknamed the Jolly Green Giant for its unique green exterior tile, the building sits west of Eighth Avenue because city zoning codes banned printing presses east of that thoroughfare when the structure was erected in the early 1930s. Vestigial six-foot-square concrete columns bespeak the structure's original design to harbor massive printing presses, although none ever arrived, as McGraw-Hill abandoned printing its own magazines by the time it occupied the quarters.

So thoroughly downscale are the new digs that my associate Ned Rochon, a Princeton grad who replaces John Gerfin, types his new phone number on his Time Inc. business cards to conceal from outsiders that he now draws his paycheck from the more plebian McGraw-Hill. The Time Inc. mystique dies hard.

TRADING PACES

Severance pay softens the move for me and presents the opportunity to adjust priorities and reshape lives. For the first time in my life, I can put serious money in the bank or invest in—*what*?

My severance package comes to about $6,500 after taxes, or around $49,900 in 2015 dollars, and opens doors closed until then. *Voila*, Irene and I have our first stake for investing in the stock market.

Long before that stake arrives, I need to get up to speed on financial matters while toiling in *H&H*'s finance section and begin reading financial books voraciously. It is a throwback to my Public Library U. days at the Development Committee, and once again, reading comes to my rescue. Looking back on that 1960s reading list yields the conclusion that these books remain relevant for today's investors.

How I Made $2,000,000 in the Stock Market first comes to hand, and this slim 148-page volume makes a lasting impression. Written by Nicolas Darvas, a Hungarian economist and dancer, the book spells out Darvas's "box" trading system of using stop-loss orders to protect against losses while letting winning stocks run to the upside. His method lets him reap a large fortune (for those days). Since Irene and I have little extra money at that time, it is all academic. Others on my early 1960s reading list include:

- *The Battle for Investment Survival* by Gerald M. Loeb, a terrific read emphasizing that nothing lasts forever on Wall Street and urging investors to be eternally vigilant for economic and market changes
- *My Own Story* by Bernard Baruch, the autobiography of a legendary stock market trader from the early 1900s who becomes an adviser to presidents and famously said, "I buy my straw hats in the fall," meaning he focused on out-of-favor stocks when they are cheap
- *The Intelligent Investor* by Benjamin Graham, then still a relatively unknown securities analyst; he becomes the patron saint of legendary long-term investor Warren Buffett, who buys into Berkshire Hathaway starting in 1962
- *Extraordinary Popular Delusions and the Madness of Crowds*, written by Scottish journalist and author Charles Mackay in 1841, tracing the trajectories of historical delusions and follies, among which he counts the South Sea Company and Mississippi Company stock bubbles of the early 1700s and Holland's Tulipmania. "Men … go mad in herds," he writes presciently, "while they only recover their senses slowly, and one by one."

All but Ben Graham's tome reside in my study today, and if you take time to thumb through the above books, you will rapidly become convinced that any intelligent individual investor with even a small amount of capital can both beat the market and earn a significant increment on his or her stake. Thus I embark on an experiment in stock trading, first and foremost to make money but also to learn to handle myself and my money in the market. Slowly, imperceptibly, over the next five years, my personal goals change from the pursuit of personal profit to the goal of being Manhattan's gift to investors by writing an investment advisory market letter. But both goals require accumulating that initial stake.

My Time Inc. going-away present of about $6,500 provides both substance and opportunity.

Not long after the McGraw-Hill move, I open a brokerage account with a Merrill Lynch office at Forty-First Street and Broadway. One investing strategy absorbed from my brother-in-law Chuck Adams is to put just a few eggs in a basket and watch that basket very closely. In this vein, I stroll the long crosstown block from the McGraw-Hill Building to the Merrill office to spend many lunch hours fixating on the tape scrolling across one office wall, searching for the symbols of the pink chips I select. A dozen or so investors join me in this stressful pastime, all older and most certainly wiser.

In that early evolution as an investor, I first gravitate toward buying a package of three conservative insurance and telephone stocks, vowing to hold as per my reading for the long-term, then defined by the IRS as six months. REITs are totally off the radar for me and the market generally. I buy ten shares of each company in August 1964, meaning I am an odd-lotter paying extra commissions for the privilege of buying less than round lots of one hundred shares. Jerry, my customer's man, isn't thrilled because my total outlay of less than one thousand dollars means a paltry payday for him.

Seven months later in March 1965, I pull the rip cord on this foray because my conservative trio is down 27 percent. This is a fast way to lose money, even though my total shrinkage is only $257. Let's shorten the holding time, I say, and buy forty shares of a stock moving up, General Bronze (symbol GLZ), at an average $29.57 a share. A month later, GLZ is at $36, and I cash in profits of $218, or 18 percent. Maybe this is easier than I thought.

I switch to test the Darvas's box system. A subsequent trade in Magnavox (MAG), a favorite color TV play, nets an 11 percent loss. Undeterred, I float the first short sale of my life, in New Mexico and Arizona Land (NZ), an ASE-listed Western land play, and net a modest 7 percent gain on a three-week holding. It is a puzzlement. Even though the market is generally rising, my longs aren't working.

For me, the Darvas system turns out to be totally unreliable. Darvas advises placing stop-loss orders ordering the broker to automatically sell a stock if quotations touch a predetermined price, generally 7 to 10 percent below the initial purchase price. For instance, if one pays fifty dollars for a share, a stop-loss would be entered at forty-five or so, limiting the purchaser's loss to no more than 10 percent of the investment. Darvas claims he invented his system because he was traveling the world with his dance troupe and often out of touch with the market. For me, the stop-loss system becomes a one-way street to more commissions. Stop already!

Emboldened by the NZ gain, I venture into a second short sale, of fifty shares of Control Data (CDA), an emerging computer stock, at $35.50 on July 8, 1965.

In a short sale, the investor borrows and then sells shares he or she does not own, hoping to buy shares back later at a cheaper price and pocket the difference. But shorting is not for sissies because the stock price can theoretically rise to the moon and the buy-in can cost way more than the initial investment. In my case, CDA swings sharply upward the next day and I cover at $39.25 for a $237 loss or 13 percent in one day. Ugh!

I try both long and short positions in McKesson & Robbins (MCK), a drug company, and lose on both long and short sides. But longs in Collins Radio (CRI) and Western Equities (WE) both turn profits of 10 and 15 percent respectively. In December 1965, I buy twenty-two shares of Fairchild Camera (FCI), another high-tech darling, at $144.25 and marvel as it soars in ensuing weeks and months, finally closing out the position at $190.75 in early March 1966 for a total $956 or nearly 30 percent gain.

Stepping up the ante, I go back into techs a few days later, putting up $4,817 to buy one hundred shares of Valley Metallurgical Processing (VMP) at $47.75 on March 7, 1966, only to see it fall to forty-three dollars within less than six weeks, for a 12 percent loss. By this time, Northwest Airlines is ending a bitter strike, and I risk $3,830 to go long a post-split thirty-six shares at $105.63 on May 6, 1966. Five months later, the stock is down and I sell on October 24 at $87.88 for a $700 or 18 percent loss.

Finally, I short one hundred shares of Control Data one more time, at $26.13 on Thursday, October 27, 1966, because CDA is now down by one-third since the earlier encounter. CDA bites me again, and I cover six trading days later, on November 4, at $27.38 or a 7 percent loss. Later I realize I have shorted CDA only a quarter-point from its all-time low!

Totaling all this frenetic activity over two years shows $367.60 net loss. Jerry, my customer's man, has made more than I, cashing $647 in commissions.

I make gains on only four of eleven long holdings, or a little better than one-third of the time. Short sales are worse with only one gain in four short-side excursions. Somehow I must boost these percentages.

Still this trading spree is small tuition for learning that buying stocks as a nonprofessional outsider is mainly a loser's game. And my stock timing needs lots of work. My foray starts as a way to make money and ends as training in how I might be able to make the market work for the little guy. But in November 1966, it is a game I do not choose to continue. I close my Merrill account and shift to a broker nearer my home, Blair & Company in Paramus, New Jersey.

A bear market swing is ending as 1966 slides into 1967, and I take a $448 profit on a trade in twenty shares at $97.58 of Ling-Temco-Vought, an aerospace conglomerate then in the spotlight for the audacious tactics of founder Jimmie Ling. In a reprise, I buy another 37.5 LTV shares at $84.94 in April 1967, a $3,187 ticket, and watch as shares soar to $137.06 by August, cashing a $1,955 gain for my biggest win so far.

By that time, I have switched jobs to Standard & Poor's Corporation and have access to a quote machine for the first time. After a couple of small gains and losses, I hear the story of Fedders Corporation (symbol FJQ) from a fellow analyst, who's excited by the loose-leaf tear-sheet he's written about the stock. Fedders is closing several smaller plants to move air-conditioner production to a monster plant, supposedly far more efficient, fronting the New Jersey Turnpike near Exit 10 and profits appear headed much higher.

So I buy 120 FJQ shares at twenty-four dollars in August 1967 and am transfixed as shares move up and up and up, finally selling the shares in three smaller tranches between April and October 1968 for a $3,557 profit, a 123 percent gain. This is the way the market should work.

In April 1968, I use some FJQ profits to acquire three hundred shares of Consolidated Leasing at $12.48 and again let my profits run, cashing a $2,554 gain or 68 percent in February 1969. In July 1968, Kenton Corporation beckons and I purchase fifty shares at $25.59 and am again rewarded as shares zoom to $67.68, bringing a $2,064 gain or 155 percent.

In the two-year bull market from November 1966 to November 1968, I initiate fifteen buys and make profits on thirteen, an astounding 87 percent success rate never duplicated since. Nothing fattens the wallet like a bull market. This five-year trading spurt ultimately nets about $10,725 in gains.

During these years, I am mostly a one-stock man, meaning I try to pick one stock at a time and ride it to ultimate sale in line with earlier insights from my brother-in-law Chuck Adams. Diversification is not yet instilled in my stock repertoire. Naturally there are some clunkers, and I've included a full record of my trading in appendix II.

My stock picks derive from many sources: news and stock research reading, conversations with colleagues at S&P, and a stock charting service then published by S&P. My take is that one must look at everything and cannot rely upon any single source for investment ideas.

My secret sauce? The insight from Darvas and others to let profits run and take small losses on weaker stocks makes all the difference.

THE SEED

Some former colleagues adopt different agendas and use their severance packages to invest in themselves and launch out with their own new businesses.

Arthur Swarm Goldman, *H&H* market research director, uses the funds to set himself up as a high-level housing consultant, organizing industry round tables where builders, developers, materials manufacturers, planners, and lenders discuss ways to improve housing quality. He and I are never good friends so I have little contact with him after the split.

Jan White, our art director, takes the opportunity to become a consultant on magazine design and creates a series of winning mastheads for Audit when I set sail with my own ship. Over the ensuing forty years, Jan writes about a dozen books on his specialty, including the widely quoted *Editing by Design: Word-and-Picture Communication for Editors and Designers*. (Jan died December 30, 2014, at age 86.)

Of most interest to me is the path of Ed Birkner, also from marketing. He sets up shop as Marketing Information Network (MIN) and begins publishing a newsletter titled *MINFAX*. Ed knows hundreds of private homebuilders and organizes the January 1961 Turn Table dinner in Chicago that marked my coming out as an *H&H* associate. His MIN also sponsors conferences that, judging from the crowds, are enormously profitable.

As my sojourn at McGraw-Hill turns increasingly uninspiring, I transfer to S&P in April 1967 and begin meeting with Ed in the second half of 1968. I gradually form a plan to emulate him with an advisory service appealing to readers wanting to follow publicly traded home-builders. By that time, Kaufman and Broad Building Corporation, Forest City Enterprises, and a host of other housing companies are estab-lishing their niches in the capital markets, and I am assigned by *H&H*, my old employer, to assemble and write an annual review of earnings and activities of this emerging group.

It is a short step to convince myself that hundreds or even thousands of investors care enough to buy an investment letter cluing them in to this emerging investment opportunity.

Thus does the germ of starting my own enterprise implant in my psyche.

My rat hole becomes a stock market disgorging homebuilding companies.

GAME CHANGER

In October 1965, two disparate events refine these plans.

First, in early October, Harvard-trained Robert Lusk, head of high-profile homebuilder Lusk Corporation and the first homebuilder to recruit Harvard's prestigious business school for management talent, summons creditors to a meeting in Tucson, Arizona. Lusk Corp. will lose $2.7 million on $26 million sales in its June 1965 fiscal year, creditors are told, and the company does not have enough cash to pay $1.25 million in unsecured debts.

But two mortgage REITs, Continental Mortgage Investors and First Mortgage Investors, pledge to continue interim financing if creditors agree to wait a bit. A group of creditors are not persuaded, and eight days later, they file suit to put Lusk Corp. into bankruptcy.

Lusk Corp.'s failure comes just months after another anxious lender, Marine Midland Bank, topples Bill Zeckendorf's Webb & Knapp Incorporated, then a high-flying aggressive New York City commercial developer and office owner, into the bankruptcy tank in May 1965. At *H&H*, we want to know the details behind Lusk Corp.'s demise and I am tapped to track down the story.

For three days before Thanksgiving 1965, I trudge from Tucson law office to mortgage office to accountant office piecing together the tragic subplots leading to Lusk's denouement. I am never able to get Bob Lusk's personal take on events, although I cannot shake the impression that Bob Lusk either has just left every office minutes before I arrive or is expected momentarily.

Back in New York, I pen a four-page midbook feature replete with a half-page graph and titled "Why the Roof Collapsed on Lusk Corp." During the writing, I am puzzled by the complex accounting issues raised by Lusk's byzantine structure and the distinctions, if any, between *earnings*, *profits*, and *net income*, terms which Lusk accountants use with varying nuances. I resolve to learn enough to end my puzzlement.

The midbook article graces the January 1966 *H&H* issue and subsequently is chosen by editors to represent *H&H* in a prestigious annual magazine awards contest. We lose.

Second, on October 18, 1965, McGraw-Hill agrees to acquire Standard & Poor's Corporation, then one of the nation's largest and best known financial publishers and investment counselors. I learn of the deal during a trip to Atlanta and immediately decide to explore any intercompany opportunities this may open.

Early in 1966, *H&H* publisher Eugene Weyeneth makes clear that any staffer seeking an in-house transfer has automatically submitted his or her resignation. S&P isn't mentioned, but the inference is clear: any transfer to S&P is off-limits.

In spring 1966, I am dispatched to Crystal Lake, Illinois, about forty-five miles northwest of Chicago's Loop, to examine the results Roger Ladd and his Ladd Enterprises experience by bringing costs of building a house from the field into their office for close analysis. Ladd's work cuts costs and improves efficiencies of building homes targeted for airline pilots based at O'Hare Field. The trek yields more insights into homebuilder accounting and another well-received midbook feature.

BACK TO SCHOOL

In spring 1966, I sit for tests leading to enrollment at New York University Graduate School of Business Administration, and in September 1966, at age thirty-six and with a wife and three children ranging from seven to fourteen years old, I go back to school after fifteen years off campus.

This time, it's evening school at New York University's business school, then located on Trinity Place in lower Manhattan adjoining the American Stock Exchange and across from Trinity Church graveyard. The location requires a long and sometimes steamy subway ride from the McGraw-Hill Building at Eighth Avenue and Forty-Second Street on the Eighth Avenue Line. When classes dismiss at about 9:00 p.m., I must return to the Eighth Avenue subway station—now nearly deserted and oozing vulnerability—and repeat this ride back uptown to the Port Authority Bus Terminal for a one-hour bus jaunt, arriving home between 10:00 and 11:00 p.m.

Today my notebooks from those three-plus years are packed away somewhere and the classes come only occasionally to mind. I remember most vividly investment classes taught by Professor Douglas Bellemore and advanced accounting taught by Professor Lee Seidler.

Bellemore is a registered investment adviser and practicing invest-ment counsel, a profession that has fallen in popularity because it re-quires the client to affirm every investment decision (as contrasted to dis-cretionary decision power held by most investment advisers). Author of a well-written book titled *The Strategic Investor*, Bellemore often strokes his bald head as he lectures.

Learning that I once worked for Time Inc., Bellemore asks me in the first half of 1968 to perform a lengthy analysis of Time Inc., probably for use in his day job. Many professors coax this kind of enforced work from students, a lucrative practice that likely continues. The Time study lets me compare circulation and ad revenues for *Fortune*, Time's business pub, to *Forbes* and *Business Week*, its two main rivals, and convinces me that business publications are an area of consumer growth.

Bellemore requires each student to analyze the stock of an industrial, rail, and utility company to complete the course, and I recall typing my utility analysis until about 5:00 a.m. before leaving for Columbus, Ohio, to attend the funeral of Irene's father, Harry Applegate, who dies prema-turely at age sixty-two in May 1968 from lung cancer, probably induced by a life's work as a welder, iron worker, and designer of steel projects. A scrupulously honest man who somehow finds time to shop for groceries and run the family checkbook, Harry loved pinochle, gin rummy, and any other card game to keep the party rolling. Harry's death is a tragic loss for his wife, Gladys Applegate, widowed at age sixty. She will live gloriously another thirty-five years.

Seidler, then a general partner at Bear Stearns & Company, lectures from a series of real-life case studies he has compiled. One involves two related companies who report earnings by buying shares of each other, Pac-Man style, below book value, resulting in reportable income for both under then-prevailing accounting rules. Neither is earning real money, however.

Another involves a two-decade manipulation of earnings by moguls of a movie company who capitalize costs of unsuccessful movies, reporting only income from their winners until accounting rules force them to fess up to their turkeys, at which time earnings plunge and Mogul One is replaced by Mogul Two, who starts the game all over again.

The course preps me for the intricacies of real estate accounting that lie ahead, a sentiment I impart when I meet Professor Seidler many years later at the Winthrop Realty Trust annual meeting, where he serves as trustee. Unhappily, his case studies are long gone.

Whenever possible, I tailor required papers to help in opening my new company. One is titled "Reporting of Income in an Industry under Duress: The Cement Industry," another accounting case. The best is "Development of a Marketing Plan for a New Investment Advisory Company—Based upon Audit Publications for Investors," completed May 1969 and containing an invaluable record of the research leading up to forming our own company. This double use of time works miracles.

Meantime Irene decides to complete the final two years of her long-delayed college degree in education and enrolls at William Paterson University in Wayne, New Jersey. She somehow manages to balance managing the household, caring for three growing children, and attending both daytime and evening classes to graduate magna cum laude. Somehow our schedules mesh, and from the fall 1966 to spring 1970, we live a hectic syncopated family life.

Sometimes it takes this intense focus, with every household member striving for a specific goal, to surface the best in everyone. Somehow, we all overcome.

OPPORTUNITY DOCKS

The sale of *H&H* to McGraw-Hill dislodges any loyalty I have toward any corporate employer. I never really become comfortable at McGraw-Hill, whose corporate culture and accent upon trade magazines is polar opposite to the Yalie elitism at Time. So I start following job ads closely and in spring 1967 find an opening at Standard & Poor's Corporation that suits my talents and experience. Remember, McGraw-Hill acquires S&P in late 1965 and this seems a major plus, although our publisher decrees that any *H&H* staffer seeking an internal transfer has in effect submitted his or her resignation.

Undeterred, I interview for the S&P position and am selected. There follow several weeks of very delicate negotiations within McGraw-Hill's human resources department to make the switch. I am determined to go ahead with the move in spite of our publisher's decree. Somehow everything falls into place, and I start work at S&P in the second week of April 1967—just in time for a four-week stock market spill occasioned by the Israel-Egypt Seven Days' War. Not long afterward, the HR man who shepherded my transfer is sent to work in a McGraw-Hill outpost in Missouri, proof perhaps that *H&H*'s publisher had some fangs after all. But *voila*, I now work on Wall Street, sort of.

More proof that if you don't ask, you don't get.

S&P is located in a nondescript office at 345 Hudson Street on the western fringes of Greenwich Village in lower Manhattan—an unlovely spot in the printing district picked many years before when S&P printed its advisory services on site. But the job has three plusses. First, it is closer to the NYU classrooms in downtown Manhattan, cutting my evening school commute.

Second, the work teaches gut-level investment basics and explains why S&P alumni fill many key spots on Wall Street. At first, I write short and medium-length articles for *The Outlook* investment service from meaty reports by field analysts based on company visits. After a few months, I am promoted to field analyst and spend my days pumping company CFOs or treasurers on a lengthy list of items from assets to yearly expectations. Reports from these visits run ten to fifteen pages and are circulated internally so everyone knows in exquisite detail what each company is telling the Street.

My company call list includes Farrington Corporation to check out its progress in developing an optical scanning system that works. Farrington's technology relies on a computer's ability to read handwritten letters filled into preprinted blocks, but this method is soon overtaken by early barcode scanners.

At another call, I learn American Bank Note prints beautifully engraved stock certificates but that business is imperiled by the looming arrival of computerized book-entry stock registries. Oddly, another branch of S&P is beavering away to perfect a universal securities numbering system, called CUSIP, that eventually facilitates this transition. ABN's check printing remains a business staple, however.

Details matter, immensely. Most memorably, I am able to ferret out a major glitch in Babcock & Wilcox's nuclear reactor vessel manufacturing, a hot technology of the day, that briefly sinks the stock of this old-line industrial. After a productive visit to company officers, I routinely check related news for any loose ends and find this brief item:

"Died—John Doe, vice president."

Mr. Doe, whose real name is lost in the mists, turns up on B&W's organization chart as a vice president of its nuclear reactor vessel operations in Akron, Ohio.

Strange, my contact didn't mention this death to me.

I find a local newspaper story reporting Mr. Doe committed suicide. Now I know something is wrong.

Finally I locate a contact who says Mr. Doe committed suicide on the morning he was to tour B&W higher-ups through his southern Ohio production facilities.

Things are going terribly off track there. Nuclear reactor vessels are manufactured in two halves and then welded into a completed boiler to receive nuclear fuel, but B&W's welds are failing safety tests at an alarming rate. To meet production schedules, Mr. Doe orders the huge vessel halves barged down the Ohio River to New Orleans and then loaded on ocean liners bound for the Netherlands for reliable welding. Eventually, the paired vessels retrace their tortuous route back to Ohio.

The whole mess is frightfully expensive for B&W.

I immediately put out a "Halt purchases—sell" on B&W to alert S&P analysts and investment counselors of the problem. It is a small but important victory for detail digging.

My brother-in-law Chuck Adams, then in love with the romance of Wall Street, remarks, "It sounds like stocks are just so many sacks of wheat at S&P," after hearing my description of daily duties at S&P.

"Yes," I agree. "Stocks are sacks of wheat to be weighed and measured. No difference." Chuck's words echo today as a reminder never to fall in love with any single stock.

Third and most important, the S&P tenure comes with access to a stock ticker, constantly spewing old-fashioned ticker tape. It is the first time I am able to be live on a minute-by-minute basis with daily market undulations. At the time, this access is greatly liberating since I am trading fairly actively. But viewed from the distance of many decades, the ticker is of no consequence for longer-term investing and in fact may hinder investment success by encouraging frequent price checking that obscures longer trends.

Those twenty-one months at S&P coincide with a bull market to remember, one which more than doubles my $6,500 initial stake. *Voila* again, the *H&H* severance is now multiplied and brings our dream company, Audit, closer to reality. Appendix II replicates my exact trading record, good and bad.

The major downside to those three years of night school is the huge commitment of evening time. Classes generally run from 5:30 or 6:00

p.m. to 8:30 or 9:00 p.m. two or three nights a week, meaning that I do not arrive home until 10:00 p.m. or later. This cuts out much valuable evening time during the coming-of-age years for our three children. The oldest, Rick, is fourteen when the night school grind begins and a newly-minted high school graduate of seventeen when it ends. Daughter Carla is three years younger at fourteen years, while youngest son Doug is ten when I complete my MBA work in September 1969. (The diploma is dated October 1969 but isn't actually received until a June 1970 graduation at Madison Square Garden.) In retrospect, I can see the biggest loser of all is Irene, who busies herself with finishing her college diploma at William Paterson University during those night-school years. The unkindest cut is that this stacking of activities leaves me unable to attend Irene's graduation in June 1970. Irene, however, is able to attend my graduation at Madison Square Garden. What a trooper!

THE FLOWERING

Irene and I were not born with innate entrepreneurial fires burning deep within, so trying to understand what course of events stokes those fires, what aspirations motivates us to take risks that only 2 or 3 percent of US citizens ever take, requires a longer look backward.

At the time of our move to New Jersey, we still had no real entrepreneurial drive. None of our six siblings, none of our thirty-five uncles or aunts, none of their twenty-eight spouses, and none of our ninety-six cousins—165 persons in total—ever go into business for themselves with one prominent exception detailed here.

We have models in the many forebears who pursued farming, often for their entire lives. Despite the low estate in which farming is generally held today, the task of wresting a living from the land is a noble entrepreneurial calling. The farmer tends his or her crops at the mercy of the weather, and drought, wind, or hail can undo the farmer's most persistent labor. Prices for farm produce tend always to be too low in the eyes of the farmer, and hence there is never enough cash money. The upside is that the farm family can nearly sustain itself, raising the chickens, hogs, cows, corn, wheat, oats, soybeans, fruit trees, and gardens needed to keep from starving. But all these crops and animals must be tended daily, so there is scant letup from the daily chores that stretch from dawn to dusk. Best of all, the farmer is totally independent. God is his or her only real boss, making the farmer the true prototypical entrepreneur.

The list of Miller, Applegate, and Campbell farmers is short but illustrious, spanning seven decades from the 1880s to the 1950s. Irene's great-grandfather George "Doc" Miller, a veterinarian, farmed tracts near Johnstown, Ohio, so successfully that he donated land for both the Miller United Methodist Church and for five working farms to each of his five sons. One of those sons was Lenn Frank Miller, Irene's grandfather.

My grandfather Isaac Pressley Campbell farmed about ninety acres near West Sunbury, Pennsylvania, in Butler County for half a century from the 1880s until his death in 1934, and he was as happy-go-lucky a man as I'd ever met, albeit briefly, as a boy. And Irene's father, Harry Applegate, briefly farmed a one-hundred-acre tract on the outskirts of New Albany, Ohio, for a time while Irene was growing up, which she also remembers as a joyous time.

Our other two grandfathers were never far from the land either. My grandfather Christopher Columbus Miller turned to farming to heal infirmities from years of pick-axing narrow coal seams while lying on his side, a disgraceful working condition that happily was outlawed long ago; unhappily, he died in his fifties.

Irene's grandfather John Wesley Applegate stands as the only truly independent businessman in our combined lineage. He ran a well-drilling business around Newark, Ohio, again using his wits and labor to find and drill water wells that operated on a hand pump, not a spigot.

He was an independent businessman with indispensable skills sought in his community long before city water systems became the norm.

But Grandfather Applegate's business contained a palpable downside for Irene's father, Harry Applegate. An extraordinarily bright man, Harry was offered a scholarship at Cleveland's Case School of Applied Science (now Case Western Reserve University) about 1925 or 1926. Better yet, he could live at the home of his sister Ethel, who was living in the Cleveland suburb of Shaker Heights, saving room and board. But Irene's grandfather, wanting reliable and cheap labor, insisted that Harry turn down the scholarship, stay home, and work in the family well-drilling business. Three years later, with the Great Depression looming, he fired Harry just after he had married and his new bride was expecting. Left to support his family, Harry set up shop as a farmer outside New Albany. Irene never forgives her grandfather. So Harry Applegate might have become the engineer that our younger son Doug is today.

But the flip side is that Harry would likely never have met his bride, Gladys, had he gone off to study in Cleveland. Life is so chock-a-block with such ironies that we should leave such woulda-coulda-shouldas to our daydreams.

By late 1967 or early 1968, our stock investments are doing so well that Irene and I begin to believe we can follow Ed Birkner's example and launch out with a new newsletter-publishing company advising investors in housing and real estate stocks. The signals are all bullish. More housing and real estate companies are coming public, I'm gaining valuable analytical experience at S&P, and my 1968 analysis of business magazines, part of the Time Inc. analysis for Professor Bellemore, convinces me that business and stock market readership is growing.

Our entrepreneurial seed is bursting into life. We are ready to be *entrepreneurs*, a word derived from the French word for *undertaker*, referring not to a mortician but one who undertakes great enterprises or ventures.

To mount a new investment advisory in the hurly-burly of Manhattan's Wall Street club, which devours newcomers with unceremonious haste, one must be either a bit touched in the head or believe with missionary zeal that he or she can add something new and better than anyone else is providing. For me, the latter applies. I see a role asking public company CEOs and CFOs all the impertinent but necessary and uncomfortable questions to uncover the often hidden motives behind corporate actions and then writing investor advisories with an "ass to boot" in Rip Manning mode.

My goal is to translate journalistic truth-seeking to Wall Street and the stock market, to bring a truly independent view that hopefully improves investment results for individual investors and protects the sheep from being shorn by the Street's ubiquitous sharpies, to operate as much as possible outside the system. Wall Street is treacherous journalistic terrain because company managements must disclose only *material* facts in a legal sense, and many personal motives and dealings remain private. My goal is to illumine those hidden recesses as they may weigh upon the merits of any investment.

The search for truth has many permutations, and I want to pursue as many as possible.

But before I can take the family wealth and invest in a new business, Irene makes me pledge to put enough income aside to make sure that we could live for a year if the new enterprise never produces a dime. That is probably the best financial decision we ever make.

We decide to include two others in our new company: my brother-in-law Chuck Adams and John Meggitt.

Chuck Adams comes because we may later want to advise on drug and medical stocks; he has over fifteen years of experience in the medical institutional field at both state and national levels and holds an MPH degree from the University of Michigan.

John Meggitt comes aboard to add his computer skills and business experience; a Cambridge University PhD, he's recently started his own computer company, Programmed Control Corporation of Princeton, New Jersey, after a career with Electronics Associates and IBM.

Both are gifted founders' shares, but over time, their participation declines, Chuck because the medical idea never materializes and John because he's too busy running an expanding company. We buy their minority shares back a few years later at book value.

The name "Audit" is picked during a brainstorming session to imply unvarnished truth-telling in sometimes-suspect financial markets. The name is duly included in the corporation papers for Audit Publications, Incorporated, because we intend to be an investment publisher. Audit becomes our trademark of sorts in the years ahead.

The seed is now fully gestated. Our leap into entrepreneurship is at hand.

In December 1968, I scout for an office in a Manhattan office market with a reported 0.25 percent vacancy and settle on the best of a poor lot, a two-room furnished suite at 685 Fifth Avenue at Fifty-Fourth Street. The 685 Fifth building is owned by real estate wizards who renovate an aging building hoping to squeeze as many dollars as possible from tenants. The rent is exorbitant and requires a $950 deposit, but there are zero alternatives.

My undated letter resigning as an assistant to the vice president of S&P, addressed to unit head Saul Smerling, says:

> "Eight years ago I left a comfortable position in the Midwest to strike out for New York City and all the uncertainties that involved. Today I must again pull up stakes and move on to new uncertainties and new opportunities, and accordingly I am submitting my

resignation from the staff of Standard & Poor's effective at the close of business Friday, January 10 [1969].

"I am becoming editor of a new investment publication specializing in the residential construction and real estate industry, an area presently undergoing great ferment and restructuring. It is my conviction that the array of investment opportunities in this industry is and will continue to widen significantly and for that reason the proposed publication has great promise. Obviously the risks of an untried publication are great but I have given the matter great thought and am determined to give it a whirl.

"I have greatly enjoyed my association with you and everyone else at Standard & Poor's, and the new publication intends to become a subscriber to a number of S&P services. Be assured that it took more than an offer for a few more dollars on The Street to forsake these associations."

Smerling asks only one question: "Who's financing your new publication?"

"I am," I reply.

And it stays that way for well over two decades, the enterprise being financed from the Campbell purse. The newly minted entrepreneurs, Ken and Irene Campbell, put about $6,500 of capital up to chase their entrepreneurial dream. The spiffy Fifth Avenue address and high hopes for success are woefully mismatched against Audit's thin capital backing.

I liquidate most of my stock portfolio at what turns out to be near the bull market peak and pocket $10,727 stock gains, which, with my initial $6,500 stake, gives us about $17,250 ($116,000 in 2015 dollars) to prepare to open our doors.

With serendipity like this, how can the fledgling Audit fail?

Chapter 8
THE CHASE

The day after my S&P resignation becomes effective, on Saturday, January 11, 1969, I begin my new life as an entrepreneur by jetting to Houston for a three-day look-in at the National Association of Home Builders (NAHB) convention. The NAHB meeting in the Astrohall convention center adjoining the Astrodome will be old news by the time I can get our first newsletter off the presses, but the convention presents an unusual opportunity to be seen and catch up with homebuilding company leaders, attend another of Ed Birkner's Turn Table dinners, and scatter my proud new business card to all takers.

The convention air is electric as homebuilders, land developers, and related companies are crowding into the stock market. Pittsburgh-based Ryan Homes Incorporated goes public on November 28, 1968, selling 515,000 shares at $26 to gross $13.4 million, and Centex Corporation of Dallas, controlled by trusts for children of Texas oilmen John and Clint Murchison Jr., is teed up to come public as Audit opens for business. (Ryan is now part of NVR Incorporated (symbol NVR), and Centex is part of PulteGroup Incorporated (symbol PHM).)

A total fifty-eight housing-related companies raise $498 million from the public during 1968, and the go-public fever is so hot they raise another $493 million in the first five months of 1969—nearly one billion dollars of new housing capital, or about $6.66 billion in 2015 dollars, in just seventeen months.

I fly home Tuesday, January 14, in time to take tests on both Tuesday and Wednesday evenings at NYU. I still have a couple of courses to wind up before tackling a thesis.

So it comes to pass that on Thursday, January 16, 1969—two weeks past my thirty-ninth birthday—I make the trek from the Port Authority via subway to my new shop in two rented rooms on the third floor at 685 Fifth Avenue but with the actual building entrance on East Fifty-Fourth Street.

How many businesses can say they began life on Fifth Avenue?

Thus begins the chase for investment values. Until now, the chase has been to find suitable stocks for personal investment and gain. Now the chase shifts to finding stocks to recommend to our potential news-letter subscribers, not yet in evidence.

Two priorities command my attention that first day: hire a sec-retary (accomplished within a few days) and submit a Form ADV to register Audit Publications Incorporated as an investment adviser with the Securities and Exchange Commission. We cannot begin publish-ing—i.e., really go into business—until the SEC approves our regis-tration, which automatically becomes effective thirty days after filing unless the commission asks questions. During our run-up planning, we debate vigorously whether or not Audit should register with the Feds and conclude an advisory newsletter has much higher value-added potential than an advertising-supported publication. Hence we must register to get in the game.

A GOOD FIRST DAY

That first day, I meet, at invitation of Cornelius C. "Neil" Rose Jr., an International Paper Corporation vice president and former mortgage banker, whom I had met previously, with an IP corporate development officer and soon am retained at five hundred dollars a month by International Paper. Then the nation's largest private landowner with seven million acres of timberland, IP seeks to boost returns from its enormous land holding. To that end, IP buys American Central Corporation, a Michigan land developer run by Don Foote, and agrees to acquire California homebuilder Donald Bren. I am to advise IP on these and other potential real estate investments. The retainer covers my rent and contributes no little comfort to my transition from corporate employee to full-fledged entrepreneur. A very good first day's work.

Within six months, Neil Rose moves to North American Mortgage Investors, a newly formed mortgage REIT, when it comes public in June 1969. Later Neil contributes with distinction to my book on REITs (see chapter 10, "The Book").

And within a few weeks, I agree to write a monthly business column and assemble an annual review of housing industry earnings for *Professional Builder*, a major competitor to my former employer, also for a five-hundred-dollar monthly fee. Secretarial and operating costs are now covered.

On Friday, January 17, I make a one-day swing to Lexington, Kentucky, for a looksee at new wares displayed by members of the Mobile Home Manufacturers Association at their annual gathering, again to spread around that prized new business card.

At the end of January 1969, we draw a balance sheet showing $8,059 of assets ($51,000 in 2015 dollars), including $3,318 in cash. We are advised to opt for "thin" capitalization, and thus the balance sheet shows only $1,000 of shareholders' equity and a $5,556 note payable to shareholders (us). We figure that Audit loses $523.86 during that first January.

Thus Audit begins with its total funding coming from the Campbell pocket. Over the years, Audit makes a couple of desultory efforts to obtain outside capital or joint venture with larger organizations but nothing ever connects. Throughout its entire twenty-four and a half years of independence, Audit is essentially funded, good years and bad, from the Campbell wallet.

One negative is that Audit's finances are always at the mercy of the marketplace for investment newsletters, with good years inevitably followed by bad. This roller-coaster means we are not always able to give our children everything they want, but we do not starve despite a couple of close shaves. The tightest moment comes sometime in the 1970s when Irene is forced to raid Rick's coin collection to buy food.

Starting about mid-1970, Irene takes over the duties of chief financial officer, a formidable assignment for someone trained as a teacher and most definitely not as a financier. For over twenty years, she juggles bill paying while keeping enough cash in the Audit checking account to retain solvency. She accomplishes this daunting task so smoothly that I never have to worry. These are the things parents never tell their children at the time.

The positive result is that Audit is never beholden to any outside influence, always free to call situations as it sees them without worrying about a nasty phone call from upstairs. Such freedom is a gift enjoyed by very few in this life. In truth, our bosses are our subscribers and clients, a truth often forgotten by so many nouveaux entrepreneurs.

To many neophyte entrepreneurs, being the boss means freedom to set their own hours untouched by the demands of anyone else. They see the boss lifestyle as pleasant, financially rewarding, and worthy of emulation.

My view, formed by helming Audit, is exactly the opposite. Being the boss gives you the privilege of working longer hours than anyone else. Mother Gladys Applegate, when visiting, often remarks that she heard my typewriter tap-tap-tapping the last thing before she fell asleep and the first thing when she awakened. A publisher's life is often a keyboard ride on a squirrel cage. As we learn during the lean years, bosses must pay their staffs ahead of themselves to make sure they don't jump ship. In the mid-1970s and again in the early 1990s, this aspect manifests itself in belt-tightening days. And most crucially, the boss really has a whole host of bosses—they are called clients or subscribers or customers or whatever. No matter what business, your clients set the terms and prices of whatever product or service you deliver. Fail to deliver, and your proud venture certainly becomes part of business history.

Thus begins our quest for that elusive quality of truth on Wall Street. We have chosen to settle on the *buy side* of the Street, representing investors against the constant outpouring of research, predominantly optimistic, disgorging from *sell side* brokerage houses. The answer to the question "What is truth?" generally lies in balancing the sell side's optimism and the buy side's innate conservatism. As a buy sider, we must hold our own counsel and restrain adopting the sell side's urgings.

The Street's buy side–sell side bifurcation is a constant, in evidence today just as much as in 1969.

Can we rely upon company executives to tell the truth? It's probably best to assume they tell their version of reality, skewed to sell their particular vision of the truth. Independent certified public auditors vouch for management's presentation of financial statements. Their numbers carry the hard reality of truth, tempered by the SEC's mantra: "Past performance is no guarantee of future results."

Still, nothing's foolproof, and over the years, a few companies succeed in hoodwinking their auditors. Equity Funding Corporation of America creates millions of dollars in fraudulent insurance policies without detection in 1973, and Enron Corporation successfully coopts accountants in 2001 to tell a complex version of obscured "truth." As analyst and adviser, we accept the version put forth by accountant and management as a first cut of truth, to be proven by inquiry.

In 1969, the market remains skeptical because investors have been burned recently by two widely publicized frauds. In 1963, Billy Sol Estes scams lenders by creating false ammonia tank mortgages in Texas. Also in 1963, Tino De Angelis fills Bayonne, New Jersey, storage tanks with water to claim more salad oil than he owns. These twin scandals are fresh in investors' memories when I set up shop. Moreover, real estate companies are in poor standing because of the Webb & Knapp and Lusk Corp. failures. One broker tells me he avoids real estate stocks because "builders go broke."

We begin operating in the paper age: no fax, no Internet, no Google searches. We cannot afford a Quotron machine or stock ticker. Information in the form of company reports or SEC filings arrives by snail mail or, in rare instances, Wall Street deliverymen known as "runners." The SEC forbids companies to give forward earnings estimates or guidance to the Street, and earnings estimates are closely guarded.

Daily trading volume runs about four or five million shares a day on the New York Stock Exchange, but even then, brokerage back offices are falling behind in transferring paper stock certificates. A year later concerns about Wall Street's back-office paper snarls are so widespread that several larger firms are forced into shotgun mergers to survive and Congress creates the Securities Investor Protection Corporation, or SIPC, to assure investors they may leave funds with sell-side firms.

On the plus side, analysts and company execs coexist in an easy relationship that lets managements pass on sensitive information to the Street informally without having to issue press releases covering every tiny event.

In short, Wall Street is an informal setting where a new face with honesty, energy, and élan can make a name fairly quickly. As a fresh face, I hope to win friends and influence investors.

FINDING CUSTOMERS

I choose the newsletter format because letters can be printed quickly and delivered to subscribers while the information and opinions remain fresh and actionable. But in a world before faxes, before e-mails, before instant communication, I must rely upon a paper chain to convey my thoughts to subscribers. That paper chain works like this. The publisher prepares an original manuscript and delivers this *mechanical* to a commercial printer, who prints the newsletters, folds and stuffs them into an envelope, applies mailing labels and postage, and delivers the bundled product to the US Postal Service. In 2015, we call it "snail mail."

For our maiden promotional newsletter, we assemble a list of 3,174 carefully selected names in homebuilding, mobile home, securities, and mortgage businesses and deliver them, along with mechanicals of the first copy of *Audit of Housing Investments,* to our printer on the evening of Wednesday, February l9, 1969.

And then I watch and push, push and watch, and then push and watch some more.

Our printer, a shop named Benson, fiddles and diddles and dithers and frets with our precious copy, our lifeblood, for nearly two weeks, finally dumping our maiden newsletter into the mails on Monday, March 3. It is old news already!

We receive our first subscription order a week later, on March 10.

I promptly switch to a second printer who guarantees twenty-four-hour turnaround, prepare a second promotional mailing, to a different list of 1,500 persons, and send this to our new printer March 19. This mailing goes smoother, and we finally start receiving return orders.

Originally, I conceive a monthly service but quickly switch to a semimonthly schedule to maximize nimbleness for subscribers and address rapidly changing markets. The first *Audit* is offered at annual subscriptions just below one hundred dollars because I perceive that many prospects can approve subscriptions below that amount without having to seek higher-level approval. Thus this first newsletter is offered at seventy-five dollars for an annual subscription for charter subscribers and ninety-six dollars annually thereafter (about $495 and $635 in 2015 dollars). Combined with my retainers, this formula puts enough dollars in the till to keep Audit above water in that maiden year.

That initial issue carries a front-page article titled "Why? An Editor's View."

> "We never pick up a new publication without asking ourselves, 'Why?' and so we want to answer that question for you straight out. *Audit of Housing Investments* is on your desk because in our experience no single periodical pulls together for investors, analysts and housing executives a concise monthly summary of the significant investment news of a major but fragmented industry. Hence one objective is simply to lighten your reading load.
>
> "We have singled out housing and real estate for initial investment attention because, in our view, institutional investors and member firms ignore at their peril this giant industry in ferment.
>
> "Too, we confess some disturbance at the fact that the investment community and the housing and real estate fraternity seldom speak the same language … In this context our name. *Audit* expresses our aim to provide an independent view of sometimes conflicting worlds and to bring to you monthly an authoritative, non-analytical report on the investment news

institutional investors, analysts, and housing executives need to know."

Notice that word *nonanalytical*. At that early stage, I plan a factual newsletter supplemented by a series of company research reports at much higher prices targeted mainly for institutional investors. That strategy fizzles within two months as newsletter subscribers make very clear they want analytical information and opinions, period.

And they want it more frequently than monthly. Hence within two months, we change the newsletter into semimonthly mode, moving from an eight-page monthly format to a four-page twice-monthly format.

Our arrival quickly casts us into the go-public turmoil then engulfing housing. At the January NAHB convention, one large homebuilder tells me: "Either myself or my staff have been in New York once a week for a solid year. I wish I had known you were in existence so you could have saved us some traveling."

To help companies with go-public ambitions, we initially publish a booklet titled *The Cost of Capital*, tabulating offering spreads and brokerage commissions on well over one hundred recent housing-related stock and bond offerings. It becomes a moderate seller.

But I am neither geared nor staffed to be a New York gofer for homebuilders across the land. "If you have nothing else to do, you chase deals," a friend tells me, and I find it sound advice then and now.

By our third mailing in early April, the newsletter has fifty subscribers, almost exactly 1 percent of the 4,700 direct mail pieces. It feels as if we are on our way.

THE MOUSE

My chase for investment values, now on behalf of my subscribers, begins when from my rat hole emerges, not a rat, not a REIT, but a *mouse*. Operating company Walt Disney Productions, famed creator of Mickey

Mouse and friends, captures my fancy as the purest of pure Florida land plays.

Following the successful launch of Disneyland in Anaheim, southeast of Los Angles, in 1955, Walt Disney rues "the one major mistake at Disneyland: the company did not control the development of the property surrounding this great tourist magnet," Audit says in April 1969.

When the company leaps from the West Coast to the East Coast for a "Florida project," it uses dummy corporations and helpful individuals to purchase most of the eventual 27,443 acres, much of which is platted into five-acre lots, south of Orlando, Florida. The *Orlando Sentinel* breaks the story of Disney's stealth land buys in October 1965, forcing Disney to go public with its plans to build the Walt Disney World theme park and resort on the huge assemblage.

By early 1969, Walt Disney Productions (NYSE: DIS) is busily preparing the site for construction but skeptics doubt the tiny movie company (its market capitalization is only $360 million) can actually raise enough money to pull off its grandiose vision. Florida land schemes and dreams are burned deeply into the American psyche by numerous past failures. Worse, the master visionary, Walt Disney himself, dies in December 1966, and the company mantle falls to his brother, Roy Disney, whose skills are largely unknown.

I ponder all these negatives and become a believer after reading Disney's annual reports and experiencing Disney's fastidious attention to detail.

In *Audit*'s Early April 1969 issue, our third, with WDW opening still over two years into the future, I try to put some numbers on the undertaking into perspective for investors.

"The initial investment of $165 million [$1.08 billion in 2015 dollars] would more than double predevelopment

assets of $120 million … some Floridians are confi-
dently predicting that Disney investment will top $600
million in the following years …

"The Florida tract is 119 times larger than the
California park [Disneyland] … the Theme Park and
attendant hotel-motel and service facilities will occupy
only 800 acres, or less than 3% of the site …

"In fiscal 1968 [September] the park [Disneyland]
accounted for $0.70 [or 46%] of $1.51/share earnings
[adjusted for a subsequent 2-for-1 split] … If Disney is
able to maintain this same rate of return on the initial
$165 million Florida investment, Disney World could
be contributing in the neighborhood of $0.98–$1.08/
share to DIS earnings four or five years out."

Our call, with DIS stock at $38.50 was:

"For these reasons DIS rates in *Audit*'s judgment as the outstanding
long-term commitment among Florida developers today."

On April 30, 1969, DIS meets analysts and the press in Orlando
to unveil specific plans and target October 1, 1971, as WDW's official
opening date. I prevail on longtime friend Lee Schooler to drive two
hours from his retirement home in Lighthouse Point, Florida, to represent Audit at the conference. A veteran newsman, Schooler buttonholes
DIS Chairman Roy Disney after the formalities. He garners a wealth of
specific info on the company's high hopes and confides that DIS plans
depreciating WDW assets over fifteen years instead of Disneyland's
twelve years. That spells higher earnings for DIS. The two old-timers
seem to hit it off famously, and the serendipitous contact is a coup for
our small start-up.

We put his new analytical insights into a special report issued May

9, 1969, recommending DIS "only for patient long-term investors." By then, DIS shares are up to $41.25. Our thesis is that WDW will be a place to stay, in contrast to Disneyland's "place to visit" status, and that DIS aims to capture considerable extra spending for lodging, meals, and recreation by building hotels and other tourist attractions.

We project DIS earnings will rise to about $3.00 per share in FY 1972, the first full year after opening, so the current price works out to 13.8 times our estimate four years out.

"As the appreciated land value in Walt Disney World becomes better defined, we feel certain the stock will sell at a considerably higher multiple. Long term investors should accumulate the shares on any decline," says Audit.

More wrinkles emerge later in the Walt Disney World (WDW) story. U.S. Steel Corporation signs on to use a new unitized modular steel system to build two hotels with 1,559 rooms adjoining WDW, and in December 1970, I travel to Orlando for a long-awaited on-the-ground peek. The system works, and we publish a two and one-half page review. Best of all, the system lets WDW keep on schedule by building in fifteen months what would take twenty-four to thirty months using normal construction methods.

The Mouse issues $150 million of low-coupon debentures convertible into common at well over two times book value, plus tapping retained cash flow, to finance Walt Disney World, whose cost rises from $165 to $230 million. The financing confounds doubters who fear that DIS cannot raise enough money to finish its Florida project.

As opening day nears, I visit Orlando one or two times more. On opening day, Friday, October 1, 1971, DIS stock closes at $108.88, up a stunning 183 percent from our opening call in April 1969, over two years ago.

But opening weekend crowds disappoint bulls and calls into question

DIS estimates that eight to ten million visitors will flock to WDW in its first year.

DIS stock tanks 8.6 percent to $99.50 when trading resumes Monday, October 4.

On October 18, we tell subscribers, "Small opening crowds are reason for caution but not panic ... At 97-7/8 [share price] we would add to long-term holdings on further weakness."

But crowds soon materialize, and the Thanksgiving weekend is a blowout. DIS shares rebound smartly to close the year 1971 at $137-1/2, up another 38 percent from that October 4 panic sell-off.

Disney, the company, is off and running on its way to building a global entertainment powerhouse valued in 2015 at $144.8 billion by stock market investors.

DIS, the stock, is also flying, and our chase for investment values opens with a super-winner.

MORE PICKS

But, as so often happens in the real stock market, our other initial picks are a mixed bag.

On May 8, 1969, Audit publishes a report saying "speculative purchases in risk accounts of Giffen Industries at 34 (OTC) might work out well." Giffen, which I describe as "a hitherto little known acquisition-minded company" and "a high-risk turnaround situation with unusual profit potentials," pays $50.3 million for 51 percent of Keller Industries, a troubled building products producer, at sixty dollars a share in March. On May 5, Giffen tells the New York Society of Security Analysts (NYSSA) that it believes Keller can be turned around by late summer.

But a week later, Giffen asks to rescind its stock deal, saying its internal review of Keller dictates its new stance. Keller stock nosedives to $32.50 on the NYSE, and Giffen now faces a quick $22.8 million bath.

I quickly put out an update on May 13 saying "we would now stand aside on both issues." Seven months later, the lawyers settle the case and Giffen ends the year at 22 bid, down 35 percent.

My takeaway from this disaster: be very wary of stories emanating from small unknown companies that leap into the spotlight from "nowhere." Above all, don't put your name on a buy recommendation for a company you don't know cold.

The cement business looks attractive. I have just done a long cement-industry accounting case study as part of my NYU work—and recommend Lone Star Cement (symbol LCE) at $27 on May 8 as "very attractive for intermediate and longer term accounts," and Alpha Portland Cement (APC) on May 5 at $24 as a "speculative purchase based on strong recovery in its cement and aggregate business plus present and potential benefits of an aggressive acquisition program."

Lone Star disappoints short-term and drifts down to $22.13 by year-end but rallies during 1970 to end that year at $26.38, justifying the call.

Alpha, one of the highest leveraged cements then extant, recently buys Slattery Associates, a New York City excavation, foundation, and highway general contractor expected to generate about fifty cents' earnings in 1969, versus APC's skimpy six cents' earnings in 1968. Intriguingly, APC is also negotiating to buy closely held Long Island shopping center developer Kimco Corporation, which then holds about 6.9 percent of APC's common. Kimco owns interests in about seventy shopping centers and hopes to help Alpha, then suffering a fuel shortage, to fire its kilns, by providing hazardous waste from its centers to keep the kilns burning. But Kimco has no thought of coming public at that time via a back-door takeover, according to Kimco cofounder Milton Cooper. As the Kimco deal unwinds, APC stock falls 25 percent to eighteen dollars by year-end.

More than two decades later, Kimco creates the modern REIT

industry almost single-handedly by coming public at the depth of a real estate recession, in November 1991, and begins a long run as one of Wall Street's favorite real estate stocks (see chapter 25, "The Partners"). We will never know how REIT history might have been rewritten if Kimco had been persuaded to come public in 1969 as part of Alpha Portland.

Deltona Corporation (DLT: ASE) is my final call in that burst of May 1969 special reports and by far the most nettlesome. If any company can ride Disney's coattails to profitable growth in Florida, I conclude DLT should be it.

Hence, Audit issues a six-page report, calling DLT a "strong hold at current levels [$46.88] and we would be a buyer on any reaction," on May 5. The price is relatively lofty at twenty-six-times our estimated $1.80 per share fully diluted earnings.

DLT is then a smaller but quality play among Florida land install-ment sellers. The three Mackle brothers—Elliott, Frank, and Robert, who organized and subsequently left General Development, then king of the Florida land purveyors—run DLT to minimize manifest risks in selling Florida building lots with ten-dollar down payments. For DLT, cash down payments average 17.5 percent of lot and house sales at their premier Marco Island community, and cancellation rates on lot receiv-ables are slightly below industry average. Better, only about 58 percent of DLT revenues come from land sales, with bulk lumber retailing and mobile home manufacturing providing sizable cash flow.

By the end of 1969, DLT shares have moved up 29 percent to $60.50, and I am happy with the call.

But installment lot sales come under attack February 2, 1970, from Dr. Abraham Briloff, accountancy professor at Baruch College in Manhattan, who rips installment land sale accounting in an adjec-tive-larded exposé in *Barron's*. DLT shares fall 13 percent to 43 dol-lars per share the day after the article and end the month at $42.38.

Consumer advocates enter the fray, claiming that unsuspecting buyers are being fast-talked into buying unwanted lots. Then during one brutal week in late May 1970, DLT shares shed 46 percent of value as the company acknowledges a difficult year. Shares rally to close 1970 at $37.75, down 19.5 percent from the original *buy* advisory, and I put them in *hold* mode.

The tally is as follows: one super winner (Disney); one okay but volatile pick (Deltona); one okay cement pick (Lone Star); one disappointing cement pick (Alpha); and one misfire (Giffen). Overall, we let our profits run on Disney to balance the lesser picks.

During this burst of activity, our office rent remains extravagant and mismatched with revenues, so we decide to move, shifting downtown to 500 Fifth Avenue, at Forty-Second Street, in September 1969 to share quarters with a fledgling public relations company begun by a chap named Bruce Marcus. Bruce is a charming, affable dreamer who rents the top floor—Suite 4916, the records show—and sets up shop in an oversized suite whose furnishings are always "on order from Denmark." I place my typewriter on the windowsill behind my desk so it is always at the ready.

One evening near Christmas, Irene arrives for dinner and remarks that the northern view of Midtown Manhattan from my office window is "spectacular."

I look up, and, sure enough, it is!

In over three months of toil at that typewriter, I'd never once lifted my eyes from the keyboard and words flowing onto paper to absorb the beauty of holiday lights from my prime vantage point. At that moment in time, I am in publish-or-perish mode, period. Shame on me!

For the year 1969, revenue weighs in at $36,377 ($230,200 in 2015 dollars), and the accountant figures we lost $1,161. But *Audit of Housing Investments* now counts 196 subscribers, and subscriptions are trending up. My salary draw is $6,625, about one-third my S&P pay. We believe 1970 will be better.

(Bruce Marcus goes on to author sixteen books and found *The Marcus Letter*, a respected journal on the marketing of professional services. He dies December 1, 2014 at age 89.)

But as that maiden year winds down, my chase for investment values shifts abruptly as dozens of mortgage REITs burst from my rat hole.

Chapter 9
THE LETTER

As 1969 eases into 1970, *Audit of Housing Investments* is being overrun by mortgage REITs.

In planning the advisory service, I figure that investors will want to read news and advice about housing, a big slice of the American economy now coming public, and that several dozen private homebuilders and land developers and mortgage companies will emerge from my rat hole.

I am 100 percent wrong!

Instead, short-term mortgage REITs march from my rat hole so incessantly and persistently that keeping score taxes my precomputer resources.

THE MORTGAGE CRASH-IN

The 1960 law creating real estate investment trusts is conceived and achieved after Herculean efforts by a small band of Boston commercial real estate operatives, yet mortgage trusts are first to capture broader investor fancy.

The two groups resemble oil and water; commercial real estate operators are borrowers, while mortgage trusts are lenders, and ne'er the twain shall meet.

But when real estate assets are defined as "interests in real property and interests in mortgages on real property" to win wider support for

REIT legislation in 1960 (see chapter 6, "The Break"), the door opens for mortgage trusts.

Two short-term mortgage trusts seize the law's opening and rush stock offers to market. First Mortgage Investors (FMI) raises $15 million with its September 1961 offer, and Continental Mortgage Investors (CMI) follows with a $22.5 million offer in March 1962, as detailed in chapter 6.

But the stock market break in May 1962 kills new REIT offerings for nearly six years afterward, and without competition, FMI and CMI establish themselves as short-term mortgage lending powerhouses. From 1962 to 1968, they consistently increase earnings, dividends, and stock prices. FMI doubles share earnings and dividends in the five years to January 1968 for a 15.2 percent annual rate. CMI bests that by tripling income and dividends per share for a gaudy 24.6 percent annual rate through March 1968. Their stellar track records put them in a class by themselves.

CMI's track record qualifies it to list on the NYSE in May 1965, elevating company and industry visibility to a wider investor audience. Shares of most early equity REITs languish in the thinly traded over-the-counter pink sheet market.

Thus short-term mortgage REITs appear to investors in early 1968 as greyhounds with great track records, juicy dividend yields, and a bigger future in a growing construction market starving for money because many savings and loan associations have departed.

Equity REITs pale in comparison and are typecast as small, slow-growth tortoises.

What matters most to investors is that mortgage REITs post sterling earnings and dividend growth during the 1960s and appear to offer a unique combination of growth and dividend yield with limited risk.

Mortgage REITs appear to be the better mousetrap. Buy, baby, buy!

The REIT revolution is about to take an unexpected turn.

THE ICEBREAKER

In June 1968, Alan J. Smith, a clever Englishman who becomes captivated by the potential of mortgage REITs while working for Continental Mortgage, persuades Ken Melis and his midtier brokerage New York Securities to underwrite a twenty-five-million-dollar offering of common stock and debentures by his creation, Associated Mortgage Investors (AMI).

AMI catches the eye of growth and income investors and before 1968 ends two other mortgage REITs—General Mortgage and Republic Mortgage, both sponsored by independent mortgage groups in Baltimore and Miami--complete stock offerings of fifteen million and thirty-three million dollars in November and December respectively. Although tiny from today's perspective, these offerings get their backers into the emerging REIT game.

The honey attracting the sponsor bees is a menu of fees for advising a trust on running a mortgage portfolio. Basic advisory fees are sweetest, ranging from 1.0 to 1.2 percent of average portfolio assets. To that, add mortgage servicing, mortgage brokerage, insurance brokerage, and title fees and the like. They add to a feast of fees.

That basic 1.0 or 1.2 percent advisory fee sets up another inherent conflict of interest if and when trust assets are levered one, two, or more times with borrowed money. Depending on the lending spread, a levered trust may pay out more in extra advisory fees than the trust actually earns in dollars after paying interest on its borrowings. Too, shareholders bear all the risk of defaults on a larger portfolio while the external adviser is insulated from such risk. (By July 1971, Audit surveys eighty-five trust advisory fee arrangements and finds seventy-four trusts combine an asset-based fee with incentive fees tied to return on shareholder equity. We analyze trust fee arrangements annually afterward and publish a popular guide to REIT fees.)

And finally there's presumed conflict over which entity gets the best investment opportunities when the REIT's sponsor remains active in the mortgage business. Trustees try to solve this conflict by insisting on rights of first refusal on carefully defined loan types, and this system seems to work.

All this complexity appears as so much legal gibberish to investors and AMI, and its two followers catapult mortgage REITs into prominence in late 1968 just as Audit is searching for office space to open its doors.

The net result is mortgage REITs are already stalking the stage when *Audit of Housing Investments*, which quickly becomes just *Audit* to readers, makes its appearance in March 1969. From my protective vantage point, the entrance of mortgage REITs threatens to draw precious investor attention away from the homebuilding and development companies that I hope will provide the initial book of subscribers—my planned bread and butter.

Fortunately, the first half of 1969 is relatively quiet for the mortgage REITs—*only* nine REIT IPO offerings in the first half raise slightly over two hundred million dollars and are duly recorded in *Audit*. Subscription growth remains solid.

THE MESSAGE

On June 26, 1969, my rosy picture darkens when Larwin Mortgage Investors sells forty million dollars of IPO stock.

Larwin Mortgage is sponsored by California homebuilder Larwin Group, which agrees in March 1969 to merge into financial conglomerate CNA Financial for one hundred million dollars in CNA stock. Larwin, then the nation's largest private homebuilder with seventy-five million dollars in sales, is led by Larry Weinberg, well known to me from *H&H* days as a keenly astute financial player.

To me, Larwin is a prime candidate to lead a parade of private homebuilders into the stock market.

Instead, Larry Weinberg rewrites my script, and his June entry into mortgage REITs conveys a chilling message for my new enterprise.

Large merchant homebuilders want to be major players in this emerging REIT field but would rather tie their more cyclical homebuilding businesses to industrial or financial blue chips.

I cannot ignore Larry's inconvenient message.

THE THESIS

Almost simultaneously in June 1969, I complete class work toward my MBA at New York University and start to write my thesis over two six-week back-to-back summer semesters. Two of my classmates say they will wait until the fall to start their theses but never come back. Sad.

What thesis topic to pick? The heightened investor interest in mortgage REITs points in that direction, and so in June 1969, I plunge into a thesis titled "An Analysis of Risk and Return Potentials of Mortgage Real Estate Investment Trusts."

The thesis involves crunching quarterly earnings records for the relatively few mortgage REITs then in existence on NYU's giant IBM computer. The effort generates reams of computer printouts, which I analyze with aid of neighbor Larry Fussell, an experienced statistical analyst.

That analysis concludes that each level of debt leverage in a mortgage REIT's capital structure results in *lower* incremental returns on new investments. In other words, a REIT whose debt is two-times its equity capital base is palpably riskier than one whose debt is only one-times its equity base because the REIT earns less on the incremental dollar invested than the potential risk inherent in the larger asset base.

Consequences of this insight do not manifest themselves until years later.

When the 131-page thesis is completed and accepted in August 1969, my thesis adviser urges me to continue toward my doctorate because "your thesis is already long enough to qualify for a doctoral dissertation."

"No, thanks," I reply. "I have a company to build."

Once the thesis is finished, I undertake to expand it into a longer investment research report and publish this in November 1969 under the title *Mortgage Trusts: Lenders with a Plus.* The report, now grown to 178 pages and bound in a blue cover adorned with red lettering, surveys the market for short-term construction lending and concludes that:

> "…the trusts have stepped into a vacuum in the C&D (construction and development loan) market left by the withdrawal of the S&Ls (savings and loan associations) and we believe fears of a glut in funds in the C&D market are extremely overblown.
>
> "If all the trusts currently operating or with proposed registration statements pending [then totaling fifty-two trusts] with the SEC leveraged themselves to a 4-to-1 debt/equity ratio, they would supply about 13.5% of the [C&D] funds required.
>
> "Beyond this bright lending future, we believe the tax-exempt status of the trusts places them in a unique position to become major providers of debt and venture capital packages to the real estate development industry … the trusts will swing from straight interim lending to lending with equity participations … [they] are "lenders with a plus."

My investment conclusion was:

> "The bulk of operating trusts present a potential of
> above-average current dividend yield generally exceed-
> ing 7.5% … and relatively low P/E ratios that offer the
> prospect of moderate appreciation of 15%–25% over the
> next year or so … Since most trusts are selling at or only
> slightly above book value, and since trusts historically
> have seldom sold below this mark, we view the downside
> risk from current levels as minimal."

All those computer runs don't prevent me from drinking the
Kool-Aid.

Lenders with a Plus turns out to be a fairly brisk seller at $27.50 a
copy, and our modest print run of six hundred is exhausted in short order. A memo at the end of 1970 notes that we have sold 584 copies and
have only 13 copies on hand.

Lenders with a Plus also sends a strong message that the thirst for
knowledge and facts about mortgage REITs is near insatiable and that
Audit's best path to success lies in gearing up to satisfy this aridity. *Voila*,
a modest best seller!

INSTANT INDUSTRY

Meantime, the content of *Audit* is becoming overwhelmed by reports of
new mortgage REIT IPOs. Wall Street is in business to raise money for
eager new entrepreneurial businesses, and with investors snapping up
every stock with "REIT" or "mortgage" or "trust" in its name, investment bankers scour the countryside to locate worthy mortgage operatives
wanting to tap the money pot.

After a relatively slow first half of 1969 in which nine mortgage
REITs raise $204 million in IPOs, the pace quickens in the third quarter

with five offerings fetching nearly $200 million equity, including the $100 million September stock offering at twenty dollars a share by Diversified Mortgage Investors (DMI), which, along with DMI's concurrent sale of $50 million convertible debentures, makes DMI the largest single REIT offering until that date.

DMI is the second REIT created by Neil and Monte Wallace, the brains behind Continental Mortgage's march to industry leadership. DMI becomes an instant "hot stock" with a 40 percent opening-day leap from its twenty-dollar share offering price because investors see it as a low-multiple way to buy the Continental management team, as top officers of the two trusts overlap. But CMI's top brass outsmart themselves because CMI's industry-best thirty-six price/earnings multiple is quickly cut in half as CMI stock plunges 42 percent from $31.25 to $18.13 before stabilizing.

DMI meanwhile gets off to a slow operating start because it must build a new management team from scratch and its stock falls back to its IPO price of twenty dollars a share by the time The Letter debuts in March 1970. DMI pledges to pursue medium- to longer-term mortgages and within a year develops into a specialist in recreation homesite loans, land acquisition loans generally to major residential communities built out over many years, and short-term fully amortizing standing permanent loans.

But IPOs in 1969's closing three months more than double that blazing third-quarter pace when a dozen new mortgage REITs, plus one doozie of an equity trust offering, come public by raising $472 million. The mix of sponsoring organizations shifts sharply as six leading mortgage bankers from all corners of the country take the plunge into mortgage REITs. Part of real estate's arcana, mortgage bankers originate local loans on homes and small commercial buildings and consolidate the loans into multi-million-dollar packages for sale to ultimate investors.

They are called "bankers" because loan bundling exposes them to risk from adverse interest rate swings.

The audacious six hail from all corners of the land and soak up $156 million in equity capital: Lomas & Nettleton from Dallas (a $28 million raise); Alison, Colwell, and Palomar from Southern California ($18.6, $15, and $15 million respectively); Atico from Miami ($15 million); and Citizens from Detroit ($21 million).

But what catches my eye is a charge by commercial banks and insurance companies into the REIT parade, the robins presaging a huge migration into REITs by their comrades in banking and insurance.

The insurance contingent is led by Mortgage Trust of America, formed via a huge $63 million rights offering to holders of sponsor Transamerica Corporation in San Francisco, and Fidelity Mortgage Investors backed by Jacksonville life company George Washington Corporation, in turn controlled by Wilmington Trust Company of Delaware.

Breaking the ice for major banks are two offerings: Cameron Brown, mortgage arm of First Union National BanCorp of Charlotte ($43.75 million); and Unionamerica, Incorporated, Los Angeles, one-bank holding company that stamps its name on the $25 million Unionamerica Mortgage and Equity Trust.

And finally New York City–based conglomerate City Investing Company pulls $68 million from the market for City Investing Mortgage (later just CI Mortgage). Clearly mortgage REITs are the flavor of the year, and *Audit* strains to bring details of each new REIT to subscribers.

Along with a $20 million offer from an independent, these new short-term mortgage trusts garner $372 million equity capital to pour into the C&D (construction and development mortgage loan) market during that fourth quarter of 1969, a high-water mark for IPOs not exceeded during the ensuing deluge.

Equity REITs, which own properties directly, labor to get into the race for new dollars with a single entry. Hubbard Real Estate Investments, managed by a subsidiary of Merrill Lynch, raises $100 million in November 1969 with most proceeds earmarked to buy properties net leased to longtime Merrill clients: warehouses for Chrysler Corporation and retail stores for W.T. Grant Company, Safeway Stores, and Broadway Hale Stores.

The market is clearly infatuated with mortgage REITs and can't buy enough of their stock … or advice on mortgage REIT stocks. An instant industry is forming before my eyes, and *Audit* must become information central. REITs are charging wholesale from my rat hole and revise my personal mission with *Audit*.

THE STRIKE

At *Audit*, we begin planning a second service named *Realty Trust Review*, or simply *RTR*. After long crafting of promotional material, mailing lists, and content—more work than preceded the original launch of *Audit*—we deliver mechanicals for a four-page complementary maiden issue of *RTR* to the post office at 5:00 p.m. on March 17, 1970. The printer is instructed to run and deliver several thousand initial copies to potential subscribers.

The launch is a major gamble of both time and money for our young publishing venture, still striving for steady profitable footing.

The next day marks our nineteenth wedding anniversary, and Irene and I plan to celebrate. Imagine my dismay when I arrive home that evening for a celebration and instead learn from the evening news that New York City postal workers are planning to strike at midnight, March 18.

We celebrate anyway. Our marriage is far more important than any money we may lose.

And strike the postal workers did. Leaders of the strike movement are based in New York City, and the New York post office effectively shuts down at midnight.

It marks the first and only postal strike in US history!

What a downer!

At first, I think we have just blown an obscene portion of our tiny free cash on prospecting for a new service that may never see the light of day. The vision of our precious promo issue sitting in some postal tub for the strike's duration haunts that evening.

The next morning, I start hoping against hope that maybe, just maybe, enough issues made it out of New York before midnight to salvage something of the effort.

The following day, the telephone begins ringing with subscription orders from persons across the land, phoning in their replies because they know their return cards likely will never make it back to us and they don't want to be left behind.

By the end of the third day, we know we have a winner, and within a week, over one hundred new subscribers enroll. The strike drags on for two weeks and cripples US mail delivery, but we are indifferent. The telephone trumps snail mail, for now and forever.

The Letter is off and running. *Voila* again!

Realty Trust Review's first issue notes that a "Nonstop Listing Parade Boosts Growth Potential"; that twenty-seven new realty trusts, both of the mortgage and equity variety, have been formed the past year; and that eighteen REITs are now listed on either the New York Stock Exchange or American Stock Exchange (known as NYSE MKT since October 1, 2008).

From a standing start, the instant industry's market valuation now stands at $1.6 billion. That's fancy stepping for an industry that didn't really exist two years before.

"In short, you'll be hearing a great deal more about the trusts," the maiden issue proclaims. That issue promises the "longest listing parade in years," bringing more REITs to either the New York or American Stock Exchanges.

Noting that listed REITs tend to sell at higher ratios above book value than nonlisted trusts, the issue says, "Simply put, a high ratio lets a trust buy other assets (either dollars for a mortgage trust or book equity for an ownership trust) cheaper than a trust with a low ratio can buy those same assets. This is the essence of equity leverage."

Under the headline "And Now, Enter the Life Insurance Giants," the issue reports that "the word on Wall Street is that the big life companies are poised to leap into realty trust operations." Both Connecticut General Insurance Company and Mutual of New York, two major life companies, each register one-hundred-million-dollar offers of stocks and bonds for mortgage trusts they plan to sponsor. Both sponsors are substantially larger than the two life companies then sponsoring mortgage REITs, American Century and Fidelity Mortgage. Both plan to focus on longer-term mortgages and equities. ConnGen, the report notes, owns half of the Columbia new town then building between Baltimore and Washington, and recently formed ConnGen Properties to operate as a realty developer.

This duo is soon followed by insurers Equitable Life, State Mutual, and Northwestern Mutual Life, as do major banks like Banker's Trust and Chase Manhattan of New York City, Continental Illinois of Chicago, and Bank of America of San Francisco, along with dozens of lesser known names. Eventually over one hundred commercial banks, insurance companies, mortgage companies, and fellow travelers sell six billion dollars in REIT common stock and debentures.

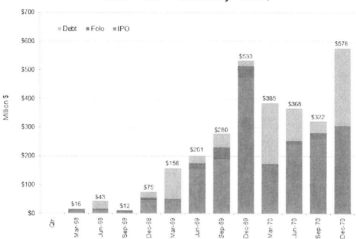

Exhibit 9.1 -- REIT Equity & Debt Offerings
1968 - 1970 -- Quarterly - Mil. $

Exhibit 9.1 traces REIT debt and stock offerings, with stock offerings classed as either initial public offerings (IPOs) or subsequent follow-on secondary capital raises (shown as "Folo" in exhibit 9.1) from 1968 through 1970, when *RTR* completed its first tumultuous year.

The *RTR* success establishes summer 1970 as a season to remember. Three graduation ceremonies crowd our calendars. Elder son, Rick Campbell, finishes work at Ridgewood High School, and Irene Campbell completes her work at William Paterson College (now University) and graduates magna cum laude with the frustration that my packed schedule prevents me from attending her graduation. NYU passes out my diploma "with distinction" in a jammed June ceremony in Madison Square Garden, which Irene proudly attends.

I know nobody in that throng except my family.

THE TROUBLES

By midsummer 1970, troubles surface for the mortgage REIT's. In late June, both Penn Central Transportation Corporation (PC) and Four Seasons Nursing Centers of America seek bankruptcy protection. *RTR* covers the investment implications in the July 21 issue under the headline, "Mortgage Trusts Face Their Summer of Discontent."

RTR probes to find out how bad these twin bankruptcies may be for REIT investors. While rail giant Penn Central becomes the largest corporate failure until that time, the conglomerate is deeply entrenched in real estate through subsidiaries controlling Florida land developer and builder Arvida Corporation, major Dallas homebuilder and developer Great Southwest Corporation, and GSC affiliate Macco Realty of Los Angeles. GSC tells the market it has borrowed construction loans from seventeen REITs—only three of which can be identified. While these Penn Central subsidiaries aren't yet drawn into the Penn Central bankruptcy, Penn Central's principal realty subsidiary borrows $300 million from a group of banks in anticipation of public financing that never materializes—and becomes unlikely.

Four Seasons, builder of nursing centers, originates construction loans via Midland Mortgage, Oklahoma City–based as is Four Seasons, to at least four mortgage trusts with the highest exposure being 6 percent of Midland's assets.

"In distress situations the first mortgage lender holds all the cards," we note in a three-page examination. Continental and First Mortgage, the mortgage REITs with the longest track records, have lost only 0.07 percent and 0.01 percent of funds advanced over nearly a decade of lending.

> "What has changed this time is that the failures involve
> large and highly visible public companies. With a larger

and larger share of housing and construction now being done by public companies, many more distress situations can be expected to be put on view for investors in the future."

Our advice is "The publicity in some of the cases mentioned above has indeed brought trusts like Midland and MIG (Mortgage Investors Group) into a range where they may be bought for their longer-term potentials."

A month later, troubles emerge from a different quarter: Washington. "The Bank Trusts Catch Mr. Patman's (Jaundiced) Eye," reads the August 21 *RTR* headline, telling how US Congressman Wright Patman "is trying to rally fellow Congressman to limit commercial bank-sponsored realty trusts."

"A frightening colossus has been spawned," *RTR* quotes the populist-leaning Texan head of the House Banking Committee charging on the House floor. "The possibilities for self-dealing, both those disclosed and the undisclosed ones, are shocking … This relatively new development is laden with grave danger to the entire economy … It is further evidence of the predatory intent of a few large banks to control and dictate, by horrendous conflicts of interest, the nation's economic forces."

While there is no love lost between Mr. Patman and commercial banks, the Texan's charges "fail to win any wide open support among his fellow Congressmen. But … Mr. Patman's tenacity in pursuing his opponents is widely known," concludes *RTR*.

RTR's summary is: "All in all, we feel the very fact that the relentless Texan is watching the bank trusts closely probably will brake new offerings by other banks."

But Patman's blast has no measureable impact, and by September, we report "Backlog of Trust Offerings Builds Again." Fidelco Growth, backed by a Pennsylvania bank, sells twenty million dollars in new shares, and two other large banks, Citizens & Southern in Atlanta and Bankers Trust in New York, register fifty- and twenty-five-million-dollar offerings. And the adviser to Mortgage Investors Group in Los Angeles agrees to be bought by Continental Illinois Bank of Chicago.

Take that, Mr. Patman!

RTR's acceptance continues, and the wave of industry news forces us to double the monthly issue size to eight pages. Success plus more pages to fill engenders enough confidence in our future that I expand staff at mid-1970. Bernard Solas, a former Value Line writer who knows everyone on Wall Street, comes aboard as director of research, and his Bronx neighbor Faye Kreisman becomes head of statistics and mechanical preparation.

As our growth makes continued co-occupancy untenable in our aerie at 500 Fifth Avenue, we search for new quarters, now in a high-vacancy market, and find space on a low floor in the New York Central Building at 230 Park Avenue papered with eviction notices for the former tenant. The rent is favorable, and so, in August 1970, we take occupancy on Park Avenue.

That same summer, we settle on a new printer specializing in newsletters, Fermaprint, located in a basement space at 50 East Forty-Second Street, only four blocks from our new office. A punctual Prussian named Carl Waring runs Fermaprint, and he insists upon precise publishing schedules; at his behest, we settle into a routine of mailing *RTR* on the fourth Friday of each month and the renamed *Audit Report* on the first and third Fridays. The schedule lets actionable buy and sell calls reach all subscribers before Monday's market opens.

In late August, son Rick enrolls to study math at Massachusetts Institute of Technology, and we pack an aqua couch into the back of the family station wagon and deposit it in his Cambridge dorm room. We never see it again, but that's okay, we think.

Printed on dark-blue paper to foil copy machines, *RTR* affectionately establishes itself as "Old Black and Blue" by the end of 1970.

THE BAZAAR

To accommodate Fermaprint's schedule, *RTR*'s eight-page monthly issue contains comprehensive stats covering market price, earnings and price/earnings ratios, dividend yields, and market capitalization for eighty-two REITs by the end of 1970, arrayed by investment goals.

By the end of 1970, eighty-two REITs with a $2.8 billion market cap emerge from my rat hole. Market cap rises 75 percent in the nine months since *RTR*'s debut, with short-term mortgage trusts dominating at 60 percent of market value. My statistical tape measure of the REIT industry at the end of 1970 by investment goal shows this profile, with market value in million dollars:

Table 9.1: REIT Industry Profile, December 1970

Trust type	No.	Mkt. Cap.	Percent
Short-term mortgage REITs.	45	$1,680	60%
Independent	9	429	15
Mortgage banker	14	390	14
Commercial bank	13	521	19
Miscellaneous financial	9	340	12
Equity and mortgage hybrid REITs	23	478	17
Intermediate term mortgage	2	158	6
Long-term mortgage	12	472	17
Totals	**82**	**$2,789**	**100%**

Source: *Realty Trust Review* data, December 28, 1970, subsequently computed.

For good measure, the stat issue now tracks prices for a messy bazaar of warrants and convertibles that give investors endless arbitrage opportunities for anyone willing to expend the intellectual firepower and time to untangle this unruly farrago.

This exotic list, which ends 1970 at twenty-seven warrants and twenty-four convertibles, eventually grows to eighty-two warrants and forty-five convertibles. It arises from efforts to solve one of Wall Street's enduring conundrums: how to offset a typical 10 percent offering sales load?

Since mortgage REITs are viewed as closed-end investment companies, the offering load subtracts 10 percent from a REIT's purchase price. Thus a trust share sold at $20.00 will have only about $18.00 in net asset value to invest.

The dizzying array of warrants and convertibles are intended to make up for this instant discount by giving the buyer a piece of paper that may be worth something someday—if the share price rises over time. But the practice creates an eclectic and exotic smorgasbord of securities.

The warrants let stock purchasers buy an additional share at some premium price—$23.00 to $25.00 was common for REITs sold initially at $20.00—within five or so years from the offering date. Convertible debentures accomplish the same purpose by giving the buyer a shot at recouping that instant discount by converting a debenture at a higher price.

Through *RTR*, Audit hopes to provide investors with a road map into this arcane marketplace, but because most warrants and convertibles aren't listed for daily trading, we must rely for monthly quotes upon a brokerage firm making markets in these securities.

The broker we select is Drexel Burnham and the junk bond operation run by Michael Milken from his famed Beverly Hills X-shaped trading desk. Looking back from the distance of forty-plus years, I wonder if we always got accurate quotes, although no one ever challenges our prices. But Michael Milken and his minions are clearly not disinterested middlemen in this esoteric game (see chapter 23, "The Surprises").

In the November 25, 1970, issue, *RTR* presents a tutorial on trust warrants under the title, "Trust Warrants: Most of That Leverage Is a Mirage."

"The typical warrant speculator looks for a leverage factor of 2-to-1, or a warrant that is priced at one-half the price of its companion stock," the analysis reads, on the theory that the warrant will double if the stock rises 50 percent. "Among the over two dozen trust warrants now traded, leverage ratios of 4-to-1 and more are the rule."

And while this should make trust warrants happy hunting grounds for speculators, "the history of trust warrants has been one of shrinking premiums," and the oldest REIT warrant then traded, the First Mortgage $11.25 warrant of 1977, generally ranges from a miniscule 3 percent premium to 5 percent discount.

Our take was:

> "The risk/reward ratio still appears unfavorable in almost all instances except this First Mortgage warrant … The warrants [at $11] should move in tandem [with the $23.25 FMI stock price], giving a possible 65%–75% capital gain, 'making the warrant slightly more attractive than the stock' after considering the stock's 8.8% dividend yield."

Happily, this warrant/convertible bazaar folds with the subsequent mortgage REIT washout never to return.

By the end of 1970, *RTR* attracts nearly four hundred subscribers, still at sixty dollars annually for a monthly letter but bumped to eighty-four dollars annually when we go to twice-monthly issues in mid-1971. Audit revenues more than double to $92,000, and while we still operate at a small loss, the foundation has been set for a better 1971.

Best of all, prices of both short-term mortgage and equity trusts are tilting upward as 1970 ends, according to an index compiled by brokerage Paine Webber Jackson & Curtis, which we publish under special permission.

We create something new and exciting, an active and vital investment newsletter bringing advice and news about an instant industry to a body of engaged subscribers, mostly real estate or Wall Street pros.

From 2015's perspective, it's clear the 1970 institutional sponsors of mortgage REITs were thrilled to off-load their riskiest loans to externally managed affiliates because they shed a layer of risk while cashing preset investment advisory fees. But the to-and-fro of analyzing a tidal wave of new REIT IPOs in 1970 obscures that macro insight.

Exhibit 9.2 Paine-Webber REIT Index
December 1966- December 1970

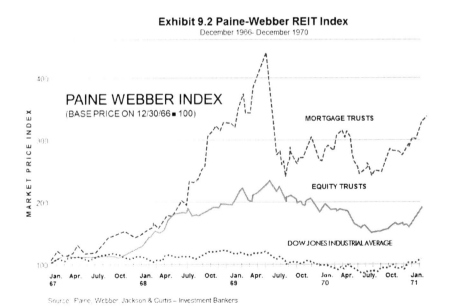

Source: Paine, Webber, Jackson & Curtis – Investment Bankers

From that auspicious launch, postal strike notwithstanding, *The Letter*, renamed *Realty Stock Review* in the 1980s, becomes our biggest seller by far, its physical unattractiveness notwithstanding.

My rat hole is teeming with new REITs, and *The Letter* is watching their every move.

Best of all, *The Letter* opens doors to two spinouts: the Book and the Fund.

Chapter 10
THE BOOK

The book, the book, my kingdom for the book.

Countless aspiring writers dream of penning *the book*, be it the great American novel or the great American nonfiction classic. Many are called, but few are chosen book of the year or of the month.

The wide acceptance of both *RTR* and the investment report *Lenders with a Plus* starts me thinking about ways to broaden the audience for publications dealing with REITs. At about the same time, the head of New York University's evening school asks me to teach a class in REITs. Not being immune to the marketplace, NYU wants to hold classes in REITs and needs a recognized practitioner to teach and attract students. There is no stipend, only hard work, but the role carries the fancy title of adjunct professor and has launched more than one successful book. "It's a time-honored way of doing a book," a friend advises. "A lot of people have done it." *Voila* again, a practical way to begin working on a book about REITs arrives serendipitously.

NEW WORLD

I do not make the decision to create a book lightly. Any book is a far more ambitious undertaking than an investment newsletter, and going this route forces my tiny firm to cast out into deeper waters, hoping to navigate *mare incognita* and land safely on *terra firma*. The commitment requires penetrating research into the foreboding world of books.

Writing and editing must be sustained over months and perhaps years, a polar opposite from our familiar world of periodical newsletters generated on a weekly schedule. Can our tiny staff of five or so cope with the mountain-sized job of preparing a book and still deliver newsletters on time? I bet we can!

Printing a book requires alignment with printers equipped with monster presses able to deliver such basics as binding, hard covers, and dust jackets. I know nothing of this world and feel *Audit's* small size puts us at great disadvantage relative to these giants. In 1971, book-printing methods are closer to Gutenberg than to e-books.

Marketing poses the highest hurdle because books are then sold primarily through established bookstores generally owned by thousands of small and sometimes specialized entrepreneurs in cities across the land. Some larger bookstore chains are emerging. A newsletter can be easily marketed via direct mail to readily available mailing lists of prospects, but with books, we are neophytes. Especially concerning is the quaint book industry practice that allows bookstores to return unsold books within a year for a full refund. I worry that a book on the specialized topic of REITs might not sell well via bookstores and thus open Audit to major cash hemorrhages down the line.

Weighing in favor of going ahead is my insight that a book lasts for the ages. Once printed and in circulation, a nonfiction book stands as the definitive reference work for its given topic until refuted or its subject matter becomes obsolete or overtaken by subsequent events. A book is a legacy of unsurpassed value, a portable and divisible monument easily accessible to all. Given the fresh arrival of REITs upon the investment stage, I determine, perhaps hard-headedly, to forge ahead with the first book on REITs. Damn the torpedoes and full speed ahead!

THE MAYPOLE

My first step is to design a course syllabus using the maypole method, one advocated by one-time boss Gurney Breckenfeld. In Gurney's version, the author fashions any long-form written work by treating all strands of the story—interviews, documents, witness descriptions, commentary, and so on—as colored ribbons to be woven around the central maypole of the story's overarching theme.

When all strands are in place, the article or book should form a resplendent mosaic of reds and greens, blues and yellows, silvers and golds, a shining work of art attracting readers from all spectra. The maypole festival, in which dancers interweave their multicolored ribbons around a central pole, welcomes spring in many towns and villages in northern Europe and the British Isles, but to me, no work of art better represents the incandescent potential of the maypole than Andrew Wyeth's singular painting, *The Snow Hill*. While Wyeth set his painting in the snow, the winter cold does not dampen the enthusiastic fellowship of the maypole dancers. To me, Wyeth's canvas conveys my soaring hopes for the book.

The maypole analogy gives me the outline for my course syllabus.

The course covers about twelve weeks at a midtown location, each lecture lasting about two hours from 6:00 to 8:00 p.m. In a reprise of my NYU study days, I am again keeping evening hours, away from home and family, for the greater good—or so it seems at the time. To preserve my golden thoughts, I tape and transcribe each lecture to capture both the substance of the lecture itself and student questions.

Each class draws about twenty-five to thirty students, nearly all working at Wall Street firms or commercial banks and all seeking to advance their careers in the nascent REIT business. One student, Paul Nussbaum, goes on to serve as CEO of Patriot American, a 1990s hotel REIT that has a great run until the credit crunch of the late 1990s forces

Paul out amid a messy restructuring. Others find lower-level spots inside REITs.

Every element of the course aims to sustain the planned part 1 of the book, titled "The Trust Business."

That title becomes my maypole.

Each lecture and resulting chapter is designed to ensnare the attention of those eager, upwardly mobile young professionals who fill my classroom. They crowd into the classroom each evening to challenge my every word, primed with complex, sometimes off-the-wall questions. They are proxies for readers of the book.

REGULATION LITE

I kick off lecture 1 by portraying these new REITs as institutions largely free from traditional regulatory limits. I believe this idea will fire the aspirations of the young men and women in my class, who live daily in the highly regulated worlds of Wall Street and banking. Delivered February 19, 1971, the lecture explores nuances and potentials of the REIT structure and forms the basis for a chapter "Perspective on the Trusts." I sketch the possibilities in the world of REITs. Examples from the topic list include: tax exempt pools of capital, removal of geographic limits, competitors without fetters, no governmental regulation, liquidity from illiquidity, and tailor-made trusts.

The transcript says I tell students, "There is almost no regulation of them [REITs] other than the IRS rules, plus ... they are under SEC (Securities and Exchange Commission) rules when they go public and if they are listed on an exchange they come under rules of the various exchanges."

To the question of the size of the short-term construction and development market, I quote several studies and conclude that "we are talking about a business that right now is about $29 to $36 billion [$174 to $216 billion in 2015 dollars] per year. Short-term trusts have about $2 billion equity capital. If you levered that 3-to-1, which is about as high as you will get, you have $8 billion. So now you are looking at an entity that probably represents 20% at a maximum of the short-term C&D market."

Lecture 2 analyzes strengths and weaknesses of various trust types. With respect to equity trusts, I tell students that equity trusts are already finding opportunities within the new law. "What is happening right now is that a number of trusts are saying, 'There is nothing in that law that says we cannot use the trust format to be an active developer so long as we do not sell, so long as we are not in the business of trading and selling property.' So what you have is the trust moving backward one step in the development chain and a number of them buying unimproved real estate, perhaps in Manhattan but more typically in the suburbs of major metropolitan areas and developing the land for their own account."

For subsequent lectures, I pick topics on which Wall Street and realty "experts" can speak from first-hand experience and are of lasting value to anyone interested in either a career or investment in REITs and real estate. Five practitioners accept my invitation and agree to speak on hot topics of the day.

WHAT WALL STREET WANTS

"Framing an Underwriting Proposal" is a topic I know will excite my students because half of them are somehow involved in trying to get a new REIT off the ground, either underwriting a trust for a Wall Street house or trying to find out what elements will pass muster with an underwriter. For the session, I prepare a case study of a medium-sized Midwestern commercial bank seeking to find an investment banker to sell shares of a new short-term mortgage trust and let students critique the sponsor's strengths and weaknesses.

The case study advises Wall Street underwriters to evaluate "the proposed sponsor and its construction lending experience … coupled with an assessment of the determination with which management of the bank or institution approaches sponsorship of a real estate trust. In a number of instances the institution's management finds that it has in effect committed prestige and reputation of the institution to the success of the trust."

Fred Joseph arrives for the second hour that evening to critique both the case study and the students' insights. At age thirty-four and not much older than most students, Joseph is already one of Wall Street's brightest luminaries in underwriting as head of real estate investment banking at Shearson, Hammill, & Company. He is not encouraging to the case study's hypothetical bank sponsor.

"Let me say this is a very typical proposal," Joseph observes. "We have been receiving two or three such proposals a week (Campbell, 1971. 97)… Nevertheless, like everyone else, we are being very choosy about managing additional underwritings, because we know there's a limit to the number of trusts we can offer successfully. At some point, either our selling network and our clients are going to be saturated with trust shares, or we're going to get to the point where our continuing relationships with our existing trust clients will preclude our doing any new trusts. (Campbell, 1971. 98)

"Most investment bankers who have done trusts are spending a great deal of time looking at prospective trust deals and turning down the vast majority. We [Shearson] have been doing one about every three months recently and hope to slow it down by only agreeing to sponsor the most viable and attractive potential trusts. (Campbell, 1971. 98)

"Naturally a sponsor has a better chance if he presents an underwriter with a 'unique' trust," Joseph analyzes the proposal, "and although that word is over-used, all trust managements seem to try to be unique in some respect … It is probably easier, and more feasible, to give the public … advantages—participations, experienced management, lower fees, equity investment by the principals in shares of the trust—to create a generally favorable impression of the trust." (Campbell, 1971. 100)

Looking ahead, Joseph opines, "As a long-term proposition, there probably is more money willing to invest in trusts than the trusts are going to be able to invest effectively. They have been the first really effective technique for using Wall Street-type liquid capital to invest meaningfully in real estate, which has traditionally been a capital short area of the economy. It has taken ten years for the impact Congress intended … but the limiting factor is going to be the long-term need for capital in real estate." (Campbell, 1971. 102-103)

As to the future of equity REITs, Joseph adds, "I am not favorably disposed toward equity trusts because I do not believe that the public understands them very well yet … Eventually the public will be more interested in buying equity trust shares. Many people say that Wall Street should take the lead in educating the public on equity trusts, but it appears to be more the problem with equity trust sponsors, not the underwriters. Most underwriters … don't particularly want to be crusaders." (Campbell, 1971. 103)

(Joseph later becomes CEO of Drexel Burnham Lambert just in time to see that firm collapse in the Michael Milken scandal of the late 1980s and dies in November 2009 at age 72.)

BORROWING AND LENDING

For a second hot topic of "liability management," Cornelius C. "Neil" Rose Jr. seeks to answer the question for my students of whether smart liability management is the reason shares of his trust, North American Mortgage Investors (NAMI), trade at a lofty two times their $13.47 per share book value. Rose's spot as chairman trustee makes him responsible for liability management for NAMI, then fourth largest short-term REIT with a $117 million market value. Rose sees mortgage trusts growing both through equity leveraging and debt leveraging. He defines equity leveraging as "the process of selling new equity at a premium over the book value of existing equity, and thereby leveraging earnings per share, book value per share, and market value per share." (Campbell, 1971. 106) Debt leveraging is borrowing new capital while maintaining a constant spread between lending and borrowing rates.

Speaking against a backdrop of falling interest rates, Rose sees a one-to-one debt-to-equity ratio as probably optimal for a mortgage trust. "The real issue in the conflict-of-interest area lies on the liability side of the balance sheet," he contends. "In a period of declining interest rates, the only way a trust can compensate for declining returns is to double up on leverage." If the trust sponsor also operates in the mortgage business, the sponsor may have little incentive to allow the trust to grow its business. "That to me is the real conflict of interest," he asserts (Campbell, 1971. 115) Rose however never sets specific limits on debt leveraging, which ultimately becomes a major issue for mortgage REITs as the economy later buckles under the 1973 OPEC oil embargo.

But Merrill Taub, a key executive of brokerage firm Donaldson, Lufkin, and Jenrette, reminds students in his session with my class that not every successful REIT is forced to run the "go public" gauntlet. Speaking to the topic "the rationale for private trusts," Taub describes how DLJ set up a private REIT to help a pension fund client invest ten million dollars in real estate. Research convinced DLJ that a private REIT of scale, set initially at forty million dollars equity, could provide diversification with a 10 percent annual yield to pension clients.

Acting on that conviction, DLJ births a new private REIT, Institutional Investors Trust (IIT), and sells its shares to a blue-chip roster of pension funds: TRW Corporation, Pittsburgh National Bank, First National Bank of Minneapolis, General Mills, Dow Chemical, North American Rockwell, Mead Corporation, and Ohio State

Teachers Retirement System. Taub is chosen to lead the trust's manager, Institutional Property Advisers.

Taub describes IIT's investment strategy: "We said, 'Let's take 80 percent of our funds and commit it to long-term situations, either a permanent mortgage or subordinated ground situation.' All of them had various kickers. The remaining 20 percent was to be committed to loans with profit participations of various types. Finally we determined to use our leveraged money for the conventional construction and development loan business. The theory was to build an earnings base that would net 10 percent to 11 percent and build on top of this base as many layers of leverage as we could." (Campbell, 1971. 158)

I am subsequently engaged to provide monthly estimated pricing of IIT shares compared with comparable public trusts because IIT trustees seek to track valuation of their shares. This arrangement ends when IIT goes public in July 1972.

Internal Revenue Service rules governing what REITs can and cannot do are evolving and complex, so I tap a savvy attorney to wrestle with and simplify "tax and accounting issues" for my students. Martin J. Oppenheimer, tax specialist at the Manhattan firm of Oppenheimer and Townsend and formerly with Davis, Polk, and Wardwell, agrees to provide needed insight into the ways IRS speaks to trust managers.

The IRS issues two types of rulings, he opines: formal rulings published in the *Internal Revenue Bulletin* available to the public and private rulings that "belong to the recipient and if he does not want to share it with others, he is not required to do so. A number of trade associations try to collect and circulate such private rulings so that all members of an industry may see what the service is saying privately. NAREIF [predecessor to NAREIT] has tried to encourage trusts who receive private rulings to share them with the rest of the industry but the incidence of such sharing has been relatively low to date." (The IRS ended this two-tier system in 1976, and today "private" rulings are permitted to be provided publicly if identifying information is redacted.)

THE ANALYST

Having covered key elements of trust operations, I now need a seasoned Wall Street analyst to explore "investment analysis of trusts." William R. Harman, a REIT analyst at Evans & Company, whose office happens to be nearby, agrees to provide an insider's look at how Wall Street picks one trust over another to recommend to its clients.

Harman believes that short-term REITs can be largely bought and sold on the basis of dividend yield within the then-current range of 6.5 to 10.0 percent. He advises my students that "Any trust that has exhibited an above-average record of earnings growth and appears capable of continuing this performance should not, in my opinion, sell at a yield higher than 8.5% in our current market environment. … Profitable investments can be made very simply by owning shares of well managed short-term trusts that have the ability to produce the large amount of loans necessary for growth in portfolio size and that have sources of low cost short-term borrowings available to finance portfolio growth. (Campbell, 1971. 245)

"Since I consider the primary function of REIT shares to be the flow through of income to the investor, it is consistent to speak of their valuation in terms of yield capitalization rather than the price/earnings ratio …" (Campbell, 1971. 244-245)

Harman is less bullish concerning equity REITs, saying "Since equity trusts cannot generate a high rate of income and their real estate holdings would likely be valued on a discount basis, they are not for performance-oriented investors but for those seeking an above-average dividend return and the peace of mind in knowing that their funds are in commercial real estate properties whose liquidating value should be higher than book value." (Campbell, 1971. 244)

With Harman's presentation, I also include a paper on REITs titled "Mixed Asset Portfolios and Real Estate Investment" by Harris Friedman, an assistant economist at the Boston Federal Home Loan Bank Board who writes extensively about REITs.

Around these building blocks, I assemble several chapters of original research. I lead the opening chapter "Perspective on the Trusts" with words putting REITs in the context of the wider financial community. The completed chapter runs twelve pages beginning with this sentence: "The ageless and arcane world of real estate is very gradually shedding its veils which have shielded its operations from the investing public for so many years."

My lengthy second paragraph, here broken into shorter paragraphs for readability, tells why realty operatives are shedding their veils:

> "[A]t all times these disclosures of operating and financial secrets by real estate men have one object: to get investors to put up the money to finance their operations. Disclosure has a long established tradition with the large manufacturing and financial companies which comprise the vast bulk of securities available to investors. But disclosure has typically been anathema to the true real estate person. The true real estate person, either developer or builder, building owner or manager, typically operates at the center of an incredible complex of partnerships, interlocking corporations, personal trusts and joint ventures.

> "Part of this is pure protection: each project is structured to stand on its own and anyone with a claim against the developer—from subcontractor to mortgage

lender—must look only to the project for settlement of his claim.

"Part is due to the frequent necessity to bring new financial partners into every new venture and thus tailor a corporate entity for that venture.

"Part is due to the desire to minimize income taxes by taking advantage of the lower tax rate the Federal government applies to companies earning less than $25,000 annually.

"Part is due to the fact that many real estate operators have never had a single continuous fund source and thus were forced to operate with bits of construction financing from one source, permanent financing from another, and land purchase money from a third.

"And some part is due to the fact that many real estate men and women operate with such fragile financial underpinnings that the entire structure would fall apart if exposed to inspection as a whole by outsiders." (Campbell, 1971. 1)

With the advent of the real estate investment trust, all that is ending.

"Beginning about 1968, all this began to change as real estate operators began learning they could, in some measure, by-pass the traditional sources of funds—and especially mortgage funds—by "going public"—i.e., create a company or other vehicle for raising funds directly from the investing public." (Campbell, 1971. 1-2)

The rest of that opening chapter details how REITs were created by real estate operatives to provide a readily available source for continuous financing.

Under the heading "Real Estate as the Pros See It," chapter 2 leads, "Real estate professionals may skip this chapter; others should not." The chapter presents interviews with highly visible real estate operatives and financiers on their daily lives.

James Boisi, the real estate man in charge of the New York Central's holdings on Manhattan's Park Avenue uptown from Forty-Fifth Street, says, "The real estate man wants to take 100 [land cost] and add 900 [building cost] and get 1,300 [capitalized value of the resulting cash flow]." While relative proportions have changed since, creating such value remains the realty developer's grail. (Campbell, 1971. 13)

Albert Keidel Jr., senior vice president of shopping mall developer The Rouse Company, an indirect predecessor of today's similarly named company, asserts, "The market value of a shopping center, if the job is reasonably well done, will be a quarter to a third higher than the total cost of production—not a bad margin. And this product has a unique feature which very few other manufactured products have. Its value will continue to grow, with an expanding cash flow and increasing return on investment." (Campbell, 1971. 22)

THE DOWNSIDE

Since I do not want the book to come off the page as a bullish puff piece for REITs, I develop a twenty-two-page chapter "Measuring the Downside," examining investor risks in four recent and highly publicized property debacles involving REITs.

Seven trusts invest $12.6 million ($77.5 million in 2015 dollars) in various properties of Four Seasons Nursing Centers of America when it seeks Chapter X bankruptcy protection in June 1970 (see chapter 9, "The Letter"). Yet a year later, our analysis "demonstrated that first mortgage lenders, providing either construction or permanent financing, have perhaps the least risk of loss in a major bankruptcy. All seven trusts stand to come out of the bankruptcy in better condition than the company's chattel mortgage lenders, the company's unsecured trade creditors, and the company's shareholders." Our computations show that the seven return an average 29.5 percent in the year following the Four Seasons filing, with only one of the seven recording negative returns. The S&P 500 returned 31.4 percent over the same span.

Southeastern Mortgage Investors Trust, a short-term mortgage REIT, leverages its equity to an industry-high 1.75 times with short-term debt to invest in mortgages in the southeastern United States. When 1966 unfolds as a year of crisis in mortgage and realty markets, real estate owned mainly through foreclosure rises to 4.8 percent of assets. Trustees cut dividends nearly in half and take over the adviser, but by year-end 1967, foreclosed or troubled loans total 30.6 percent of investments. Share price sinks from the nine- to eleven-dollar range to the three- to five-dollar range, and eventually Southeastern is taken over by new backers who convert it to a development company. Share prices never recover.

Prudent Resources (later Prudent Real Estate Trust), an ASE listed REIT, ends its November 1968 year with record earnings and dividends, and its shares soar to $31.13. In April and May 1969, it pays $1.15 million cash down payment on the purchase of two properties, agreeing to pay or assume $3.1 million in debt, pending a stock offering. But underwriters can never sell one million new shares, and the situation deteriorates until Prudent shares touch a six-dollar low in July 1971.

My summations of these cases is:

1. *Cash balances and cash flow*: A dominant feature of the three cases is that shareholders are not shown detailed reconciliations

of cash flow.... [Reconciliations are now required for all public companies.] ." (Campbell, 1971. 213)

2. *Current principal payments.* The level of principal payments due within one year will normally be a most significant number for inspection ...(Campbell, 1971. 215)

3. *Correction time*: Once the carefully orchestrated growth pattern of a trust shifts into reverse, shareholders should expect a long period of convalescence ... Reassurances [by management] are not intentionally misleading ... Rather reversals in real estate normally occur for such fundamental economic or operational reasons that even the best intentioned and capable managements are seldom able to cope with them. (Campbell, 1971. 215)

4. *Risk of adverse stock market swings.* The stock market is a special risk for trusts since the quantity and price of new equity capital depend directly upon a trust's share price [prices below book or net asset value typically dampen or preclude raising new capital]. The Prudent Resources case illustrates dramatically the impact the market can have upon a trust's funding plans. (Campbell, 1971. 195)

These warning signs are as true in 2015 as when written.

Eventually the lectures plus interviews with prominent real estate professionals and research into the history of REITs produce 247 pages of prose and statistics on REITs. At about five hundred words per page, part 1, "The Trust Business" section of the book totals about 123,500 words.

THE TRUSTS

For part 2 of the book, I conceive two-page analyses, titled "Profiles of Individual Trusts," of every significant REIT. By then, 115 REITs march from my rat hole with about $4.2 billion market value ($24.6 billion in 2015 dollars). The left-hand page of this layout contains a narrative description of all essential factual elements of each trust: basic position, investment policy, portfolio, trustees and officers, investment adviser (if any), underwritings of equity and debt capital, share data, and offices.

There is just one problem: such descriptions do not exist anywhere.

Bernard Solas, then director of research, takes the lead on digging these details from prospectuses and annual reports. We enlist two part-timers, Jeffrey Morris and Winifred Wilkinson, and set out to produce these narrative descriptions ourselves.

The second or right-hand page of each planned trust two-page spread is conceived as a computerized analysis of quarterly operating results. My thesis is that precise quarterly measurement of each trust's investment spread between return on investments and interest costs will let us and investors scope out the most efficient and profitable trusts.

Unfortunately, no computer program exists for this purpose either.

So I set about working with Dr. John E. Meggitt, president of Programmed Control Corporation (later Prophet 21), a newly formed Princeton, New Jersey, computer firm, who is introduced by my brother-in-law Charles Adams.

John is a remarkably skilled programmer, having started his own business after stints with Electronic Associates and IBM, and also remarkably patient with my computer illiteracy. This collaboration means driving the ninety minutes each way to Princeton once or twice a week after a full working day to huddle with John on ways to develop a program to process financial info for each REIT.

Eventually, we persevere, and the book is able to present such vital information as portfolio yields, operating margins, price/earnings ratios, and dividend yields for each trust for every quarter of their operations. That intensive work with John cements a lifelong friendship. No one has been able to publish such detailed REIT analyses before, and we are extremely proud of the accomplishment.

Eventually these REIT descriptions fill another 220 pages.

Books, by necessity, require the basics of typesetters and printers to bring their words and dreams to fruition. For typesetting, we locate Ridge Type Service, run by a fiercely competitive woman named Dot Murtaugh, in our hometown of Ridgewood, New Jersey, and her operation sets the book in type. When we start, Dot runs Ridge Type from her living room but later moves to a larger office.

My better-half, Irene, steps in as our red-check proofreader, and it's a tribute to her diligence that thirty-eight years after publication of the book, we've never had a major error called to our attention. A friend, Leonard Harlan, suggests a printer near Miami, Florida, and after much talk, we entrust all 467 pages of the book to New World Manufacturing Company in Hallandale, Florida, for publishing and binding in a gray hard cover, without a dust jacket. The initial press run is five thousand copies, and the completed book tips our postal scales at slightly over two and one-quarter pounds.

THE BOOK

I want to title the work *America's Newest Billionaires*, but my longtime friend Bob Elfers suggests adding the book's topic to the title and we settle upon *The Real Estate Trusts: America's Newest Billionaires*.

The title turns out an all-time winner.

The Real Estate Trusts: America's Newest Billionaires (October 1971: 467 pages), of which I am billed as editor and principal author, becomes an instant best seller when introduced at twenty-four dollars per copy (about $140 in 2015 dollars) at the October 1971 NAREIT annual convention in the Fairmont Hotel in San Francisco.

ANB, as our staff quickly begins calling it, more than any other single product, establishes our still-tiny company's credibility as the go-to source for reliable REIT information and advice.

The price is reduced to sixteen dollars about a year later, and all five thousand copies of the book are sold within a year or two. *Voila* again, we have another big winner!

In 2015, only three of the 115 REITs profiled in the book remain active in business under their 1971 names: American Realty Trust, now trading as American Realty Investors, Inc. (NYSE: ARL); Pennsylvania REIT (NYSE: PEI); and Washington REIT (NYSE: WRE). Today's General Growth Properties (NYSE:GGP) is a second iteration of the similarly named trust of 1971, and First Union Equity & Mortgage Real Estate, now named Winthrop Realty Trust, is liquidating. A complete list of those 1971 REITs appears in appendix IV-A.

Federal Realty Investment Trust (NYSE: FRT), now a REIT powerhouse, operates in 1971 but doesn't join the *RTR* list until February 1974 with a $5.9 million market cap.

While the book's facts and figures stand as artifacts of a long-gone era in the maturation and investment acceptance of REITs, its insights and general advice remain as valid in 2015 as in 1971.

In real estate, in REITs, and in the stock market, the facts and situations may change, but basic principles rarely do. The book does a good job of honing in on those basics, then and now.

And its success leads directly to *the Fund* connection.

Chapter 11
THE FUND

Three weeks before the book's winning debut, Robert Birch visits me in my Manhattan office. Birch is president of Gardner and Preston Moss (GPM), a Boston investment advisory firm founded and then still run by Boston Brahmin John L. "Jack" Gardner, descendant of the famed Gardner family. Birch does not come to chitchat.

Birch asks me to participate in forming a proposed new leveraged closed-end fund to be named The REIT Income Fund. Birch proposes that *Audit* serve as subadviser to the fund, while a subsidiary of GPM will act as day-to-day fund manager.

"The idea is a natural for REITs," Birch presses, "because you can give preferred shareholders a fat, fixed yield while common shareholders get some income plus all the potential appreciation."

He sees mortgage REITs as generating a "steadily rising income stream" that makes the planned fund a long-term winner.

Three Harvard Business School students bring the idea to GPM for creating a closed-end fund investing in a portfolio of high-yielding mortgage REITs and capitalized with both preferred and common stock. Their concept is that preferred stock will receive a fixed 8.75 percent return and appeal to conservative income investors. In the meantime, common shares will receive all capital appreciation plus any leftover income and appeal to more aggressive capital-gains investors.

At the time, mortgage trusts yield between 7.1 and 8.9 percent, so it appears that a diversified mortgage trust portfolio leveraged one-third by the prefs can cover the preferred dividend and leave some appreciation on the table for common holders. But this hope comes with a caveat. Since the common shares are leveraged with the preferred, they carry higher risk. Both common and preferred shares are to be publicly traded, and the common later lists on the American Stock Exchange.

The proposal essentially applies the techniques of so-called duo-funds, a few of which are prospering at the time, to these new-fangled REITs. The lure of being part of a trailblazing fund is appealing.

I also like the makeup of the fund's planned board of directors, including such REIT and real estate luminaries as Martin Bucksbaum, founder and head of General Growth Properties, the largest enclosed mall REIT of the day; Morton Zuckerman, a magical name in Boston office development and later chairman of high-multiple Boston Properties; and Lester C. Thurow, a precocious Oxford and Harvard-educated economist then an MIT professor beginning an illustrious writing and teaching career.

Two of the fund's five directors—Philip Eiseman and David Scribner—represent preferred holders, an important fact I note only in passing.

Coping With Conflict: Signing on means I must become a salesman for the fund, participating in a road show quarterbacked by underwriters Piper, Jaffray, and Hopwood of Minneapolis, to sell Fund shares to investors across the country. As an ingrained buy-sider and receiver of countless road show stock appeals, I am queasy about becoming a pitch man for selling new stock.

I must also cope with the inherent conflict of carrying water on both shoulders as editor of a successful advisory letter *and* purveyor of advice to a fund whose managers will be buying and selling REIT shares daily without any input by me.

To balance my competing obligations, I settle on a deal giving GPM direct access to our growing proprietary computer database and providing only my personal industry overview without commenting on individual stocks to the fund's manager.

My lawyer, Andy Davis, also insists that my advisory service *Realty Trust Review* give up publishing two very specific model portfolios begun the year before to guide investors through the burgeoning roster of REITs. One portfolio aims to help investors seeking long-term inflation protection, and the other targets intermediate-term aggressive investors; both are very specific, tracking prices and dividends monthly.

I agree, and both portfolios are closed out with the June 26, 1972, *RTR* with a note saying, "We have concluded that continuance of the model portfolios would be inconsistent with our new subadvisory relationship with REIT Income Fund."

I am happy to report that both portfolios have outperformed the Dow-Jones Industrials since inception thirteen months previously. Perhaps, presciently, the long-term "conservative" stock group rises 23.8 percent over that span, easily besting the Dow-Jones Industrial Average's 0.8 percent gain. The more aggressive short-term package trails with only a 7.3 percent rise because June prices dip as market leader Continental Illinois Realty says it expects a 40 percent earnings decline in its June quarter.

No subscriber comments or complains about losing this hand-holding feature.

These arrangements overcome my fears about conflicts with my subscribers, and I go all-in for a limited role as fund subadviser with a modest retainer.

Start the road show!

THE ROAD SHOW

We first travel to San Francisco to try to entice Dean Witter into the syndicate, but one of their veteran salesmen harbors deep reservations about REITs and Witter declines. Many smaller regional firms climb aboard however, and that hectic road show takes me to Chicago, Kansas City, and San Francisco (again) on a whirlwind tour.

Back in my Manhattan office during a lull, I am startled by an unexpected 9:00 a.m. call from Robert Birch.

"Can you be on a 2:30 plane to London?" he asks. "If you have any trouble getting a passport, we have some connections that can get one for you."

"What's going on?" I counter. "I thought we were only selling shares in the States."

"A very big broker in England wants to join the syndicate, and we want to let him in," Birch replies. Birch speaks with a distinct British accent, and while I don't know his personal history, I suspect he has called in some chits from across the pond to maximize initial sales of the fund.

"I'm in," I reply. I don't tell him I have never been to London before.

The catch is that I must get to JFK Airport on Long Island by noon, and my passport is at home thirty miles away, along with needed wardrobe changes.

Thanks to Irene's agility in tossing some duds into a suitcase and rushing my passport into my hands through heavy traffic on three-hours' notice, I make the flight before the door closes. Bernie Solas, Audit's number-two man, hops into the car, and on the way to the airport, I impart voluminous instructions on what needs doing during my hastily arranged absence.

Birch's scent is right on. The United Kingdom brokerage, James Capel, has some eager clients, and that trip turns up some big orders.

So on June 8, 1972, the REIT Income Fund materializes on the investment scene with $25.1 million initial capital ($144 million in 2015 dollars), the result of selling 1.436 million common shares at $10.00 and 215,648 preference shares at $50.00 per share, net of $2.1 million selling costs.

Voila, voila! The fund emerges alive.

One considerable fringe benefit of this new affiliation is that I must attend quarterly board meetings in Boston. Since son Rick is then attending MIT, Irene and I get to see our college student son more frequently than would otherwise have been possible.

Subsequently, the fund floats two more stock offerings, raising $15.2 million gross on December 6, 1972, and $25.1 million gross on October 19, 1973, at $11.90 and $8.97 per common share respectively. I am able to duck these sales campaigns, however. That brings total funds raised to $65.4 million gross ($361 million in 2015 dollars) and just a shade under $60 million after offering expenses of about 8.25 percent.

All $5.4 million offering costs are charged against common shareholder capital under accounting rules, increasing the effective balance sheet leverage.

LOCKED-IN LEVERAGE

Unfortunately, gross invested assets never exceed $51 million, including bonds and commercial paper during the fund's life, because of a steadily weakening market for REIT shares after the October 1973 capital raise.

In six sickening quarters from March 1973 to September 1974, the fund's common shares shed 90 percent of their net asset value, slicing NAV from $10.11 to $1.01 per share.

GPM's portfolio managers move aggressively to combat sharp price declines by boosting liquid commercial paper to 44 percent of investments during the December 1973 quarter while cutting more volatile short-term mortgage trusts back from 46 to 34 percent of holdings. They fail to catch the falling knife however, and their shifts cannot stanch the bleeding.

REIT Income Fund shares live in the basement for the second half of the 1970s. From a low $0.93 NAV in the December 1974 quarter, share NAV eventually climbs back over $4 per share five and one-half years later, in June 1980. That recovery marks a fourfold increase for investors who buy at the bottom but also translates into a 60 percent loss for initial holders. Exhibit 11.1 traces the fund's common share NAV record during its life:

Exhibit 11.1 -- REIT Income Fund:
NAV Per Share 1972 - 1980

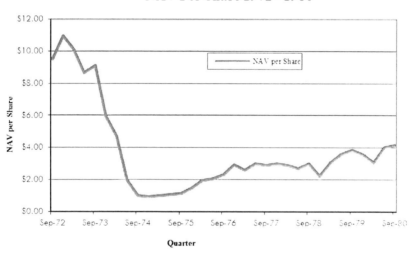

Fund shareholders are locked into a reverse-leverage vise they cannot undo because the fund can only call the preferred shares at a 5 percent premium to par. As a result, I resolve never again to get into a situation where leverage is locked in for a long time, ten years in this case.

One disheartening result is that common share dividends are deferred following the December 1973 quarter—the very quarter in which the fund raises $25.1 million from investors, or three-eighths of its total capital. During that quarter, fund net assets drop to 184 percent of preferred liquidating value, a level preventing the fund from paying common share dividends under SEC rules requiring 200 percent coverage. Exhibit 11.2 tells this story.

Exhibit 11.2-- REIT Income Fund:
% Asset Coverage of Preferred Shares 1972 - 1980

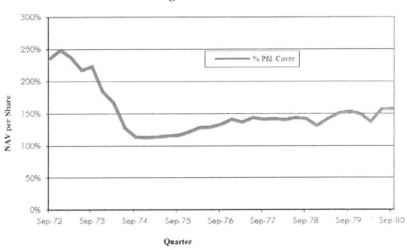

Common dividends never resume even though fund managers make valiant efforts to recoup these losses in the second half of the 1970s and eventually build coverage back to 157 percent by September 1980.

This frightening plunge for common shareholders attests to the terrors of locked-in negative leverage. Because the fund's preferred holders have a prior claim on $26.7 million of fund assets, common holders suck wind when REIT shares prices fall.

Losses are doubled for common shareholders while preferred holders have set aside for them 200 percent of assets needed to cover their stake. And REIT Income Fund is just one of a dozen or so similarly situated duo-funds, including two other REIT imitators, caught in this reverse leverage vise.

The plunge in the fund's common shares turns quarterly board meetings into tense pitched debates, akin to witnessing an execution and leaving no love lost in any quarter. Although I am technically not aligned with either side, the tension drains all joy from those required quarterly junkets to Boston.

The tensions begin when the two fund directors elected by preferred shareholders quibble with common share directors. The dispute quickly escalates when these preferred directors insist on bringing their lawyer to board meetings.

At that first dual-lawyer meeting, barristers for the prefs quickly bristle over legal niceties with lawyers representing both common holders and the adviser. Board meetings thereafter turn into legally charged debates filled with abstruse legal language but little meaningful action.

The fund board meetings cease to be any fun.

TAX ALCHEMY

Eventually the fund runs up over thirty million dollars in capital losses, nearly half the total capital raised. But losses of such magnitude are not all bad for the fund, thanks to the alchemy of the US tax code.

That transpires because an active traffic exists, then and in 2015, in tax losses whether derived from operations or from capital declines. The IRS, of course, strictly limits how and when losses can be used to offset income and gains, but this traffic in losses goes on to this day.

Of the two kinds of losses, capital losses have enormous allure to companies and especially to venture capitalists, which start new companies and hope to see their babies grow into profitable companies generating mouthwatering capital gains.

When that happens, the venture capitalists start searching for a company or fund with preexisting capital losses to offset a heavy tax bite. By this tax alchemy, net realized capital losses are good and the fund has gobs of them—over $8.00 per share at the trough.

Vulture investors start doing what vultures do: target that fat carcass.

In October 1979, a Los Angeles investment banker says he owns 5.6 percent of the fund's shares.

But Atlanta financier J. B. Fuqua, head of Fuqua Industries, buys 630,000 or 17 percent of the fund's shares, and in December 1979, executives of the fund, now renamed RET Income Fund because it no longer specializes in REITs, sign a deal to merge RET into Cyprus Corporation, an investment company controlled by Fuqua.

In January 1980, S. Craig Lindner, son of Cincinnati financier Carl Lindner of American Financial Corporation, proposes acquiring RET's 3.8 million shares for five dollars a share, or about nineteen million dollars.

Fuqua wins the face-off, and in summer 1980, RET officers ask common and preferred holders to approve merger into Cyprus.

The fund's investment adviser, GPM REIT Managers, Incorporated, is sold to J. B. Fuqua in June 1980, subject to approval by both classes of shareholders. Winning approval involves distributing numerous goodies all around.

To make sure preferred holders sign on to the new regime, preferred shareholders cash a $6.00-a-share special distribution and get a 23 percent bump in their annual dividend to $5.40 a share, giving them a 12.2 percent yield on their net forty-four-dollar investment. Additionally, they receive a 38 percent boost in preferred liquidating value from $50.00 to $60.00 per share and have the pref's term extended for another ten years. Very sweet!

Common shareholders have their leverage, via the prefs, extended for ten years and hope to benefit from Mr. Fuqua's expertise in running a fully diversified portfolio. A talented buyer and fixer of companies, Mr. Fuqua earns enough during his lifetime to endow the Fuqua School of Business at Duke University with gifts of nearly $40 million. (Fuqua dies in April 2006 at age 87.)

My eight-year stint with the fund ends on a high note. Since I bought thirty shares or about 3 percent of GPM REIT Managers way back when, I'm in line for a slice of sale proceeds that ultimately comes to $24,637 ($65,500 in 2015 dollars) when the final check arrives in May 1981—nearly nine years after the fund launch.

Voila, the alchemy of the tax code turns losses into gains.

I decide that Judge Learned Hand is right: "There is nothing sinister in arranging affairs as to keep taxes as low as possible."

The unexpected check is legal. And I am always legal.

I cash the check. Thank you, Uncle Sam.

What a wondrously giving rat hole!

The fund is worth more dead than alive.

The fund experience whets my appetite for more focus on portfolios via fund management—but I must wait a decade and a half before another fund opportunity arrives.

Chapter 12
THE MODS

The intertwined stories of Operation Breakthrough and Stirling Homex are so pregnant with implications for today's housing they must be retold here. Bear with me, I shall be brief.

Incoming president Richard Nixon gambles after taking office in January 1969 by picking defeated rival George Romney as his secretary of Housing and Urban Development (HUD). A forceful, free-swinging man claiming to be descended from a long line of homebuilders, Romney rises to fame by downsizing gas-guzzling autos built by American Motors.

Once ensconced in HUD in spring 1969, Romney unveils an Operation Breakthrough program aiming to industrialize housing's archaic site-bound production methods to tap economies of scale and efficiency. His call for proposals evokes an astonishing 621 responses, including 236 proposing prototype construction and 385 seeking further research or experimentation.

On February 26, 1970, Operation Breakthrough selects twenty-two private companies and developers to pioneer construction of an estimated two thousand dwelling units using industrialized homebuilding techniques. Selection bequeaths a modest subsidy plus publicity for the panelized and modular homebuilders who are selected but also brings into the spotlight manufacturers of plumbing cores and other specialized products.

A handful of selectees are consortia formed by blue chip industrial companies: Aluminum Company of America, Boise-Cascade, General Electric Company, Hercules Incorporated, Republic Steel Corporation, and TRW Systems Group.

A second group consists of consortia assembled by prominent on-site and panelized building companies, such as stick-builders Forest City Enterprises and Levitt Building, panelized builders National Homes and Scholz Homes, and Rouse-Wates, combining skills of the developer of the new town Columbia south of Baltimore and a British industrialized building company.

THE LONER

And then comes Stirling Homex Corporation ("STIR" or simply "Homex").

The timing raises eyebrows because a week before its selection, on February 19, 1970, modular homebuilder Homex sells 1.175 million shares of stock at $16.50 to raise $19.4 million ($122 million in 2015 dollars). But only 400,000 shares are sold by Homex directly, netting only $6.6 million new money for Homex; remaining shares are sold by certain shareholders.

It's a hot offering and Homex stock, trading under the symbol STIR, more than doubles on day 1 to close at $36.50 bid. Shares finally peak at $51.50 before settling back; by late May, they are quoted at $11.50 bid, down 30 percent from the offer.

The offering price values Homex's 8.9 million shares at about $147 million ($922 million in 2015 dollars) and about sixty-nine times the $0.24 per share earned in its July 1970 fiscal year. At STIR's exuberant peak price, Homex's 8.9 million shares are worth nearly $458 million in equity market value. For the record, Homex reports only $22.6 million in sales in its July 1970 fiscal year, up 117 percent from $10.4 million the year before, with net income of $2.04 million or $0.24 per share, up 88 percent.

The Breakthrough buzz clearly levitates Homex shares.

Did somebody on Wall Street know something in advance? We shall never get a clear answer.

Organized only three years earlier by brother builders David and William Stirling of Avon, New York, south of Rochester, Homex tells HUD it is ready to go ahead with a demonstration building project sans partners, one of only two finalists to go it alone. Homex will not require partners, it says, because it has already developed not one but two factory-built housing systems since its founding three years earlier, in 1968. Both systems aim to provide affordable housing for low- and middle-income families, hence Homex's initial successes are sales to public housing and other government agencies.

Homex's low-rise system employs twelve-by-twenty-four-foot factory-produced wood-frame modular units, which can be stacked two high; other mod builders are producing similar units, so the low-rise system seems low-tech for its day.

THE INNOVATOR

But its new high-rise product brings true pioneering to the industrialized housing space: a unique reverse-sequence erection system in which lightweight modules are assembled at grade level and hoisted into place via electronically controlled jacks. Homex thus eliminates the need for expensive cranes to stack boxes from the top, the high-rise norm until then.

Homex says its high-rise system also employs an integral steel-frame concept that does not require supporting megastructure and is presently engineered for towers up to twenty stories tall. To streamline modular production at its 215,000-square-foot plant in Avon, Homex signs a unique agreement with the United Brotherhood of Carpenters and Joiners, pledging to use Brotherhood members without discrimination both in its plant and on job sites.

Clearly, Homex has its eye on a quantum leap in building technology.

My staff and I go with the flow and produce in June 1970 a 165-page book, *Profits and the Factory Built House: An Investment Probe*, analyzing the historic record of previous efforts to industrialize housing production and fifty competitors for Breakthrough grants. The book flops because I misprice it. The study first is offered in a glossy bright-yellow soft cover at three hundred dollars per copy, but this price proves wildly extravagant for the market. We rebind it with a black hard cover and reoffer it at $37.50 and sell slightly over two hundred copies.

Homex believes passionately that innovative shipping will be key in establishing modular housing. In a headline-grabbing event in July 1970, Homex gets railroads to agree to form "unit trains" that are never uncoupled and bypass city rail switching yards to expedite transit of Homex modules from Avon to Corinth, Mississippi, where thirty-three townhouses designed to be erected in twenty-four hours are put up for poor African-American tornado victims.

Homex believes rail shipment by such unit trains can effectively triple the three-hundred-mile radius feasible for truck shipment of modules.

The Mississippi shipments bear more fruit in March 1971 when Homex cuts a deal with the Harrison County (MS) Development Commission to build a 350,000-square-foot manufacturing plant for it at Gulfport, Mississippi. Homex plans to ship modules by water along the crescent-shaped Gulf Coast from Texas to Florida and up the Mississippi River and its tributaries into the Midwest. The planned Gulfport plant more than doubles the size of Homex's 215,000-square-foot plant in Avon. The plant will effectively triple Homex's production capacity to the $250 to $300 million annual range.

STIR is scaled for great success or great failure, notes the *Audit Report* in March 1971. "Overhead is said to be more nearly suited to a company with a quarter-billion dollars in sales instead of one-tenth that size," *Audit* states on March 8, 1971.

> "An aggressive and polished public relations program has turned some analysts off by its sheer size. And the accounting system is criticized because it lets the company book manufacturing profits on units built for firm contracts, even though the modules may be held at the company's plant for weeks or months before they are shipped to the site for erection."

On that date in 1971, *Audit* opines that Homex is taking the right tack:

> "We view SH's heavy investment in people as a plus for the future. The same holds for the external communications program with the industry, government, and Wall Street. If STIR didn't have a highly effective program on all counts, we'd worry more. As for the accounting, it's no different than percentage of completion methods for on-site builders."

THE MODS

Sadly, subsequent events reveal my accounting judgment to be 100 percent wrong.

Needing more money to finance inventory buildup of completed but uninstalled modules, Homex registers a common stock offering in spring 1971. But the SEC forces Homex to disclose that it has accumulated about 6,600 completed but unshipped modules at its Avon plant. Only

31.3 percent of the 9,650 modules produced in the twenty-one months through April 1971 are installed on site, while the remaining 6,600 are stored either at Avon or on building sites.

That prospectus also shows that unbilled receivables have tripled to $18.9 million. *Unbilled receivables* is an exotic accounting category meaning work has been completed and profits booked for investor reports, but the customer has not yet been billed.

"Clearly STIR cash collections have been running well behind reported sales," I tell investors on May 17, 1971. With shares trading at $19.50, I advise investors, "We are expressing no opinion or recommendation on current action to be taken on the shares … Holdings based on earlier advisories should not be disturbed."

Despite these storm warnings, underwriter Merrill Lynch is able to sell $20 million of convertible preferred stock, instead of common, on July 31, 1971.

But disaster lurks for Homex. First, the economy begins softening and housing starts fall. In October 1971, Homex reports a 54 percent earnings spurt to $0.37 a share in its July 1971 year on a 63 percent sales gain to $36.9 million. Margins clearly are under pressure, but order backlog is up about $200 million and the number of unshipped modules at the Avon plant is down to about 6,000.

By February 1972, Homex says it is developing new models for sale to private condominium and hotel builders, and salesmen fan out across the country to sell units to private developers, even though nearly all competitors are ramping efforts to sell modules to public housing agencies and other public buyers. We call the shares "unassessable at this time."

When I visit the Avon plant, on a date not recorded, I puzzle at that huge buildup of unsold modular units choking two large fields adjoining the plant. They are all sold, company execs assert, and only await completion of site work before they are shipped.

Each unit is impervious to weather damage before shipping because all are wrapped in polyethylene, they assure me. Profits have been booked, per accounting rules. But quarter after quarter, uninstalled inventory keeps building until it reaches nearly 50 percent of assets. "Where are the shipments?" I, among many others, ask.

SOGGY MODS

In April 1972, Homex reports a $2.07 million loss in its February 1972 quarter on a 68 percent plunge in sales to only $3.26 million. The reason is that auditors decide not all conditions had been met to let the company report income on several major contracts.

The next month, in May 1972, I pass on word that "we hear that Stirling Homex has been effectively taken over by its banks."

On May 10, 1972, Homex reports its inventory of uninstalled modules is now up to 10,000 boxes, which it hopes to reduce to 5,500 by the end of the calendar year. Worse, Homex says "recent experience indicates that modules stored for extended periods of time often require refurbishing" and provides $7.4 million or $0.70 per share for such rework.

Homex stock sinks like a polyethylene-wrapped stone, the company seeks bankruptcy court protection in July 1972, and Homex stock is kaput.

When court officials open the modular units sitting in those Avon fields, I am told they find the units are sealed so tightly against the air they have become miniature terrariums, creating moisture and even rain inside.

The modules are unusable, and I hear local fire departments enjoy their biggest training fire ever as the Homex mods vanish in smoke.

Such epic public failures attract scrutiny, and two and one-half years later, in December 1974, David Stirling and Homex's general counsel are indicted for making payoffs by arranging $200,000 in bank loans to seven carpenter union officials. Union officers use the money to buy STIR shares on the IPO at $9.50 per share, a $7.00 or 42 percent discount below the offering price.

More troubles follow, and in July 1975, the SEC charges David Stirling and five other former Homex officers with creating phantom sales, using illegal bugging equipment, and making illegal political contributions.

David Stirling Jr. is sentenced to one year in prison in March 1977 for stock fraud that cost investors $40 million; he tells the court he relied upon financial experts and intended no harm. David's brother William and three others also are sentenced to jail terms, according to the *New York Times*.

Bottom line, David Stirling and his executives believe so mightily in the merits of their new system that they bend major rules to win acceptance. They join the scores of inventors and creators who, innocent to the rules and rituals of Wall Street, run afoul of its arcane regulations and moral imperatives. The means do not justify the ends, then and now, as any experienced lawyer will tell them.

We publish a 207 page update of *Profits and the Factory Built House* in July 1972, and this time around, the book is a winner, selling over 750 copies. The Homex obituary fills four and one-half pages.

TODAY'S MODS

But Romney's Operation Breakthrough comes with a long-tail payoff. Today, a significant portion of one-family homes in rural areas are double-wide modules, making cheap housing available to persons in many locales without other options.

And Forest City Enterprises (FCE:A NYSE), a Breakthrough survivor now with an eight-billion-dollar market value and planning to convert to REIT status in 2016, is building a 363-unit apartment tower artfully named "B2," in Brooklyn, New York, that, at thirty-two stories, will be the world's tallest modular apartment building. FCE is using variations of its experience from the 1970s, over forty years ago. FCE has the smarts to make this modular experiment work this time, since its 1960 IPO makes it the oldest public real estate company still operating.

Construction halts on B2 in the fall of 2014, and both Forest City and its module maker partner rush to court to air perceived grievances on both sides. An early settlement seems unlikely. In February 2015, FCE writes off the modular plant and related losses to the tune of $146 million.

B2 is now set to open in the third quarter of 2016.

Will mods make the grade in Brooklyn? Stay tuned.

Chapter 13
THE SELL

Whatever goes up must come down.

And whatever security an investor buys must inevitably be sold.

"Buy low; sell high," runs the hoary Wall Street aphorism, but the real question is when.

Countless books, learned treatises, and periodical articles provide myriad answers to this quandary over the years. Most are academic and pedantic, scant help in the real world.

As the 1970s bull market in mortgage trusts begins showing strains, I am left to answer this ageless question in the unrelenting real-world laboratory of a faltering marketplace.

I assay the market from both a short- and long-run view. In the short-run, the market is a highly sensitive voting machine, as millions of investors vote minute-by-minute with their dollars on deviations from estimates, growth opportunities, and potential dangers. Sometimes these short-termers overreact, sometimes they are wrong, but they're never in doubt.

The long-run is diametrically opposite. Investors parse economic and company data searching for longer-lasting trends that can win big profits. The market is a weighing machine over longer periods, judging the strengths and long-run growth prospects of businesses with uncanny accuracy. Accept as fact that while markets may err in the short-run, they seldom miss in the long-run.

All my training focuses me on analyzing longer trends for all securities, including REITs.

But the long-run consists of hundreds of daily and weekly data points and news events. As editor of an investment advisory service, I must live the long term day-by-day, making daily, weekly, and monthly market calls. This is my market laboratory, my daily torture chamber. Bear with me as events unfold for the REITs until the weight of evidence mandates *the sell*.

Not that I am unprepared. I make a few good sell calls in the 1960s for my own account. Now the tables are turned: I must make good sell— as well as buy—calls on behalf of several hundred subscribers whose personal circumstances and market moxie are unknown.

In those first years of Audit's life, we confront choppy markets for both REITs and homebuilders. The market heads south almost as soon as I sell our personal holdings in January 1969 to fund Audit. Interest rates rise sharply, and the prime lending rate jumps by 2.0 percent to 8.5 percent in the first half of 1969, depressing stock prices.

Mortgage trusts, as measured by the Paine Webber Index, a variable divisor stock index constructed like the Dow-Jones Industrials and maintained by the brokerage firm Paine, Webber, Jackson & Curtis, rocket to a high of 442 on the index by mid-May 1969.

With the advantage of hindsight, Paine Webber in an undated commentary describes the market's next steps in this fashion:

> "Whether investors became enthusiastic because the prices of mortgage trusts began to rise sharply or vice versa is a mute question. In any case hindsight tells us

that in May 1969 the prices of such shares were too high.

"At that time a number of commentators were criticizing the REITs. Further a large backlog of new issues in registration dampened the market for REIT shares. Then the general market fell.

"Over the ensuing ten weeks, the Dow Jones Industrials fell 16 percent, but in the same time period the mortgage trust index went down 45 percent. Of course a good portion of the fall was probably a necessary adjustment."

But here the mortgage trust script takes an unexpected turn in Paine Webber's eyes: "From July 1969, when mortgage trusts reach their bottom, through July 1970 the mortgage trust index rose about 11%," continues the Paine Webber analysis. "This is a remarkable record considering that the Dow Jones Industrial Average fell another 13% in the same period [following the Penn Central Railroad's unexpected bankruptcy filing in June 1970]."

DOUBLE TOP

But from July 1970 to October 1971, the PW Mortgage Trust Index rises some 81 percent while the Dow Jones Industrials gain only 31 percent. On October 14, 1971, the PW Mortgage Index reaches a second peak at 443. The number is a single point above that previous high of 442 a full twenty-eight months earlier, in mid-May 1969.

Stock market chartists are extremely wary at that point, fearing a dreaded "double-top" in which prices equal those of a previous peak because the market lacks enough firepower to push upward to new highs. Traders who study the market's price and volume trends mostly avoid stocks or indices reaching double-tops because almost universally prices will decline for an extended period following the second zenith.

In my stock trading in the 1960s, I am exposed to these technical market trends by reading *Technical Analysis of Stock Trends*, a classic book first published in 1951 by Robert D. Edwards and John Magee. But I have moved beyond charting and attach little significance to the PW reading of 443 in October 1971, which is just another number to be plotted with precision on the Paine Webber Index chart we present to subscribers. That chart adorns the very first issue of *Realty Trust Review* and is included with month-end statistical pricing letters after we go to two monthly issues in July 1971.

END OF A STREAK

On November 17, 1971, just one month after the book's winning debut and five weeks after the double-top, Durand A. Holladay, managing trustee of the largest mortgage REIT Continental Mortgage Investors (CMI), tells a *New York Times* reporter that CMI's earnings for the next six months will fall 12 to 20 percent behind year-ago results. The news shocks the market because the shortfall snaps a string of thirty-eight consecutive quarterly earnings gains. Holladay blames the end of CMI's near-decade run of good news to falling interest rates that make it difficult to replace maturing higher-yield loans and the rapid proliferation of competing trusts, which he says produce an unhealthy and unprofitable contest for construction loan volume at a time of fluctuating interest rates.

Many new trusts "have relaxed, if not totally eliminated" traditional criteria for underwriting construction loans in their haste to meet earnings projections, he avers.

CMI's admission of mortality storms the New York Stock Exchange floor like a whirlwind and shares of all sixteen NYSE-listed REITs fall, slicing about $260 million from their market value. The ten largest losers that day are all mortgage REITs. CMI shares shed $74.4 million of market value as its shares plunge 4-1/2 points or 24 percent to close at 14-1/2.

RTR sees CMI's plaint through different eyes than management. "CMI's sheer size has forced it to move away from its traditional markets among smaller builder-developers and compete for larger and larger projects, putting it head-to-head with larger national banks and regional banks," we comment in the November 29 issue. "And sheer size makes rolling over loans more and more difficult; with a portfolio approaching $400 million, CMI had to originate $100 million new loans each quarter merely to keep even."

RTR also analyzes CMI's net lending spread and leverage and concludes that "CMI's leverage ratio has to be thought of as approximately 3–1 … CMI's ratios are among the highest in the industry." Our conclusion: "The effect … has been to make CMI vulnerable to declines in portfolio yield, for leverage tends to magnify itself on the downside." We recommend a basket of lower-levered trusts not including CMI.

It's a tough call but still too early for any broadside sell.

Other concerns weigh on REIT investors at the same time. The Federal Cost of Living Council decides after long deliberation to unfreeze commercial and industrial rents from cost-of-living controls, and the IRS is deep into a long-awaited revision of REIT rules.

Moreover CMI's blast fails to achieve one major goal of stemming the tide of new competing mortgage trust IPOs. Six new REITs sell shares publicly in December 1971 alone, pushing IPO capital raised to $377 million and $818 million for the quarter and year. Existing trusts add another $79 million in follow-on equity offers plus $913 million in debt, lifting total REIT capital raises to $1.8 billion for 1971. CMI stock ends the year at $13.63 a share, down 25.3 percent for the year but still a healthy 40 percent premium-to-book value.

Mortgage REITs' stock prices end 1971 with a 29.7 percent yearly gain as measured by the Paine Webber REIT Index, although year-end prices are down just over 10 percent from the pre-Holladay peak.

Much later, Holladay tells me, "We knew what was wrong and what we had to do, but we kept on doing the same thing."

The king is dead. Long live the king!

Thus mortgage REITs enter 1972 as show-me stocks while investors await evidence pro or con about CMI's assertions.

FOLLOW THE CASH

As 1972 opens, *RTR* begins to focus on monthly dividends, figuring that dividends will equal earnings under the REIT pass-through tax system, and examine monthly declarations in excruciating detail in each monthly statistical issue.

That dividend tracking shows payouts remaining generally strong during 1972, although a few glitches emerge along the way. In March, four of thirty-four declarations, or nearly 12 percent, are down year-over-year, including an expected 4.3 percent dip by Continental Mortgage and cuts of 11 percent by short-term mortgage trust First Memphis and of 19 percent by equity trust Mutual REIT.

The negative side of warrant exercise first appears with a 14.9 percent cut by ICM Realty in March because warrant exercise boosts the number of shares qualified to receive the payout well above the number of average shares used in computing earnings per share.

Warrant exercise becomes a significant reason for dividend dips as 1972 wears on, illustrating the negative consequences of industry reliance upon warrants to produce an exotic bazaar of shares, warrants, and convertibles for investors (chapter 9).

By year-end 1972, our tally shows 66 percent of the year's 409 declarations up from year-ago payouts while only twenty-seven or 6.6 percent show declines. For "mature" trusts over one year old, 78 percent or 144 of 184 declarations are on the upside, while 17 or 9 percent show declines.

Most declines trace to warrant exercise, and in December, we note "some evidence of a slowing rate of gain [in payout growth]. This does not pain us because most REITs should show moderate growth rates in dividends instead of the super-heated rate of a growth stock."

In June 1972, the Housing and Urban Development Department begins including REITs in its monthly study of the mortgage market, finding the REITs holding $4.1 billion or 14 percent of $28.7 billion construction loans outstanding by March 1972. REITs also count $1.55 billion long-term mortgages and $1.3 billion land loans in their $6.9 billion holdings.

REITs thus account for about 14 percent of the $28.7 billion total construction loans counted in the HUD survey. Add $4.9 billion land loans and the $33.6 billion combined C&D plus land loan market is not much different from the market's size found in my 1969 study three years earlier.

The HUD survey provides some evidence that the flood of new REIT money into short-term construction loans has not eroded the overall market despite CMI's claim of diluted underwriting standards.

One note of caution surfaces in HUD's finding that REITs hold a much higher 26 percent of all $4.9 billion land loans, waving a modest red flag but certainly not meriting a "sell" on REITs.

REIT shares move up modestly during the year with mortgage REITs ending 1972 at 424 on the Paine Webber Index, up 6.8 percent, while equity REITs rise a more modest 4.2 percent to 200 on the PW Index. On a total return basis, including the 9.2 percent average REIT dividend yield, REITs return 15.9 percent to investors in 1972, trailing the Dow Industrials by 2.0 percent and the S&P 500 by 3.7 percent.

These are strong numbers for investors, and 1972 provides no reason to consider a "sell."

From my vantage point, one of the best pieces of news is that new

REIT offerings start tailing off during 1972. IPOs fall every quarter, ending just shy of $500 million, the lowest year since 1968. In total, REITs raise only $1.1 billion for the year, including debt, down 39 percent from the $1.8 billion of 1971.

We sigh in relief because it's become apparent that the deluge of REIT IPOs is the number one threat to a viable industry. In this context, less is best.

THE "PROBLEM" PROBLEM

The new year, 1973, starts on a bullish note when the Paine Webber Mortgage Index touches a recovery high of 436 on January 11, a reading within 1.5 percent of two previous highs of 442 in May 1969 and 443 in October 1971.

Some market technicians see this as a rare triple-top—more foreboding than a double-top—but since I am not a chartist, this highly bearish stock price tracing goes unnoticed by me and our staff. Our January month-end price survey notes that REIT shares are bearing up well under twin threats of renewed inflation and rising interest rates.

Ominously, our dividend tally finds the rate of increase is "showing signs of slowing."

REITs end January 1973 at a $6.9 billion market cap ($38.5 billion in 2015 dollars), a mark not seen again for nearly two decades. Short-term mortgage trusts make up almost exactly half, with intermediate and long-term mortgage trusts weighing in at 30 percent and equity and combination trusts at 20 percent.

This auspicious New Year start is dashed in late March 1973 when Chase Manhattan Mortgage & Realty Trust drops a bombshell, reporting a 12 percent earnings decline because of a money market squeeze. Short-term commercial paper rates leap 0.75 percent in the year's first seventy-five days while the Nixon Administration pressures banks to put a lid on their prime lending rate.

"Their money costs soared in the face of jackrabbit commercial paper rates while their loan portfolio yields, mostly tied to an artificially depressed prime, could move up very slowly," we explain to subscribers. The news slices 20 percent from Chase REIT's stock market valuation.

That same month, problem loans hurt earnings at two smaller trusts. Associated Mortgage, whose June 1968 IPO set off the mortgage REIT frenzy, tells investors three problem loans amount to about 20 percent of its loan portfolio, and the stock sinks to a 19 percent discount to book value. GREIT Realty, an equity trust that ventures into lending, says it's taken over 1,382 Houston apartments and cut its dividend by 25 percent; GREIT shares drop 28 percent on the news.

From then on, 1973 becomes the Year of the Problem Loan.

And problem loans are poison for investors.

There is one caveat as we repeatedly remind subscribers. Problem properties and nonearning loans are ordinary business events for mortgage REITs almost from the get-go, following *Realty Trust Review's* launch in March 1970. Four Seasons Nursing Centers of America's bankruptcy in June 1970 provides a perfect case study to examine just exactly how hardy the seven mortgage lenders snarled in that debacle are. My study a year later for the book *America's Newest Billionaires* (chapter 10) convinces me that mortgage trusts can weather most adversities if managers have done their underwriting job correctly.

Then, just as the book is going to press in July 1971, an earnings burp by Continental Illinois Realty (CIR), a major mortgage trust, reminds me that the first mortgage lien on properties held by mortgage lenders gives them an impregnable priority claim on properties in the event of troubles. CIR reports that a nonearning loan will cut earnings by 40 percent in its June 1971 quarter, but after inquiring, I feel CIR's first lien position will prevent principal loss and the brief earnings hit won't interrupt CIR's longer-term performance.

Hence I do not pull the "sell" rip cord when CIR's problem loans surface.

Problem loans are loans that fall behind in scheduled payments. In accounting lingo, they become *nonaccruing* or *nonearning* loans. But to the Street and to our staff at *RTR*, they are simply problem loans.

Their presence creates big problems for investors because these underperforming assets sap earnings, reduce those all-important dividends, and ultimately bring lower stock prices. In short, problem loans, no matter how small or innocuous, pose big problems for investors.

"To repeat, there's risk in today's market and each investor must choose how much risk he or she can absorb," we advise on March 26, 1973, under the heading "Straight Talk about Reit Earnings in a Chaotic Money Market." "That's a personal decision this service cannot make for you. There's a caution light flashing and you should heed it if you don't like the prospect of a decline in share quotations."

Caution light, yes; sell signal, no.

"Most trusts are experiencing problem loans … and they are showing more candor to the investing public than ever before," we note on April 16, 1973, in introducing a new feature tracking bad loans held by companies analyzed in our continuing REIT reviews. That first sweep finds an average 1.9 percent problem loans among eighteen REITs, but two of the eighteen trusts report over 5 percent in bad loans. "Losses have been minimal to non-existent for most trusts," we observe. "This points up that short-term construction lending contains risk and the test is ability to cope with problems."

By year-end 1973, we comb through financials of 153 REITs and turn up names of eighteen, or 12 percent, of coverage with over 5 percent nonearning assets. Fewer than half or 44 percent report zero bum investments.

The Street's search for problem loans reaches manic proportions, absent quarterly earnings conference calls to maintain open communication between company managements and analysts. In late April 1973, one analyst alerts clients that General Growth Properties, then the largest enclosed shopping mall owner, could be hurt by the closing of an army base in Des Moines, Iowa. "General Growth didn't know of any military base near a GGP center," we report, "but is building a center called Army Post Plaza named in honor of a long-defunct military base. Notwithstanding that fact, GGP shares were off 16.7% last month."

In late May, trust shares drop another sharp 5.7 percent, matching the Dow Jones Industrials decline, as confidence ebbs when reports circulate that DeBoer Associates, headed by Jack DeBoer and then among the nation's five largest apartment builders, "has gotten into difficulties." Details are very sketchy but about a dozen REITs loan or commit about sixty million dollars to several DeBoer projects. Creditors paper over the troubles with a new sixteen-million-dollar line, of which about three million represents new money. "Most important, the project, not the developer, is what counts in a real estate loan," we observe without advising selling any of the suspect dozen.

"I am trapped between fear and greed," a subscriber writes plaintively in late June 1973. "I do not want the REITs that I already own to fall, but I want bargains in REITs that I plan to purchase."

"This inner tug-of-war is repeated throughout the history of market swings and individual investor psychology," I reply. "We have always felt REIT investors should be willing to average down (i.e., add to positions if a stock's price declines) in quality issues whose fundamentals remain unimpaired ... We do not yet believe this general bear market has exhausted itself and thus would concur on your sideline stance (for planned purchases)."

In August 1973, the DeBoer name pops up again as two trusts say they own the land, subordinated to first mortgages, beneath several apartments owned by DeBoer. "Major institutions like the First National

City Bank and Ford Foundation of New York are moving to shore up finances of these projects," we write in advising purchase of ICM Realty, one of the landholders, for "stable income, low price volatility, and long-term appreciation." (Jack DeBoer later pioneers the extended-stay hospitality business by founding Summerfield Suites and Candlewood Suites all-suite hotel chains.)

In the meantime, REITs discover "how tough it is for trusts to raise money, and how high the price of money can go," *RTR* observes. By then, more REITs need the money to honor forward-lending commitments. REITs raise a sequentially low $52 million in 1973's third quarter, nearly all coming from two highly unusual offerings. Guardian Mortgage garners $19.9 million by selling 600,000 shares at $33.13 a share by letting new buyers receive a previously declared dividend, while Barnett Mortgage sells $30 million of 8.5 percent debentures convertible at $39.00 or a 63 percent premium to current share price; after five years, the debentures would convert at 80 percent of average share price, a highly unusual provision.

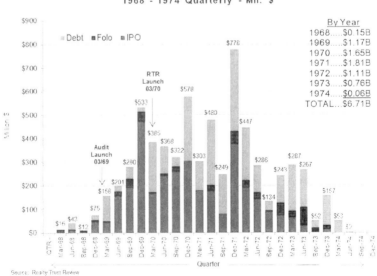

Exhibit 13.1 -- REIT Capital Raises
1968 - 1974 Quarterly - Mil. $

By Year
1968.....$0.15B
1969.....$1.17B
1970.....$1.65B
1971.....$1.81B
1972.....$1.11B
1973.....$0.76B
1974.....$0.06B
TOTAL...$6.71B

Source: Realty Trust Review

"Where do we go from here?" writes a puzzled subscriber in September 1973. "I am loaded with REITs—and love them—for income. Mine are 8–15 points below what I paid and most will not recover until the political clouds have departed. It is not all the fault of Watergate, etc."

Coming in the early stages of the Watergate investigation, the answer is imponderable. But I try: "Focus attention on the ability of trusts you own to maintain (and perhaps increase) quarterly dividends, not on share prices. The real test of your investment is what happens to the payouts after your initial investment."

ENTER OPEC, INTRUSIVELY

Then on October 6, 1973, Egypt and Syria attack Israel on that nation's holiest day, Yom Kippur. The Organization of Petroleum Exporting Countries (OPEC), dominated by Arab nations, announces a series of production cuts and oil price hikes that effectively quadruple oil prices to about $12 a barrel. Although the Yom Kippur War ends within three weeks, the oil price shock in concert with Watergate uncertainty sends all US stocks down, the Dow Jones Industrials plunging 14 percent in October. REIT shares are not immune, falling 15 percent.

After October 1973, mortgage REIT share prices fall slowly, broken by occasional rallies common to all bear markets. More and more parts of the US economy shudder in response. Economic data begins falling more sharply, and it slowly becomes clear that the systemic risk unfolding after the OPEC oil embargo begets ruinous impact on properties by boosting operating costs and required rents while diminishing tenant ability to pay. New construction falls precipitously, and too much mortgage money is chasing too few deals. Slipping mortgage REIT prices underscore that part of the story.

The bad news for REITs continues in early November when Cameron-Brown Investment and Fidelity Mortgage, two large institutionally sponsored mortgage trusts, plunge 20.5 percent and 16.6 percent respectively when *Barron's* and the *Wall Street Journal* report major problem loans causing large earnings declines. In reporting the events, *RTR* says, "Existence of a problem loan is not in itself reason for selling a REIT or to prevent investing in REITs … Most trusts have absorbed 3%–5% of portfolio in problem loans without major earnings damage."

By Thanksgiving 1973, it's apparent the energy shock is having profound impact throughout the economy, including long lines at service stations. Amid this energy crisis bear market, I peer into my investment crystal ball:

> "The energy shortage may be more long-lasting than either a war or a recession. There's the possibility that price and wage controls could make semi-utilities out of some basic industries like steel, railroads, petroleum and the like. If that is the shape of the future, then here is the investment posture that seems to make the most sense:
>
> "REITs with leveraged, variable-rate assets should do well … This points toward equity trusts and we favor those owning major urban center office and industrial buildings because apartments are sometimes vulnerable to tenant actions such as rent strikes, etc. Names: First Union, Washington REIT and Pennsylvania REIT suggest themselves.
>
> "Conversely highly leveraged short-term mortgage REITs probably are vulnerable."

Mortgage REITs now stand at 290 on the PW Index, down 33 percent from that January 11 high of 436.

But no across-the-board sell yet, although no vote of confidence either.

The problem loan hammer drops four days before Christmas 1973 when Walter J. Kassuba, the nation's third largest apartment builder with an estimated six-thousand-unit annual volume, seeks bankruptcy court protection.

"Kassuba Bankruptcy: The News May Be Worse than the Facts for Trusts," we report in a December 27 special report to subscribers. We find fourteen trusts holding $135 million of paper to Walter J. Kassuba. "With over $500 million real estate assets involved, the Kassuba bankruptcy is by far the largest real estate bankruptcy since the widely watched failure of Webb & Knapp a decade ago … over 200 mortgage lenders hold about 300 mortgages and leases on about 119 properties under construction or in operation with about 36,000 dwelling units."

The $135 million mortgage REIT involvement with Kassuba breaks down 32.5 percent first mortgage standing or permanent loans, 21.3 percent first mortgage construction loans, 10.0 percent first mortgage land and development loans, 26.2 percent subordinated land purchase/leasebacks, and 10.0 percent junior and wraparound loans. Numerous legal uncertainties mean "it is not possible to assess with any precision the ultimate earnings impact on individual trusts," *RTR* observes. NJB Prime Investors, sponsored by a smallish New Jersey bank, has the most exposure with 18.3 percent of assets involved with Kassuba.

Thus the Year of the Problem Loan rings out with a plethora of problem loans.

Everything is down for the year 1973, with REITs falling at about twice the rate of the broad market. Dow Jones Industrials sink 16.9 percent in price for the year while equity REITs slump 30.0 percent and mortgage REITs plunge 40.1 percent, as measured by the Paine Webber Indices. When dividends are added back, all REITs are down 28.8 percent versus the Dow's 13.0 percent.

REIT market value slumps by one-third from that exuberant $6.9 billion January 1973 high to end 1973 at $4.6 billion.

At *RTR*, we feel the strong equity REIT relative performance validates our shift toward this group after mid-1973, while the huge slippage in mortgage trusts builds angst about the coming year. Our December dividend tally finds payouts falling for the second month running because of Fidelity Mortgage's omission and sizable cuts by a half-dozen others.

We await 1974 with trepidation.

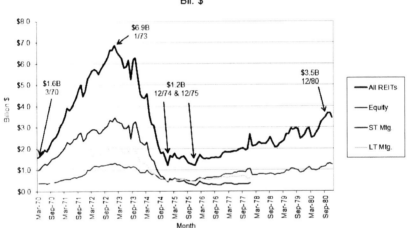

Exhibit 13.2: REIT Market Capitalization in the 1970s
Bil. $

Source: Realty Trust Review & Author's Calculations

THE SELL

"The year 1973 was a near-wipeout for REIT investors but the year-end panic selling already shows signs of lifting and a recovery for 1974 appears favorable," we open our first 1974 issue.

We are 100 percent premature in calling the demise of this super-bear.

That initial 1974 issue contains an ambitious tally of total returns for 130 trusts active over the previous four years, 1970 through 1973. The totals reveal equity trusts as turtles, slow of foot but steady, while the short-term mortgage brethren are more volatile hares, leaping ahead and then falling flat in the stretch. The average annual record and four-year compound annual growth rate (CAGR) are as follows:

TABLE 13.1: FOUR-YEAR REIT TRACK RECORD BY SECTORS, 1970–1973

	1970	1971	1972	1973	4-Yr.Growth
Equity REITs	+ 4.2%	+18.9%	+11.8%	-23.3%	+1.52%
Short-term Mtg.	+29.9	+39.1	+22.3	-31.7	+10.84%
Long-term Mtg.	+ 1.7	+39.4	+13.4	-30.9	+2.66%
All REITs	**+18.9%**	**+33.4%**	**+17.2%**	**-28.8%**	**+7.26%**
Dow Jones Indus.	+8.3%	+9.7%	+16.3%	-12.4%	+4.86%
S&P 500	+3.1%	+14.9%	+18.9%	-14.8%	+4.70%

Source: *Realty Trust Review*, January 14, 1974, and author's computations for DJI and S&P.

The respite is brief. The *Wall Street Journal*, on January 21, prints a page 1 article headlining fears that REITs face a "major shakeout." Since *shakeout* is such a loaded word, *RTR* draws from the article's author Priscilla S. Meyer her view that the word "indicates a situation in which perhaps six REITs would not survive as REITs and perhaps another dozen or so would encounter serious problems. To her, a 'shakeout' is less than a disaster."

REIT investors are not frightened by the journal's loaded words, and REIT shares slide only 0.9 percent for January.

Conservatism sets in. Accountants begin forcing trusts to recognize problem loans earlier and insist on appraisals of any doubtful property, forcing trusts to boost loss reserves. Banks become skittish and force tiny Dominion Mortgage to cut back its line. Three highly leveraged short-term trusts seek merger with lower-leveraged sister trusts to boost balance sheet strength.

In March 1974, *RTR* reports that many REITs involved in the complex

DeBoer and Kassuba workouts are gradually working out of their hold-ings. "Incidence of new problem loans is receding," we state on March 11. Associated Mortgage, the REIT that fathered the mortgage REIT boom and bubble, seeks bankruptcy protection March 15, 1974, but by then AMI stock hasn't traded since October 1973 and its nine-million-dollar market cap is so tiny that hardly anyone notices or cares.

REITs rise 5 percent during March 1974 and are essentially flat for the year to date.

Then the commercial paper market delivers a knockout blow by collapsing for many REIT and other issuers.

The collapse impels our first and only all-points sell.

"Special Recommendation: Avoid New Purchases of All Short-Term Mortgage Reits," we headline a special two-page bulletin to subscribers on April 4, 1974.

Commercial paper, or uncollateralized corporate notes, usually back-stopped by bank credit lines, is the most volatile of REIT financing sources. Our computer runs show REIT commercial paper standing at $3.9 billion, a major portion of REIT debt capital. The commercial paper market is "a snake-pit of rumors, reports of rating changes and withdrawals, collapses of Eurodollar backup facilities," we report.

The commercial paper market collapse "has clouded the outlook for mortgage REIT shareholders and we do not believe subscribers should expose themselves to the greatest risks of devastating surprises," we tell subscribers.

Exhibit 13.3 REIT Stock Prices 1966 – 1975
Paine Webber /Audit Index: December 1966 = 100

Already two REITs run into deep trouble trying to raise capital to fund loan commitments. Great American Management & Investment is forced to pull a planned convertible preferred offering March 28 and cuts its dividend 38 percent; shares drop 40 percent the two following days.

First Mortgage Investors, the oldest short-term mortgage REIT dating from 1961, is putting together a four-hundred-million-dollar credit line to replace its commercial paper after Moody's yanks its credit rating.

If these two trusts cannot make it in this new tougher financing world, I figure there's scant hope for smaller and newer trusts. "This pattern is repeated in many other trusts: portfolio problems are coming under control, but the uncertain financing outlook increases the risk sharply for shareholders," the bulletin concludes. "The recent interest rate increase can only hurt mortgage REIT earnings. The equity trusts, untouched by problem loans, are the only group we would consider for new investment at present."

I reason that the near-halt in fund access spells declining growth in new loans for short-term mortgage trusts. With this earnings driver now headed south, the game is effectively over for these mortgage lenders—hence the sell bulletin.

Despite its careful wording to "Avoid new purchases," the bulletin is interpreted as a "sell" by most readers.

It remains the only blanket advisory issued in *Realty Trust/Stock Review's* twenty-year history.

Subscribers, especially those affiliated with mortgage REITs, howl with anger that the call is unwarranted and premature, but I stand firm and never withdraw the advice.

The sell signal comes at 214 on the PW Mortgage Index, down 51 percent from the 436 January 1973 peak, but it still saves subscribers over three-quarters of their investment dollars as mortgage REIT stocks die in the second half of 1974 on their way to a low of 51 for a 76 percent debacle after the sell.

Equity REITs fare slightly better, falling 59 percent after the sell to close at 55.

Taking away the punch bowl is never fun, but it is a necessary part of investing. For every buy, there is a time to sell.

The rest of 1974 is an unremitting, dismal slog into Death Valley.

We survey problem loans held by 122 REITs in the May 28 issue and find more concentration than expected. REITs report slightly over one billion dollars in nonearning investments or 6.05 percent of the $16.9 billion investments surveyed.

Short-term mortgage REITs account for over 80 percent of problem loans.

A total of twenty-five trusts reports over 10 percent of their portfolios not earning income, while thirty-three trusts, predominantly equity and long-term mortgage, have zero impacted investments.

In June 1974, Paine Webber gives up on computing its signature REIT index because the firm sees no future in REITs and asks if *Realty Trust Review* wants to take over. I jump at the opportunity, and the index is renamed the Audit Investment Index.

Cash is tight at Audit, but Irene and I resolve to take our three children on a brief vacation drive through New England in August. We get as far as Route 128 north of Boston when the radiator of our family car begins boiling, necessitating a tow to nearby Gloucester where mechanics deliver the ugly news. The vehicle must stay two days in dry dock for repairs.

With no choice, we finally scrounge a room in the crowded artist's haven that is Gloucester and Cape Ann and explore its charms via bus. Irene loves the ambiance. At a charming waterfront restaurant, Irene orders crab, only to wind up deathly ill, whether from an allergy or tainted seafood we never learn.

Finally, the radiator is repaired, and we complete our truncated vacation, humbled by the knowledge that unexpected events can alter mortal plans within an instant.

All this takes place against the backdrop of the worst bear market since the Great Depression, fueled in no small part by the Watergate scandal and President Nixon's resignation in August 1974. By year-end 1974, the Dow Jones Industrials shed 27.6 percent of their value and the S&P 500 falls 29.7 percent; both are among the worst drubbings in the broad stock market since the Great Depression.

Equity REITs, the best performers in our problem loan surveys, fall a grinding 60.7 percent on the Paine Webber Index for the year. Some in the group are tempted by high mortgage returns and fall by the wayside in ensuing years. Most remain viable and live for another day.

Short-term mortgage REITs collapse a sickening 79.9 percent—call it 80 percent—for the year 1974.

Every one of the fifty-nine new short-term mortgage REITs emerging from my rat hole after 1968, without exception, live on only as either trading sardines for vulture investors or bankruptcy court subjects. Only one of twenty-nine long-term mortgage REITs from the era survives today; Hotel Investors ultimately morphs into Starwood Hotel & Resorts, still listed in 2015 under its 1974 symbol, HOT.

Wall Street memories are long, and no one has ever been courageous enough to attempt to revive this particular brand of short-term mortgage REIT.

Realty Trust Review subscriptions plummet from a peak near 1,750 in the glory days to just below 1,200 at the end of 1974, a 30 percent shrinkage that throws Audit into a modest $2,740 loss on $217,800 revenues ($1 million in 2015 dollars) for the year.

Subscribers are bailing every day, and I worry about what 1975 will bring.

Is Audit about to join the ranks of the detritus from this unsparing bear market?

Is five years of hard work about to go down the tubes?

Is my string of serendipitous successes about to run out?

And above all, can I find a new job if I must?

We take the staff to a Christmas luncheon December 20, but no one is really in a festive mood.

At year-end 1974, I consider crawling into my rat hole and never emerging.

The REIT revolution is dead, executed by OPEC and too many bad loans.

1975? The unknown haunts our holidays—but I have a strong opener for the year.

Chapter 14
THE GIFT

A serendipitous gift arrives for the 1975 New Year.

The unsolicited gift arrives just before Christmas when a *Wall $treet Week* producer calls to invite me to appear on a planned national TV program about REITs.

At that time, *Wall $treet Week* is the nation's first and most widely watched national financial show. It is beamed to over 250 PBS stations nationwide at 8:00 p.m. Fridays from the Maryland Center for Public Broadcasting in Owings Mills, Maryland.

Watching *W$W* becomes a Friday ritual for Irene and me when we are home because it provides a relaxing end-of-week perspective on current investment trends.

W$W is the brainchild of Louis Rukeyser, a political and foreign correspondent for the *Baltimore Sun* and economic correspondent for ABC Television, which originates *W$W* in 1970 and hosts the show.

The half-hourly format never varies. A panel of four Wall Street "experts" opine on market action of the past week during the first fifteen minutes and then question an investment guru in some specialized field for the remaining quarter-hour. I will be the guest guru for one show.

In its early years, *W$W* counts over three million viewers weekly and is amid its skein of glory days when my guest invitation arrives.

Turning down the gift overture seems out of the question.

I accept. I do not lobby for the guest slot and to this day have zero clues on how the show's producers settled upon issuing my invitation, although years spent peering into my rat hole for REITs most certainly plays some part.

W$W staffers subsequently descend upon our office and ask a torrent of questions about my investment views and background before the deal is finally sealed.

On Friday, February 21, 1975, the start of the President's Day holiday weekend, Irene and I drive to Towson, Maryland, just north of Baltimore to the home of friends who invite us to stay the weekend.

About 5:00 p.m., a black limo arrives and tools us to the *W$W* studio in Owings Mills, where we meet that night's panelists and warm up with real estate scuttlebutt over a light repast before taping begins at 7:00 p.m. Frank Cappiello, then head of a national investment advisory firm and an original and enduring panelist, hosts that evening's show because Rukeyser is taking the holiday weekend off.

WHAT'S UP WITH HOUSING?

The show is titled "Housing: Crunch Becomes Crush" to capitalize on viewer interest in a then-ongoing housing collapse of 35 percent to 1.34 million units in 1974. To the first question of why housing is in such a slump, I reply: "We got this way, Frank, because we were up so very high. We were at the top of the Alps, at the Matterhorn, and we skied down the valley. We had three years back-to-back with two million starts or more [1971 to 1973]. It's never happened in the United States before, and, you know, basic law of economics—What goes up must come down. So we had some overbuilding, and we're correcting that right now. A lot of other reasons but that's the basic one."

"Where will the money for a recovery come from?" Capiello persists.

Money to fuel a housing rebound will come primarily from the savings and loan industry, I opine. "We had record inflows into the savings and loans in California last month. The money is coming in because it always happens this way. When the consumer gets frightened, he begins saving. Once the money comes back in, it will go into housing."

Capiello presses on about a housing recovery. "Do you see much future for townhouses or condos? Is this part of your scenario for the housing boom?"

"Interesting," I reply. "Condos have been really buoyed because everybody said they're the answer to high land cost. But a number of surveys recently say that condominium buyers want to live in a single-family home within five years. So I tend to view condos as a more transitional form of housing. I don't think condos will be a major part of housing; they're going to be there for a long time, but they will not be major."

WHITHER REITS?

Calling REITs a "disaster industry," Panelist Carter Randall, then a senior vice president at Baltimore's Equitable Trust Co., presses a key question: "What future do you see for this industry? Will it have to change its structure and in numbers of companies?"

"I tend to think the equity trusts or the property trusts are going to have quite a bright future, and the long-term mortgage trusts will be with us for a long time. But the short-term trusts will see significant consolidation or departures. Their structure is going to be changed. And that tends to get the most publicity because about half of the assets of the REITs are in short-term REITs right now."

"Then they're in trouble, really, aren't they?" persists Randall.

"They're in the same trouble that I think virtually all construction lenders are right now," I retort.

NAME THOSE NAMES

"Historically the building stocks have been one of the most spectacular performing groups from bear market bottoms," observes Robert Nurock, a technically oriented adviser who creates the *Wall $treet Week* Index (a.k.a. "The Elves" in Rukeyser's droll rendition). "I'm wondering if you think that they will be good performers this time? And if so, which stocks in the groups would you be looking at?"

"I think that real estate stocks tend to move in much different cycles than do other industrial securities. For instance, the real estate group did not share in the 1964–65 bull market. My tendency is to think that most investors will wait for a while. The REITs have not really shared in this rally. The homebuilders and some other building groups have, but not the REITs."

"Are there any particular ones you might favor at this juncture?" Nurock persists.

"Well, in the REIT group, we like the big five insurance-company-sponsored ones."

I then recommend "in alphabetical order" five institutionally sponsored long-term mortgage trusts: Connecticut General Mortgage and Realty, Equitable Life Mortgage, MassMutual Mortgage, MONY Mortgage, and Northwestern Life Mortgage.

"In the equity REIT group, we look very highly on General Growth Properties and First Union Real Estate."

"It's interesting," muses Capiello, "that when you referred to the REITs, every single one was life insurance linked. They were all part of the life insurance complex. Why don't you recommend bank REITs?"

"In the life insurance REITs, we see managements that have been long-term mortgage investors for hundreds of years. They know their business, and they're investing in a commodity which is quite common and familiar to them, a long-term mortgage. Most of the bank-sponsored REITs happen to be in the short-term construction area, and that's a very specialized field. We've just not been as impressed with their performance."

"Ken," asks Capiello, "if the average investor is bullish on real estate, how would you recommend a guy with ten or fifteen thousand dollars enter the real estate market? Or should he?"

"Aside from the long-term mortgage REITs, which I mentioned, the only other group we would like would be the investment builders. General Growth Properties, which I mentioned, is basically a developer in REIT clothing, an investment builder, which holds shopping centers and some apartments for its own account ... good standard real estate."

"How would you look at apartments?"

"The tendency has been to make them numbers games," I respond, "and not have a good insight into their operating and management expenses. I don't know of an apartment builder that I'd want to have an investor go into right now, because the economics of apartments are very bad right now. Rents have lagged the Consumer Price Index dramatically. Rents on new apartments are up only about 10 percent in the last five years. So the cash flow coming out of apartments is terribly poor."

CASH FLOW CONUNDRUM

Panelist Joel Stern, a financial economist and then consultant with Chase Manhattan Bank, inquires about how we analyze land development companies. "If you're looking at say Dillingham or Amfac that have a large proportion of their assets in land and land development, don't you think that earnings per share don't count? Don't you think that what really matters is such things as free cash flow?"

"I'm glad you asked that," I retort, "because I made a speech to the partners of a large accounting firm a year or two ago in which I advocated cash flow accounting, at least as an adjunct to security analysis, and the accountants were turned off by that view. And I might say the SEC has been turned off. They keep insisting upon accrual basis accounting. And the real estate analysts should come back to cash as closely as they can. We tend to look at price to cash flow on virtually all [land development] stocks."

"Ken, I think we might mention that the SEC will not allow cash flow representations in prospectuses relating to real estate companies," moderator Frank Capiello notes. "So it's really a moot point for the investor because you can't show the figures."

"I think that you're absolutely right," I affirm.

"Ken, we have only a little time left," says Capiello. "Is this a good time for someone to buy a house?"

"We've been at the top," I advise, "we're down in the valley. I think you buy a house now, sure. There are bargains around. They generally aren't advertised, but they're there."

THE GIFT

Over the years, *W$W* has been criticized because stocks mentioned by guests tend to rise in the days before the program's airing, spike on the Monday following broadcast, and perform poorly afterward.

For my part, I have no regrets for the seven names "tipped" to the TV audience that evening. The seven return a total 16.7 percent for investors by year-end 1975, with Equitable Life outdistancing the others and Northwestern Mutual lagging. Four of the seven stocks rise in price by year-end 1975, and all seven hold or increase payouts.

None of the seven REITs I mention that evening ever get into big-time trouble, but ultimately the large life insurance companies decide to close out their trusts and all go private within five years.

General Growth is sold at a huge profit in 1985, and First Union is ultimately taken over in 1994 because its share price lags well below the net asset value of its properties.

For me, the gift invitation affords a feel-good opportunity to speak to a national TV audience. Upon rereading, the transcript reveals that the back-and-forth questioning that evening contributed in some small way to investor understanding of the nuances of investing in real estate stocks. And the stock tips that night, if viewed as a package portfolio, yield good results.

Still the unforgiving time limit and the showbiz nature of such forums limit their value to investors. My takeaway is that individual investors should try to draw ideas and trends from such shows but should not buy a security based on a TV tip without doing much more inquiry.

W$W*'s pioneering of financial news doubtless opens airwaves for today's daily telecasts by CNBC and Bloomberg News of trading on the New York Stock Exchange. In the end, *W$W's unvarying format becomes so predictable the show is cancelled in 2005.

Voila, my *W$W* gift appearance comes off without a gaffe.

My presence fails to spark TV stardom but lets me introduce Audit's wares to a wider national TV audience, and the results are scintillating. Audit loses only a net eleven subscriptions to *Realty Trust Review* during that dreaded year of 1975, off less than 1 percent to a year-end 1975 count of 1,171. Subscription revenue rises 45 percent to $125,980 ($543,000 in 2015 dollars), the highest of the decade, thanks in part to a 28 percent September subscription rate increase.

Thus my lonely rat hole watch begets a gift TV slot that keeps on giving.

Thank you, *W$W*. You cure my 1975-phobia.

In the *W$W* afterglow, pressure from the problem loan explosion fades for a few weeks but quickly resumes as busted deals continue their relentless march from my rat hole as 1975 unfolds.

Back to reality we go.

Chapter 15
THE SEMINAR

REIT problem loans double between January and May 1975 to $7.1 billion and now consume 37 percent of all REIT assets, a frightening deterioration in the health of mortgage REITs in less than six months.

REIT stocks rebound sharply from their December 1974 lows, and by May, equity REITs are up 17 percent. But the newswire brings distressing tidings. In May 1975, Chase Manhattan Trust, once the largest REIT with a $298 million market value at the January 1973 peak, rattles the market by hiring bankruptcy specialist Weil, Gotshal, and Manges to separate its legal counsel from the law firm advising sponsor Chase Manhattan Bank. Chase Trust loses 94 percent of its market value to $17.7 million by the time it switches lawyers.

"Retention of a firm well known for its expertise in bankruptcy and near-bankruptcy situations was not lost on banks," we comment in the May 23 *Realty Trust Review*.

"Nearly every trust has consulted bankruptcy counsel," one prominent banker told us. "The banks are aware of this and act accordingly. There's no cause for panic."

To assess the outlook for investors, we convene a one-day seminar called "REITs—What's Ahead" in the Empire Room of the Waldorf Astoria Hotel in Manhattan. The date is Friday, June 6, 1975, and well over one hundred investors pay $150 to listen to and question a blue-ribbon roster of speakers.

Half the attendees are scared to death; the other half are looking for speculative plays at a perceived market bottom. There is no talk of a REIT revolution here.

HOW LONG A WORKOUT?

"The problem up until now has been one of dealing with an unknown," I open the session by summarizing a special nine-page, single-spaced research report pulled together for the event. "As we size it up, we now have probably unearthed about 90 percent of the problem loans that will surface in the REIT industry. We project that the explosion of nonaccruing loans will probably peak somewhere in the fourth quarter around $7.5 to $8.0 billion worth." (I am too optimistic. Nonearning loans hit $9.5 billion by the end of 1975 and peak at $10.1 billion a year after the seminar, in June 1976.)

After noting that management judgment is paramount in deciding when to stop accruals, I continue, "There's probably a sort of reverse one-upmanship surfacing here in which REITs are vying to show how bad off they are, so that if their pallor is extremely pale and they can say they are on their deathbeds, they hope to wring significant interest rate reductions from their bank lenders."

The housing crunch is mainly to blame, I continue. About one-third of problem loans are either one-family or condominium homes, "many conceived at the crest of the 1971–73 housing boom and targeted for sale to an affluent, energy-rich economy." Another 12 percent of bad loans finance apartments, and 19 percent are land acquisition or development loans, mainly for residential projects.

"Nearly all were hit by record inflation in building costs, which surged through the economy in 1973–74," I report. "This increased physical construction costs by 10 to 25 percent for a great majority of projects.

Material shortages compounded difficulties by delaying construction, thereby increasing their 'soft' financing costs as well."

Trust leverage is a killer. "Nonearning investments began hitting REITs when the typical REIT was leveraged 2.7-to-1 and the short-term mortgage trusts leveraged nearly 4-to-1," my research finds. "As nonearning investments soared over 20 percent of portfolio, it's easy to see that they thus equaled 100 percent of shareholders' equity."

I end this litany with three brief examples of problem loans:

- A $2.6 million land loan in Washington DC acquired by American Century Mortgage is down-zoned from office building to multiple residential use and written down 23 percent by the trust.
- A $5.5 million six-story wood-frame walk-up apartment project with 350 units, built in the Columbus, Ohio, subdivision where I formerly lived, is denied a certificate of occupancy by the Ohio Fire Marshall who declares, "No one in Ohio will ever live in a six-story, wood-frame walk-up." (He wins his lawsuit, and the apartments are leveled, costing First Mortgage Investors its investment.)
- An $8.0 million land loan to finance a 1,120-unit condominium in Sailboat Key, Florida, near Miami, runs into major community opposition and is foreclosed, hurting the three REITs who share the loan.

FIVE HIGH-PROFILE PROBLEMS

To assess workout time, I unveil a detailed look at five high-profile problem properties whose loans are shared by several REITs; four are properties I can visit regularly on my travels or can monitor easily. This hands-on look helps me estimate the industry's workout time and underscore the conditions and actions that torpedo the mortgage REITs.

"The workout time cannot be assessed in the abstract or by reference to some widely followed economic variable (e.g., housing starts or GNP [then gross national product, now gross domestic product or GDP])," I say. "Since many projects were conceived for an affluent, energy-rich economy, return to those conditions would be most helpful. Affluence could recover with GNP, but it's doubtful if energy will ever become cheap or plentiful again. Housing starts and revival of housing may improve liquidity, especially in single-family homes. This will aid urban single-family lot tracts but have far less impact upon secondary homesite and resort developments. The best approach is to assess prospects for selected specific projects. This brief inspection illustrates two points.

"*First*, some nationally known old-line developers were attracted into building some uneconomic projects; four builders of these projects were public companies, and two were listed on the NYSE.

"*Second*, projects were developed with a high level of aesthetic sensitivity, front-end expenses, and equity investment by the developers. It appears developers put about $74 million into these five projects, or about 22 percent of the $346 million invested [$1.54 billion in 2015 dollars]. That's considerably higher than the estimated average for all distressed properties. Virtually all that $74 million is effectively lost, and it appears mortgage lenders eventually will see about $42 million in losses, or about 15 percent of their funding. Please don't extrapolate that estimate across total REIT problem investments, but it does illustrate the fact that mortgage lenders can and do lose money." Here are our estimates in millions:

TABLE 15.1: SUMMARY OF FIVE HIGH-PROFILE PROBLEM PROPERTIES—MIL. $

	Mortgages	Equity	Tot. Inv.	E Mtg. Loss	REIT Loans
1166 Ave. Americas	$ 45.0	$ 22.8	$ 67.8	None	None
Blue Hill	30.0	22.0	52.0	None	$ 8.0
Colony North	*96.2	E10.0	106.2	$17.0	E32.6
Sandestin	21.8	E6.0	27.8	5.0	19.7
Palmas del Mar	78.7	13.0	91.7	20.0	E70.0
Totals	$271.7	$73.8	$345.5	$42.0	$130.3

E = Estimated. * Includes $43.23 million funded and $53 million required to complete. Source: Author's computations from property data.

A brief look at this quintet of losers shows what went wrong: missed market timing, terrible site selection, cost overruns, and grandiose resort planning.

A. *Missed Market Timing: Urban Office building—1166 Avenue of the Americas, Manhattan*

Status in June 1975

Tishman Realty & Construction, NYSE listed major investment builder, and joint venture partners began constructing this forty-four-story office building at Forty-Sixth Street with 1.43 million square feet net rentable space in 1970 and completed it during 1974 when its target rental market was in near-disaster mode. Tishman took charges totaling $29.7 million in 1974 while the vacant shell, which I pass nearly every morning on my walk to the office, stands untenanted. First National City Bank of New York, lead lender on a $45 million construction loan, sues to force a group headed by North American Mortgage Investors to close an interim permanent mortgage loan but loses and lenders take control of the tower in 1975.

Outlook: 2–3 year workout. [*2015 Status:* Our estimate is on target, and the tower is sold as a commercial condominium in 1977–78.]

B. *Misguided Site Selection: Suburban office building—Blue Hill, Pearl River, New York*

Status in June 1975

Uris Building Corp., NYSE listed developer and one of Manhattan's largest office owners, conceived this project to capture the flow of businesses out of New York City in 1967–68 and compete for back-office space for the New York Stock Exchange. In January 1970, Uris completed financing arrangements with a group of pension funds administered by First National City Bank, joining Uris as equity sponsors putting up $22 million. A $30 million construction loan was taken up by Union Bank of Los Angeles, which subsequently sold $4 million participations each to mortgage REITs Sutro Mortgage Trust and Colwell Mortgage Trust.

Uris selected a bucolic 242-acre site in Pearl River, Rockland County, New York, about thirty-five miles from Times Square overlooking prestigious Blue Hill golf course but without any surrounding office uses and only one-half mile from the New Jersey state line. At the time, New York had a state income tax but sponsors figured New Jersey had to adopt an income tax soon. On this site, only seven miles from my New Jersey home, Uris erected the 1.2 million-square-foot Blue Hill office complex, built to a stunning Skidmore, Owings, & Merrill design, consisting of One Blue Hill Plaza, a 550,000-square-foot, twenty-one-story tower linked by a 135,000-square-foot concourse to six-story Two Blue Hill Plaza, also with 550,000 square feet.

Exhibit 15.1: Blue Hill Office Project, Pearl River, NY: Howard J. Rubenstein Associates, Inc., 1976.

Only 5 percent of the space is rented initially at rates from $7.85 to $9.15 per square foot, and in April 1974, Uris deeds its interest in Blue Hill to Union Bank and the pension funds, in lieu of foreclosure. A new rental agent is hired, and in November 1976, I attend a luncheon on the twenty-first floor announcing a new leasing campaign. The lookout is stunning, but the remote location is a clear strategic blunder.

Ironically, Western Union, Union Camp, BVD Corp., and several other major national corporations attest their desire for suburban locations and relocate their corporate headquarters across the state line into lower-tax Montvale, New Jersey, about four miles distant.

Outlook: 3-5 year workout. [*2015 Status:* Uris also forfeits its namesake Manhattan office tower to foreclosure, and ultimately the losses force the company's sale at a big discount. In 1981, Wichita developer George Ablah buys Blue Hill from the bank for about $20 to $25 million, or about half its cost, fills the space with aggressive leasing, and sells four years later for about $200 million, according to my estimates.]

C. *Cost Overruns: Urban Apartment—The Colony North, Fort Lee, New Jersey*

Status in June 1975

New York City private developer Hyman Shapiro, builder of 5,000 apartments in New York City, began work on this four-tower complex containing 1,088 apartments about 1972 following the success of an initial 250-unit tower on a stunning site on the Palisades just south of the George Washington Bridge, affording panoramic views of Manhattan. The site is about twenty miles from my home.

Post–oil embargo inflationary pressures cause cost overruns, especially on very expensive foundations straddling the New Jersey Palisades, and work is halted in November 1974. Lead lender C.I. Mortgage Group, a REIT, began foreclosure in February 1975. Court records show lenders have advanced $34.4 million and another $53 million is required to complete. The finished apartment complex is valued at about $79 million versus the total mortgage funds of $96.2 million, handing mortgage lenders a loss of about $17 million if and when completed. Lenders are negotiating to bring in a new contractor.

Outlook: three- to four-year workout. [*2015 Status:* Our estimate is spot-on; a new contractor finishes Colony North in 1977, and in 1978, the apartments rent smartly. Today Colony is indistinguishable from its toney neighbors.]

D. *Highly Leveraged Land Play: Onshore Resort Community— Sandestin, Destin, Florida*

Status in June 1975

Evans & Mitchell Industries (EMI), a public company based in Atlanta, in 1971 acquired 1,700 acres in the Florida panhandle sixty miles from Pensacola. The site fronted on the Gulf of Mexico and eight miles of Choctawhatchee Bay, part of the Intracoastal Waterway. EMI paid about $1,100 per acre, putting $267,000 or 11 percent down over $2.15 million of purchase money mortgages. EMI planned a balanced community about equally divided between permanent residences and vacation retreats. Development lenders included Cabot, Cabot, & Forbes Land Trust ($6 million) and Chase Manhattan Trust ($13.7 million). In April 1974, EMI runs short of cash and its major lenders, including Citizens & Southern Realty Trust and C&S Bank, agreed to a major debt restructuring. The plan founders, and in August 1974, Evans & Mitchell files Chapter XI bankruptcy and is now in Chapter X.

Outlook: a build out of eight to ten years, assuming a sound developer versus an original six to eight years. [*2015 Status:* The workout estimate is about right. Today, Sandestin is a thriving leisure community centered around the Sandestin Golf and Beach Resort.]

E. *Grandiose Planning: Offshore Destination Resort—Palmas del Mar, Puerto Rico*

Status in June 1975

Sea Pines Co., nationally prominent publicly traded developer of affluent golf and tennis mecca Hilton Head Island in South Carolina, began assembling land on the east coast of Puerto Rico about forty-seven miles southeast of San Juan in 1969 and ultimately bought 2,777 acres at about $4,500 per acre, or $125 million land cost. The key plot was a former coconut plantation stretching six miles along the Caribbean coast. The trade winds provide a constant breeze and two hills on the tract concentrate this prevailing breeze into a wind tunnel that keeps the property comfortable most of the time. Sea Pines described it as "a place so removed from the problems and frustrations of the urban environment that its fascinating blend of beauty and leisure must be sampled to be truly understood … In terms of character and feeling, it is closer to Portofino, Marbella, or St. Tropez."

As befits this idyllic site, a comprehensive master plan includes a new harbor carved into the coastline, a resort inn and villas, a championship tennis center, two eighteen-hole golf courses wending among the palms, an airport, and a 297-acre tropical forest set aside for environmental conservation. Complex problems of providing utility services and telephone, highways, and other urban services to the site required major front-end cash. In January 1974, sales began—just as the full force of the energy shortage hit—with homesites priced from $14,000 to $116,000 and villas at $50,000 to $130,000.

Exhibit 15.2: Palmas del Mar resort, Humacao, Puerto Rico: Website publicity photo, 2015.

Initial sales were strong (185 homesites and 191 villas in the first two months), but sales declined from this hot pace in the face of worsening economic conditions. When I visit in October 1974, it's clear that the project is experiencing cash flow difficulties. In February 1975, Sea Pines restructures the debt of five subsidiaries, including Palmas del Mar, giving Chase Manhattan Trust an option to buy 50 percent of the subsidiary's stock for nominal consideration. Total debt outstanding isn't clear, but it appears lenders have perhaps $90 million at stake, the largest portion being an estimated $60 million by Chase Manhattan Trust. In May 1975, Sea Pines wrote off its $13 million investment in Palmas, Sea Pines President Charles E. Fraser saying Puerto Rico was a "bottomless pit," and lenders take over soon thereafter.

1975 Outlook: an eight- to fifteen-year workout versus a ten-year development initially. [*2015 Status:* We are too optimistic. Chase Manhattan Trust retains Palmas and seeks Chapter XI bankruptcy protection in February 1979, finally selling Palmas in 1984 to Maxxam Inc. (MXM), a Houston company then listed on the American Stock Exchange and controlled by activist investor Charles E. Hurwitz. Irene and I visit in the early 1980s but find few activities. Maxxam goes private in 2009, and its last publicly filed 10K for 2008 shows about 1,000 of the 2,700 acres remain undeveloped. Palmas reports a $12.5 million operating loss for 2008 on $10.5 million revenues. Today many more activities are in place at the now-mature resort, and in 2014, Charles Hurwitz tells me that Palmas is doing very nicely.

PIED PIPER OF BANKRUPTCY?

With this hard-nosed but realistic estimate of workout times for REIT problem loans in seminar attendees' minds, a reluctant Harvey R. Miller then strides to our June 1975 seminar dais to answer two burning questions: Will there be more REIT bankruptcies to add to the two already filed? If so, does the shareholder or bondholder win?

No lawyer in captivity is better able than Harvey to provide answers to my eager REIT mavens because, as the lead bankruptcy partner at powerhouse law firm Weil, Gotshal, and Manges, he represents the two REITs, Associated Mortgage and Fidelity Mortgage, who've already fled into Chapter XI bankruptcy protection by then.

"First let me say that it is with a substantial amount of reservations that I decided to come here today," Harvey opens his remarks as transcribed in *REITs: What's Ahead*. "Several months ago, I made the mistake of appearing at the NAREIT Lawyer's Conference, and the next thing I knew, my friend, Mr. Campbell, had quoted something that I had said, and I suddenly became the Pied Piper of bankruptcies … It got my partners upset." (*REITs: What's Ahead*, 1975. C-1)

"Let me apologize to Harvey publicly if I've tried to cast him as the Pied Piper of bankruptcy," I reply. (My report never used that colorful term but quoted Harvey as saying, "Chapter XI is a real tactical weapon that every trust with bank debt should consider.") "When I first met Harvey, I found a man who had an absolute total grasp of a topic of which investors have extremely limited knowledge. I asked him here today because he's the best man I know for this assignment." (*REITs: What's Ahead*, 1975. C-13)

"Chapter XI is a realistic alternative in the case of a REIT which has no secured debt [the case for nearly all mortgage REITs]," Miller begins. "It's built on secured debtors who are having cash flow problems ... and essentially need time to work out of their real estate. You really need time, and you do get time in a Chapter XI proceeding. You get a lot more time in a Chapter X proceeding ... Whether you file a petition or not really has to do with the attitude of your lenders. (*REITs: What's Ahead*, 1975. C-10)

"Ken asked why AMI [Associated Mortgage Investors, filed March 15, 1974] and FMI [Fidelity Mortgage Investors, filed January 30, 1975] filed Chapter XI petitions. Well, the answer was really very simple. Each of these REITs had reached a point where it was impossible for them to continue in good faith and pay interest at the rate that the institutional creditors were asking [generally 130 percent of the prime rate] ... (*REITs: What's Ahead*, 1975. C-9)

"In the case of AMI, the filing was preceded by five and one-half months of very intensive negotiations that finally broke down. We had ten million dollars of matured debentures, and the only alternative was to seek some sort of relief ...(*REITs: What's Ahead*, 1975. C-10)

"In the case of FMI, every effort was made to try and reach an accommodation in development of a new revolver. The FMI petition was filed at about ten minutes to five o'clock and not filed until the institutional creditors had in effect laid down the gauntlet in saying you have to sign the agreement [which would have been in default the minute it was executed]." (*REITs: What's Ahead*, 1975. C-10)

What do bondholders get in a bankruptcy?

Harvey says AMI's Chapter XI plan, which became effective the week of our seminar, posed "major problems because several institutional creditors insisted that the subordinated lenders or debenture holders receive nothing so long as the senior creditors had not been paid. A plan would have been impossible ... under that type of situation. The plan adopted was difficult and is atypical because it provides 100 percent repayment to both bank debt and the ten million dollars subordinated debentures, with the two classes of debt getting 20 and 5 percent cash payments initially. Banks are projected to get all their money in four years while debenture holders wait another year … (*REITs: What's Ahead*, 1975. C-11-12)

"The 100 percent plan was adopted primarily, in my unofficial view," says Miller, "in order … to satisfy the [Securities and Exchange] commission's view that there must be something for the subordinated debenture holders … The plan is saying that AMI is essentially out of business, that AMI is not going to be a real estate investment trust, it's not going to be a commercial corporation. It's going to conduct an orderly liquidation of its assets with proceeds used for creditors." (*REITs: What's Ahead*, 1975. C-12)

Harvey is peppered with twenty questions from my audience, including this twister: "Could a REIT borrower use debentures of that REIT to repay his loan?"

"In other words, can you set off one obligation against another," Harvey simplifies the issue. "There is a provision in the bankruptcy act which authorizes set-offs. The debts have to be mutual, and the credits have to be mutual. If there is mutuality, they can be set off." (*REITs: What's Ahead*, 1975. C-14)

[After a distinguished career, Harvey R. Miller dies April 27, 2015, at age eighty-two; see appendix VI.]

A MORTGAGE MAVEN'S VIEW

Our next seminar speaker, President Jack E. Sonnenblick of Sonnenblick-Goldman Corporation, nationally known mortgage banker and sponsor of North American Mortgage Investors, checks in with his take on what went wrong.

"The trusts were put under pressure by the Street for continuous upticks in earnings quarter by quarter. In their zealousness to put out money, they were funding their own points; they were funding their own interest. The borrowers had no money on the line, and the worst thing you can do in any deal is to have the entrepreneur not have anything at stake. If he has money on the line, he'll fight like hell to protect it," analyzes Sonnenblick. (*REITs: What's Ahead*, 1975. D-10)

"Another factor was a lack of experience in negotiating. Mortgage brokers would walk into a construction lender and receive a commitment within twenty-four hours. Under these circumstances, prudent underwriting standards are impossible to maintain. These fellows just didn't know how to negotiate. In prior years, we used to have a lot of fun negotiating. We would fight over the amount and the rate and the terms and the guarantee and the holdback and twenty-eight other items.

"What happened when the broker presented a deal to a trust, if it wasn't accepted as applied, he would threaten to run down the hall to another trust to make the deal. It was just a real lack of negotiations and in many cases inexperience." (*REITs: What's Ahead*, 1975. D-10)

Jack's outlook is: "With respect to the short-term lenders, the future is in the hands of the commercial banks, especially those that have revolving credit agreements. The banks are keeping those trusts alive, and they are generally in a liquidating position, hoping that by keeping them going, they will be able to get their money back. Interest costs are secondary; they are only kidding themselves with respect to recouping of interest." (*REITs: What's Ahead*, 1975. D-11)

Jack's forecast is: "Currently very, very bearish." (*REITs: What's Ahead*, 1975. D-11)

(Jack Sonnenblick dies in April 2015 at age ninety-one; see appendix VI.)

ACCOUNTING FOR LOSSES

One of the hottest topics as our seminar convenes is whether REITs, alone among all financial entities, should be forced to follow new and onerous rules in accounting for losses on their problem loans and properties.

The issue is in flux as we convene our seminar. Edmund R. "Randy" Noonan, a partner in Peat, Marwick, Mitchell, & Co., whom I had met in conjunction with Stirling Homex (Chapter 12, "The Mods"), arrives to try to explain why the three bodies governing accounting—the American Institute of Certified Public Accountants (AICPA), Financial Accounting Standards Board (FASB), and the accounting division of the Securities and Exchange Commission (SEC)—cannot agree on rules for computing loss reserves.

His explanation boils down to a pungent farrago of overlapping jurisdictions, but he believes that rules being agreed to would require mortgage trusts—and only trusts—to include estimated carrying costs in computing the value of problem loans and foreclosures. These rules would force REITs to increase their REIT loss reserves and heighten the prospect that some mortgage REITs would show negative equity on their balance sheets and thus automatically go into default on both bank credit lines and debentures.

Three weeks later, on June 27, 1975, the Accounting Standards division of AICPA issues a statement of position on "Accounting Practices of Real Estate Investment Trusts" that in effect would require significantly higher loan loss reserves for REITs.

NAREIT president Sylvan M. Cohen, then president of Pennsylvania REIT, fires back with a lengthy letter to AICPA asserting "there is a growing tendency to overreaction on the subject of anticipated losses" on approximately $7.7 billion nonearning assets within the REIT industry's $21.2 billion assets ($94.4 billion in 2015 dollars). (*REITs: What's Ahead*, 1975. B-17)

"Now the AICPA proposes that future carrying costs be provided uniformly, but only within the REIT industry," Cohen writes.

"If the concept underlying treatment of future carrying costs has any validity for REIT loans," Cohen concludes, "it should apply equally to all loans, whether or not secured by real estate mortgages or other financial institutions such as commercial banks. To do otherwise would create a serious problem of discrimination and more investor confusion." (*REITs: What's Ahead*, 1975. B-20)

THE BANKER'S SIDE

Next to arrive as seminar speaker is Brian F. Lantier, bank analyst for First Boston Corporation, a major underwriter of bank securities.

I note that Audit invited nine of the nation's ten largest banks to appear at our seminar and all declined, some citing scheduling conflicts. "The prevailing message I get is that they wanted to cool it," I conclude.

"I just have to believe that Ken in his subconscious figured that if he couldn't get bankers to come up here and commit *hara-kari*, maybe we can get their underwriters," opens Lantier. "What better deal than to get an analyst from an investment banker, which happens to be one of the major bank underwriters ... So he has me between a rock and a hard place." (*REITs: What's Ahead*, 1975. E-3)

Lantier pours cold water on the idea that banks did shoddy underwriting in lending mortgage trusts something over seven billion dollars. "It's pretty difficult for us now, even in hindsight, to go back and say bankers should have built in lending contingencies for a 12 percent prime rate, for an oil embargo, etc. I don't think that's really fair ..." (*REITs: What's Ahead*, 1975. E-3)

Brian predicts that banks may attempt to get out of their REIT credit lines in 1976 if the Financial Accounting Standards Board enforces on banks the proposed accounting guidelines [mandating higher loan loss reserves], which have been handed down as they apply to

REITs. "We're told the bank audit guide is currently being revised and there's a question whether the net carrying value and interest discount method as defined by Randy Noonan of Peat Marwick earlier may be applicable to commercial banks." (*REITs: What's Ahead*, 1975. E-5)

"The accounting treatment being lobbied for by REITs is, in effect, undermining all of the things that the senior creditors are attempting to do in working out of their problems with the REITs," says Lantier. (*REITs: What's Ahead*, 1975. E-12)

Disclosure of bank exposure to REIT loans is then a hot disclosure item, and both Chemical Bank and Manufacturers' Hanover Bank of Manhattan recently postponed debt offerings because of investor concern over their REIT involvement.

Lantier is less committal about nitty-gritty issues, such as bank renegotiation of their REIT lines and asset swaps with REITs that reduce bank loans. He is happy to see lines being renegotiated and hails a new credit line with First Mortgage Investors as a "pacesetter" in this regard.

QUESTIONS, QUESTIONS

At end of a very long day, Bernie Solas, Audit's director of research, and I stand to answer any questions thrown to us. Seminar attendees keep us on our toes for nearly two hours, firing questions about our outlook for nearly fifty REITs.

"Please comment on the quality of the Chase Manhattan Trust portfolio," is an early request.

I point out that the portfolio appears "extremely aggressive. Approximately 52 percent of the $450 million in nonearning loans are either in condominiums or resort recreational communities. About 20 percent of their nonearning loans are in the Sandestin and Palmas del Mar projects discussed earlier. I can say good things about all the rest of it, but these two projects just make it very difficult for me to be optimistic at all for that portfolio." (*REITs: What's Ahead*, 1975. F-8)

Many questions focus on bonds, then trading at an average 43 percent of par. Since REITs have $4.5 billion of subordinated debentures in the market, bondholders are thus over $2.5 billion under water.

To a specific question about First Virginia Mortgage bonds, Bernie Solas replies, "I think that First Virginia is having so many problems and has been close to a bankruptcy candidate; it would not be one of my first choices, to say the least, in the bond area." (*REITs: What's Ahead*, 1975. F-11) (First Virginia, later renamed Nova Realty, seeks bankruptcy protection in October 1980.)

Asked to assess the adequacy of the industry's loss reserves, I point out that the industry's loss reserves average about 9 percent of nonearning investments while some industry observers say reserves should be 20 to 25 percent of nonperforming assets. (*REITs: What's Ahead*, 1975. F-14)

Asked to comment on C.I. Mortgage, sponsored by conglomerate City Investing, Bernie Solas advises, "Several real estate people say that President Jim Tomai is an excellent real estate lender, but maybe they grew too fast, too many undertakings, both here and in the sister trust, C. I. Realty, and the net result is that some of the loans don't smack of top real estate lender's marks." (*REITs: What's Ahead*, 1975. F-16)

"Is it possible that we are seeing the trough of the REIT collapse right now?" I am asked.

"Yes, I think with about 90 percent probability; in this real estate market, I see a very long saucer kind of recovery," I respond. "I just don't think it is reasonable to see anything of recovery in two years for many of these pieces of real estate." (*REITs: What's Ahead*, 1975. F-18)

Asked about bank exposure, I say, "The nine major money-center banks have about 50 percent of the exposure in the revolving credit area, and those nine are the six in New York City: First National City, Chase, Chemical, Bankers Trust, Manufacturers' Hanover, and Morgan Guaranty. Morgan has an extremely low level of exposure. The three other money-center banks are: in Chicago, First of Chicago and Continental Illinois; and in San Francisco, Bank of America." This group of nine commits $4.5 billion to the REITs. (*REITs: What's Ahead*, 1975. F-21)

The seminar probes the big questions of that day and through the eyes of key players sheds much-needed light into murky corners of the mortgage REIT collapse of the Stressful Seventies.

Irene diligently tapes every word, and we subsequently gather the transcripts of that exhausting day into a booklet titled *Reits: What's Ahead* and publish the proceedings as a 148-page soft-cover book at $29.50. The book is as well received as the seminar.

Within a week, *Realty Trust Review* reports, on June 13, 1975, that "bank lenders are nearly unanimous on the need to keep troubled REITs alive. Their latest vehicles are contingent-interest deals, now coming in a bewildering complexity for investors that will effectively keep interest charges from eroding shareholders' equity for many REITs ...

"The new spirit of cooperation between banks and their REITs is being greeted exuberantly by investors because the restructuring of bank revolving credit agreements is bringing sharply lower interest rates with it."

Did those barbed questions asked in our unofficial seminar help change those banker hearts of stone? Or did Harvey Miller turn their heads by ardently advocating that pressured REITs consider Chapter XI bankruptcy?

We shall never know. But something changed that week.

In the wings an inquiry looms, and it is ominously official.

Chapter 16
THE INQUIRY

In the spring of 1976, with the recession recovery rolling through the economy, politicians are still fighting the last war (as they are wont to do), asking a pointed question: Were banks to blame for the collapse of the mortgage REITs?

Bill S. 2721 is introduced in the Senate to require bank holding companies, or BHCs, to engage in activities "so closely and directly related to banking or managing or controlling banks as to be a proper and necessary incident thereto …" The bill would make REIT sponsorship out of bounds for BHCs.

The bill immediately becomes a political flash point for lawmakers and lobbyists because it would lock some really tight handcuffs on bank holding companies.

Regulating banks stands as one of the hardiest strains in American politics, stemming from long-simmering fears that Eastern banks are somehow depriving Western farmers and settlers of the fruits of their labors. President Andrew Jackson's battle to close the Second Bank of the United States in the 1830s and William Jennings Bryan's fiery "Cross of Gold" speech to the 1896 Democratic National Convention remain landmark events in populist antibanking sentiment.

Representative Wright Patman (D, Texas), whom we met in chapter 9, "The Letter," epitomized antibanking fervor in Congress, although the

House Banking Committee he chaired largely ignored his more virulent antibanking ideas and legislation.

S. 2721 fits into this mold, and controversy is the expected norm when Washington's powerful banking lobby begins revving up its opposition.

The rhythm of politics demands that every crisis beget a Congressional hearing to affix blame. The Senate Committee on Banking, Housing, and Urban Affairs seeks to find someone to testify on the topic.

But Wall Street's investment banks duck their invitation to testify out of fear of arousing the powerful banking lobby.

Finally, committee staffers come upon my name, and I am invited to tackle the topic publicly and comment on the hot-potato bill to limit bank and bank holding company sponsorship of mortgage REITs.

A chorus of critics contends that regulators should never have let bank names be used by affiliated REITs because using a bank's name creates an implicit but false belief among investors that the banks will stand behind the REIT offspring.

HOT POTATO INVITE

The invitation comes with many fishhooks because banks have sponsored nearly two dozen mortgage REITs, including such household bank names as Chase Manhattan Bank, Continental Illinois Bank, Bank of America, and Bankers Trust. The first three stamp their names or variations on their trusts, while Bankers Trust wraps its REIT in plain vanilla initials as "BT." Other bank sponsors of REITs use variations of these two approaches. The implication is that banks and bank holding companies are clearly trying to use their good names and reputations to make bank-spawned REITs a success, even though these REITs are legally independent entities controlled by separate boards and with assets and liabilities removed from their bank sponsor's balance sheets. Moreover, these "independent" REITs can borrow from their sponsoring bank as well as other banks. Clearly Congress is zeroing in on an apparent conflict, albeit four or five years too late.

The other side of the coin is that many managers of bank-sponsored REITs subscribe to *Realty Trust Review* and our other services. If I testify, I run the risk that they could pull their subscriptions.

I decide that our name "Audit" implies independence and that we have made no secret of our intent to call issues as we see them without regard to financial consequences.

I accept the challenge.

LONELY WITNESS

Hence on the bright spring morning of May 27, 1976, I take the airline shuttle to Washington in the gray dawn and a cab to the Senate office building where the hearing is scheduled, arriving about 8:30 a.m. for a scheduled 10:00 a.m. hearing—no limousines, no entourage of publicity agents, just one lone man lugging a briefcase. After breakfast in a basement cafeteria, I arrive in the hearing room at 10:00 a.m.

The hearing room scene is something never seen on television: no TV cameras, no journalists jockeying for position, no hoopla. Instead, the hearing room is occupied by only a few Senate staffers looking to kill a bit of time. And instead of a full panel of senators, only Committee Chairman Senator William Proxmire of Wisconsin appears to hear my pearls of wisdom.

If the banking lobby is terrified by my appearance, its panic is not in evidence.

Senator Proxmire, who seems to be sponsoring the bill, makes a name for himself in Washington by giving a monthly Golden Fleece Award to whatever project he deems an egregious waste of taxpayer dollars. His first award pans an $84,000 National Science Foundation grant to study why people fall in love.

Happily, I am not there to receive one of the Senator's Golden Fleece Awards.

"The honey which drew the commercial banks, along with many others, into sponsorship of REITs was a generous fee structure," I charge in a prepared statement. After citing Audit's analysis of profit margins earned by bank advisers to REITs, I add, "Put another way, these data indicate that perhaps only 30 to 40 percent of advisory fees were actually used to provide investment advice, loan underwriting, loan monitoring, and other services in many instances ... I should point out that REITs are the only entities BHCs (bank holding companies) may advise which can borrow from the banking system and whose results are not consolidated with the BHC."

Under the heading of "Potential Conflicts of Interest," I say, "It is almost impossible to prove instances of unequal risk allocation, but the fear has persisted that banks could, and perhaps did, direct their riskier loan applications to sponsored REITs ... The only way to prevent fear of future overloading of risk would be to prevent BHCs from acting as advisers to REITs, as is here proposed."

Further on, I testify: "It is clear that BHCs undertaking to sponsor REITs in reality try to serve three masters: their depositors, their shareholders, and the shareholders of an independent REIT. Experience of the past years demonstrates that this is impossible and should be banned in the future."

Asked for recommendations, I state: "It is clear that the concept of 'adviser' or 'sponsor' must disappear altogether for REITs. Each REIT must be given independence and single-mindedness ... This will serve the banking system and REIT shareholders best."

After a few perfunctory questions, I am dismissed—no newspaper photos, no camera-toting TV journalists, no blogs, no fuss. I flag a cab to the airport and am back at my Manhattan desk by 2:00 p.m. that afternoon.

My testimony is not reported in the general press, and the trade press takes scant notice. What looms as a big deal beforehand turns out to have no more impact than putting my hand into a bucket of water and then withdrawing it.

Back home, I turn my full attention to house hunting. In March 1976, while celebrating our twenty-fifth wedding anniversary and with the house full of relatives, Irene blows out her knee making the sharp turn from the kitchen to the stairway at our split-level at 542 Lynn Street in Ridgewood, New Jersey. An earlier fall while skiing had weakened the knee. The doctor puts her on crutches, a convalescence lasting six months and forcing us to immediately find a new home with only one floor.

The search ends in early June when we buy the house at 16 Glenwood Road in nearby Upper Saddle River and move in August 1976. The commute is longer, and for years, I get up in the gray dawn to catch the 6:20 a.m. bus from Elmer's Store to NYC, the only daily bus from USR. The new home has an extra two rooms, nestled in the woods beyond the garage, and son Doug immediately claims them as his pad.

No major legislation ensues from my brief visit to the Senate, but the REIT collapse effectively ends forever the idea of REIT sponsorship by banks or anyone else.

REITs are free at last.

Bottom line, equity REITs become free to blossom only when the era of REIT sponsorship ends with the collapse of short-term mortgage lending REITs in the 1970s.

Voila, unknowingly, my Senate testimony voices a prophetic truth.

Chapter 17
THE LEMONADE

Charge!

As short-term mortgage REITs begin a slow-motion tailspin in early 1974, I start mapping a survival strategy.

Charging is built into my genes. Never say die. Markets always come back. Tomorrow will be a better day. Power forward!

I was born under the sign of Capricorn the Goat, and the general description of Capricorn males seems largely in tune with my psyche, even though I am not an astrological devotee.

"Capricorn is one of the most stable and (mostly) serious of the zodiacal types," runs Astrology Insights' description of Capricorns. "These independent rocklike characters … are normally confident, strong willed, and calm. These hardworking, unemotional, shrewd, practical, responsible, persevering … persons are capable of persisting for as long as is necessary to accomplish a goal they have set for themselves …"

Leaving aside the inflated flattery of such astrological chatter, this description of Capricorns reflects many personal traits.

My unwillingness to take "No" shows in an incident about that time. Wanting to show off to my brother Jim, who was visiting with his wife, Judy, from my hometown Butler, Pennsylvania, I invite them on the spur of the moment to dinner at the famed Windows on the World restaurant atop the World Trade Center. Arriving about 6:00 p.m., well before peak dinner hour, we ask the maître d'hotel for a table.

"No, sir, all these tables are reserved," he says with a haughty glance at about two hundred vacant tables. Jim and Judy are so deeply disappointed I decide to make a second try.

Putting a twenty-dollar bill in the palm of my hand, I shake the maître d'hotel's hand with these words: "My name is Campbell. Are you sure there isn't a table for us?"

"Oh, Mr. Campbell," he replies smoothly. "Your table is ready. Right this way," and leads us to a window-side table looking up Fifth Avenue toward midtown.

You don't ask; you don't get.

So pronounced is this Capricorn congruence that I briefly consider titling this treatise *Nixon Was a Capricorn, Too* in reference to former President Richard Nixon, whose repeated bounce-backs from multiple humiliations—including the ultimate disgrace of being the only person forced to resign the US presidency—make his name synonymous with persistence and perseverance.

That unswerving single-mindedness marks Capricorns through the ages: Joan of Arc, Albert Schweitzer, Horatio Alger, Howard Hughes, J. Edgar Hoover, Barry Goldwater, Walter Mondale, Mohammed Ali, and Martin Luther King Jr.

Joseph Stalin and Mao Tse Tung count as Capricorns, too.

I aim to decouple Audit's future from the market gyrations of REIT stocks. I lived with that market risk for six years; now it's time to step out and diversify.

The biggest risk by far for any single-line company like Audit is that if its business sector falters or dies, it leaves the owner without a viable business. When they stopped making buggy whips, most buggy whip makers fail. The 1973–74 collapse of mortgage REITs leaves my tiny enterprise very close to buggy whip-hood.

I attempt to do what any good entrepreneur does when markets reverse 180 degrees: turn the lemons into lemonade.

THE THIRD OWNER

I decide to capitalize upon the items REITs possess in excess—problem properties and troubled loans—and take advantage of one of real estate's hoariest aphorisms: "The third owner makes all the money."

This adage works because most property developers borrow up to or beyond their means to build the project of their dreams. Consider the usual sequence.

The first property owner-developer goes all out to erect the most sumptuous, opulent, sophisticated building he or she can conjure, pushing the design envelope to maximize bells and whistles to attract tenants. Failure is almost guaranteed from the first mortgage draw.

Unless the developer is unusually disciplined, cost overruns surface and the developer is forced to raise asking rents. Tenants balk at the higher rents, and sooner or later, the developer turns his or her Taj Mahal over to the bank, which becomes the second owner, either legally by deed transfer or effectively under a "lender in possession" agreement.

This second-owner bank slogs through the mess and spends more money to remedy the property's deficiencies, writes down the real estate to its estimated market value, and thereby cuts asking rents. Then this second owner puts the renovated property back on the market as promptly as possible because banks aren't permitted to be long-term owners of nonbank property.

Finally the bank sells this renovated property to a third owner. Recall how the third owners of Blue Hill office and Colony North apartments (chapter 15, "The Seminar") won big profits by repeating this metronomic, almost inexorable, real estate truism. Whether the property or bad loan is sold by auction, sealed bid, or off-market negotiations makes little difference. The third owner gets either an upgraded, market-ready property or a fixer-upper, usually at some fraction of the original cost.

This discounted cost usually translates into a good profit for the third owner.

A real-life example exists not far from my home. When housing was hot a few years ago, a homebuilder constructed a 9,200 square-foot home in an upscale neighborhood on Philadelphia's Main Line, listing his dream product for $4.25 million.

Zero takers appear, largely because the house sits on a small lot with groundwater problems.

The bank takes control under a defaulted $2.6 million loan and after months of on-again, off-again foreclosure sale dates, recently transfers the loan to another builder for $600,000, approximating the building lot's value. This new and third owner hopes to remedy the water problem and sell at a profit. At this writing, the home is listed at two million dollars.

Thousands upon thousands of bargain-hunting realty operatives scour foreclosure notices fervently in hopes of becoming the prized third owners of a problem property. But real estate doesn't have the equivalent of yard sales or discount warehouses.

Hence my simple concept: Audit will become the clearinghouse for information about REIT problem properties and loans. We will ferret out the tiniest detail of the smallest problem property and print the gruesome details for all to see. We will search regulatory filings by public companies, digest the minutiae of bank reports, and offer the very best data we can find to real estate professionals. No matter how the awkward details may embarrass some developers or banks, we will print them faithfully. Helping clean up these abortions on the landscape is a greater good than protecting reputations.

We will become the storehouse for all things problem property, the repository for every scrap of troubled loan detail.

If the real estate gods are angry, we will render the offal of this market madness to them as sacrifice for their peace.

We will become Information Central for Problem Properties and Loans!

THE FIRST LEMONADE

The initial offering from Audit's little lemonade stand is *Real Estate Disclosure Digest*, based on my experience that trouble in the real estate business always unearths opportunities that attract hordes of eager bottom-fishers. *REDD*, as we quickly dub it, seeks to capitalize on the equal parts of greed and optimism animating thousands of real estate entrepreneurs around the world. Conceived as a vehicle to provide a wide range of nonadvisory property-level information to subscribers, *REDD* debuts in February 1974 as an open-end service with each issue containing as many pages of information as needed.

REDD finds a ready audience when introduced at a discounted $195 annual subscription versus $240 regular tab.

We bill this first lemonade offering as: "A New Service to Help You in the Tougher Real Estate Credit Markets Ahead."

> "*Real Estate Disclosure Digest*, for the first time, lets you discover and use the intimate details of hundreds of current real estate transactions and financings. These transactions reflect the combined ingenuity of hundreds of real estate professionals, always adapting to real estate's unique qualities and credit markets.
>
> "*Disclosure Digest* keeps you abreast of these fast-paced events by finding and assembling for you an enormous wealth of detail now buried in public filings

and announcements of hundreds of real estate companies and real estate trusts. Their disclosure is a required
by-product of real estate's penchant for going public in
recent years, yet often the facts remain hidden under
tons of chaff and trivia. Worse, no individual professional in real estate financing or development can take
time from his or her regular duties to ferret them out.

"Audit Investment Research Inc. is taking the lead
in bringing the essential details needed by professionals
through *Disclosure Digest* because it has a unique vantage point: it already reviews this flood of material as an
investment adviser specializing in real estate securities.

- *"REDD* promises to deliver a diverse range of topics: financing
  details in credit lines and mortgages, along with …
- "Advisory and management fees for REITs, partnerships and
  other entities;
- "Defaults and foreclosures by REITs and other lenders, indexed
  by location, property type and borrower if given;
- "Joint ventures and partnerships—terms, participants, etc."

REDD represents a heady undertaking for our still tiny enterprise,
but by then, we are receiving tons of SEC filings via microfiche. These
plasticized five-by-seven-inch cards, or fiches, hold about fifty pages of
microfilmed printed matter and, with the aid of a bulky fiche reader
and indefatigable digging by staffer Faye Kreisman, we access a hither-
to-hidden realm of intimate details lurking behind the blander sanitized
versions of company public reports. These fiche are our raw materials
for *REDD*.

Because *REDD* is open-ended, it strains staff resources to get voluminous issues, running sixteen, twenty, or more pages, out the door twice a month. But consumers have a way of finding valuable products, and *REDD* gains momentum much the way a bobsled gains speed during a downhill run.

REDD continues its mission of printing nitty-gritty details of problem properties and company comings and goings for six years, finally merging at the end of 1979 with an expanded *Housing & Realty Investor* covering housing companies. While early issues are now lost in the mists, I estimate that *REDD* compiles and prints nearly nine hundred pages of vital data upon problem properties, financings, and many more intimate disclosures from the bowels of public real estate companies and REITs.

Great literature it is not; pragmatic prose it is.

THE NITTY GRITTY

Many *REDD* subscribers want even more property-level detail, and we break out a separate service called *Disclosure Reports on Problem Properties* in April 1976. This service consists of detailed descriptions of problem properties arranged coupon-style with eight separate property reports per page. This super-targeted service offered at $168 annually is moderately successful with a limited audience.

Thanks to *REDD* and *DRPP*, *voila*, we are able to cover most of a 15 percent *RTR* subscription shortfall in both 1976 and 1977 and sustain operations without personnel cuts.

DRPP—pardon the confusing initials—brings subscribers up-close and personal reports on individual problem properties, all color-coded by property type: yellow for commercial properties, gray for condominiums, green for apartments, and pink for land developments, which turn out to be the most numerous entries.

Two entries we rescue from the obscurity of public documents and print in *DRPP* illustrate the pervasive carpetbagger nature of 1970s mortgage lending as REITs based in one part of the country parachute into unfamiliar territory in search of borrowers. Why such a feeding frenzy? Wall Street underwriters are pressuring the mortgage REITs they've brought public to show investors a growing pipeline of commitments, future loan funding, and, presumably, earnings, all designed to drive stock prices higher. With over one hundred mortgage REITs now in this game, results are predictably negative.

This example shows a New York City-based REIT wrestling with an uncompleted Jacksonville, Florida, apartment:

TYPE: Apartments   **DATE**: 3/4/77 39DR-7 (Identifier #)
SITE: Jacksonville, FL   Update of 24DR 2/76
NAME: Barcelona
DESC: $2,253,000 carrying value on 236-unit rental apartments. Acquired 8/75. Construction approximately 85% complete at 10/76.
HOLDER: C.I. Mortgage Group, 717 Fifth Avenue, New York, NY 10022 James V. Tomai, Pres. 212/935-9100
SOURCE: 10/76 10K

A second example portrays a Los Angeles mortgage REIT grappling with foreclosed land next to an already-foreclosed apartment complex in Houston:

TYPE: Land   **ISSUED**: 5/7/76 20DR-7 (Identifier #)
LOCATION: Houston, Tex.
NAME: Not available
DESC: $184,442 investment in 6.7 acres unimproved land, planned for development of apartment project. Adjacent to 240-unit apartment project acquired by trust. Trust believes land is ideal for future expansion of this project. Foreclosed 3/75 and held at 12/75.
HOLDER: Colwell Mortgage Trust, 3223 W. Sixth St., Los Angeles, CA 90020. Stephen H. Dolley, Pres. 213/381-1261.
SOURCE: 12/75 Ann.&10K

It is bred into real estate's bones that some builder will find these rough-cut gems and make a good profit by finishing and renting these projects.

Thumbing through the 296 pages of property-level information contained in *DRPP* between May 1976 and April 1977, when publication ceases, confirms that these examples represent typical REIT problem properties of the day.

At eight entries per page, our *DRPP* lemonade stand thus brings data on 2,368 problem properties to bargain hunters everywhere.

SWAPS AND PROPS

Just in time for Christmas 1976, we complete a 181-page research report *REITs, Their Banks and Bondholders*, or *RTBB*, and offer *RTR* subscribers early copies at $150 versus $225 regular price. The research report expands a ten-page paper titled *REITs and Their Banks: What's Ahead* prepared for our *REITs: What's Ahead* seminar eighteen months earlier.

During that eighteen months, numerous REITs begin swapping assets to their banks to satisfy debt, much to the consternation of REIT shareholders, who wonder if their REITs are getting fair value in these privately negotiated and complex exchanges. Banks, of course, maintain the swaps are needed to get their dollars back while propping up their otherwise-broke borrowers. REITs defend them as survival necessities.

RTBB surveys 130 REITs and presents a picture of a highly bifurcated REIT industry with fifty-eight trusts, mostly short-term lending entities, in deep debt trouble with negative equity and huge loss reserves, while the remaining seventy-two REITs are in relatively good financial shape. The data:

TABLE 17:1: REIT DEBT STATUS, 3Q 1976—BIL. $

REIT Credit status	No.	——Debt Outstanding —— Banks	Senior	Subor.	Total	Share Equity	Loss Reserves
Reduced interest	58	$7.0	$0.7	$1.1	$8.8	$d0.05	$1.90
Full rate credit	34	0.9	0.6	0.2	1.6	0.70	0.15
Open lines full rate	38	0.7	1.7	0.3	2.7	1.57	0.07
Totals	130	$8.5	$3.0	$1.55	$13.1	$2.23	$2.15

d = Deficit. Source: Audit Investment Research, Inc.: *REITs, Their Banks and Bondholders*, p. 3–8: 1977.

REMEMBER THE BONDHOLDERS

"Bondholders are the forgotten investors in the REIT debacle," I assert in my introduction.

> "It appears that about half of ... subordinated debt is held by initial purchasers who are either (1) retired individuals who've invested their life savings in REIT bonds, (2) trustees who hold bonds in trust for very elderly, legally incompetent or deceased persons; and (3) pension and profit sharing trusts.
>
> "It does no good to say that REIT bonds shouldn't have been sold to these persons in the first place, nor to suggest—as some do—that most REIT bonds are now held by speculators. Both assertions beg the question of how all parties can preserve as much principal as

possible for these bond investors." (*REITs, Their Banks and Bondholders*, 1977. i)

By then, *Realty Trust Review* can report that a list of forty-four REIT convertible debentures with about $450 million par value sells at an average 54.3 percent of par at the end of 1976, up 40 percent from the low 38.7 percent of par at the December 1974 market nadir. This pricing indicates that convertible bond investors still sustain hope their conversion rights will pay off since thirty-six straight or nonconvertible REIT bonds with $1.02 billion face value trade at only 42.1 percent of par at the same time.

Most short-term mortgage REITs either are or soon will be in in default under their unsecured credit lines. At one time, most of the nation's money-center banks and nearly all the Manhattan-based giants had REIT lines equaling 100 percent and in some instances 200 percent of their equity capital. Naturally, Washington is concerned about whether banks can survive.

Banks are negotiating arrangements under which they swap selected REIT assets for reduction of debt, and details of these swaps are eagerly awaited by both investors and real estate bottom-fishers. Investors suspect that REITs are swapping their best assets to banks to get the biggest debt reduction, leaving the REITs and their shareholders with the dregs. The lack of transparency in these deals multiplies suspicions.

We undertake an excruciatingly detailed examination of the exact position of each REIT with its banks, based upon official reports filed with the SEC. Our factual findings include the following.:

REITs report $177 million gains on $1.13 billion of completed swaps, meaning banks are taking about a 23 percent haircut on their swaps and indicating REITs are reaping more than fair value for swapped assets. Another $1.8 billion swaps are pending or in the works at the report deadline. Our major conclusion is:

> "Return of 100% of principal to all creditors, in accordance with priority rules of a bankruptcy court, should become first order for all creditors and managers of deeply troubled REITs. Payment of interest should be strictly secondary in these situations. Any other course will commit all parties to squeezing as many dollars as possible from the principal of thousands of smaller investors." (*REITs, Their Banks and Bondholders*, 1977. 11)

Our conclusion rankles some bankers, who argue that their senior creditor position entitles them to first dibs on the assets and dollars residing in REITs. But we sustain our stance during the days ahead because by that time I have testified as an expert witness in some cases highlighting the extreme losses inflicted on elderly and infirm bondholders. Enough is enough!

The soft-cover investment research report is well received by both stock and bond market investors and the real estate community. It is proud lemonade.

THE ROAD BACK

From the gloom and speculative fever of that June 1975 seminar, REIT stocks very gradually begin an ascent from the market basement.

In 1975, equity REITs—the only REIT game left in town after the debacle—rise a modest 8.3 percent while the S&P 500 rebounds a startling 31.5 percent.

The next year of 1976, REITs begin catching up with a strong 36.2 percent gain, besting the S&P 500's 19.1 percent increase.

In 1977, REITs rise a further 14.0 percent while the S&P 500 falters by falling 11.5 percent.

The equity REITs keep this string of gains going in 1978, up another 2.7 percent while the S&P climbs only 1.1 percent.

This four-year winning skein gives equity REITs a 72.7 percent spurt in the first four years after the meltdown while the S&P 500 rises only 40.2 percent.

The strong performance convinces serious REIT investors to climb out of their bomb shelters, and in June 1977, we begin compiling and publishing extremely detailed two-page summaries of every REIT left standing under the title *REIT Evaluations.*

The first packet of *Evaluations* contains profiles of twenty REITs ranging from American Fletcher Mortgage, a bank-sponsored mortgage trust that eliminates dividends in September 1974 as it struggles with land development and condominium loans, to United Realty Trust, a long-term mortgage trust whose low leverage lets it continue dividends during the deluge. Formerly named Larwin Realty & Mortgage Trust, United is advised by a subsidiary of CNA Financial. Each evaluation contains maximum detail on the subject's nonearning loans and foreclosed properties.

American Fletcher reports 93.4 percent of assets aren't earning income, and, not surprisingly, its shares at eighty-eight-cents are dying and carry "extreme risk." United's non- and low-earning assets consume 43.2 percent of total assets, but United stock, at $8.88 a share, is moving skyward and suitable for "moderate yield and recovery potential."

When we've cycled around all REITs left standing, we update all evaluations and publish the lot in a new soft-cover research report under the banner *New Opportunities in Realty Trusts,* or *NORT.* The book weighs in at 296 pages and is in heavy demand from its first offer in July 1978 at ninety-six dollars a copy. *NORT* reviews 118 equity and mortgage REITs, including specific data on the valuable net operating tax loss carry-forwards (NOLs) now being racked up by some former mortgage REITs who've become involuntary property owners. Today in 2015, *NORT* still provides invaluable insights into a REIT industry struggling to recover from its worst recession.

"The world of realty trusts has turned upside down since I wrote the last sentence in October 1971 of our last full-dress book on trusts, *The Real Estate Trusts: America's Newest Billionaires*," I write in *NORT's* introduction. (*New Opportunities in Realty Trusts*, 1978. vi)

> "In less than two and one-half years the bloom faded and trust shares sagged sharply when the October 1973 oil embargo triggered an inventory boom sending the prime rate soaring to 12%. The impact upon realty trusts was especially severe and it became all too clear that the trusts had had too much money chasing too few good deals.
>
> "Many cynics jested that my sequel would have to be titled, *America's Newest Paupers*.

"But it became apparent that stock and bond markets investors have very short memories. Investment success is about 2% reflection on the past and about 98% projection of the future," I opine. Our detailed trust-by-trust look in *REIT Evaluations* convinces us that "a panoply of new opportunities has opened for realty trust investors. An enormous range of investment goals can now be served by realty trust securities.

"No longer blessed with youthful innocence, the realty trusts now go forward to a more promising future. That is the genesis of *New Opportunities in Realty Trusts*." (*New Opportunities in Realty Trusts*, 1978. vi)

NORT becomes our best lemonade offering yet, turning into something of an investment Bible.

Another *voila*: working the investment field and staying close to unlovely facts pays off. There's no answer to troubles other than plowing ahead and living each day as if nothing has happened.

Humpty Dumpty is beginning to recover from his great fall. Maybe the REIT revolution can get some traction after all.

TRACKING PROBLEM LOANS

During the long months of recovery, we faithfully tally nonearning loans and properties with each monthly statistical issue of *Realty Trust Review.*

While this seems a thankless chore through the lonely months and years of the second half of the Sickly Seventies, amassing these monthly data now lets anyone interested track the unfolding horror show of the denouement of the mortgage REITs.

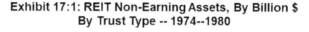

**Exhibit 17:1: REIT Non-Earning Assets, By Billion $
By Trust Type -- 1974--1980**

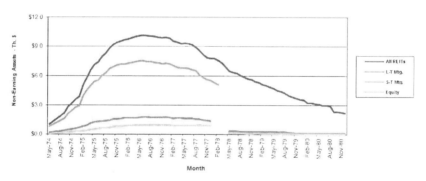

From that initial reading of slightly over $1.03 billion nonaccruing assets, or 6.05 percent of industry assets, in May 1974, problem assets skyrocket to $7.1 billion, or 37.0 percent of assets a year later, when we stage our *REITs: What's Ahead* seminar. With scarcely a pause, this measure of futility moves inexorably skyward for another year, peaking at $10.16 billion or 55.5 percent of industry assets in June 1976. Total problem loans fall slowly afterward but because better assets are either being sold or swapped to banks, the industry's percentage of nonearning assets keeps slowly rising until peaking at 58.9 percent in September 1977.

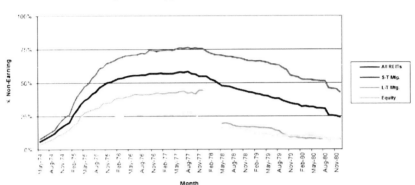

Exhibit 17:2: REIT Non-Earning Assets, By % of Total By Trust Type -- 1974 - 1980

Short-term mortgage trusts, accounting for about half of industry assets, see idle assets soar to 76.0 percent of total assets in October 1977. By then, the short-term trusts are effectively out of business and most have converted to operating companies that can use their mounting operating tax-loss carry-forwards.

Long-term mortgage trusts fare far better than their short-term brethren and see nonearning assets peak at 43.8 percent of assets in July 1977.

Equity REITs fare the best by far, and although a number are enticed into construction lending, those that avoid the mortgage morass come through the debacle unscathed. Idle assets peak at 28.0 percent of assets in August of 1977, completing the pattern of nonearning assets peaking in 1977's third quarter.

Exhibits 17.1 and 17.2 trace the rise and fall of REIT bad assets in the 1970s.

THE SWEETEST LEMONADE

Audit's five year run hosting this most unusual of lemonade stands yields the desired result. Revenues top $200,000 every year from 1975 to 1979 except one. Two years have large profits, two years show modest loses, and 1975 brings a larger loss, but on balance, our company loses less than $5,000 during the soggy second half of the 1970s.

Best, we are able to keep staff intact. No lemonade ever tasted so sweet.

We emerge intact from the Sickly Seventies.

Our small staff produces over 6,900 pages of advice and information on REITs during the 1970s, about 29 percent being our unique blend of REIT lemonade. My rat hole is a busy burrow indeed. At about four to five hundred words per page, this output equals about 2,750,000 to 3,450,000 words.

But there are only two true measures of an investment publisher's success: *First*, how many readers do you have? On this score, *Realty Trust Review*, our most popular service, peaks at 1,023 long-term subscribers (excluding short-term trials) at the end of 1973 and ends the Sickly Seventies six years later with 743 long-term readers, down 27 percent for the decade but hardly Armageddon considering the REIT bloodbath. Our lemonade fills the revenue gap. But since no other publishers venture into the shark-infested waters of REITs and we essentially remain the only game in town, our services carry outsized impact upon participants in this ascendant industry. Multiply circulation by four or five to reach a true estimate of *RTR's* real punch.

Second, did subscribers profit from your market calls? There's no real way to answer this honestly because we never keep track of our investment calls. I recently bumped into a Wall Street trader and long-ago subscriber at a conference, and he told me, "Ken, I made a lot of money from your black-and-blue service because you laid out all the facts and it was easy to pick the right stocks." I rest my case.

Thus we publish our way out of perdition.

AT THE COUNTINGHOUSE

Audit operates on the proverbial shoestring during the 1970s, due in no small part to the extremely volatile market for REITs during the decade and the collapse of the mortgage trusts in the second half. This hurt subscription revenues from the two main advisory services and forces us to "make lemonade" from the lemons presented to us. New services and research reports—our lemonade—help fill the void, but revenues still fall 17 percent in 1978. We survive by appealing to the many specialized audiences unearthed by the epic eclipse of the mortgage REITs.

We lose a small amount of money that year, but the loss is paltry compared to the deficit in 1975, our worst year.

From an operating standpoint, we acquire for $18,000 our first computer in 1974, a first-generation Wang as big as a desk and running disks the size of dinner plates. It stores only minibytes but lets us computerize subscription lists, a major help. The Wang is also very sensitive to static, leaving Irene traumatized with an abiding fear of losing data. Staff is loyal and proficient: Bernie Solas, a CFA who joined from Value Line until his September 1978 departure, and Faye Kreisman, Bernie's neighbor, who becomes highly efficient in running the Wang and reading microfiche.

On a personal level, Audit provides the wherewithal to pay all family bills, help son Rick and daughter Carla through college, where both work to pay substantial chunks of their tuition bills, and add some modest amenities by decade's end. Had Irene and I known in January 1969 what we were in for, most likely, we would have kept our money in the bank and lived happily ever after. We set out to publish for a homebuilding audience and wound up becoming nationally recognized sources of information for real estate investment trusts.

The 1970s are both cornerstone and prologue, and not a single one of the multiple advances since 1980 would have transpired without survival in the 1970s.

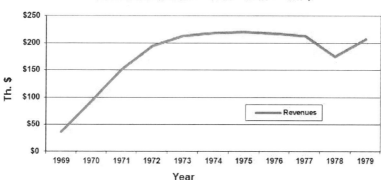

Exhibit 17.3: Audit Investments Inc.
Annual Revenues -- 1969 - 1979 -- Th. $

After searching our records, I present here a graph showing rapid growth of revenues in the first three years after the founding of Audit in 1969, followed by a leveling. For the decade, we took in $1.94 million in revenue, equivalent to $8.77 million in 2015 dollars. Net income was something else, and the financial statements provided by Sanford Goldstein & Co. show a minuscule loss of $360 for the decade. Without the losses of 1975 and 1978, we would have fared quite well for a fledgling business.

Of far greater importance than the accounting results is that we establish Audit as a nationally recognized source for factual and analytical research on the nascent REIT industry. That reputation becomes our most important asset.

EQUITY BEATS DEBT

Property-owning equity REITs not only survive the worst recession of the postwar years until then but provide strong evidence that conservatively managed and financed owners of commercial property can, like Noah, emerge still breathing from the deluge. During the second half of the 1970s, I drove through downtown New Orleans with a life insurance company executive who pointed out that every major office building was in foreclosure. Since life insurance companies could then lend up to 75 percent of a building's value, his comments implied that every realty developer had lost their entire equity stake in these landmark towers. My takeaway: 75 percent debt leverage, or a three-to-one debt-to-equity ratio, is too high for the best real estate when the deluge arrives. Lower the leverage, and you survive.

The experience of those conservative early-1970s equity trusts profoundly rebuts then-prevailing wisdom that the only way small individual investors should approach real estate is via fixed income mortgages. This "wisdom" persists despite the abject failure of mortgage bonds to protect small individual investors in the 1920s and 1930s (see appendix I, "History of the New York Real Estate Securities Exchange").

The proof is in the numbers: Equity REITs fall 44 percent in price from December 1971, when the National Association of REITs initiates its REIT price indices, through year-end 1974 before soaring 117 percent in the decade's second half. When dividends are included, equity REITs handily beat the Standard & Poor's 500 Index for the Sickly Seventies on a compounded annual growth basis.

TABLE 17.2: EQUITY REIT PERFORMANCE, 1972–1979 — ANNUAL PERCENTAGE RATES

	1972–74	1975–79	1970–79
Equity REITs			
Price Change	-17.6%	+16.7%	+2.4%
Dividends	+ 7.2	+ 9.7	+ 8.7
Total Return	-10.5%	+26.4%	+11.1%
S&P 500			
Price Change	-12.4%	+9.5%	+0.7%
Dividends	+3.1	+5.2	+4.3
Total Return	-9.4%	+14.7%	+5.9%
REIT Advantage	**-1.1%**	**+11.7%**	**+6.1%**

Source: Author's calculations from total return indices for NAREIT All Equity REIT Index and S&P 500.

Simply put, investors in property-owning equity REITs make money if held for the long term through the economy's purge by fire in the 1970s. Exhibit 17.4 tells this story graphically from 1966 through 1979. After participating tepidly in the mortgage trust boom of the early 1970s, equity REITs mount a significant recovery advance in the decade's second half and wind up slightly above their early 1969 peak as shown in Exhibit 17.4.

That performance teaches a lesson for me and every investor: Don't panic in downturns, keep your powder dry and hold for the longer term. Equity REITs are an investment class with legs.

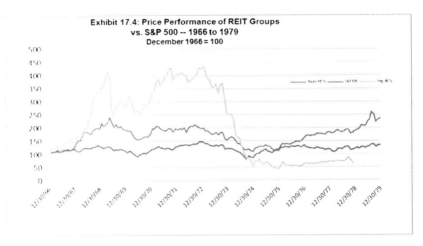

Exhibit 17.4: Price Performance of REIT Groups vs. S&P 500 -- 1966 to 1979 December 1966 = 100

Or consider the experience of investors in the six largest equity REITs at the December 1974 market bottom. Five of this sextet—Continental Illinois Properties, First Union Real Estate, Hubbard Real Estate, ICM Realty, and that first listed REIT, Real Estate Investment Trust of America—sell down to a 53 percent discount to book value at the December 1974 bottom. The sixth, General Growth Properties, maintains its strong attraction for investors through the sell-off and trades at "merely" twice book value at the market's low point.

Five years later, every one of this six is up at least 50 percent in price, and the six average a 145 percent price gain over this half-decade span. GGP rises 192 percent to trade 248 percent above book value during the second half of the 1970s. Even that scintillating gain plays second fiddle to Continental Illinois Properties, which is bought by a British pension plan in August 1979 for a 321 percent gain over this span. All six narrow their book-value discount to at least single digits except Hubbard, which is hobbled by its 24 percent of assets snared in the 1975 W.T. Grant bankruptcy.

These six comprise the vanguard for a new industry based on property-owning equity REITs, but it will take another test by the cruel realty cycle in the 1980s before the promise of tradable equity real estate securities is realized.

Short-term construction and development mortgage trusts disappear, never to return, and construction lending largely reverts to banks and insurance companies. A decade later, a new generation of mortgage REITs investing in collateralized mortgage obligations (CMOs) and other mortgage variations appears.

All that is beyond my knowledge as we ring in the New Year 1980. We at Audit live to fight another day as the 1980s beckon and scavengers circle the dregs of the sickliest of the former mortgage REITs.

As my brother-in-law Charles Adams is wont to say, "Halitosis is better than no breath at all." Exigencies bring out the best in people. You think best with your back to the wall.

Farewell to the Sickly Seventies.

The 1980s open with scavengers for companies replacing scavengers for properties.

Chapter 18
THE REIT CHASERS

The Reit chasers move in within months of the mortgage REIT eclipse of December 1974. Since the seismic market crash of 1974 ultimately forces most short-term mortgage REITs to forfeit their preferred tax status as REITs, I refer to them as lower-case Reits in the next three chapters.

From 1969 through 1974, I focus on watching well over one hundred REITs scamper from my rat hole, the 1960 law letting realty operatives claim pass-through tax treatment by organizing as real estate investment trusts. While the law is written with property owners in mind, most REITs scampering out of my rat hole from 1968 to 1973 aim to lend construction mortgage money to real estate developers. This unleashes a money torrent ultimately bringing ruinous lending competition when the economy and construction collapse after the OPEC cartel triples oil prices in October 1973.

REITs now sit on the cusp of dramatic and life-altering trauma and turmoil, objects of a relentless scavenger hunt, ultimately creating a new REIT industry.

From 1975 onward, I know one thing for certain: my rat pack divides into two distinct herds, the Biblical sheep and goats, now called survivor and bait trusts.

THE SURVIVORS

About seventy trusts owning equity in property or lending long-term mortgages remain as qualified REITs and are relatively unscathed, although a goodly number are caught with too-high debt and problem loans that siphon 20 to 30 percent of their income. Since only about one-half of survivors continue regular dividends into the middle of 1975, net book value—the difference between invested assets and liabilities—becomes the lens through which post-crash investors judge survivor trusts.

Reflecting uncertainties of the day, stock prices of survivors sag dramatically to half or less of stated book value, and all but the hardiest become targets of stock market bottom-fishers.

I and my *Realty Trust Review* colleagues see enormous investment potential for survivor stocks, especially trusts owning properties directly. As they are called property or equity trusts, we reason they should hold most of their book value and generate eye-popping gains because most have sidestepped the construction mortgage morass.

In those dark days, their stocks sell at an average 55 percent discount to a modestly impaired book value during mid-1975, and we see this as an unprecedented bargain that should give investors potential to double their money in two to three years. Our job at *RTR* is to dig into management strategies and asset quality to pinpoint survivors with highest potential gains.

We are cautiously optimistic on stocks of long-term mortgage lenders because we cannot estimate the depth of hidden losses, even though most are managed by life insurance company veterans—from the ranks of Equitable Life, MassMutual Life, Northwestern Mutual Life, and others—with long and successful track records in mortgage lending.

THE BAIT

All former construction and mortgage lenders, totaling about sixty trusts, face eclipse as their days in the sun set. Up to their eyeballs in debt and drowning in problem properties approaching 80 percent or more of assets, they count scant income with which to wrestle with impatient bank lenders who want their money back—yesterday. Nearly all end their qualification as REITs and become lowercase *Reits* in my lexicon.

Their main value is ownership of mortgages on completed buildings and building sites. *If* real estate recovers and *if* they can make peace with their banks, these assets have potential value far beyond today's worth.

Both groups struggle to attract investors. The income-seeking individuals who bought mortgage trusts gradually drift into other vehicles, disillusioned and now seeing REITs as an unmentionable four-letter word. They won't return to REITs for a decade or longer. A very few of these individual investors move into survivor trusts, but these trusts are largely managed to generate unexciting and stable but sluggish income growth. Survivors thus battle to find a new base of investor backing.

Bait trusts have the opposite problem. Investors they emphatically want to avoid find them with impunity. Discounts to book value running 75 to 90 percent are Wall Street's neon billboards, blinking *Buy Me Now! Buy Me!* to every passing investor. But investors who care to peek beneath the hood find, as we do, that those bargains are often mirages and will take tons of patience—measured in years, not weeks or months—to cash big gains from fallen angels.

Enter the vulture investors, often called "bottom-fishers" or "raiders." In today's politically correct world, we call them "activist investors." For them, bait trusts are fair game. As in the animal kingdom, Wall Street is home to investors whose raw meat is the carrion of broken or busted companies. But it's important to distinguish the many varying goals animating these activist investors.

Vulture investors, like their namesake raptors, subsist almost entirely by feeding on the carrion of broken or busted companies. Nothing brings out vultures like dead meat. And by feasting on the dead meat of walking dead companies, they remove from our environment lots of messy, smelly, and unwanted carcasses. They clean up the list, almost always making a profit but rarely creating anything of value.

Junk men and other scavengers, on the other hand, perform distasteful but useful and necessary societal chores: cleaning dirt and trash from streets and tidying our living spaces by collecting garbage and trash divested by the exigencies of living. Webster defines scavengers as junkmen, people who collect secondhand, worn, or discarded articles or other waste that may be used again in another form.

Scavengers, to my thinking, are redevelopers, adapters, creators of value where others see only cast-offs. Vultures, on the other hand, keep the landscape clean but add little value to society.

I see them as Reit chasers and Reit catchers because they pursue those mangy, battered, barely surviving busted Reits of 1975, who live on only at sufferance of their banks. Over the next decade, the Reit chasers and catchers twist and turn and merge the bait trusts into something of value. Most important, they purge the stock list of the wreckage and aroma, thus giving survivor trusts room to grow and prosper.

Midway through 1975, a Reit catcher investor might survey a feast of carrion from the bloodless verdict of Wall Street's market, including these two morsels:

Look at Chase Manhattan Mortgage & Realty Trust, NYSE symbol CMR, once the toast and giant of the trust industry befitting its link to the storied Rockefeller family's Chase Manhattan Bank when its stock traded over $41.00 a share, now available to all takers at $4.63. You want bargains? CMR's stock changes hands at about 10 percent of its December 1973 high. Better, Chase Trust is getting right with its auditors, already writing down book value by 78 percent to $5.89 a share. Market cap is a relatively hefty $22.6 million, but with debt a towering 31.1 times equity, CMR offers a chance to control nearly $1 billion in real estate and loans for a fraction of the cost. What's not to like?

Or ogle Great American Management & Investments, trading under GAA, down an eye-popping 97 percent from $30.50 in December 1973 to a mere $1.00. You can own one share of this prize for less than the cost of three thirty-five-cent trips on New York City's subway. GAMI is taking a few licks, writing down book value by 12 percent to $14.78, so you can buy shares at a 93 percent discount to book, a better deal than the 77 percent average discount for all mortgage trusts. Market cap is only $3.0 million, so for a mere $1.51 million, you theoretically can own 51 percent and control $474 million of real estate and loans that are "only" 73 percent nonearning. With debt *only* 11.9 times equity, GAMI sports the fourth highest leverage among trusts. This bargain has oodles of upside as real estate recovers.

Six months after the crash, our June 27, 1975, *Realty Trust Review* bulges with data on 131 such bargains. About two-thirds—eighty-five trusts—sell below $5.00 a share, a Wall Street never-never land where brokers generally won't extend margin loans to buyers and most white-shoe brokers won't even take an order.

Only four REITs are valued by Wall Street at over $15.00 a share: long-term mortgage trusts Equitable Life Mortgage & Realty Investors (EQ: $17.75), Connecticut General Mortgage & Realty Investments (CGM: $16.00), shopping center owner General Growth Properties (GGP: $17.25), and short-term mortgage REIT Lomas & Nettleton Mortgage Investors (LOM: $15.38). Together, they account for $346 million market value or over 20 percent of the entire REIT industry.

Yet three of this quartet of high-priced REITs can arguably be called bargains because they sell at less than book value. The pair of long-term lenders trade at an average 28 percent discount to net asset value while short-term lender Lomas & Nettleton weighs in at 55 percent discount to book, weak but one of the best among peers.

General Growth sits in a class by itself, its stock cruising at an altitude of 156 percent premium to book net of accumulated depreciation, the highest ratio among only five REITs trading above book value. Martin Bucksbaum, the soft-spoken, genial former merchant, and his brother Matthew Bucksbaum, who founded GGP, are well liked in Wall Street because they build a lengthy no-surprise track record with Midwestern shopping malls. Four years later, the Bucksbaums sell ten GGP malls to an insurance company and repeat by selling seventeen more malls to a second insurer five years later. After some downtime, the Bucksbaum brothers return to public markets in the 1990s with a second iteration of GGP.

Others in this elite group include Federal Realty Investment Trust (NYSE: FRT) and Washington REIT (NYSE: WRE), both survivors to this day as standout long-term performers cranking out earnings and dividends for shareholders. The other pair of premium-priced equity trusts in 1975, New Plan Realty and Riviere Realty, both subsequently merge into other entities.

On paper, those June 1975 "bargains" seem irresistible. But the bargains are only a chimera because looming losses aren't yet reflected in financial statements. As happens so frequently during those years, auditors, despite their best efforts, cannot catch up with reality in their reports. As a result, *RTR* data, based on latest financial statements, paints a misleading picture to would-be Reit catchers.

Recognizing this data lag, we at *RTR* try to give subscribers a handle on the magnitude of prospective losses in our company reviews, but twenty-twenty hindsight tells me our staff did only an okay job. As property REITs lead trusts out of the 1970s collapse, we at *RTR* start ignoring depreciation—as real estate professionals had done for years—in earnings reports and move to full cash flow reporting in 1981. That story is told more fully in chapter 21, "The Value Seeker."

THE TRANSFORMERS

Despite these hidden dangers, well over 150 Reit chasers and catchers ultimately put their money on the line to chase these bargains. For the next decade, they scramble to find values hidden in nearly two hundred stocks, bonds, and warrants, the flotsam left by the collapse of the mortgage REITs. Most bonds and warrants trade in subterranean over-the-counter markets where successfully executing trades in a desired piece of paper often depends more upon whom you know than what you know. More often than not, two or more Reit catchers wind up chasing the same security or find other bargain hunters ahead of them when they finally complete their cherished buy. The Reit catchers, often fairly young and making their first foray into securities market activism, find nothing easy or transparent about this chase.

Realty Stock Review's monthly statistical issue, pulled together with lavish labor by our staff from REIT financial reports and multiple Wall Street sources, becomes something of a must-read for the Reit catchers. *RTR*'s news columns, chronicling who is buying what or whom, tingle with the vibrancy of this byzantine marketplace.

By early 1978, most trusts make peace with their banks, and the foreclosure tide is receding ever so slowly, letting control-minded investors venture into the treacherous REIT market with some impunity and glimmers of real estate and share price recovery on the horizon. Almost every *Realty Trust Review* issue enfolds news of some new block purchases, and periodically, we stand back and tally all available 13-D filings so subscribers can survey the forest as well as the trees.

"New buying groups are surfacing almost every day now," *RTR* reports on January 13, 1978 (an ominous Friday the 13th), along with a brief list comprising stakes in six Reits by four outside buyers.

Managers of three other trusts report defensive purchases at the same time, effectively signaling the end of trust managers relying for control upon OPM—other people's money that assents meekly to management fees and perks.

On August 11, 1978, we assemble our first roster of major block purchasers, listing sixteen purchasers of 5 percent-plus blocks in fourteen different REITs. Block buyers now have $10.1 million rolling in the market, a microscopic 0.4 percent of the industry's $2.37 billion market cap. See Appendix III for that initial list.

Holdings range up to 19.3 percent of outstanding shares (in Transco Realty Trust, a REIT deemed too small for inclusion in *RTR*), which in a surprising turnabout holds $1.9 million stock, or 15.6 percent, in $12.4 million Hospital Mortgage Group. The buyout game is on!

Six-plus years down the road, by November 1984, when we gather our final list of block buyers, the roster has grown to 147 different block positions in 79 different current and former REITs. Appendix III displays the November 1983 list.

Block buyers now have $1.75 billion invested in REIT workout and recovery candidates, or about 27 percent of the $6.46 billion relevant market cap ($14.6 billion in 2015 dollars).

In those intervening half-dozen years, block buyers transform the old REIT industry, merging, consolidating, or simply liquidating the seventy-plus unprofitable and unfundable mortgage REITs, turning some into viable equity REITs or simply selling the detritus. Not a single mortgage REIT, whether short- or long-term, survives, and all vanish from the stock list. All equity-and-mortgage combination trusts also disappear from the Wall Street scene, and the concept of a sponsored or externally advised trust happily joins the buggy-whip as virtually extinct.

By the end of 1984, a new equity or property REIT industry now emerges whose $6.5 billion market valuation is nearly eightfold larger than the December 1974 nadir.

THE REIT CHASERS

Block buyers quickly separate themselves into two groups, passive investors looking to profit from a real estate recovery, and active investors looking to make something happen. Our *RTR* subscribers largely reside in the passive camp and get particular attention. In my mind, they are the Reit chasers, looking for good values and upside. While many assemble 5-percent-plus blocks of stocks, they aren't about to take over management.

Both Reit chasers and Reit catchers have a field day. Like the exuberant youth tearing through a manure pile because he's sure there's a pony in there somewhere, most make good money and a few build strong companies thriving to this day.

A main asset of the zombie Reits they chase is the huge net operating tax loss carry-forwards (NOLs) racked up by all trusts. It works like this. When a REIT loses money, either from poor operations or jettisoning bum assets, it creates net operating losses. These losses can be carried back into past years in some cases and applied to taxes due in future profitable years. An investor or business with substantial cash flow and income can purchase control of an NOL-rich Reit and save considerable income taxes by consolidating the two entities. Of course, the IRS enforces strict rules on trafficking in tax losses, but pursuing trust NOLs becomes a favorite investment sport in the late 1970s and into the 1980s.

Six boldface name activist investors cut their first deals in this fertile public market hunting ground. Despite their reputation as takeover activists, neither Richard Rainwater, Carl Lindner, nor David Murdoch ever stay the course long enough to seize control of a busted REIT. Trading, not takeovers, is Ivan Boesky's cup of tea, while Warren Buffett and a future president earn big gains with their idiosyncratic styles.

Super investor Richard Rainwater, captaining the investment ship for the wealthy Bass Brothers of Texas at age thirty-three, launches in June 1976 a $7-per-share tender offer for 300,000 shares, or 22 percent, of San Francisco Real Estate Investors, a $62 million asset REIT owning nearly one million square feet of office buildings and mortgage loans. SFREI shareholders snub the offer, and Rainwater uncharacteristically backs off, turning his attention to non-REIT companies. Lee National Corp., a smallish but aggressive Manhattan realty player, at the same time, says it will mount a tender for shares of API Trust, formerly Arlen Property Investors, but never follows through. These misfires cause tenders to fall out of favor among REIT block buyers for a time until the tender tactic resurfaces three years later.

Hedge fund manager Ivan Boesky takes a swing at REITs and buys a 7.2 percent stake in Prudent REIT in April 1979 but doesn't pursue his quarry, which ultimately lands in the lap of another Reit catcher. In 1984, he acquires blocks in two operating companies, Canal Randolph and Southland Financial, but backs off the chase.

I meet Boesky only once during those years to gauge his intentions. It is noontime in his lower Manhattan office, and I arrive at the very moment the SEC has shut down trading in one of his stocks and he is frantically trying to trade the name in London. He barks questions to his US securities lawyer on one line—"Can I trade this stock in London?"—while simultaneously firing the same query to someone in London on a second line. The stress of needing instant answers on both lines is palpable, and while the stock's name is never mentioned, it's clear big dollars are riding on the outcome.

I leave after fifteen minutes because it's clear Boesky is in no mood to talk REITs. I pigeonhole Boesky as a classic trader with no intent of taking control of a REIT. (In November 1986, Boesky pleads guilty to using illegal inside information about pending mergers to amass a $200 million fortune and is sentenced to three and a half years in prison, although he serves only two years. His cooperation with the SEC helps that agency topple junk bond king Michael Milken and Drexel Burnham Lambert.)

Other boldface raider names of the era come up empty.

Carl Lindner, a feared raider of the day, takes a pass at Eastover Corp. through a subsidiary of his American Financial Corp. but is turned away by Leland Speed, one of the era's biggest winners, as detailed in chapter 20, "The Biggest Winners." Later, Lindner takes positions in First Mortgage, North American Mortgage, Kenilworth Realty, and Triton Group (formerly Chase Manhattan Mortgage), hoping to use the vast financial resources of his Great American Life Insurance Co. subsidiary to extend backup financing to hard-pressed REITs convertible into major ownership positions. It's a clever business ploy that brings results in some instances.

David Murdoch, an Arizona realty developer who takes an unsuccessful run at DMG, Inc., successor to Diversified Mortgage Investors, drops out of the Reit chase. But in 1985, Murdoch captures control of Hawaii's Castle & Cooke and with it the iconic Dole Pineapple empire.

Manhattan hedge fund manager Robert Wilson buys 5-percent-plus stakes in a few Reits, including C. I. Realty, owner of several valuable Manhattan office towers, but never controls any one entity. Wilson puts out the word that he's besieged by so many Wall Street stock pickers that he limits analysts to one good idea a year. I see him as a Boesky-type trader.

All-American-value investor Warren Buffett joins the chase. Buffett is no stranger to REITs, having served on the General Growth Properties board at its September 1970 IPO. I first meet Buffett at a New York reception at which Martin Bucksbaum, GGP's founder and guiding light, introduces Buffett and other GGP directors to real estate analysts. Buffett is clearly the main attraction, known primarily then for his late-1960s takeover of Berkshire Hathaway Corp. Buffett stays with GGP only a couple of years. "I got out of there fast," Buffett tells me many years later, without elaboration.

Buffett is a heavy hitter, so I am taken aback when, between March 1979 and January 1980, Buffett and then-wife Susan Buffett personally accumulate 46,900 shares of $5.3 million microcap mortgage Reit, Citinational Development Trust, sponsored by small but prestigious City National Bank of Beverly Hills, California. The 7.8 percent Buffett stake fits neatly into Buffett's fabled "margin of safety" investment maxims: big discount to book value, bank debt a miniscule $500,000, and the trust announcing intention to liquidate and return capital to shareholders, which it subsequently does.

In June 1981, Buffett switches buying to Central Mortgage & Realty, paying about $5.25 a share, a net of a $6.00 liquidating dividend for 47,500 shares of a former mortgage lender struggling with foreclosures. Central almost duplicates Citinational's valuation stats: stock trading in June 1981 at $7.13, or a 54 percent discount to the $15.94 book value, debt paid down to $400,000, and management vowing to liquidate holdings. Over the next two years, Central pays another $9.87 to shareholders and then, in October 1984, sells control of the shell at $0.52 a share. The buyers are an investment publisher named Ken Campbell and an Irish investor group, which is another long and sad story told in chapter 23, "The Surprises."

In these two forays, Buffett makes no active move to take control. "Just give me my rightful shareholder due," he implicitly says, "and I'll be on my way."

Buffett is not alone among big names questing for painless and passive profits from the REIT carnage. On August 8, 1980, *Realty Trust Review* exposes the identity of another REIT investor with hopes of remaining incognito:

"Portrait of a Reit Investor: Large Gain on One
Issue to Outweigh Losses on Others

"While reading *Barron's* this week, we were intrigued
by a table detailing the 1979 capital gains schedule for
one taxpayer. The more we thought about it, the more
we thought that this person could be characterized as
the typical (successful) REIT investor.

"During the year, he sold a total of 11 issues long-
term, for a net capital gain of $234,455 on an invest-
ment of $720,399. While he did quite well on three
bank issues, for a total gain of $82,046, his most strik-
ing investments were in three REIT shares. He took
a whopping loss in Guardian Mortgage shares, losing
$25,359 of his initial investment of $26,373 (the shares
were purchased at an average price of $26.37). He took
a proportionally smaller loss on his Moraga [a former
REIT] shares, losing $41,752 of the initial investment
of $58,708 (purchased at $19.57 a share each—if he'd
purchased them when we recommended them, at $3, he
would have done quite well).

"But his moment of glory far out-weighed these
minor losses. Having purchased Continental Illinois
Properties at $11.54, he tendered his shares at $30, for
a gigantic $203,099 gain, by far his largest transaction
[and 87% of his total net gains].

"This is what all REIT investors aim for, the large
gains far outstripping losses on other shares. The name
of this particular investor?

"Ronald W. Reagan."

Vistas from Ken Campbell's Life Journey

1951-57

The Columbus Citizen

The Columbus Citizen SUNDAY, APRIL 21, 1957

Lincoln Village Annexation Plan Called 'Cheap Politi'

By KENNETH CAMPBELL

At City Hall

'What's Next?' Becomes Big Question As Court Rules On Franklin Township

By KENNETH CAMPBELL

Campbell

City in Traffic Chains...
Engineer Proposes Ban on Downtown Parking at Curb

Higher Fares, Shuttle Busses Also Suggested As Possible Aids

By KENNETH CAMPBELL

Dedicated to developing a better community through organized citizen effort.

DEVELOPMENT *f* COMMITTEE
for Greater Columbus

ROBERT F. MOTT, *Executive Director*

| 0 South Third Street | CA 1-7871 | Columbus 15, Ohio |

1957-61

URBAN RENEWAL PROGRESS REPORT

OCTOBER, 1960

Annexation Puzzler: Will $ Limit Growth?

Annual **PROGRESS** *Report*

MAY, 1958

DEVELOPMENT COMMITTEE FOR GREATER COLUMBUS

House & Home
May 1961

MANAGING EDITOR
Gurney Breckenfeld

EXECUTIVE EDITOR
Edward Birkner

ASSISTANT MANAGING EDITORS
John F. Goldsmith
Walter F. Wagner Jr.

ART DIRECTOR
Jan V. White

ASSOCIATE EDITORS
Jonathan Aley
Kenneth D. Campbell
James P. Gallagher
Maxwell C. Huntoon Jr.
Robert W. Murray Jr.
Richard W. O'Neill
Richard Saunders (Washington)

Photo by Fred Schnell

1961-67

1970's –
Audit
Investment
Brochure
Painting by:
Linda Verhagen

1970 – Irene Campbell greets
visitors at an Audit sales booth

1975 –
Ken with
Wall $treet Week
host, Frank Capiello

1972 –
Ken (seated right)
with REIT Income
Board Directors

1971 –
The Book

1972 –
The Mods

1969 –
Expanded Thesis

"The Last REIT Watcher"
Forbes, 1979

1981 – *Fortune Magazine*   1983 – Proxy

HAMILTON INVESTMENT TRUST
567 Morris Avenue
P.O. Box 819
Elizabeth, New Jersey 07207

NOTICE OF SPECIAL MEETING OF SHAREHOLDERS
To be held on February 16, 1983

To the Shareholders of
Hamilton Investment Trust:

NOTICE IS HEREBY GIVEN that a Special Meeting of Shareholders of Hamilton Investment Trust ("Hamilton") will be held at First National State Bank of New Jersey, 550 Broad Street, Newark, New Jersey 07102 on February 16, 1983, at 10:00 A.M., local time, for the following purposes:

The King of the REIT-Watchers

Former journalist Kenneth Campbell, 51, has been a REIT-watcher since 1961, when he wrote an article about the first wave of trusts. Now he writes a newsletter, *Realty Stock Review*, which comes out twice a month and is considered the last word on REITs. (A year's subscription costs $185.) Campbell views trusts primarily as income vehicles and considers their record of dividend payments as important as the value of the real estate. Although he's impressed with the capabilities of Lomas & Nettleton and Public Storage, sponsors of two new REITs, he thinks investors should stick to the ones with track records.

REITS,
Their Banks
and
Bondholders

New Opportunities in Realty Trusts

1977 – The Disaster   **1978 – New Opportunities**

I SURVIVED
HIGH Y...
CONVERTI...
CONFEREN...

1983 –
Predator Ball Memento

1988 – *Money Magazine*

By day, Campbell tangles with property cash-flow projections and vacancy rates. At night, he likes to curl up with the *Record's* crossword puzzle in his Upper Saddle River, N.J. home.

Photo by Ken Krebs

Campbell

Dillmeier

Campbell & Dillmeier
REAL ESTATE INVESTMENT BANKING

230 Park Avenue
New York, New York 10169
Telephone (212)986-6112

Kenneth P. Campbell

Robert L. Dillmeier

Old Dominion Real Estate
Investment Trust

Piedmont Real Estate Investment
Trust

Campbell & Dillmeier

BRT Realty Trust

Campbell & Dillmeier

Sunstates Corporation

Treco, Inc.

Campbell & Dillmeier

Johnstown American
Companies

Marshall Homes Company

Johnstown Mortgage Company

Campbell & Dillmeier

Growth Realty Companies

The British Land Company

Campbell & Dillmeier

Pacific Southern Mortgage
Trust

Old Stone Corporation

Campbell & Dillmeier

Gould Investors Trust

NOVA Real Estate Investment
Trust

Campbell & Dillmeier

WMI Equity Investors

Eaton Vance Corp.

Campbell & Dillmeier

Monetary Realty Trust

American Realty
Trust

Campbell & Dillmeier

Regent Investors

Campbell & Dillmeier

Kenyon Investment Corporation

Sunstates Corporation

Campbell & Dillmeier

Hamilton Investment Trust

Johnstown Financial
Corporation

Lane Company

Campbell & Dillmeier

CAMPBELL RADNOR ADVISORS
1992

CRA
REAL ESTATE SECURITIES

NAREIT Industry
Leadership Award 1996

CLARION · CRA
SECURITIES

1998

ING REAL ESTATE

1998 -
Closing of Sale to ING

Sept. 26
2003

Feb. 25
2004

Aug. 20
2007

CBRE
CLARION
SECURITIES
CBRE Clarion Securities
201 King of Prussia Road
Suite 600
Radnor, PA 19087

July 01, 2011

To Our Investor Clients and Friends:

I am very pleased to announce that the purchase of our firm by CB Richard Ellis (CBRE) was completed on July 1st. As most of you are aware, our firm has been managing real estate securities portfolios for more than a quarter century. Our business has mirrored the growth and development of the listed real estate market into a dynamic global asset class. During this span, we have had the privilege to serve our investor clients as Campbell Radnor Advisors, Clarion Real Estate Securities and, for the past 12+ years, as ING Clarion Real Estate Securities. Our transition from ING to our new home within the CBRE organization is now complete and we now look forward to serving you as CBRE Clarion Securities.

2011

Robert L. Dillmeier &
Kenneth D. Campbell

LIFE'S PARTNERS

Jarrett B. Kling,
Kenneth D. Campbell, &
T. Ritson Ferguson

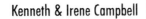

Kenneth & Irene Campbell

2013
Extended
Campbell Family

Chapter 19
THE REIT CATCHERS

Only a very few Reit chasers in this chaotic, no-holds-barred free-for-all capture control of one or more tattered REITs. Sometimes feared, sometimes honored, the catchers of these Reits, a.k.a. sick REITs, merit closer inspection because their motives and actions ultimately popularize property ownership by stock market investors and remove the curse from the word *REIT.*

Their combined efforts propel REITs on the road to stock market redemption. Redemption follows a simple rhythm repeated endlessly in the stock market. Stocks of busted companies become dirt cheap, attracting investors who believe so strongly that they can fix either assets or management's business plan that they put their money on the line and buy shares of these fallen angels. Ultimately they become the new mogul, oust the old mogul, fire old staff, and embark on new business tracks. Jobs are lost at first, but more jobs are created *if*—that pesky word—their revamped business plan works.

Most Reit catchers are young, in their thirties or early forties, looking to make fame or fortune in this free-form scavenger hunt, attracted from nearly all corners of the globe by the lure of cheap real estate.

Some succeed; some fail. I witness and chronicle in the pages of *Realty Trust/Stock Review* perhaps one hundred takeover attempts in the late 1970s and 1980s to resuscitate busted REITs into the stuff of dreams. It is humankind's ageless quest for fame and fortune, for success and riches, for recognition and self-validation.

At root, these Reit catchers hope that one plus one—money plus management—equals three or four or, if things go really well, five, in total return for shareholders. Read on for stories of ten different value routes that burn in my memory after nearly forty years. I give each a final grade on that one-plus-one scoring grid, based on the total return these Reit catchers deliver for their long-suffering shareholders. I score each Reit catcher company through the end of the 1980s unless their public record ended earlier. Since 1989 ended during a deep real estate recession, this terminal date creates some potential negative skew. Of the five companies scored through 1989, three ended with negative scores versus only two in the plus column. You, perceptive reader, must factor this potential bias into your thinking as you read on.

THE WALL STREETER

Our *Realty Trust Review* fingers Carl Icahn's first takeover target—except I am oblivious to the event, which transpires in this fashion.

Marvin Olshan, a well-connected name partner in law firm Olshan Grundman Frome (now Olshan Frome Wolosky) and whom we meet later (chapter 23, "The Surprises"), buys stock through the small brokerage firm of Carl Icahn & Co. in the late 1970s and asks that certificates be delivered to him since back-office paperwork is strangling many brokerages. Weeks and months pass, and no certificates arrive. Deeply concerned, Olshan rings up Carl Icahn, whom he knows slightly, and asks what's going on. Carl blames the snafu on another firm and then asks Olshan, known for his roster of real estate clients, what he thinks about REIT stocks, then struggling to recover from their massive 1973–1974 crash.

Olshan believes at the time that assets underlying most REIT stocks are worth about 50 percent more than their stock prices, and, reaching into his drawer, pulls out his latest copy of *Realty Trust Review*. Thumbing through the pages of "Old Black and Blue," he comes upon the name of Baird & Warner atop the list of mortgage banker-sponsored REITs, then trading over-the-counter at around eight dollars a share. "Take a look at Baird & Warner," he says before ending the conversation.

Within a short time, Carl Icahn, founder of the options and risk arbitrage house bearing his name, begins buying Baird shares in his first foray into activist investing at age forty-two. By December 1978, Icahn buys a 22.5 percent stake in $51-million asset Baird & Warner Mortgage & Realty Investors, sponsored by a Chicago mortgage banker. The 235,000-share block costs him about $7.50 a share, or $1.75 million. Baird resists, and in the spring of 1979, trustees propose liquidating the trust to thwart Icahn's hostile stock purchases. But Icahn uses a special trust bylaw to call an election for his handpicked slate of new trustees. In May 1979, Icahn wins the election and takes control. In June 1979, Icahn renames the trust Bayswater Realty, adopting the name of a famed central London precinct.

In January 1980, I meet Icahn after the market close at a midtown Manhattan restaurant to try to penetrate his intentions for Baird. It is my job to chase the Chasers and try to read between the lines of their carefully drafted statements of intent in official 13-D filings. But Icahn either has a short attention span, is distracted by more pressing matters, or ducks my questions politely but intentionally. He is already well-coached by his lawyers, and it's clear he's uncomfortable facing nosy security analysts asking pesky questions. The interview ends without any new insights or knowledge.

Once in charge of Bayswater, Icahn begins liquidating assets and using proceeds to buy a 1.1 percent stake in Hammermill Paper Co. in March 1980, in tandem with other Icahn entities. The Securities and Exchange Commission comes calling to ask questions about the

Hammermill deal, but the probe comes to naught. By year-end 1981, Bayswater joins other Icahn entities to tender for a block of Simplicity Pattern.

In Chicago, Icahn finds more real estate to his liking, and in early 1982, the Bayswater-Icahn team buys a 14.3 percent block in iconic upscale Chicago retailer Marshall Field & Co. Field sues in vain to halt Icahn's buying, and when Icahn ups his holdings to 19.4 percent by February 1982, Field escapes his embrace by finding a white knight buyer in BAT, British American Tobacco, in June 1982, and Bayswater earns a slice of the profits.

Score: Chicago insiders, 1; Icahn, 1.

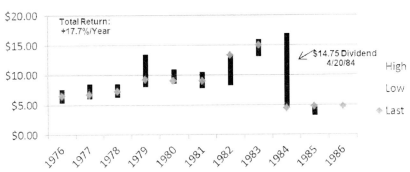

Exhibit 19.1: Baird/Bayswater (O: BAYS)
Annual Stock Prices 1976 - 1986

By this time, Icahn owns 67 percent of Bayswater and begins talking about taking this small entity private by offering in September 1982 to buy the 281,723 shares or 33 percent he doesn't own for $13 a share. Minority shareholders, suspecting more hidden value in Bayswater shares, resist the idea and tender less than half of minority shares.

There follows a protracted and tense standoff between Icahn and minority holders that ends eighteen months later when, in April 1984, Bayswater distributes $14.75 per share in a special cash dividend. After that, the stock settles into a $4 to $5 trading range, indicating total value well above Ichan's previous $13 a share offer. Trading dries up afterward, and we delist the stock in May 1986; Icahn ultimately gets his wish and takes the company private.

Icahn earns about 18 percent compounded annual total return for his Bayswater shareholders over an eight-year involvement, without counting any heartburn from the standoff with minority holders. His maiden voyage in activist seas lets him hone skills ultimately making him one of America's wealthiest investors.

Icahn's final score: 1 + 1 = +4.

THE CANADIANS

From Toronto, suave George Mann leads his Unicorp Canada Corporation into control positions in four equity REITs.

Mann's foray surfaces in December 1978 when he reports buying 9.2 percent of GREIT Realty Trust (ASE, symbol GRT), a smallish $7.1 million market cap trust with $35 million assets then focusing on shopping centers after a disastrous turn into mortgage lending. Mann's stake in this old-line REIT founded in December 1960 is valued at $656,000.

Within three months, Mann strikes at two more trusts, buying in February and March 1979 respectively blocks in two more trusts: a 6.4 percent position for $1.9 million in the granddaddy of all trusts, $44 million asset Real Estate Investment Trust of America (REITA), now headed by Henri J. Bourneuf, which owns urban office and retail properties; and a 6.0 percent block for $1.7 million in $63 million asset San Francisco Real Estate Investors (ASE: SFI), a newer trust liquidating its mortgages to focus on office buildings.

In August 1979, Mann establishes a 5.0 percent position at a cost of $3.7 million in $199 million asset First Union Real Estate Equity and Mortgage Investments (NYSE: FUR), another old-line equity REIT specializing in downtown offices and shopping malls.

Thus in less than a year, Mann ponies up over $8.0 million to buy headline-grabbing blocks in a quartet of equity REITs. Mann is clearly in the game to stay.

Mann's eye for value is uncanny. All but San Francisco continue dividends uninterrupted during the mid-1970s mortgage meltdown, and in February 1979, they sell at an average 38 percent discount to net book value, including accumulated depreciation. At the time, we call First Union "a high quality holding for dividend income and moderate appreciation potential" and estimate that GREIT shares, then trading at $7.13, "have a break-up value in the ... $13 to $19 range on a free-and-clear basis." We see REITA shares, where new management is settling in, as "conservative income holdings" although "recovery will take some time."

All four trust managers resist Mann's entreaties early on, but Mann, a courtly and canny investor whose vocabulary doesn't include the word *no*, keeps pressing his case. By April 1981, Mann owns 50.1 percent of GREIT and 41 percent of San Francisco and begins the legal process of creating a new company, Unicorp American Corp. to consolidate his US holdings. But it takes until mid-November 1981 before Unicorp begins trading on the American Stock Exchange under the UAC symbol.

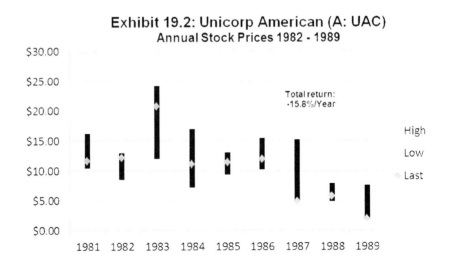

Exhibit 19.2: Unicorp American (A: UAC)
Annual Stock Prices 1982 - 1989

But First Union (FUR), an early Mann target, launches bitter legal resistance, and UAC sells its 24.5 percent stake in February 1982 to settle litigation with FUR. Mann, exhibiting a true Canadian's thirst for oil and gas exploration, has UAC buy 14 percent of a Canadian exploration company in May 1982.

Next San Francisco REI, a Mann subsidiary, tenders in November 1982 for 51 percent control of REITA but is initially rebuffed. Mann keeps pouring money into REITA shares, and REITA agrees in June 1983 to merge into SFREI. The merger isn't completed until December 1984 when both REITA and Institutional Investors, a troubled mortgage REIT, merge into UAC, creating a $327 million company at appraised value owning over two million square feet of urban offices and 1.7 million square feet of shopping centers.

Mann's strategy is to sell properties to generate income and cash flow to reinvest into operating businesses. In 1983, Mann begins buying stakes in savings and loans in Florida and California, and in July 1987, UAC borrows to pay $150 million for 90 percent of a $2.3 billion Manhattan savings bank and a 43 percent interest in a medical buildings company. After initial enthusiasm lifts UAC shares to near $25 and $60 million market value in late 1983, UAC stock falls out of favor with American investors. In July 1987, we feel that "significantly higher leverage could increase the risk character of UAC common."

The real estate recession of the late 1980s deals unkindly with highly leveraged companies, and Mann's UAC comes full cycle. UAC common closes the 1980s decade at $2.00 a share, down 92 percent from a peak $24.25 in 1983.

For Mann, the persistent Canadian, it marks a bitter round trip. He loses about 15 percent a year for his eight-year sojourn south of the border. A gentleman at all times, Mann's thirst for leverage turns against him.

Mann's final score: 1 + 1 = (2).

Mann is not the only Reit catcher from north of the border. From Vancouver come the *Belzberg Brothers*—Hyman, Samuel, and William, then aged fifty-four, fifty-one, and forty-eight respectively—to target $54 million long-term mortgage lender State Mutual Investors, sponsored by a Massachusetts insurance company, and in April 1979, they agree to take control by injecting $14 million new cash and properties by buying 5.03 million new shares or 50.1 percent at $5.03 a share.

Exhibit 19.3: State Mut./First City (N: FCP)
Annual Stock Prices 1977 - 1988

They rename the trust First City Properties in July 1981 and convert it into a California homebuilder and land developer by buying an Anaheim business park and undeveloped land in San Juan Capistrano. Additional deals add more land and properties in both California and Arizona, giving the Belzberg brothers 69 percent control. West Coast homebuilding earnings let FCP use most of its $20.4 million tax losses.

Unfortunately, the brothers also venture separately into a West Coast savings and loan, Far West Financial of Beverly Hills, California, run by brother William, and as a real estate recession bites in the second half of the 1980s, the S&L becomes a major concern and is ultimately seized by the federal government.

The brothers go their separate ways in 1991. Sam remains in the real estate business and through his Balfour Corp. buys land from the Resolution Trust Corporation (RTC), set up to sell assets from failed S&Ls, and develops land and house building lots in seven US cities. Balfour is sold in 1997 for a solid profit to Blackstone Group, a New York City hedge fund operator.

Once among the most feared raiders of their day, the business-like Belzberg brothers do well in diverting a broken REIT into businesses they know well, homebuilding and realty developing, earning about 10 percent a year during their stay in the United States.

The Belzberg's final score: 1 + 1 = +3.

THE BRIT

From London comes clever investment banker Tony Gumbiner, pushing the joys of selling stock at big discounts to market price to raise a pot of money to repay stressed bankers. Gumbiner ultimately uses his discount stock scheme, which is not repeated by any American investment banker, to take control of two trusts with $315 million assets and flips a 26 percent stake in a third trust for $9.3 million to the Canadian acquirer, George Mann.

A perennially upbeat man, standing not much over five and one-half feet and weighing perhaps eleven or twelve stone (155 to 165 pounds), Gumbiner trudges through Wall Street's canyons lugging a pair of twenty-five-pound barrister's briefcases to sell his novel discount stock idea to investment bankers skeptical because it breaks a hoary US tradition of never diluting shareholder equity. I catch up with him one evening when he's staying in the three-story penthouse in Manhattan's Helmsley Palace Hotel after a long day of peddling his pet idea and find him relaxing with a cool drink. He ruminates: "Someone's got to do the work of opening the eyes of Wall Street."

Gumbiner confides details of his biography to enhance an aura of sophisticated success. A British barrister, he domiciles most of his US deals in the Cayman Islands to capture that enclave's favorable tax laws for British citizens. His wife is a citizen of Monaco, where he dwells and enjoys time on his yacht. Monaco residency, he acknowledges, confers on him a second layer of tax benefits.

Acting through Hallwood Securities Ltd. of London, Gumbiner signs his first breakthrough deal in August 1980 with $175 million asset First Pennsylvania Mortgage Trust, sponsored by banker First Pennsylvania Corp. The deal is numbingly complex, but he swears it will bring redemption to First Penn.

With First Penn's three million shares trading at $1.50 and only $0.22 net book value, First Penn agrees to offer holders the right to buy, for $7, a unit of seven new shares and seven warrants exercisable at $1. The carrot enticing holders to accept such massive dilution: banks will accept the $20.7 million raised in full settlement of $46.5 million debt, or a 57 percent discount. Hallwood guarantees that its backup investors will buy all unsold shares. Hallwood gets three million, or 1 percent, of diluted shares as underwriting fee. Following the deal, First Penn's 33.4 million diluted shares have a $1.57 book value.

First Penn pulls off the deal and in December 1980 vacates investment purgatory. Impressed, trustees of two other hard-pressed REITs sign up to drink Gumbiner's magic discount elixir. Hallwood pulls off a deal by raising $18.6 million for $140 million UMET Trust, previously sponsored by bank holding company Unionamerica Corp. of Los Angeles, in February 1982, and raising $25 million for $153 million Institutional Investors Trust, sponsored by Wall Street brokerage Donaldson, Lufkin, and Jenrette, in July 1983.

Gumbiner tops off this marathon by merging First Penn and UMET in May 1984 into a new entity named Hallwood Group Inc., listed on the NYSE (symbol HWG). A 26 percent stock position earned by restructuring Institutional Investors Trust is sold to George Mann's Unicorp American for $9.3 million, providing cash to his investors.

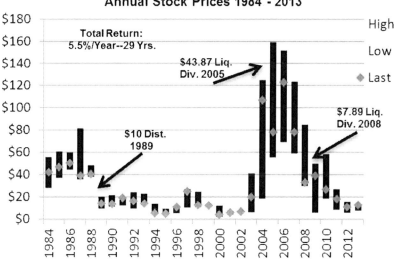

Exhibit 19.4: Hallwood Group Inc. (N: HWG)
Annual Stock Prices 1984 - 2013

Gumbiner emulates Mann's game plan: liquidate the real estate and use the proceeds to operate as an investment banking and holding company. In May 1984, when Hallwood lists on the NYSE under HWG symbol, we bull the stock by headlining it as a "play upon recycling of real estate assets." We add HWG to our Recovery/Turnaround sector "because the market has sold both common and preferred stocks to new lows since the merger that created HWG." We continue recommending this "wallflower" stock through the end of 1984, by which time Hallwood restructures a troubled oil and gas exploration company and is working to resurrect a Swiss hotel company.

By February 1987, we recommend the shares for contrarians, cautioning that the main obstacle to using its $2.36 per share tax-loss carry-forward is "the complexity and attendant time required to complete major merchant banking deals."

The late 1980s real estate recession deals harshly with Hallwood, whose shares peak in August 1987 at a 1980s high of $81.67, adjusted for subsequent splits, after a favorable *Barron's Business and Financial Weekly* write-up but then trace a long glide downward.

The October 1987 flash crash, when the Dow Jones Industrials plunge nearly 23 percent in a single day, kills many realty stocks, and Hallwood's price is cut in half to a split-adjusted $40 by November's end. We remove shares from *Realty Stock Review* in February 1988 because "interviews with HWG indicate that many of HWG's stable of investors in its recovery financing business have effectively gone out of this market," following the October 1987 market collapse.

We are wrong.

Hallwood stock finishes the 1980s at a disappointing split-adjusted $13.67 a share during a grueling real estate recession. For Gumbiner, the recession tests his grand plan of recycling real estate assets into investment banking, despite the allure of cashing in lucrative tax losses.

Gumbiner's discount stock format however clicks when Hallwood translates it into rebuilding the fortunes of other companies. During the late 1980s recession, Hallwood raises nearly $300 million in seven discounted stock offerings, restructuring retailer Hecks Inc., Holiday Inns' licensee Brock Hotel Corp., semiconductor supplier GCA Corp., banks in Alaska and Texas, and Saxon Oil Co. Late in the 1980s, Hallwood also acquires controlling interest in Chuck E. Cheese restaurant and entertainment operator, later sold in a 1997 public offering.

The Saxon Oil transaction gives entrée to the energy business, and today, Hallwood owns three oil and gas subsidiaries, boasting that it is an innovator and pioneer in exploration and production of unconventional shale oil and gas in onshore fields. HWG stock enjoys a huge surge in 2005, peaking at a split-adjusted $159 a share before making a $43.87 a share liquidating dividend. Another $7.89 is paid in 2008. HWG goes private in April 2014 at $12.39 a share.

During its twenty-nine-year run as a public company, Gumbiner's Hallwood earns about 5.5 percent a year for shareholders, about half the 10.2 percent total return for the Standard & Poor's 500 over those years. The investment banking business model produces volatile earnings and stock prices but generates shareholder profits overall.

Gumbiner's final score: 1 + 1 = +2.

THE TRADER MAN

My initial book outline omits any mention of Gene Erlo Phillips and his tortuous, ill-starred run as the most prolific and snakebitten Reit catcher of them all. Perhaps there's deep-seated fear that I missed all those blinking red lights. Perhaps deep down, I want to airbrush the unpleasantness of real estate's largest failure of the 1980s.

But this cautionary tale deserves telling and you must judge whether my reporting and advice in *Realty Stock Review* alerted investors fairly and timely as extraordinary events unfold.

Born in 1938 in the small South Carolina town of Draytonville, Phillips graduates with a chemical engineering degree from Clemson University and attends Virginia Tech graduate school before turning to homebuilding and real estate development, borrowing $30 million by his mid-thirties. His November 1973 bankruptcy filing in Spartanburg becomes South Carolina's largest to that date. After helping a Greensboro, North Carolina, company locate properties suitable for swapping into realty partnerships, Phillips and his 15 percent partner, William Friedman, operating as Syntek Corp., astutely spot and take advantage of the worst bond deal of the 1970s to wrest control of a $180 million mortgage REIT, Citizens & Southern Realty Investors (C&S), from its sponsoring Atlanta bank of the same name.

C&S Realty managers take the unfortunate advice of their investment bankers in 1972 by selling a package of $30 million "synthetic convert-ibles": 6.75 percent debentures usable at par to exercise 300,000 Series A warrants to buy one hundred C&S shares at—as stated in the crucial fine print—"80 percent of the daily mean between the high and low sales prices ... on the principal national securities exchange ... on the ten consecutive trading days ending prior to October 15, 1977." C&S sells the warrants when C&S shares trade about $38 a share, so C&S adds downside protection by inserting a clause giving it the option, but not the obligation, to call the warrants at $25 if this exercise price is below $33.

That floating exercise price dooms C&S Realty.

When witching day arrives on October 15, 1977, that average price is counted not in dollars but in pennies, about forty-four of them.

Warrant holders, if they choose, can theoretically own 67.9 million new shares or nearly eighteen times the 3.83 million C&S shares then outstanding. With the bonds trading at 38 to 41 percent of par, an investor can theoretically buy 226 C&S shares at an effective eighteen cents per share. Of course, a bondholder would give up creditor status in a very troubled REIT for the privilege of equity ownership.

Thereupon frenzied negotiations ensue over several months between trustees for the defaulted bonds, unsecured bank lenders, and manage-ment, resulting in the trust agreeing in July 1978 to restructure bank debt and exchange old Series A warrants for new Series B warrants, letting holders buy fifty shares at two dollars for five years. Holders of 258,000 warrants swap for the new B warrants, and C&S reserves 12.9 million shares for warrant exercise, or about 80 percent of the potential 16.2 million fully diluted shares. C&S severs ties with its bank sponsor and renames itself Southmark Properties (NYSE: SM).

Once this deal is set, significant numbers of investors begin trading their warrants for stock, effectively doubling share count to 6.4 million shares by the end of 1979.

By April 1980, Syntek Corp., the investment fund owned by forty-two-year-old Phillips and Friedman, controls 42 percent of Southmark via stock and warrants, and by October 1980, Southmark agrees to surrender control to Phillips by exchanging 2.5 million shares for recreational land, office buildings, and receivables held by Syntek.

Once in full control, Phillips switches Southmark into full acquisition mode. His plan: Buy properties cheap to sell at fat profits. In August 1981, SM buys an option for a 69 percent controlling interest in $98 million asset North American Mortgage, plus 27 percent of smallish Riviere Realty and 7.5 percent of Growth Realty.

Phillips wants into the lucrative real estate syndication business, which is all the rage in the early 1980s. Syndicators sell limited partnership units, effectively conveying tax losses that offset earned income for wealthy purchasers, part of President Ronald Reagan's plan to stimulate the economy. In October 1981, SM issues a new preferred stock to buy about $30 million net assets in three realty partnerships managed by Lexton-Ancira Funds.

In November 1981, Phillips takes a page from Carl Lindner's financing book and lends $9 million—at 18 percent interest—to asset-rich but illiquid American Realty Trust (ART) to let it cure loan defaults. Phillips gets three ART board seats, and ART agrees to issue new ART shares constituting 37 percent of total shares to SM if ART cannot come up with the cash to repay the loan. (Southmark exercises this option in July 1984, upping its ART ownership to 64 percent.)

In December 1981, Phillips caps his hectic year by swapping control blocks in two trusts. SM buys a 22.5 percent stake in ART shares from Leland Speed's Eastover Corp. while selling his 22 percent stake in Riviere Realty to Speed. The deal gives Phillips 35 percent ownership of ART while Eastover takes effective control of Riviere.

A second goal of Phillips is to capture as much cheap commercial real estate as possible so he can sell the properties at handsome markups to buyers funded by savings and loans who traditionally are not sophisticated commercial lenders. Noting that SM's ability to fund and then resell distressed or undervalued assets makes it the third best performing realty stock for 1981, *Realty Stock Review* asks in its February 12, 1982, issue, "Can SM Keep Up Its Torrid Sales Pace in Today's High Rate Climate?"

"Nothing's for sure, but so far, SM has been able to find buyers [for distressed real estate] where others can't," we answer. "If it continues, SM could salt away profits rapidly and build book value. That makes SM an aggressive capital gains vehicle."

Phillips needs more inventory and adds $150 million assets with two more deals. Later in February 1982, we report that SM pays nearly $4 million for a 10 percent block in $65 million asset former REIT Novus Property Co., and in April, SM pays $5 million cash plus a SM preferred to exercise its option to buy 69 percent of $98 million asset North American Mortgage from Carl Lindner's American Financial.

"We view real estate properties not as investments but as inventory," Phillips tells Southmark shareholders in his June 1982 annual report, elaborating on his grand design to remake SM into a property trading company.

"Properties are bought, managed and resold so as to maximize asset value for sharcholders—not to hold for their latent value," we report. "Since Phillips arrived, SM has acquired ownership in 14 companies and REITs." SM sells $132 million in property in 1982, earning $1.30 a share primary, and has $458 million assets in inventory: 3,900 apartments, 1,138 condos, and 1.3 million square feet of shopping centers."

In that June 1982 annual report, Phillips defends the volatility of SM's quarterly earnings—which fall 38 and 74 percent in the June and September 1982 quarters respectively—saying, "We expect fluctuations in earnings from one quarter to the next, according to the impact of individual property sales."

"All this activity has boosted EPS (earnings per share), although Wall Street experience with previous property trading companies may not engender a high price/earnings ratio," we comment in November 1982. "Shares are for further speculative gains."

Seeking more predictable earnings to smooth volatile trading profits, in October 1983 Phillips leaps into financial services with a twofer, acquiring $150 million asset credit life company Pacific Standard Life Insurance Co. for thirty million dollars of preferred stock and $450 million asset San Jacinto Savings of Houston and its eighteen branches for ninety-three million dollars cash and preferred stock. Both "should provide a base of recurring earnings," we observe.

Storm clouds appear early in 1984, when trustees of University Real Estate Trust, managed by a SM subsidiary acquired in 1983, spurn SM's acquisition offer and begin searching for a new adviser. No reason is given publicly but SM stock begins slipping from a peak around 12 and in our October 1984 review of SM's June fiscal year, we ask:

"So the big question is why SM stock acts like it has leprosy and whether the condition is curable."

Our answer: "The company has grown too fast and made too many large acquisitions to digest everything easily." Part of the stock's malaise—then selling at $7.63 or a paltry 4.7 times the $1.58 a share earnings of its June 1984 fiscal year—traces to issuance of fifteen million common shares over the past fifteen months because of conversion of convertible preferred stock issued in acquisitions. After inspecting all the pieces, we think SM common will benefit in the coming year as regularity of earnings becomes better known and upgrade shares to short-term and long-term buys.

We are dead wrong.

Southmark's four fat years are about over and the lean years beginning.

In retrospect, I can see I should have probed more deeply into why nameless "market" participants see trouble ahead for Phillips's nonstop property acquisition and trading machine.

I miss investor concern over SM's increasing reliance upon debt sold by Michael Milken's junk bond machine inside Drexel Burnham Lambert. Between 1983 and 1986, Southmark goes to the debt well at least seven times to raise about $750 million in both the United States and Europe. In May 1984, SM agrees to pay 15.25 percent interest to get $50 million of seven-year debentures out the door. And although Standard & Poor's boosts SM's subordinated debt rating from B- to B+ in May 1984, investors have continuing doubts about the Drexel connection.

[Years after the fact, in July 1991, new Southmark management in bankruptcy sues Michael Milken and others at Drexel Burnham Lambert charging they "saddled Southmark with a crushing burden of public debt, then encouraged Southmark to divert the proceeds of that debt from legitimate operating needs to highly speculative investments," according to Associated Press.]

And I underestimate the impact of new rules Congress passes in July 1984 to curb "abusive tax shelters" by requiring all syndications with over two-to-one tax write-offs to register with the IRS. "SM has never been known as a high write-off shelter syndicator," we say. "So far syndication sales are strong and SM sees an uptick in last year's [50 percent of operating] profit contributions."

SM tells a story of undiminished growth to the New York Society of Security Analysts on November 15, 1984, its first and only appearance before this prestigious group. I attend and report analyst reaction in *RSR*: "Attendance was good but it's too soon to gauge impact on stock prices ... The end of tax-loss benefits [as a component of reported earnings] improves EPS quality," we comment.

Accounting troubles surface in July 1985. Southmark "will restate its EPS downward by about 8%–10% for the two years and nine months through March 1985," we report. "Most revisions will be for its June 1984 fiscal year. The revision relates to the discount rate used to estimate value of receivables taken in property sales to syndications."

In November 1985, we see Southmark, its stock now rising to $8.38, as "growing into a major conglomerate." San Jacinto S&L, now grown to $2.4 billion assets, generates $18 million income, and Pacific Standard adds $2.5 million. But Phillips remains a deal junkie and SM plunges into hotels and casinos by buying 36 percent of Pratt Hotel Corp., owner of Atlantic City's Sands Hotel and Casino. Noting that debt and preferred stock now total a high 2.6 times $387 million equity, we caution that while "real estate markets have favored this real estate [trading] strategy for the past five years, lower inflation ahead may require some corrections to strategy."

The S&L industry continues to deteriorate, and in October 1986, Congress mandates strict controls on the use of syndication tax shelters, effectively ending growth for realty syndications, now about half of SM's operating income. Our December 1986 annual SM review is headlined: "Southmark Corp. Hits Bumps on the Road."

"It's been a wild ride since 1985," we report. "SM rose from $8.38 a year ago to touch $14 [where its $540 million market value trails only two other realty companies including office giant Rockefeller Center Properties], then fell all the way back to $8.75 as concerns over impact of tax reform and a regulatory slap at its Houston-based S&L subsidiary hurt."

Federal regulators, worrying about realty lending by Sun Belt S&Ls, "require SM to sign an interim operating agreement restricting San

Jacinto's commercial real estate lending to syndications and ... requiring a 43% reduction in real estate assets by June 1987." Regulators also bar San Jacinto from paying dividends to parent SM, cutting off [crucial internal] cash flow to pay dividends on SM's burgeoning preferred stock obligations. As result, SM signals it may sell San Jacinto." We rate the stock B (above average) but make no further advice to subscribers.

In 1987 and 1988, we are standoffish in our annual Southmark reviews of SM's June fiscal years, finding the company's earnings flagging, debt rising, and liquidity falling. In December 1988, SM tells the market that liquidity is perilously low after a $200 million sale of its Integon Insurance subsidiary blows up "because insurance regulators turned down a deal nearly 100% leveraged with junk bonds," we report in advising a sell. Worse, we report that SM directors must decide whether to extend or foreclose on a $10 million margin loan, secured by SM and other stock, the company made to Phillips and Friedman a year earlier. SM stock is trading at $1.75, down 62 percent for the year, and the worst performer among all realty stocks.

In January 1989, SM directors force Phillips and Friedman to resign from a company "whose cash flow has dried up. Suspicion that shaky assets may have been swept under the rug ... have left SM almost incapable of selling assets to ease its cash bind," *RSR* reports that month. SM directors agree to cancel SM's management agreement for seven REITs and companies then managed by Southmark, returning control of these entities to Phillips and Friedman. Southmark bankruptcy examiner Neal Batson later terms this an "enormous windfall" (Batson, Examiner's Perspective, 1990. 7)

In May 1989, Southmark announces a $1.1 billion loss for its March quarter, including an $829 million addition to loan loss reserves, the largest loss ever for a realty company until that time, washing away the

$1 billion Southmark spends over eight years amassing control of nearly fifty REITs and real estate entities.

Southmark takes the $1 billion earning's hit because a new auditor, hired by new management after the January 1989 shakeup, applies more stringent real estate valuation methods to reflect a worsening real estate recession and new Southmark management's inability to close several significant pending real estate sales.

"Since 1982, Southmak has recorded total earnings of $634 million," bankruptcy examiner Neal Batson later commented. "All of these were erased by the $1 billion write-down in 1989...the provision for losses of $742 million in Southmark alone [excluding subsidiaries]...was greater than its total reported profits since 1982." (Batson, Examiner's Perspective, 1990. 2, 3)

Southmark files for bankruptcy in July 1989, the largest real estate bankruptcy of the decade and rivaling only the Texaco bankruptcy in size to that time. The news devastates Southmark's 30,000 employees.

"The story of Southmark's rise and fall involved its ability to create the illusion of success and prosperity that deceived the investing public with a self-portrait of ever increasing profits, assets and net worth. That its 'ever increasing' profits, assets and net worth were illusory cannot seriously be debated," bankruptcy examiner Neal Batson summarized his inquiry. (Batson, Examiner's Perspective, 1990. 5)

Court-appointed examiner Neal Batson in July 1990 counts "approximately 550 direct and indirect, active and inactive subsidiaries and approximately 350 affiliated entities, which include numerous public and private real estate investment partnerships" that raised an estimated $950 million from investrors. (Batson, Final report, 1990. 3, 15) [SM followed the common realty practice of creating a separate subsidiary corporation for each property owned.] Batson explains how these off-balance sheet realty syndications aided Southmark's ambitious sales program in these words:

"Typically Southmark sold real estate properties to the syndicated limited partnerships [mostly formed before Southmark acquired management control] at a price significantly above the original cost of the properties. This practice enabled Southmark to record huge paper gains from the sales. As part of the consideration the partnership would issue a purchase money note to Southmark generally representing greater than 90% financing. The note would generate interest at above-market rates, thereby enabling Southmark to record additional earnings." (Batson, Examiner's Perspective, 1990. 29)

"…[I]n the syndication sales…the limited partnerships paid little cash and issued purchase money notes, generally representing 80% to 90% financing…With the syndication sales, Southmark was able to command the price for the property sold since the transaction was 'arms length' in name only. On both sides of the transactions, Southmark was the seller as well as the sponsor, de facto general partner and manager of the syndicated partnerships that purchased the properties…to the extent that payments were made on the mortgages, such payments would be funded by Southmark through increasing advances to the partnerships." (Batson, Examiner's Perspective, 1990. 84)

Batson asserts that these practices produced "illusory sales, phantom profits" ultimately resulting in "a sea of red ink." (Batson, Final Report, 1990. 54)

Phillips and Friedman "emphatically" deny Batson's allegations and say his report "contains material factual errors, unsubstantiated allegations, and misleading innuendoes," reports the *Wall Street Journal*. But the court accepts Batson's report for filing.

During its run in the sun from 1985 to 1988, SM reports selling about $2.8 billion in real estate properties for trading profits, about

27% of which were sales to realty syndications. (Batson, Examiner's Perspective, 1990. 83) The market turns up its nose at those gains. Pressured by the gathering storm of a deep realty recession, those profits are not enough to bring SM safely to shore.

The two institutions Southmark bought in 1983 to stabilize earnings sputter, turn unprofitable and ultimately are seized. San Jacinto savings is hurt when Congress in August 1989 overhauls federal S&L governance and regulators mandate major changes in S&L accounting. Finally, on the last day of November 1990, federal regulators seize $3.25 billion San Jacinto S&L, the last major S&L to fall to regulators. Pacific Standard Life Insurance Co., the second "stabilizing" institution, is placed under conservatrorship by California regulators late in 1989. During Southmark's ownership both become sinkholes for corporate cash to maintain required regulatory capital, San Jacinto to the tune of $377 million cash drain and Pacific Standard $128 million cash drain. (Batson, Examiner's Perspective, 1990. 48, 57) The $505 million total is cash Southmark could not spare.

Southmark stock ends the 1980s trading at eleven-cents a share.

Under Phillips's tutelage, Southmark loses a compounded 8.1 percent annually during the eight years through 1988. That annual loss falls to -31 percent if the bankruptcy year of 1989 is added to Phillips's watch.

Who or what kills Southmark? A vicious real estate recession and federal efforts to stamp out abusive tax shelter syndications obviously play major roles. But the management of any company is charged with building an enterprise able to withstand cyclical and legal shocks, and Southmark management relied far too heavily on two at-risk business lines: syndication sales and real estate trading. Harsh but true, SM management gets a failing grade. Balancing the two time periods measured above gives:

Phillips's final score: 1 + 1 = (3).

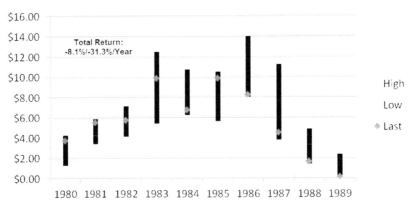

Exhibit 19.5: Southmark Corp.(N: SM)
Annual Stock Prices 1980 - 1988-89

The remnants of those seven REITs transitioned to Phillips in 1989 remain as the most visible denouement of the Southmark story. Three survive in 2015 in the Phillips orbit and trade on major securities exchanges. One is the $1.08 billion asset American Realty Investors, Inc. (NYSE: ARL), which is 84.1 percent owned by entities controlled by Gene E. Phillips Children's Trust. American Realty in turn owns 80.9 percent of Transcontinental Realty Investors, Inc. (NYSE: TCI), which owns 81.1 percent of Income Opportunity Realty Investors, Inc. (NYSE MKT: IOT). ARL's financial statements consolidate those two subsidiaries for both book and tax purposes.

The corporate coziness continues in management: Most ARL directors and officers also hold the same positions for TCI and IOT. "We have historically engaged in and will continue to engage in certain business transactions with related parties," says ARL's 2014 annual Form 10-K report to the SEC.

This interrelated trio owns at the end of September 2015 a $989 million diversified portfolio, divided 83 percent operating properties; 12 percent net loans receivable, 97 percent at face from related parties; and 5 percent investment in unconsolidated subsidiaries and receivable from a related party. Operating properties include 7,511 apartments, mostly in the Southwest, at cost of approximately $71,800 per unit and about 95 percent occupied at an average annual rent of about $10.19 per square foot; 2.2 million square feet of commercial properties plus a golf course in St. Thomas, US Virgin Islands; and 4,000 acres of land for development costing about $39,500 per acre. "We intend to pursue higher risk, higher reward investments," states ARL's 2014 10-K.

ARL's $790.4 million debt is 4.98 times $158.7 million net equity after preferred stock, a level significantly higher than most REITs in 2015. ARL's continuing operations lost 71 cents per share in 2014 after a $1.39 depreciation charge but had $2.99 per share gains on property sales and related tax benefits put ARL $2.28 a share into the black. ARL lost another $0.22 a share in the first nine months of 2015.

ARL reports $10.23 a share net book value at September 2015, this value rising to an adjusted $19.58 when real estate depreciation is added back. ARL stock ended 2014 trading at $5.46 and traded at about $5.00 in mid-2015 until a 40% surge on light volume in August 2015 lifted quotes to $7.27 a share. This price represents a 63 percent discount to adjusted book value.

ARL and its two subsidiaries are advised by an entity named Pillar Income Asset Management, Inc., owned after several corporate layers 100 percent by a trust for the children of Gene E. Phillips. "Mr. Phillips is not an officer or director of Pillar ... nor is he a trustee of the Trust," state proxy materials for the American and Transcontinental annual meetings December 9, 2014. "Mr. Phillips does serve as a representative of the Trust and is involved in daily consultation with the officers of Pillar and has significant influence over the conduct of Pillar's business ..."

This Alice-in-Wonderland situation should end, with the three entities either going private, merging, or taking separate paths. Phillips tells me in July 2015 that the trio has tried to merge, only to be thwarted by voluminous SEC staff comments. Perhaps, just perhaps, common sense will prevail sometime.

This trio of companies is likely to continue to be super-cheap as long as the interlocking ownership and what I view as the Phillips discount hangs over them. Still on the outs with media, regulators, and most institutional investors, Phillips, now aged seventy-seven, stands as the stock market's Joe Btfsplk, the trader-man with a permanent dark cloud hanging over his head in cartoonist Al Capp's legendary rendition of unbroken gloom. So for this trio, it all comes back to our 1984 question: "Why does the stock act like it has leprosy, and is the condition curable?"

For ARL and its subs, property trading remains a focus judging from its 2014 Form 10-K statement that "We are an active buyer and seller of real estate and during 2014 we acquired $48.6 million and sold $142.5 million of land and income producing properties." Is ARL stock a bargain? Not so long as those 1980s trader genes remain alive and well. The stock market dislikes realty trading profits, both in the 1980s and in 2015.

THE BIGGEST LOSERS

The 100 percent loss sustained by Southmark shareholders is matched by shareholders of a dozen REITs. Lawyer Harvey Miller's 1975 advice (chapter 15, "The Seminar") that most mortgage trusts should seriously consider filing for bankruptcy to preserve shareholders' equity plays out in slow motion. Mortgage trusts do not dive into the bankruptcy tank all at once because REIT trustees are understandably wary of the uncertain outcomes and uncontrollable costs of bankruptcy. But ultimately thirteen trusts plunge into the tank like forlorn leaves twisting in autumnal winds, one by one for varying reasons. All but two lend money for short-term construction and development mortgages.

This baker's dozen of REIT bankruptcies strings out over six and a half years, from March 1974 through October 1980. This slow-motion collapse of the mortgage REITs offers a caution to investors, whose general optimism often impels them to rush into sectors after the first few signs of distress. Investors must use patience and caution before they assume the market has sounded an all-clear.

The number of REIT bankruptcies equates to about 10 percent of the 131 REITs operating at the peak of the craze, but that percentage fails to convey the story by trust types.

Short-term mortgage trusts see eleven or 18.6 percent of their fifty-nine brethren operating at December 1974 subsequently fall into bankruptcy. In contrast, bankruptcy claims only 2.3 and 3.4 percent of forty-three equity trusts and twenty-nine long-term mortgage trusts respectively.

In total, these thirteen trusts hold $1.86 billion of assets ($5.8 billion in 2015 dollars) when they seek court protection. Southmark's July 1989 bankruptcy adds another $1 billion to this total ($2 billion in 2015 dollars).

Here for the record is the futility list of bankruptcy filings by mortgage REITs of that era and the ultimate outcome of each:

All but one trust disappear from the investment scene. The vanished include:

Continental Mortgage, a REIT granddaddy, is ultimately merged into a Michigan flat glass manufacturer to use its considerable tax-loss carry-forwards.

Chase Manhattan Trust liquidates its assets to various buyers (see Palmas del Mar in chapter 15, "The Seminar") and is acquired by conglomerate Fuqua Industries in 1984.

Both National Mortgage and First Virginia are acquired by Mississippi investor Leland Speed, who merges them into 2015's EastGroup Properties and Parkway Properties (chapter 20, "The Biggest Winners").

Only one of these entities ever becomes an investible entity again. That standout exception is Great American M&I, taken over by "grave dancer" investor Sam Zell and his partner in 1981. His deft strategic touch harvests major rewards for GAMI holders. How Zell's rescue of GAMI helps launch Zell into REIT sainthood is told in the next chapter.

TABLE 19.1: BANKRUPTCY FILINGS BY 1970-ERA MORTGAGE REITS

Trust (New Name)	Ch. XI Filed	Assets (Mil.$)	Outcome
Short-Term Mortgage Trusts			
Associated Mtg. Inv.	3/15/74	$56.1	Liquidated
Chase Man. M&R (Triton)	2/22/79	265.3	Acq.:Fuqua Ind.
Citizens Mtg. Inv. Tr.	10/5/78	66.5	Liquidated
Colwell Mtg. (CMT Invest.)	2/21/78	100.0	Control by Deltec
Continental Mtg. Inv.	3/8/76	522.6	Merged: Glass co.
Dominion M& R	6/27/77	33.9	Acq.: Southmark
Fidelity Mtg. (Lifetime)	1/30/75	206.7	Property corp.
Great Amer. Mgt.&Inv.	3/25/77	280.0	Acq.:Zell entity
Guardian Mtg. (Florida Cos.)	3/9/78	204.3	Acq.: Fairfield C.
Justice (Metroplex/Vista)	12/29/77	20.4	Acq.:Lomas&Net
National Mtg. Fund (STM)	6/30/76	30.6	Acq.: Eastover
Equity and Intermediate-Term Mortgage Trusts			
NJB Prime Inv. (Vyquest)	9/4/78	44.2	Acq. hotel co.
First Virginia (Nova Rl.)	10/30/80	29.5	Acq.:Parkway
Total Assets		**$1,860.1**	

Source: *Realty Trust/Stock Review*, various dates.

Chapter 20
THE BIGGEST WINNERS

Lest you conclude from the preceding chapter that cleaning up the 1970s REIT mess was a crap shoot with the odds on the downside, this chapter recounts notable high spots of the REIT renaissance, strategies that put outsized gains into investors' pockets, and a couple of unlikely tenders producing spectacular gains when stock market stars align.

Keep in mind we are judging each Reit catcher by total returns they produce for shareholders, not how well they line their own pockets as takeover artists.

We assume they hope to achieve one plus one—money plus management—equals three or four or, if things go really well, five in total return for long-suffering shareholders. To eliminate personal bias, I measure the Reit catchers against an objective total return yardstick over their time in charge.

We begin our stories far from Wall Street, in the offices of a modest stockbroker in Jackson, Mississippi, the unlikeliest spot of all to launch a REIT comeback.

THE CONSOLIDATOR

Leland Speed, a forty-three-year-old stockbroker in his father's Jackson, Mississippi, firm of Leland Speed, Mounger & Bartlett, knows nothing about REITs in the summer of 1975 when Jackson banker Bill Watson shows him the quarterly financial statement for First Commerce Realty Trust of New Orleans and asks: "What's wrong with this company?"

First Commerce stock is then trading over-the-counter (OTC) at the unloved price of about $7 a share or about one-third of its $21-a-share stated book value.

A real estate dabbler who's built a few small warehouses and retail properties, Speed is intrigued enough by the valuation disparity to begin buying the stock alongside major client John Head, chief investment officer at Southern Farm Bureau Casualty Insurance Company.

First Commerce stock promptly does a 45 percent swan-dive to $3.75 a share as a posted $2.40 dividend melts, first to a $1.20 rate and then to a $0.17 special payout with faint hope for more in the future.

When the stated book value shrinks by 5 percent to $19.98 a share by year-end 1975, Speed and his client buy more in an illiquid market until they amass 191,000 shares or about 18.6 percent of the company by early 1978. By this time, their investment nears $1 million, averaging about $5 a share.

Staring at losses and no immediate hope for recovery, Speed takes action in the fall of 1975. He rings up First Commerce Bank president Jimmy Jones, whom he later learns has already accepted a position with a Houston bank, and using the Southern Farm Bureau muscle, wangles an appointment. Speed tells him, "Look, this thing hasn't worked out as expected. We are far and away the largest shareholders and hard decisions need to be made. It's better if the largest shareholders take the lead on making these decisions because management has only a very small stock interest. We'll take this thing off your hands, move it out of town, give it a new name, and make those tough decisions without any reflection on the bank."

Jones accepts and offers three board seats, which Speed fills with himself and two prominent businessmen, a Jackson realty developer and a lawyer specializing in limited partnerships. Two holdover members continue on the company's board.

"It took us three years to get things right. The financial statements didn't show that the trust had $50 million of unfunded loan commitments and a bank line with twenty-one banks," recalls Speed. "It took the better part of three years to work our way out of the debt that this entailed. And it seemed to take forever to persuade the banks that the only way they would get their money back was to swap assets. Finally we got down to $5.2 million of bad assets, and I had made a deal with Jones's successor to take back $5 million, and First Commerce Bank took them back." First Commerce Realty repaid its last bank debt April 28, 1978, one of the first troubled REITs to escape debt purgatory.

Speed's group then takes full control, and true to his word, Speed moves the trust to Jackson on June 1, 1978, and changes its name to Eastover Corporation, a name borrowed from a prestigious residential neighborhood Speed had developed with his father in Jackson.

Voila! Speed takes control of a troubled REIT without much fuss and muss and sets about getting out of the hole.

"Shares are a speculation on a more aggressive workout and deals under new management," we opine on July 14, 1978.

But all is not wine and roses. "We had $10 million net assets after mortgage debt but nearly 80 percent were not accruing interest on their loans and over two-thirds were land loans," recalls Speed. "We set up shop in the cheapest space we could find—cost us $500 a month—and set out to find ways to use our $10 million of net operating tax loss carry-forwards (NOLs), which can be used to offset future income.

"It was the Jimmy Carter years, and inflation was sky high, hitting 12 or 13 percent," says Speed. "People wanted out of paper and into hard assets. That environment allowed us to sell almost anything and raise cash so we could start looking for our next targets. We made it very clear we were motivated sellers, and we were able to convert assets into cash and earning loans at fifty-cents on the dollar."

Setting out to put the cash to best use, Speed is teased "to do something creative" by investment banker Bill Smith of Paine Webber Jackson & Curtis over a drink on Peacock Alley at Manhattan's Waldorf Astoria Hotel. The "something" includes a careful look at ICM Realty, a land leaseback trust sponsored by Investors Central Management Corporation, a New York mortgage investor.

Land leasebacks are among the most exotic and potentially toxic real estate investment legal structures. Under ICM's format, the trust buys land beneath an office building or shopping center and leases the land back to the building owner, typically for fifty years or more, for an annual land rent. But ICM inserts a kicker, giving the trust an open-end override on all property rents above predetermined minimums.

Although ICM presents itself as a conservative trust, a closer look at its balance sheet reveals higher hidden leverage. ICM's formal balance sheet shows debt of $31 million or a low 0.7 times $45.5 million equity. But ICM's leasebacks are subordinated to about $250 million prior mortgage debt, giving the trust breathtaking off-balance sheet leverage.

"It was a time when everyone wanted leverage since inflation was ramping up," says Speed, "and ICM had leverage." But ICM is a stretch, being nearly four times bigger than Eastover with $28.2 million market value and still paying an annual dividend. More problematically, 57 percent of its $95 million assets earn little or no income.

But Speed and Eastover cannot stalk such prey without giving notice to the market of their actions. Federal securities laws require any investor buying over 5 percent of outstanding shares in a public company to file a Form 13-D disclosing the number of shares owned, the source of funds, and intentions for their block holding. REIT block buyers begin proliferating, and in August 1978, *Realty Stock Review* publishes its first listing of 13-D block buyers, just as Speed begins his pursuit of ICM. Our tally is short, listing only sixteen blocks valued at slightly over $10 million, and the Speed/Eastover purchases, not yet up to 5 percent, don't make the list.

Exhibit 20.1: EastGroup Properties (EGP)
Annual Stock Prices 1978 - 1989

In Jackson, using $2.1 million of its new cash hoard, Speed-helmed Eastover buys 247,000 shares or 8.2 percent of ICM on November 20, 1978, at about $8.50 per share and pays a visit to Arthur W. Viner, ICM's organizer and manager. "He wasn't happy to see me," recalls Speed.

About the same time Speed is called by Buffalo stockbroker Brent D. Baird of the Trubee Collins firm, who by April 1978 owns blocks in six—count 'em, *six*—tiny mortgage REITs, the most important being Texas First Mortgage, later renamed Parkway Properties.

Speed and Baird hit it off famously at their first luncheon. Afterward, they rough out terms of a partnership, pooling their resources to buy large and perhaps controlling blocks in struggling mortgage REITs.

Both are so excited they wonder what could go wrong and decide to let the partnership documents cool for thirty days before giving a final

"Go." Within two weeks, both are still so a-tingle they pull the rip cord and affirm their deal.

Over the next four years, through the end of 1982, they accumulate control blocks in five more REITs with $171 million assets.

Speed presses his pursuit of ICM Realty independently and reaches 25 percent by February 1980, at which time the ICM board grants him three seats and Speed becomes chairman. ICM Realty is renamed EastGroup Properties (EGP) in May 1983 and forms the base for a rejuvenated equity REIT taking shape in Speed's mind.

Operations of all controlled trusts are moved to Jackson, but the trusts are operated separately to preserve their loss carry-forwards, aggregating about $35 million. From his lawyers, Speed learns that companies with past profits can be consolidated into loss companies and merges a mixed-use development near Sugar Land, Texas, into his companies. The result is a big refund check from Uncle Sam and ownership of a development that earns $17 million upon completion during a very favorable Houston economic environment.

Ultimately Speed acquires eleven companies and REITs and merges them into either Parkway or EastGroup, the survivors. David Hoster is recruited from a smaller acquired trust to run EastGroup in 1983 and has done so ever since. Hoster guides EGP into specializing in Southern transportation-driven industrial markets. "I finally found a property type I love," enthuses eighty-two-year-old Speed. "They aren't building any new airports anymore." Now sixty-eight, Hoster will take over Speed's post as EastGroup chairman at the end of 2015.

Under Speed's tutelage, EastGroup and its predecessors, ICM Realty and Eastover Corporation, generate 15.3 percent compounded total return for EGP investors over ten years through 1989, ending the decade trading over $20 a share. EGP's strong performance trails the Standard & Poor's 500 total return of 17.6 percent during this period.

Speed's final score: 1 + 1 = +3.

Under Speed and Hoster, EastGroup keeps the good results rolling into the 1990s and through 2014, providing investors with stunning total returns since the modern REIT era dawned in 1991 and besting Warren Buffett's Berkshire Hathaway over the twenty-three years through 2014. The numbers are as follows. EastGroup's 15.5 percent compound annual return beats Berkshire by 0.5 percent, the NAREIT Equity Index by 3.9 percent, and the Standard & Poor's 500 by 5.1 percent. Fancy stepping for a trust built by stitching together a hodgepodge of struggling or busted REITs.

THE GRAVE DANCER

Sam Zell proclaims himself "The Grave Dancer" in a winter 1976 article in the unaffiliated professional journal *Real Estate Review*, a bold and shocking claim at a time when only a few real estate cognoscenti know his name.

"A review of the current list of best-selling fiction reveals a novel that needs to be written," he begins his iconoclastic article. "It would be a story of an individual or organization immersed in resurrecting the real estate corpses created by the greatest explosion of real estate lending and building in this nation's history."

Remember, Zell pens his treatise at the depths of the mid-1970s real estate recession cum depression when many realty operatives think the sky has already fallen. He continues:

> "Unfortunately this new loosening of funds was accompanied by the simultaneous blossoming of the real estate investment trust as a construction lender. When the trust form was created by Congress in 1960, its primary focus was long-term ownership [of commercial properties]. In the late 1960s however, many REITs shifted their sights to short-term construction lending.

"Neither Wall Street nor the general investing public possessed a clear understanding of the difference between an equity trust that owned real estate on a long-term basis and a short-term trust in the high-risk business of financing construction. Neither recognized that participation in the construction lending business requires much greater supervision than other types of real estate investment." (Zell, 1976. No page)

Zell then outlines the essential goal of an investor seeking to profit from the mortgage trust calamity:

"A more realistic incentive to the distressed property investor is the prospect of long-term growth in asset—'brick and mortar'—value. Given the overbuilding of 1970–1974 … another expansionary period in real estate construction in the near future is not likely. Thus an investor in a bailout situation must be asset-oriented … If these assumptions are valid, the intrinsic value of brick-and-mortar in place, well-designed and well-maintained, will grow substantially.

"The grave dance relies on the theory that a major increase in rents is probable because of a significant shift in the demand-supply equation for real estate.

"Grave dancing is an art that has many potential benefits," Zell concludes. "But one must be careful while prancing around not to fall into the open pit and join the cadaver. There is often a thin line between the dancer and the danced upon." (Zell, 1976. No page)

At the time, Zell is a mere thirty-five years old but has been running

Equity Financial and Management Company of Chicago with partner Robert Lurie for nearly a decade. His tender age belies years of bare-knuckles real estate experience.

While an undergrad at the University of Michigan, Zell pitches the developer of an eighteen-unit student housing apartment to give him and a friend free apartments if they manage the project. The developer accepts, and by graduation, Sam and two friends are managing two hundred apartments. After winning his law degree in 1966, Zell sells his business, which by then includes three thousand units under management, and returns to his native Chicago. Soon thereafter, he starts an investment firm. Bob Lurie, who works for him at Michigan, joins him in 1969.

"When I was in school, they wrote on the blackboard in big bold letters—*supply* and *demand*," Zell frequently regales audiences. "It is the most important lesson I ever learned, and we disregard it at our peril." In 1976, his confidence in a real estate revival is rooted in visualizing how supply and demand dynamics will transform a moribund market.

Zell's article captures wide attention and among those intrigued is one Ken Campbell, editor and publisher of *Realty Trust Review* in New York City. I sponsor occasional conferences for real estate and Wall Street professionals and invite Zell to present at our next conference, figuring his startling *nom de guerre* may bring in additional paying customers.

Zell arrives at the appointed time wearing a sports shirt open almost to his belt buckle, his bare chest adorned by an amulet around his neck, and accompanied by two comely attendants. It is most definitely not what my preppie Wall Street professional attendees expect.

But Zell talks gut-level truth with a raspy voice commanding attention, never sugarcoats risks, and opens his fertile mind to questioners. Attendees listen spellbound and walk away with useable ideas for approaching the downtrodden REIT stocks plus the perception that dress isn't all that important in a world of ideas.

The only negative is that Zell is a private market guy, holds the inner workings of deals close to his bosom, and has no yen to become corporate chieftain of a public real estate company.

Or so I think.

About that time, and unstated during Zell's conference gig, is Zell and Lurie's concern that real estate conditions are changing for the worse. The familiar fixed-rate, twenty-five-year mortgage is going the way of horse-drawn carriages, and lenders are demanding—horrors—a piece of the equity action. They vow to diversify ASAP.

Fast-forward to a day in November 1980 when Zell reads a *Wall Street Journal* piece saying Congress is about to pass legislation giving former REITs up to eight years, versus only five years before, to apply income against net operating loss carryovers, or NOLs. The change effectively gives trusts that have abandoned REIT status three more years to use their NOLs. Most readers shrug off the obscure news item, but for tax-oriented Zell, it is a memorable "Wow" moment.

Every real estate operative knows after one day on the job that taxes are the second most important thing in real estate behind a building's location and quality. A dollar saved or postponed in taxes is a dollar earned in their minds, even if accountants don't exactly see reality that way.

Zell starts scanning stock market lists and marks down a few names with hefty NOLs. After a few buys in some smaller public REITs that turn into dead ends, Zell finally settles upon Great American Management and Investments (GAMI), a once high-flying mortgage REIT so busted it is already in and out of bankruptcy by April 1979. That fact appeals to Zell's lawyerly instincts because the bankruptcy trip cleanses claims against GAMI from banks and creditors.

Better, GAMI owns 6,678 foreclosed garden apartments and nearly 3,000 hotel rooms. "They were not great properties but could be sold quickly," recalls Zell.

There's only one problem: Manhattan hedge fund and distressed debt specialist Morgens/Waterfall is already sitting on this turkey, buying a 13.7 percent piece of GAMI in April 1979.

Undeterred, Zell and Lurie, operating as SZRL Investments, begin buying GAMI stock.

By September 1980, Zell and Lurie own 14 percent of GAMI while their hedge fund competitor is now up to nearly 19 percent. Their competitive buying pushes GAMI's stock price from around $5 to $8.25 a share.

In December 1980, both the hedge fund and Zell take GAMI board seats. GAMI stock is a "sophisticated play on Sunbelt realty with high-leveraged fixed-rate Chapter XI plan debt," we opine.

By spring 1981, Morgens/Waterfall runs its stake to 27.5 percent while SZRL is close behind at 22.7 percent.

In September 1981, we at *RSR* confirm the two block buyers take joint control and seek to repay $124 million Chapter XI debt at about seventy-cents on the dollar. Most banks take the haircut, and GAMI cuts debt to $96 million by early December 1982, reducing the debt load to 1.1 times its $88 million equity.

But working in harness doesn't suit either party, and late in December 1982, we report that SZRL takes full control. "Shares are for further speculative recovery," *RSR* observes, noting that GAMI continues to sell properties to repay debt.

Did the Morgens/Waterfall exit result from a tense standoff between the former partners? During this period, I meet several times with Edwin Morgens and Bruce Waterfall and know them as tough negotiators, never giving an inch and never tipping their hands.

Did the partners split after a tense duel? Zell won't tell. "They were stock pickers and we were real estate operators," he says simply.

"Shares are for further speculative recovery," we advise, happy a single management team is now running GAMI.

Once in control, Zell starts selling those apartments and hotels at the highest prices he can get, taking back debt from buyers and eventually building a $227 million book of receivables, all consistent with the earlier plan to diversify away from real estate. The plan works, and by 1985, the Zell/Lurie-led GAMI buys industrial companies under arrangements in which GAMI funds 100 percent of the purchase price for 80 percent ownership and a preferential prime-plus-2-percent return on its investment. The deals let GAMI apply 80 percent of income against its nearly $120 million tax losses.

Industrial companies run the gamut: oil field tools, agricultural chemicals, plumbing and metering products, ceramic insulators, and a Florida savings and loan. Some deals work out, some don't, but GAMI slices its NOLs in half to $59 million by the end of its July 1985 fiscal year.

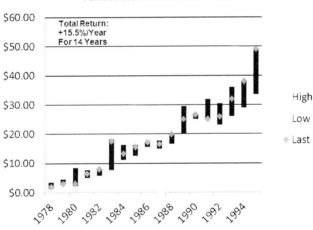

Exhibit 20.2: Great American M&I (O: GAMI)
Annual Stock Prices 1978 - 1995

"GAMI seeks to build upon a large real estate asset base to make selected acquisitions with risk-oriented, entrepreneurial partners who are highly incented to produce longer-term profits and use GAMI's tax-losses," we comment in December 1985.

Notwithstanding the sophisticated game plan and generally good execution, we delist GAMI from *RSR* in 1986. Zell keeps the public entity going until all tax-losses are used and then takes it private in April 1996 at $50 a share.

Under Zell's maiden turn as a public company exec, GAMI returns 15.5 percent annual total return in the over-the-counter market shares for holders over Zell's fourteen years of stewardship through 1995. Shares Zell started buying at about $5 a share end that period at $50. Notwithstanding the strong showing, GAMI shares lag slightly behind the 15.9 percent annual gain for the Standard & Poor's 500. Zell's astute ability to find ways to use net operating tax loss carry-forwards (NOLs) is exemplary.

Zell's final score: 1 + 1 = +4.

Zell learns his public company lessons well, and, after Robert Lurie's untimely death in 1990, returns in the early 1990s as CEO and major backer of three newly minted NYSE-listed REITs: Equity Residential Properties (symbol EQR), a $30 billion equity market value apartment trust in 2015; Equity LifeStyle Properties (ELS), a $5 billion equity market value manufactured-home community REIT; and Equity Office Properties (EOP), an office operator. The $39 billion sale of EOP in February 2007 marks the peak of the early 2000s bull market. That prescient sale establishes Zell's reputation as the consummate property seller of all time.

But to me, Zell's early strategic vision producing extraordinary returns for GAMI shareholders in the 1980s marks him as an executive wholly on the side of individual shareholders, of whom he is the largest. His net worth stands at a reported $5 billion in 2015.

When I confront Zell with my calculation that he and his partner earn $50 million in their GAMI caper, he smiles. "More."

HARPER'S WEEK

Only one pension fund takes full control of a REIT: Bouverie Properties, Inc., affiliate of Britain's National Coal Board pension plan, captures Continental Illinois Properties (CIE), property REIT sponsored by the Chicago bank of the same first two names, with a $30 a share tender offer in June 1979.

This mountaintop moment happens only because James D. Harper Jr., CIE's founder and president, busts his tail—and saves his life in the doing—cementing not one but two tender offers for the two REITs he pilots in a hectic five-day stretch.

Originally a Los Angeles commercial banker, Harper breaks away from banking to found an independent short-term mortgage trust named Mortgage Investment Group or MIG in April 1969, which raises $49.6 million by selling 2.48 million shares at $20 a share. By 1971, commercial banks are crowding into mortgage REITs; Harper engineers acquisition of MIG by top-tier Continental Illinois Bank of Chicago, and the trust is rechristened Continental Illinois Realty. Late in 1971, he creates a companion equity and long-term mortgage trust, Continental Illinois Properties, which raises $100 million by selling 4 million shares at $25 to the public.

Installed as an executive of the bank's holding company, ConIll Corp., Harper splits time between offices in Chicago and Los Angeles.

In mid-May 1979, Harper is visited in his Los Angeles office by a lawyer for a major law firm who informs him politely that two Saudi Arabian sheiks, each with $125 million on deposit with Citibank in New York City, are preparing to offer $25 per share or $100 million for all CIE shares, then selling at about $17 a share.

Harper listens carefully and thanks the lawyer for coming by but does not say yea or nay to the proposed offer.

At a hastily assembled board meeting attended by most trustees by phone, trustees review the offer and its planned timing and conclude they have no obligation to recommend any action to shareholders. At the conclusion, Harper tells them, "I think I'd better get my ass to London and see if we can get a better offer." He is on a jet within hours.

In London the following morning, still jet-lagged and groggy from sleep lost during the overnight flight, he meets with Hugh Jenkins and Wendy Luscombe, principal officers of the British Coal Board, a major United Kingdom pension plan. He gives them a current prospectus covering CIE shares, says the trust has been given notice of a proposed tender, but is careful not to "puff" the stock. Jenkins and Luscombe say they will take the matter under advisement and Harper heads for Heathrow Airport and a return flight.

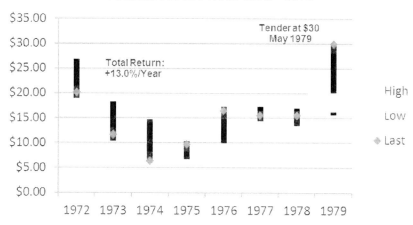

Exhibit 20.3: Continental Illinois Prop. (N: CIE) Annual Stock Prices 1972 - 1979

Within days, Brabant Inc., the entity representing the Saudi investors, begins its promised tender at $25.

On Monday, May 21, 1979, Hugh Jenkins and the Coal Board chairman arrive at Harper's Chicago office and notify him they are beginning an offer at $30 a share via their subsidiary Bouverie Properties

Inc. Almost immediately, investors hop on this higher bid, and within days, it's clear that the Coal Board will win control of CIE.

Under Harper's leadership, CIE returns 47.4 percent annual total return for the three and one-half years from 1976 through the June 1979 completion of the tender offer for CIE. Backing up the clock a bit to the end of 1973, Harper's performance yields a still-hardy 13.0 percent for six and one-half years. For a good job blended over both short and longer terms in extracting maximum value for CIE investors, I say:

Harper's final score for CIE: 1 + 1 = +3.

As this heated market drama unfolds, Harper is notified on Wednesday, May 23, at his Chicago office that William Lyon, a private Southern California homebuilder, is offering $10 a share for Continental Illinois Realty (CIR), the short-term mortgage REIT also headed by Harper. The bid more than doubles CIR's market price.

But it's not enough to Harper because he knows something hidden from public shareholders. Here is how we describe the situation in the June 22, 1979, issue of *Realty Trust Review*:

> "The trust held warrants, acquired in a 1972 financing, to buy 20% of privately held Lyon at $625/sh. Since then, Lyon was phenomenally successful and book value zoomed to $48,900/sh. by March 1979, before giving effect to the warrants. In 1977, Lyon began negotiating to repurchase the warrants and finally offered $7.3 million plus 20% of after-tax profits for three years (a package estimated to be worth $12 million or over $4.25 per CIR share). When CIR rejected this offer, Lyon moved to buy the entire trust which had book value of $5.71/sh. In other words, CIR had unique value for Lyon Co. alone.

"We detail this story because CIR very carefully had never disclosed the warrants' potential value, even while it negotiated with Lyon. Since Lyon was a private company, security analysts had no way of evaluating the warrants. All this raises the intriguing question:

"How many more goodies are carefully squirreled away in REITs?

"Right now the market is willing to believe there are many others but we advise you to be cautious. Continental Illinois Realty was uniquely aggressive with some close ties to a few borrowers; very few other trusts followed this pattern."

Exhibit 20.4: Continental Illinois Realty (N: CIR)
Annual Stock Prices 1971 - 1979

Lyon quickly raises his bid to $11 per CIR share, giving holders a 138 percent premium over the $4.63 price at which CIR traded before the fireworks explode.

Under Harper's leadership, CIR returns 81.1 percent annual total return for the three and one-half years from 1976 through the June 1979 tender offer. But since CIR shares were originally sold at $20, the $11 tender is only a half-loaf outcome. CIR's return for the six and one-half years beginning in 1973 is a pedestrian 4.9 percent. Considering that Harper's work salvages the highest recovery for any short-term mortgage trust, I come up with:

Harper's final score for CIR: 1 + 1 = +2.

Juggling *two* stock tenders keeps Harper sequestered in his Chicago office for the rest of that frenzied week, preventing him from departing on Friday evening for a customary commute to his Los Angeles home.

That Friday, May 25, 1979, American Airlines Flight #191 to Los Angeles crashes on takeoff at O'Hare International Airport, killing all 258 passengers in the worst single airline disaster in US history.

Harper's week saves his life, and in 2015, at age eighty, he lives quietly in his native Oregon and walks five miles most days. Occasionally he still cuts a real estate deal.

THE MUSCLE MONEY

In the late 1970s and early 1980s, institutions comb stock lists for prime real estate undervalued by Wall Street investors. US pension plans are fairly passive, but aggressive funds from Great Britain show more moxie, assembling significant but noncontrol blocks by providing new capital to cash-strapped REITs.

All seek ownership of sturdy income-producing commercial properties hidden inside equity and long-term mortgage trusts, their presence unacknowledged by most historians of the time.

In October 1977, a group of Scottish investment trusts, organized as Chevy Chase Property Co. Ltd. of Bermuda, pay $3.9 million for a 20 percent stake in Realty Income Trust (not today's trust of the same name) by buying 300,000 shares from an institutional holder of this $75 million combination mortgage and equity trust.

In July 1981, London's Merchant Navy Officers Pension Fund pays $14 a share to buy 847,200 newly issued shares, giving it 30 percent of CleveTrust Realty Investors. The deal injects $11.9 million new capital to let CleveTrust pay down bank debt and expand assets. But managers of the $58 million asset property and mortgage combination trust and Merchant Navy Fund fall out in February 1985 when the fund proposes liquidating the trust.

CleveTrust settles the tiff by buying the fund's shares back, paying $19 a share—a 36 percent premium to original cost.

CAN YOU TOP THIS?

All this is small change compared to the big-money competition that erupts not once but twice to buy pieces of General Growth Properties (GGP), arguably the most successful equity REIT of the 1970s and early 1980s. For most of the early 1970s, GGP stock trades in a class by itself, selling at the group's highest multiple to earnings and soaring well above net book value. When the bell rings to end 1974's stock market carnage, the highest priced equity REIT stock is General Growth Properties at $12.50 a share, a stunning 82 percent above its $6.88 initial offering price in September 1970. Its 1974 closing price is 98 percent above book value, one of only two REITs on the plus side for this important metric.

Behind this market success is the unruffled, methodical management of Martin Bucksbaum, GGP's forty-eight-year-old chief and co-founder. Born into a retailing family, Martin and brothers Matthew and Maurice Bucksbaum decide there's more money to be made as landlord than as tenant and launch into realty development.

Once he becomes head of a public company in 1970, Martin spends oodles of time walking Wall Street analysts through the comparability of stock market and private realty market valuations. He insists both markets value the same quantity: property net operating income (NOI), or property revenues less all expenses except depreciation. The stock market merely calls NOI by another name, funds from operations, or FFO. To Bucksbaum, NOI and FFO are one and the same. During my years with REIT Income Fund (chapter 11, "The Fund"), I come to appreciate Bucksbaum's low-key, zero drama formula for investment success.

But not every Wall Street investor is privy to Bucksbaum's tutorials, and while GGP stock rebounds smartly from that December 1974 low and climbs on several occasions into the mid-$20 range, Bucksbaum remains disappointed that Wall Street investors aren't more knowledgeable about pricing real estate stocks. My translation: he wants a higher stock price.

His disappointment bursts into flame in December 1978 when the brothers, then owning 15 percent of the shares, offer $30-per share cash for the 85 percent of shares they don't own.

Before that can be translated into a formal offer, Marathon Realty, a unit of Canadian Pacific Investments, informally offers $35 a share or $217 million to buy all GGP shares in July 1979. We at *RTR* see the shares as "average" pending a formal offer.

In quick succession, the brothers boost their share offer to $35.50, only to be topped by a $42 a share bid from Detroit mall magnate A. Alfred Taubman. During this frenzied bidding, GGP shares zoom to $47 a share.

But Taubman's offer is aborted and the Bucksbaums instead opt to accept Aetna Life Insurance Company's offer to buy ten GGP malls for $160 million. A shareholder sues to block the deal, but the lawsuit is ultimately settled and GGP sells the malls and pays a $15-a-share special dividend in May 1980.

The bidding frenzy "has encouraged speculation on GGP's ultimate break-up value with some [Wall Street] estimates running to $60 a share," we comment November 21, 1979. "We think it's somewhat less but there is no telling what could happen in the heat of a bidding contest."

With GGP shares falling back to $35.50, we advise: "GGP shares once again have appeal. We are raising them to No. 1 ranking."

After the big May 1980 dividend, Wall Street's typical short-termism sets in, and investors forget all the excitement and those $60-a-share breakup estimates. GGP shares once again settle into an unexciting trading range, falling as low as $12.25 in the 1982 bear market and reaching a high of $25.13 in 1983.

Exhibit 20.5: General Growth Props. (N: GGP)
Annual Stock Prices 1971 - 1984

But Bucksbaum is not done in extracting value from GGP. On Sunday evening, March 18, 1984—our thirty-third wedding anniversary—Martin Bucksbaum calls me at home to give me a heads-up: General Growth Properties will announce before Monday's market opening that it has agreed to sell nineteen enclosed malls to Equitable Life Assurance Society for $704 million ($1.6 billion in 2015 dollars). The price works out to an unprecedented valuation for shopping centers at about nineteen times mall NOI.

Bucksbaum, whose family now owns about 25 percent of GGP shares, says he expects that GGP will distribute between $25 and $30 a share when the purchase is approved by shareholders and closes, he hopes, by late summer.

The announcement is delayed a day, and GGP shares fall by fifty-cents on Monday, but when news hits the broad tape on Tuesday, GGP shares rise $1.38 a share or nearly 5 percent to a new fifty-two-week high of $30.38.

This time, no shareholder dissents. The deal closes in November 1984, and GGP distributes a $25 dividend in February 1985. The $708 million sale is the largest US realty transaction up to that time.

GGP shares trade for a period after the payout and then remaining assets are placed in a liquidating trust, which ultimately distributes another $10 a share. Adding the $15, $25, and $10 pieces puts GGP's ultimate breakup value at $50 per share, not quite $60 but a good outcome for holders.

Under Bucksbaum's leadership, GGP returns 19.3 percent annual total return over fourteen turbulent years from their late-1970 IPO through the post-crash years and GGP's final mall sale in 1984. Martin Bucksbaum stands among the most astute mall operators of his day, combining retailing vision with great people skills to achieve legendary status among early REIT leaders.

Bucksbaum's final score: 1 + 1 = +4.

Bucksbaum uses his gains to assemble a new enclosed mall portfolio and brings this new company, also named General Growth Properties, public in 1993. We breakfast during a REIT conference in Phoenix in the late 1980s, and he confides that a heart murmur surfaces in an annual physical, forcing him into an exercise program. Notwithstanding, a heart attack fatally fells him in July 1995 at age seventy-four. "Martin Bucksbaum … had a sense of pragmatic good will: he saw himself providing an innovative service, which was convenient shopping for an increasingly automobile-oriented society," the *New York Times* says in its 1995 annual review of notable deaths. "He had no more desire to stand in the way of this kind of progress than he would have wanted his family grocery business to stay small … Thus was the American postwar landscape created, not as part of a grand utopian plan but bit by bit, town by town, as Martin Bucksbaum moved across the plains, a Pied Piper of ease and convenience."

Upon reflection, the ten activists and managers portrayed in the past two chapters transform the REIT industry during the 1970s and 1980s by putting shareholder value creation front and center in assessing any future tradable real estate security. Sponsorship and external REIT management die an unlamented death. Busted short-term mortgage REITs fade precisely because the near-zero investment by their managers make them vulnerable fair game for activist investors betting their own dollars on the outcome of new directions. Investor confidence slowly revives because the men and women running the show now stand alongside shareholders in the eventual outcome.

The December 1974 mortgage REIT meltdown fades from memory as the real estate cycle self-corrects: falling returns choke supply of new office, retail and residential buildings, bringing higher rents and margins for landlords. The resulting earnings rebound for property-owning equity REITs catches investor eyes, giving investors 21.3% annual total return for the 13 years stretching into February 1987, an equity REIT bull market unduplicated in REIT history.

Win or lose, the activists usher in new and higher investor standards for judging future REITs. And their presence rescues the REIT revolution by keeping alive the concept of trading real estate securities in public stock markets.

Chapter 21
THE VALUE SEEKER

As a crusading newsletter publisher, I am a pussycat.

"Just give me the facts, ma'am," and I am on my way to deliver them to my investor subscribers in realty stocks. My capacity for copious note-taking during management meetings becomes the stuff of legend in some realty circles, and few intimate company details escape my notice. I follow the German adage, "*Was ich schreibe, ich werde erinnern*," meaning "What I write, I will remember" in longtime friend Jim Braker's translation.

I take on no crusades, with one exception: U.S real estate accounting for depreciation designed to obfuscate and often conceal true net asset values from investors in real estate securities.

Let's be very clear. The true value of the assets behind a realty security can and often is wildly different from either the net book value under accounting rules or the stock market price on any given day.

Finding true value is my constant mission.

Finding true real estate value requires understanding how and why US realty accounting, wedded to historic cost, conceals true value more often than not. Hence I implore you, gentle reader, to stick with this brief personal tour of the fight to make current values more accessible to investors in real estate securities.

IS DEPRECIATION REAL?

From the beginning of real estate securitization in the 1960s, Wall Street's understanding that "earnings" means "net income after depreciation" wars with real estate's convention that depreciation is not a real expense. This misperception begins with a company's income statement, which determines net income but carries over to the balance sheet as well.

This Wall Street misunderstanding of depreciation creates countless opportunities for incisive realty investors in the 1970s and 1980s to spot untold bargains in the stock market. In 2015, those opportunities fade as real estate becomes a more visible player in the overall stock market. But they still exist.

US property owners and realty operatives, in the 1970s and now, routinely ignore depreciation in calculating the cash flow produced by a single building or a property portfolio. Depreciation is a noncash charge for income tax purposes and is so honored by the accounting profession and the Securities and Exchange Commission (SEC). Here is how I describe the real estate versus accountant standoff in my 1971 book *The Real Estate Trusts: America's Newest Billionaires.*

> "All this [controversy] leads to the question of whether real estate really depreciates. Accountants insist that a charge for depreciation is needed to reflect the impairment of a property's ability to produce income and cash flow over a long period of time, and since real estate is a long-life asset, this charge is necessary. The Internal Revenue Service recognizes depreciation as a valid deduction for income tax purposes … (Campbell, 1971. 18)

"Most real estate people say at least for public consumption that this cash is "free" cash because the property undeniably will appreciate in value ... To which the accountant and realist say nonsense because not all income producing real estate appreciates in value and the cash flow from *all* buildings does not increase. (Campbell, 1971. 19)

"So the ceaseless quest of the real estate man or woman and the accountant to find acceptable ways of telling investors about the results of their operations goes on. The lesson is, of course, that no single number can tell the full story of a real estate operation, even the real estate person's hallowed 'net cash flow.' Analysts and investors and accountants will have to continue looking at the whole, not the part." (Campbell, 1971. 22)

Remarkably little has changed since these words were written forty-four years ago.

Moreover, in the real world of buying and selling income properties, depreciation doesn't count. A property's net operating income or NOI (defined as revenues minus hard costs for realty taxes, insurance, and the like) is valued by capitalizing NOI at an expected rate of return. If an investor wishes to earn 8 percent on his or her investment for instance, the building's NOI is capitalized at 8 percent to obtain its valuation. Thus for a building earning $1,000 NOI, this $1,000 is divided by 8 percent (1,000/0.08) to arrive at $12,500 value.

I aim to replicate the real estate professional's blind eye toward noncash depreciation and provide investors with the revered net cash flow number for a carefully selected group of property-owning REITs.

Beginning March 29, 1971, a year after inception, *Realty Trust Review* reports this net cash flow per share to public investors.

"For equity trusts, net cash flow (i.e., earnings plus depreciation and noncash charges minus mortgage amortization) has been used and any known seasonal factors applied in the annualization," we tell subscribers.

Equity trusts are tagged with a "#" hashtag symbol, which becomes a sought-after mark of distinction for equity trusts during *RTR*'s life.

Twenty equity REITs, from American Realty to Washington REIT, qualify for the hashtag that first listing, part of an ambitious computerized expansion to provide a package of Comparative Trust Statistics "intended to facilitate comparison of relative efficiency of trust management with funds available."

That hashtag continues to guide equity trust investors until inflation begins ramping up in the second half of the 1970s.

MONUMENTAL INFLATION

Annual inflation nearly triples from 4.9 percent in 1976 to 13.3 percent in 1979, and the 1980 rate is nearly as bad at 12.5 percent. At those rates, the purchasing power of a dollar is cut in half within five years. Money markets are in chaos, and yields on long-dated Treasury bonds soar to unprecedented levels.

Prices of real estate, that classic inflation hedge, head for the stratosphere.

Monumental Corporation, a Baltimore life insurance holding company, decides to cash in on July 1, 1978, by spinning out its real estate into a separate Monumental Property Trust. The trust seeks to liquidate sixteen enclosed regional malls and four village centers with 7.4 million square feet plus 16,180 apartment units.

Monumental's units start trading publicly in the $45 range, slightly above their $38.79 appraised value.

What turns everybody's head is that the $38.79 appraised value is an enormous sixteen times greater than the $2.42 per unit historic cost under generally accepted accounting principles (GAAP).

Monumental's huge value gap to historic cost accounting starts investors asking what other values might be hidden inside those overlooked equity realty trusts.

On February 23, 1979, while Monumental goes about the business of soliciting bids for its properties, we at *Realty Trust Review* conclude we'd better do something to give investors a better value guide and begin adding accumulated depreciation to net book value for those hashtag-designated equity trusts.

"The change will mean that their cash flow will now be measured as the percentage return on gross book value," we comment in a brief one-paragraph note.

Never did one paragraph stir such a storm.

The change boosts restated book value by 48 percent for large property trusts. Investors react calmly, and prices rise less than 2 percent and remain 18 percent below this adjusted version of book value.

But the change provokes a storm of mail and phone calls.

"Realty Trust Managers Must Find Ways to Value Assets for Investors," reads our *RTR* headline on March 23, 1979. The president of a very successful property trust takes me to task in these words: "Why in the world you would list stocks at so-called book value, which includes depreciation, is beyond me. I don't like this as a trustee and president because it is misleading to existing and potential shareholders … I must express my opinion to you that this is a grave mistake on your part."

I fire back in my heated article in these words:

> "If you are disturbed, I am disappointed—disappointed by the utter unreality of your balance sheet and that of

every other trust and company that owns property in
these inflationary times.

"You know and I know that "book value" computed
under historic cost accounting bears no relationship at
all to market value of properties.

"You, however, and every other trustee and manager have a fairly good idea of that market value. The
problem is that neither I nor any other outside investor
can find that value in your financial statements. This
omission forces us and every other public investor to
guess about underlying values."

I point out that most property trusts distribute some portion of depreciation in their dividends, and that most ask investors to judge them
on measures like "funds generated from operations" or "net cash flow,"
defined as they please.

"Audit has long accepted this concept for the income
statement and set up rules for computing net cash flow.
What we did a month ago is follow this argument to its
logical conclusion: we added accumulated depreciation
which trusts themselves are saying should be ignored
to provide a gross book value we believe is the most
realistic one for investors."

I cite Rouse Company, a shopping center builder and owner, and
Pacific Realty Trust as both using appraisals to convey management's
sense of value to shareholders.

"The point is that there already exist ample means to
get away from depreciation and reflect estimated market

value of properties. In today's inflationary times historic cost accounting simply isn't good enough. REIT trustees have to use their best efforts to present inflation's impact upon asset values to shareholders. The old ways are not good enough."

I end my rant by citing the Monumental story, then still playing out.

"But look at liability from my side of the fence—the investor's side. Early in 1978 the equity in Monumental Property Trust was stated at $18 million by historic cost accounting … The shareholder who sold at $18 because he believed management's historic cost accounting was surely cheated of a major gain.

"The example may be extreme but the principle is sound: Management has a duty to value its assets fairly for the guidance of shareholders."

By May 1979, word comes that bids for Monumental's properties are valued at about $64 a unit, and by July, the final tally shows shareholders will get a cool $70.50 a unit—an astounding twenty-nine times historic cost valuation.

Something is surely rotten in Denmark, and the finger points to historic cost accounting.

THE DEBATE

The furor touches tender nerves throughout the $2.3 billion REIT industry, and the National Association of Real Estate Investment Trusts asks me to debate the issue at its October 1979 annual convention in Washington DC.

I accept and learn that I will debate Sylvan Cohen, a friend and respected former NAREIT president known for high accomplishment and keen insights. A Philadelphia lawyer, Cohen founded and heads Pennsylvania REIT, one of the largest trusts then operating. Cohen also helped found and led the International Council of Shopping Centers, a major real estate group, plus many professional and charitable organizations.

The debate is billed as "Hidden Asset Values Versus Book" and takes place at 8:30 a.m. October 5, 1979. Cohen cites the expense of providing appraisals for investors and the fact that some appraisals may be off the mark, thereby misleading investors. The potential liability from misleading investors clearly drives his lawyerly stance.

"This morning's session is billed as 'Hidden Asset Values Versus Book,'" I open my rebuttal, "but the real topic is coping with inflation—that nasty word that has a tendency to make ordinary people, be they consumers, businessmen, or investors, go bananas. We have all become so consumed by the search for some protection from inflation that we tend to overlook the obvious—the fact that inflation encourages millions to think the sky's the limit, that all prices are going up and they'd better buy now.

"In case you are a doubter, here are two of many examples of how inflation is infecting the national psyche.

"The *Washington Post* published on July 8, 1979, a proposal by a University of Pittsburgh associate professor that the federal government issue one new dollar for each ten you now hold. To which a cynical friend of mine retorts that one zero isn't enough—you have to cut off *two*.

"And the US Senate just passed a new housing bill saying the Federal Housing Administration can assume that the value of a home will increase 2.5 percent every year in underwriting its new graduated payment mortgages.

"These stories evidence the fact that the madness of crowds is turning fear of inflation into a sort of mass hysteria. And real estate is right in the middle—I read a little gem the other day in *Barron's* that said, 'The only thing as good as gold these days is real estate.'

"And that pretty well sums up where we are today—amidst a rip-roaring inflation in real estate values that encourages investors to dream impossible dreams about the real estate you own. The sky's the limit, and hardly a day passes that I'm not asked to pick the next Monumental Properties—that's the real estate subsidiary of a Baltimore life insurance company whose equity is being sold for $550 million currently, a cool *twenty-nine times* the book value of the equity based on historical cost.

"Now I and every other investment analyst and adviser know that current market value of your assets is not historical property costs on your balance sheets. We know there are acceptable and rational ways of estimating that current market value. We know that it's almost impossible for us as outsiders to arrive at those current market values unless we have access to your rent rolls, your leases, and your store of knowledge about present and potential tenants. And we know that any current values you come up with through the various appraisal techniques are really estimates—subject to variation as conditions change. And finally, we know that closed-end investment companies, which is what REITs really are, usually sell below net asset value unless they are going to be liquidated.

"That's why early this year we at *Realty Trust Review* began adjusting book value upward by adding accumulated depreciation to net book value for those trusts and real estate companies that pay out depreciation as a return of capital dividend. Before making the change, we tallied a number to specific property sales and found the selling price was within 15 percent plus or minus from original cost. Thus armed, we published.

"That first issue brought more comment than any single issue in years. Most investors were in favor and urged us to press for more comprehensive current valuations by trusts themselves, or suggest other computation methods. One horrified trust manager told me: 'Ken, you're asking us to strip naked and walk in front of the firing squad,' a reference to fear that raiders might mount takeover attempts."

I note the Financial Accounting Standards Board, which is delegated by the SEC to set US accounting standards, issues its exposure drafts on "Financial Reporting and Changing Prices" and on "Constant Dollar Accounting." A task force is examining the specifics of applying these principles to real estate accounting, and the final meeting will be October 15, 1979. I then distribute an informational packet and describe how a half-dozen public realty companies, none a REIT, is coping with real estate inflation.

"So there you have it," I conclude. "Current market valuations are coming, and you can use one of several acceptable valuation methods. You can pretty well name your poison as to cost. Working together … I trust we may serve the interest of REIT investors."

CURRENT VALUES FOR SOME

Fast-forward nearly two years to summer 1981 by which time nearly two dozen companies and REITs take up my 1979 challenge and begin providing current value estimates to shareholders. In our August 28, 1981, issue, we pull these estimates together and publish them in tabular form. Exhibit 21.1 replicates that first presentation.

"The table's data are still experimental because the accounting and real estate professions haven't yet come to unanimity on how to deal with the glaring fact that inflation has boosted the market price of most real estate far above historic cost," we comment.

Exhibit 21.1 FIRST RSR CURRENT VALUE TABLE					
Name	Value Date	Current Value	Notes	Last Price	% Price to Curr. Value
QUALIFIED REITS					
BANKAMER RL	Jul-81	$44.50	a	$28.13	-36.8%
FEDERAL RLTY	Dec-80	$35.65		$19.25	-46.0%
FIRST UNION	Aug-81	$22.73		$15.38	-32.3%
INTL INCOME PROP	Dec-80	$13.59		$8.50	-37.5%
JMB REALTY	Aug-80	$29.69	b	$18.50	-37.7%
NEW PLAN RLTY	Jul-80	$20.74	b	$11.50	-44.6%
PACIFIC REALTY	May-80	$36.81	b	$28.13	-23.6%
PROPERTY CAP	Jul-79	$24.00		$23.63	-1.5%
RAMPAC	Jun-81	$41.00		$23.38	-43.0%
SANTA ANITA	Dec-80	$20.34		$15.38	-24.4%
UNIVERSITY RE	Aug-80	$13.05		$8.75	-33.0%
WELLS FARGO	Aug-81	$31.04	a	$21.00	-32.3%
REIT AVERAGE					-32.7%
NON-QUALIFIED REITS					
BAY FINCL	May-81	$17.25	a	$9.50	-44.9%
CLEVETRUST	Feb-81	$21.59	a	$10.00	-53.7%
FAIRFIELD COMM	Feb-81	$52.05		$15.88	-69.5%
GROWTH RLTY	Jun-80	$14.47	a	$4.00	-72.4%
MTG INV WASH	Mar-81	$5.48		$3.00	-45.3%
ROUSE CO	Dec-80	$20.75		$23.38	12.7%
SAUL (BF) REIT	Sep-80	$15.37		$8.25	-46.3%
UNITED NATL	Feb-81	$34.43		$15.50	-55.0%
US REALTY	Sep-80	$19.47	a	$14.25	-26.8%
NON-REIT AVERAGE					-44.6%
a -- Mortgages not revalued. B -- No indpendent concurrence.					
Source: *Realty Stock Review* tabulations, August 28, 1981.					

"Many company managements resist putting out a specific share estimate citing technical appraisal uncertainties (e.g., proper capitalization rate) and fear of touting their stock. Often this means they fear current asset value would be so far above stock price that they would be inviting unfriendly tender offers from outsiders.

"Actually this has happened only once, in June 1981, when a tender offer came within days after Connecticut General Mortgage & Realty (CGM) set a $41.40 value on its shares without taking a haircut on low-rate mortgages. Ultimately a Prudential Life unit bought CGM for $42 a share."

We bill this new table as a way investors can track market prices and assert values. Over ensuing years, single *RSR* issues containing this table are purchased more frequently than any other.

Current value guidance by public companies and REITs is here to stay.

FFO AND BEYOND

But as the 1990s arrive, investors turn more attention on the REIT income statements and NAREIT empanels an accounting taskforce to develop guidelines for Funds from Operations, or FFO, finalizing their definition in 1991. This more refined FFO substitutes for the crude but necessary cash-flow-per-share measure we at *Realty Trust Review* introduced two decades earlier, in March 1971.

But time gradually erodes adherence to this new FFO standard.

"About one-half of our members as well as a number of analysts have come to focus more on modified versions of FFO, especially when it comes to earnings guidance," NAREIT president and CEO Stephen Wechsler says in a September 24, 2014, letter to members.

"The NAREIT definition of FFO was officially recognized by the SEC in 2003 as a supplemental earnings measure and as a result companies have been able to report FFO on a per-share basis. Today, over 95% of stock-exchange listed equity REITs report FFO according to the NAREIT definition.

"The failure to provide guidance with reconciliation to NAREIT-defined FFO … (whether called normalized FFO, recurring FFO, core FFO, adjusted FFO or something else) is increasingly problematic for the REIT industry … Our review has led us to conclude that there is in fact demonstrable confusion in the investment marketplace about FFO …

"If your company currently provides earnings guidance to a company-defined version of FFO and does not provide related guidance to NAREIT-defined FFO, I urge you to consider doing so with reconciliation when you release your 2015 full-year guidance and going forward."

The outcome of Wechsler's plea is unknown as this goes to the printer.

CURRENT VALUE IN 2015

US REITs and companies still do not provide current net asset value to shareholders; cost-basis accounting remains the standard in this country as it was in 1979. In the intervening years, the accounting profession develops several alternate methods by which companies may provide the current value of properties to investors, but most public realty companies and REITs bypass them.

US investors in 2015 instead rely upon an unofficial system in which highly skilled security analysts provide net asset value, or NAV, estimates widely accepted by institutional investors in real estate securities. With about three dozen institutional analysts providing a steady stream of NAV estimates, this private system reacts swiftly to market changes in interest rates, capitalization rates, and current real estate transactions.

The US system stands in marked contrast to most foreign countries, especially Great Britain, Canada, and Australia, where company managements provide annual estimates of net asset value or, in Australia, net tangible assets. All follow newly developed International Financial Reporting Standards, or IFRS, which generally ignore depreciation as a real estate expense and require users to mark all assets to current value. Changes in current value then flow through a company's income statement.

IFRS backers try to get the United States on board by adopting their standards, but the effort runs into opposition when over two hundred industry professionals comment publicly to the Securities and Exchange Commission in 2010. The SEC lays out a work plan for possible adoption by perhaps 2015 or 2016, including making sure that the SEC does not compromise its statutory duty to oversee US accounting standards. This effort seems several years behind schedule.

Thus current value accounting still stops at the US shoreline.

George Yungmann, NAREIT senior vice president for financial standards, indicates that "over 90% of companies that prepare financial statements under IFRS report investment property at current market value. Even the U.S. pension funds report investment property at current market value now."

"Using a multiple of funds from operation, or FFO, as well as a company's net asset value measured at current value are both important factors in valuing stocks."

And FFO ignores real estate depreciation, just as IFRS proposes. Cost basis accounting still reigns for determining property values in balance sheets, however.

The only balm is that inflation today runs in the 1 to 2 percent range, well down from the double-digit days of 1979 and 1980. Will those days ever return?

Don't bet against it.

Chapter 22
THE BANKERS

One day, in summer 1981, I receive a call from Bob Dillmeier, whom I know only slightly through Bill Smith, the senior real estate investment banker at Paine Webber Jackson & Curtis. Then eleven years younger than I am at forty, Bob is about to become at liberty after a stint taking over and reorganizing a troubled private REIT originally sponsored by a Baltimore bank.

While still working at Paine Webber in the late 1970s, Bob is contacted by an institution wanting to know how it can liquidate the untraded stock of a mortgage REIT whose shares Paine Webber placed with it privately some years earlier. Using his contacts, Bob finds two Manhattan investors willing to buy the shares—but only if there is a chance of either buying more shares or attracting other shareholders to vote to change management of the REIT.

That triggers Bob and the investors to begin a nationwide tour to contact every shareholder they can locate and ask him or her to support a proxy to replace existing management. They find enough backers that their "blue proxy" slate carries the election at the annual meeting in 1978 and Bob is elected president. He and his wife, Peggy Dillmeier, move to Baltimore, and over the next two years, Bob heads a major effort to work out the trust's bank lines while gaining control of and liquidating as many assets as possible.

That task now done, the REIT is being sold to a new group of investors interested in using the trust's net operating losses (NOLs) to reduce taxes in another business. That means that Bob is exploring all options before deciding on his next career move.

His choice is complicated by the fact that he needs to spend some time working with his father's glass business. Starting in the 1930s, the senior Dillmeier began selling glass display cases to retailers and, more recently, has become the exclusive supplier to one major national retailer. The business is nicely profitable, provided this small family enterprise can meet all the needs of that one giant customer. That mandates that Bob spend time managing this business, setting up display cases at new stores as needed, and overseeing their glass supplier.

In other words, a full-time nine-to-five job is out of the question for Bob.

After several talks, we decide to form Campbell & Dillmeier (C&D) as a boutique investment banking firm serving smaller real estate companies and REITs. As we survey the field, we find many smaller REITs own assets or tax losses of interest to niche investors. At that early juncture, we see mergers and acquisitions (M&A) as the major focus of C&D. In the vernacular, we aspire to become a specialized deal shop.

M&A work is chancy at best, and most everyone in Wall Street sees chasing deals as something to be done only when there is nothing else to do. We hope that Dillmeier's expertise and my industry visibility and contacts will give us an edge in this high-risk undertaking.

To me, Bob Dillmeier brings two key assets to our projected M&A party. He possesses several years' experience as a working investment banker at a major Wall Street firm with a strong résumé of taking over and restoring viability to a broken REIT, and he is "born to the purple" in my plebian eyes, his background with a comfortable family business giving him the confidence to charge going rates for investment banking. Since my analysis of the 1970s leaves the distinct feeling that Audit's printed services are way underpriced for the value delivered to subscribers, the opportunity to upgrade pricing seems—and ultimately proves—a key attribute.

Partnerships are tricky. Bob feels strongly that partnerships should be one-on-one relationships between two trusted associates. He argues that three-cornered partnerships can turn sour if any one partner gets the impression—true or otherwise—that the other two partners are ganging up to work against his or her best interests. Partnerships of four or more are easier to control, since they become more like corporations with clearly defined partnership percentages and more defined structures.

Bob and I settle upon a two-person partnership with a single handshake on the following terms: The partners will disclose all aspects of each person's activities to the other. We never put anything in writing. Bob is a devout Catholic, and I feel his background will make him a trusted partner. This turns out to be 100 percent accurate, unlike some other partnerships, joint ventures, and business relationships I enter.

The Campbell & Dillmeier partnership works well because we devise a simple and probably foolproof way of handling money to the satisfaction of both partners. I agree to set up a broker-dealer securities firm registered with the National Association of Securities Dealers (NASD—now the Financial Industry Regulatory Authority, or FINRA) to handle the partnership's books. Investment banking fees and other income will be deposited into this broker-dealer (or BD) account, and 50 percent of net proceeds from each deal will be split between the partners. The BD pays an overhead reimbursement to Audit for using its space and facilities. When Audit moves to New Jersey in 1986, C&D rents a smaller office in 230 Park Avenue in Manhattan for meetings and client contact.

Forming C&D creates a clear conflict-of-interest issue for me. How can I continue giving investment advice to investors as editor for *Realty*

Stock Review while at the same time going "behind the curtain" to advise REITs on confidential financial matters, such as potential mergers and acquisitions that could impact stock prices? Howard G. "Gerry" Seitz, our attorney, has a simple solution: "Disclosure is the best disinfectant." Hence, any time I or Dillmeier take any advisory role or executive position in a publicly traded entity, we rigorously disclose that fact in *RSR*. It works well, and the conflict question is never raised during the decade-long life of C&D.

THE FIRST DEAL

Chasing deals already beckons, but making money chasing deals requires skill and discipline. Without those qualities, one can spend boatloads of time in the chase and wind up with dry holes. The trick is to know or sense when to end the chase, when to hold, and when to fold.

The second essential is a fallback source of income. I have that in Audit, and Bob has income from his family business, so we are both covered on this latter score.

Somehow—I cannot recall details—I arrive at a relationship to advise Pacific Southern Mortgage Trust (PSMT), a very small mortgage REIT with only $9.7 million assets based in San Diego. Two unrelated individual shareholders, both based in Providence, Rhode Island, have taken sizeable stakes in PSMT and are elected trustees. Once seated, they press vigorously to sell or liquidate PSMT so they can get their money back plus a good profit.

My job is to advise *all* the trustees on whether this is a good idea, first, and if so, how it can be accomplished. This assignment begins before I meet Dillmeier, so the idea of forming C&D merely carries on and provides additional resources for this task.

Eventually, PSMT is acquired by Old Stone Corporation, a bank holding company based in (surprise) Providence. The merger closes in June 1982, and I host a festive closing party at the Algonquin Hotel, famed site of the roundtable lunches by writers for the *New Yorker* magazine, on Manhattan's West Forty-Fourth Street at which I order Dom Perignon champagne at ninety dollars a bottle for the small crowd. The C&D tombstone ad, a financial ad recording a transaction, says that "Kenneth D. Campbell, a principal of the firm, advised the Trustees of PSMT in negotiating this transaction."

ENTER KENDALE

Starting the broker-dealer firm we envision proves a more formidable challenge. NASD rules call for the proposed firm to have minimum capital of ten thousand dollars if it does not plan on trading stocks. Complying with NASD rules requires some doing because neither of us is registered with NASD. Digging through the rules discloses that at least one individual must be a registered representative (i.e., an RR or customer's man) by passing the Series 7 securities exam. Also, the firm needs principals overseeing the two areas of operations and financial compliance. That means I must pass two more tests since NASD lets one person fill both roles. I hit the books, and within a few months, I pass all three exams and set about filling out forms to register the fledgling firm with the NASD.

I combine my first two names to name the firm "Kendale Corporation," and the NASD sanctions Kendale as a member firm sometime in early 1982.

Kendale stays in business for about ten years, or until we form Campbell-Radnor Advisors a decade later. All C&D fairness opinions are issued on Kendale letterhead, and its only other purpose is to act as conduit for investment banking fees.

WHAT'S FAIR?

As it turns out, Kendale becomes the main umbrella under which C&D issues nearly two dozen fairness opinions on pending M&A transactions negotiated by third parties. The demand for fairness opinions stuns us because we assume when setting up C&D that a small, unknown firm with only two partners will never have enough credence to be asked to issue fairness opinions.

We are wrong!

The character, varied experiences, and reputations of the two C&D principals make our opinions valuable to many REIT trustees and managements, and this business represents well over half our revenues over a decade.

Fairness opinions are among the most elusive and sought-after assignments in investment banking. Typically, two entities find each other and negotiate a merger, sale of assets, or some other transaction requiring approval by public shareholders of one or both entities. Knowing that public investors will wonder if any negotiated deal is really the best possible outcome, one or both parties will hire a well-known and respected investment banker to "opine" on the merits of the deal. The banker's opinion is circulated to public investors in a proxy statement seeking approval of the deal.

The banking firm issuing a fairness opinion assumes super risk. Essentially, the investment banking firm is putting its name out to the public and asking any disgruntled shareholder to sue. The legal profession is populated by hundreds or perhaps thousands of firms—called the "plaintiff" or "tort bar"—that make a handsome living filing class action suits alleging violation of securities laws. Smaller firms like Campbell & Dillmeier can thus be drawn into abrasive and lengthy litigation for alleged infractions.

A few high-profile tort lawyers build careers and fortunes from their practices. Former US Senator John Edwards, once a contender for the Democratic presidential nomination, made his fortune as a tort lawyer mainly in medical malpractice cases before being elected to the Senate. Peter Angelos, owner of the Baltimore Orioles major league baseball team, wins awards for numerous plaintiffs in asbestos litigation. Many other public figures amass fortunes as tort lawyers before turning to public service or other careers.

We are deeply cognizant of the risks in offering an opinion that a deal is "fair."

Bottom line, a small firm such as Kendale and Campbell & Dillmeier with tiny capital issues fairness opinions only after they turn over every imaginable rock looking for snakes. We inspect the relative values of the cash, securities, or other consideration being exchanged; comparative valuations; management's strategic plan for the merged entity; and every other relevant aspect. Only then can we put forth an opinion that a transaction "is fair from a financial point of view."

Diligence is our antidote for lawsuits, and we are never sued, proving our diligence works.

In August 1984, C&D pulls together a montage of tombstone ads for our first dozen transactions and we are surprised to learn that we have issued five fairness opinions in those dozen transactions. A copy appears in the photo section.

Knowing the protocol for tombstone ads helps one understand the important facts they convey. The client's name is always listed first in the ad, followed by the substance of the transaction being memorialized and the name of any third party. There follows a brief description of the service provided by the investment banking firm, whose logo appears as the signature for the ad. Finally, the date of the transaction's closing appears in the lower left corner.

This analysis of C&D's most complex and demanding transactions provides a good thumbnail sketch of how we operate, where we find clients, and the nature of our business.

THE REAL MCCOY

Early in 1980, I meet a young man named Hal McCoy Jr. of Greensboro, North Carolina, son and heir to a fairly large real estate business operating under the name Kenyon Investment Corporation. In March 1980, I travel to Greensboro to learn more about Kenyon's business and inspect its apartment projects and other commercial properties. All are financed by real estate syndicators who provide most equity and debt capital.

Having built a thriving business, Hal asks me if he can take the next step and merge Kenyon into a surviving REIT. I suggest Cameron Brown Investment Group (CBIG), an $11 million market value former mortgage trust based only about seventy miles distant in Raleigh, North Carolina. CBIG is well situated to consider a merger; new management has been installed and wants to convert into a holding company to facilitate a turnaround.

By October 1980, CBIG cuts bank debt to $11 million, attracting two activist investors who together buy about 12.2 percent of the trust's shares, pushing prices up sharply to $7.25 where they still trade at 23 percent discount to book value. In March 1981, CBIG completes conversion into a holding company named Sunstates Corporation (NYSE: SST).

"The new holding company adds flexibility," *Realty Stock Review* comments in June 1981, adding however that the "best assets are gone."

I meet the new Sunstates CEO sometime in 1981 for a leisurely and expensive lunch at the newly opened Grand Hyatt Hotel in Manhattan to float the idea of SST acquiring Kenyon via an exchange of stock to give Sunstates significant new earning apartment assets. He seems receptive because such a deal would place a block of stock in friendly hands and give Hal a board seat. That's a plus because Marshall Cogan and Stephen Swid, owners of General Felt Industries, boost their stake to 12.5 percent by July 1981 and appear bent on buying more to tap SST's $16.5 million net operating losses (NOLs).

By September 1981, Hal is meeting regularly with Sunstates management trying to hammer out a deal, and he is happy because SST pays bank debt down to only $4.2 million and shares still sell 37 percent below the $9.15 a share book value.

Talks go well, although Sunstates has a tough time valuing Kenyon's equity in apartment projects subject to syndicator financing. Ultimately Sunstates offers to buy Kenyon for 315,000 shares valued at about $6 a share, or about $1.9 million.

Hal accepts the deal, giving Kenyon 13.5 percent of Sunstates shares and a board seat. With bank debt essentially paid, he figures SST is in a solid position to deal with unfriendly block holders. The deal closes in December 1981.

"Kenneth D. Campbell, a principal in the undersigned, initiated this transaction and represented Kenyon," says Campbell & Dillmeier's tombstone ad.

It is C&D's first completed transaction as a team, and Bob's advice along the way helps convert an idea into a completed deal. Our fee is not recorded, but it certainly is significantly larger than a subscription.

Once Kenyon merges into Sunstates in December 1981, we maintain contact mainly through periodic talks with Hal McCoy.

A REAL PREFERRED

In January 1983, Chicago investor Clyde Wm. Engle (his preferred appellation in legal documents), acting through a controlled former mortgage trust named TRECO Incorporated (the initials standing for **T**he **R**eal **E**state **Co**mpany), acquires options to buy shares and warrants that, if exercised, represent 33 percent of Sunstates shares.

The seller of the options: my former client Hal V. McCoy Jr.

The story goes that both companies own considerable properties around Jacksonville, Treco's home base, and as result, the two staffs become friendly and want to merge.

Early in 1984, C&D is retained to advise the independent directors of Sunstates to see if fair merger terms can be found.

By this time, Engle owns 37.8 percent of Sunstates, and the only question becomes the merger consideration, not the outcome.

Setting the price and coin (whether cash, stock, or other consideration) quickly turns acrimonious. Clyde Engel, an internationally known horseman and also the man on the other side of the table representing Treco, constitutes a one-man conglomerate with interests in a dozen smaller companies in banking, financial services, two former REITs, furniture, and a chocolate factory.

Our inquiries indicate one ominous fact for Sunstates holders: Engle likes to buy out noncontrol shareholders with preferred stocks with short call protection, usually one year. Preferred stock investors, most at or near retirement age, usually seek consistent income over several years. Typical preferred holders thus resist short call periods because a quick call period upsets their income planning.

From Engle's standpoint, calling preferred stocks quickly erases his company's preferred dividend obligations and lets him use the company's cash flow for other purposes.

Sunstates' directors, along with Bob and me, are determined to prevent Engle from paying a "disappearing" preferred to SST holders.

There follow protracted and tempestuous negotiations unlike any we experience anywhere.

Late in the game, Engle sues all Sunstates directors and refuses to withdraw the suit even after an agreement on major terms is reached.

"Clyde will keep the shotgun on the table with the hammer cocked," one Sunstates director remarks. Because Sunstates opts for a directors' insurance package with very high deductibles, every director's personal net worth is on the line in the lawsuit. As a result, talks lurch along in a sticky, tension-wracked fashion.

Exhibit 22.1: CBIG/Sunstates (N: SST)
Annual Stock Prices 1980 - 1988

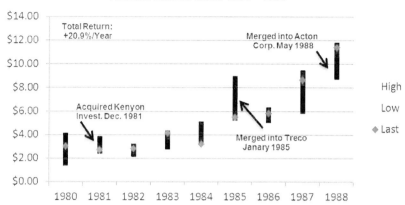

We and Sunstates want Engle to offer a five-year noncallable preferred with a relatively high coupon, while Engle angles for a lower coupon and a preferred callable at the company's option within one year.

After one long and contentious late-evening session, I fall exhausted into my hotel bed only to be awakened about 6:30 a.m. by Clyde Engle asking if we can agree to new terms. I stand firm on our demand for a five-year noncallable preferred—meaning Sunstates shareholders can count on the dividend yield for five years.

After what seems like an hour of rancorous back-and-forth, Clyde relents and the deal is sealed at a meeting later that morning. So far as we know, Campbell & Dillmeier is the only banker ever to stare down Clyde Engle and win.

"Campbell & Dillmeier is advising the independent Directors of Sunstates Corporation in this transaction," reads our tombstone.

Sunstates merges into Treco on January 31, 1985, with the combined entity assuming the Sunstates name and issuing $11.87 million of 15.0 percent cumulative preferred shares ($3.75 dividend on $25 par value) valuing SST shares at $8.50 a share, or a 33 percent premium to its market price. We celebrate our handiwork on behalf of 3,200 preferred shareholders.

Three months later, on April 1, 1985, Sunstates buys an insurance holding company whose main asset is "nonstandard" auto insurer Coronet Insurance Company of Chicago.

On April 30, 1988, Sunstates shareholders approve merging into Acton Corporation, another public entity controlled by Engle, which again adopts the Sunstates name and redeems the 15 percent preferred stock in full five years later.

The stock market takes a shine to the Sunstates-Treco-Acton trifecta, and the common stock returns nearly 21 percent annually to shareholders for the nine years from December 1979 through the Acton merger in 1988. Reported earnings are volatile, but the market senses that values of SST's underlying properties are headed north. In this case, what's good for the goose (think Sunstates preferred shareholders) is also good for the gander (think Sunstates common holders). Shareholders benefit handsomely from the strong real estate recovery from the depressed real estate and stock prices of the late 1970s, with corporate and management changes having little impact. If you find a strong recovery trend, ride it as long as you can.

Less than a year after the Sunstates face-off, Clyde Wm. Engle asks Campbell & Dillmeier to render a fairness opinion on the merger of another former REIT he controls for another preferred stock "except the preferred stock has to be callable."

We pass. If we agree to callable prefs beforehand, our reputation as tough negotiators for clients is destroyed and we lose more than any fee.

ADDING GROWTH TO GROWTH

Into our Manhattan office one day in late 1981 walks George Weinstein, whom I know briefly as managing trustee of Wisconsin REIT, a very small equity trust based in Milwaukee. George is ousted in 1980 as

Wisconsin REIT's president after a bruising proxy contest with Clyde Engle, whom we met in the preceding section and who now controls Wisconsin.

A roly-poly CPA with thin white hair and a genial disposition, George somehow always seems to know what deals are available at any given time—we never find his secret source of deal flow. He installs himself as chairman of the board of Weinstein Associates Limited, a consulting firm that includes his son Stanley. George is "in touch" with British Land Company (BLC) in London, one of the largest United Kingdom property companies, and says BLC wants to enter the US real estate market by acquiring a busted REIT.

After surveying the field, Bob and I settle on Growth Realty Companies, an $8.5 million market value Los Angeles mortgage REIT, as the most likely prospect and set about contacting Growth CEO Robert Felixson to sound out his reaction to merging Growth with a US-based subsidiary of the UK company.

Like nearly every other former mortgage trust, Felixson is struggling to repay Growth's $28.5 million bank debt, selling assets whenever he can to make banks happy. Felixson also must reckon with a $9.2 million debenture issue due April 15, 1982.

Unlike his peers, Felixson plays the appraisal game and tells investors in October 1980 that an appraisal of Growth's remaining assets indicates about $7 a share "hidden" gain above its $7.50 book value—if only Growth can sell the assets at appraised value.

Swayed by those appraisals, *Realty Stock Review* calls the stock an "attractive purchase" at 23 percent discount to book value figured on historic cost and 60 percent below the putative $14.50 per share value if appraised value turns out to be right.

All this makes Growth an attractive merger partner for BLC.

Additionally, Growth stock trades on the NYSE (symbol GRW) and has about $20.5 million or $9.74 a share net operating losses (NOLs).

Two separate groups turn up the heat on Felixson by buying blocks of stock. One buyer knocking on the door is feared acquisitor Gene E. Phillips and his Southmark Corporation (chapter 19, "The Reit Catchers") with a 7.5 percent block in September 1981.

Our merger inkle turns on how badly Felixson wants to escape his pressure cooker.

At first, Felixson says he has loads of options, crowds of people offering him deals, and he wants time to consider them all. We are skeptical and wait.

In early 1982, with that April 15 maturity of $9.2 million bonds bearing down on him, Felixson agrees to let BLC use its credit stature to try to resolve Growth's issue with its banks and public bondholders.

In March 1982, BLC uses its own loans and credit guarantees to settle with the banks and guarantees repayment of $9.25 million subordinated debt coming due on April 15. For its help, Growth sells BLC 1 million new shares at $3 a share, giving BLC a 31 percent stake, plus 950,000 stock warrants.

The transaction gives BLC voting control of Growth, and BLC names John Weston-Smith, one of its executives, as CEO and appoints George Weinstein as director.

As the deal nears its closing date in April 1982, BLC starts quibbling over the fee we have agreed upon for finding and initiating the transaction. Our fee is based upon a percentage of the amount of help BLC gives to GRW, but it becomes necessary for C&D to sign some document vital to the closing.

We refuse to sign.

After days of frenzied brinksmanship, BLC caves and we receive our agreed-upon fee, whose exact amount does not survive. The deal proves that C&D, the new kid on the M&A block, can find and complete a complex transaction even though Growth's market value is only $7.8 million, a milestone and vital ingredient in C&D's activities for the rest of the 1980s.

"Growth Realty Companies restructured its bank debt and its public subordinated debt through use of loans, guarantees and sale of new shares totaling approximately $15,000,000 provided by The British Land Company PLC," reads the C&D tombstone. "The undersigned initiated this transaction."

At the closing party, John Ritblat, the entrepreneurial founder of BLC, cracks, "Are these the blokes who held us up over a fee?"

We assure him that we are indeed "the blokes" and aren't bashful about it.

Without our keen eye for a willing target, BLC would still be stuck in London.

THE EYE DOC

Unshackled from its debt chains, Growth Realty is now ready to grow again. The name changes to British Land of America (BLA) in November 1983 when BLA acquires two large Manhattan office buildings in a share exchange with its parent while starting to sell properties outside New York City.

But by the late 1980s, British Land of America share price isn't making any progress with its $1.75 a share stock price well below the $2.75 of five years earlier in 1982. British Land decides it cannot strike gold in America because that weak share price, well below the $3.41 a share appraised net asset value, won't let it buy new properties. With recession looming over US realty, BLA and its London parent decide to focus only on New York City properties and ask numerous persons, including George Weinstein, to suggest an exit formula for non–New York properties.

In January 1988, BLA connects with James H. Desnick, a Chicago ophthalmologist. After numerous conversations, BLA agrees on February 25, 1988, to a stock swap, transferring BLA's non–New York properties into a new Desnick company named Medical Management of America, or MMA.

Only thirty-seven, Desnick wants to create the first publicly traded corporation specializing in management of medical and surgical centers dedicated exclusively to eye care. It is a lofty goal, considering that a number of states prohibit corporations from "practicing medicine." Lawyers advise that MMA may meet this restriction by having a publicly traded company own physical medical facilities while agreeing with medical practitioners to provide services at these locations.

Dr. Desnick sees MMA as expanding work he begins in 1985 in opening the Desnick Eye Center, an outpatient ophthalmic surgical center, or surgicenter, on Chicago's northwest side, performing relatively new techniques for cataract surgery. At a time when cataract removal customarily requires lengthy hospitalization, the Desnick Eye Center, as described in the MMA proxy, provides "the application of microsurgical techniques and new technologies to ophthalmic surgery resulting in less invasive procedures for the patient so that routine cataract removals can be performed safely on an outpatient basis." Combined with improvements in anesthesia, the center "enables patients to recuperate at home instead of remaining hospitalized at a much higher cost during a more extended post-operative recovery period. Because outpatient surgery is less costly than [hospital] surgery ... government agencies including Medicare and other third-party reimbursers have increasingly accepted outpatient ophthalmic surgery as an attractive alternative." (Combined BLA proxy and MMA prospectus, 1988. 86)

The result is a "transformation in the manner in which ophthalmic care is provided ... Before the IOL (intraocular lens) procedure became available, persons who underwent cataract removal would wear thick-lensed glasses which restricted vision and were heavy and cosmetically unattractive, or contact lenses." (Combined BLA proxy and MMA prospectus, 1988. 86, 87)

The Desnick Center, along with two smaller eye clinics, are wildly successful, their revenues rising from $5.4 million in 1985 to $18.5 million in 1987. As 100 percent owner, Dr. Desnick's shareholder's salary rises from $1.1 million in 1985 to $9.5 million in 1987 ($18.9 million in 2015 dollars).

The Desnick Eye Center sends buses through Chicago suburbs ferrying hundreds of elderly patients daily to the center. The center "estimates that the incidence of some level of cataract disformation is over 70% for persons aged 65 and over," says the proxy. "Approximately 90% of the surgical procedures performed at the Surgicenter are for removal of cataracts ... Cataract removal with an IOL implant is the surgical procedure most commonly performed at the Surgicenter and generates the highest fee per procedure." (Combined BLA proxy and MMA prospectus, 1988. 86, 92)

Since most patients are Medicare eligible, the center "estimates that historically over 85% of the Surgicenter's cataract patients have been covered by Medicare, and approximately 80% of the revenues collected ... have been and continue to be paid or reimbursed by Medicare. MMA expects this dependence on Medicare reimbursement to continue, and perhaps increase." (Combined BLA proxy and MMA prospectus, 1988. 92)

For each procedure, Medicare pays "several fees, including a facility fee, an IOL fee, a surgeon's fee, an anesthesiologist's fee, and smaller miscellaneous itemized fees for tests and services ... The current facility fee paid by Medicare for an IOL procedure ranges from $584 to $659 nationally ... Medicare pays a fee for each IOL prosthesis implanted which currently approximates $350 in Illinois ... physicians' fees ...

currently vary from approximately $1,400 to $2,600 throughout the country ... with an estimated national average of approximately $1,750 per procedure. The fees currently paid to [the MMA providers] for this procedure exceed the national average." (Combined BLA proxy and MMA prospectus, 1988. 92, 93)

"In general Medicare reimburses only a percentage of the total amount billed to each patient ... Since April 1, 1988, Medicare reimburses the physician only for 80% of the Medicare approved fee, and the physician is obligated to make a reasonable effort to collect the remaining 20% from each non-indigent patient or such patient's supplemental insurer." (Combined BLA proxy and MMA prospectus, 1988. 93)

Desnick sees great opportunity in consolidating this business by buying similar eye centers in other parts of the country and views taking his clinic public via a back-door merger into BLA as a way to get a Wall Street multiple for his earnings. The proxy states, "MMA currently intends to expand its business by acquiring or developing other ambulatory ophthalmic surgical treatment centers and diagnostic facilities, as well as non-surgical care facilities ... both in Illinois and in other states ... MMA anticipates that in the Chicago metropolitan area the existing and new Eye Care Centers will serve as community-based centers for patient screening and referral to the Surgicenter on a 'hub and spoke' model." (Combined BLA proxy and MMA prospectus, 1988. 90)

Independent directors of BLA retain Campbell & Dillmeier (C&D) in early March 1988 to advise whether this oddest of odd-couple marriages is fair to BLA's public shareholders.

We tackle the assignment with trepidation on three fronts.

First, we are not eye doctors and so must rely on medical professionals. We hire a prominent New Jersey ophthalmologist to review Eye Center patient charts and advise us on medical matters. After spending two days poking around the Desnick Center, he reports that, yes, there's a high propensity for Desnick's eye examinations to recommend laser cataract surgery, but that's not too unusual because most patients are over age sixty-five.

Second, we worry about that 80 percent concentration of revenues in Medicare billings. Several risks must be assessed. Medicare could cut the reimbursements over time or could at some future time find fault with MMA's operating or billing practices and limit or halt payments. To test whether Desnick's center is being too aggressive in its diagnoses, I put on my best Mike Wallace *Sixty Minutes* face and grill Desnick about that high proportion of recommended surgeries. The conversation goes something like this:

"Why be so aggressive in marketing this one new service?" I ask.

"We use relatively new technology to restore vision to persons who had no option before. Laser technology and IOLs are relatively new techniques and restore sight quickly, can be done on an outpatient basis, and eliminate costly hospital stays compared to previous methods. On that basis, it's actually cheaper than the old method and provides better results."

(In a July 8, 2015 email, Dr. Desnick adds,"There was no unique surgical technology used at my centers. Our niche was the development of outpatient, ambulatory surgery centers. This was somewhat similar to Humana, Medivision, and others. However our focus was on ophthalmology.")

"Why do such a high percentage of your patients have laser surgery?"

"It's a function of age plus neglect. Many patients think it's too expensive or too difficult to operate on their eyes and so don't do anything. When we tell them they can correct cataracts without staying in a hospital for days and that Medicare will pay 80 percent of costs, most sign up on the spot. What better gift than to restore an elderly person's vision?"

"If Mike Wallace shows up here, can you stand up to him with a straight face?"

"I believe I can. We are helping people, not doing anything illegal."

"Won't Medicare cut reimbursement rates?" we challenge. "That could hurt your revenues."

"They have already cut fees and will continue to do so. I don't see this as hurting our plan."

Third, MMA is a new company whose managers have no public company experience. Our concern is mitigated because George Weinstein and John Weston-Smith agree to serve on MMA's board, giving the new company valuable and needed management heft.

"How will you grow MMA's business?" we want to know on behalf of every potential investor.

"MMA currently intends to expand its business by acquiring or developing other ambulatory ophthalmic surgical treatment centers and disagnostic facilities through purchase, lease or constructon, and by contracting to provide MMA services to additional medical service providers both in Illinois and in other states…MMA is investigating opportunities to expand [and] intends to seek such arrangements initially in Illinois and those states where there are not significant legal or regulatory restrictions…(Combined BLA proxy and MMA prospectus, 1988. 90)

"MMA has obtained written commitments…from two financial institutions to lend to MMA up to $30 million on a revolving credit basis.…MMA currently intends to target as prospective clients either ophthalmological practices that own or operate their own surgical centers, or medium to large practices that perform surgeries in outpatient surgical facilities owned by third parties other than hospitals. MMA believes that such practices are large enough to be marketed, are relatively well established in their markets, can recruit physician employees more easily, and should generate management fees in amounts sufficient to produce positive cash flow for MMA…" (Combined BLA proxy and MMA prospectus, 1988. 90, 91)

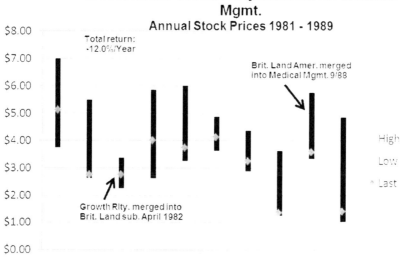

Exhibit 22.2: Growth Rlty./Brit. Land Am./Med. Mgmt.
Annual Stock Prices 1981 - 1989

We conclude Dr. Desnick is a dedicated practitioner with credible answers to our crucial questions. Hence the risks to his new enterprise seem manageable.

In late March 1988, we tell the committee orally we believe the deal is fair. But the parties do some more tinkering with deal points, lowering risk to BLA holders by holding back about 31 percent of the 5.8 million (post-split) shares to be issued contingent upon MMA reaching certain levels of pretax earnings.

We issue our fairness opinion for a proxy dated August 26, 1988. Our opinion is 100 percent correct on the facts presented but 100 percent wrong on the unexpected problems Dr. Desnick encounters in executing his business plan.

The deal is approved promptly, and Medical Management of

America, Incorporated, begins trading on the American Stock Exchange under the symbol MMA, opening at $16.88 per share (adjusted for a subsequent one-for-three reverse split) on a when-issued basis in late September 1988. That quote boosts MMA market value over $123 million, nearly three and a half times MMA's $4.98 a share pro forma book value. The price is a lofty thirty-one times its fifty-four-cent pro forma 1987 earnings. Dividend is twenty-seven-cents annually.

Sadly, that opening stock quote marks MMA's high spot. Trading is light and sporadic because only 12 percent of MMA's 7.3 million shares are owned by 1,500 former BLA holders. Dr. Desnick owns 68 percent, British Land holds another 8 percent, and MMA management another 11 percent. With such limited public float, the company struggles to attract public attention.

During its first full year, ending October 1989, MMA acquires four eye surgicenters in Miami, Florida; Munster, Indiana; and Newport Beach and Upland, California for about $10 million. But operating revenues fall 28 percent to $15.3 million due to "increased competition from other high-volume providers in the area." (Medical Management of America: 1989 Form 10-K. 13) Early in the year, MMA's vice chairman and president leave, causing a thirty-three-cents-a-share pretax severance charge. The October 1989 annual report shows MMA losing thirty-two cents a share from operations (equaling those severance payments) plus $1.12 a share red ink from selling BLA's real estate at a loss during a blossoming realty recession.

MMA's second year is much better, as operating revenues in the October 1990 year rebound 40 percent to $21.4 million despite a Medicare fee cut. MMA elects to terminate some underperforming contracts at newly acquired facilities, costing forty-four cents a share pretax. Even with this charge, MMA reports earning thirty-one cents, including twelve cents in tax-loss benefits, in its October 1990 year. But

MMA shifts its stock to the over-the-counter market and ends 1990 trading at $4.13 a share, a modest thirteen times earnings.

In October 1990, BLA proposes taking the company private, and Dr. Desnick agrees to go private at $8.25 per share. BLA holds 51 percent of non-Desnick family shares and agrees to vote for the deal. Thus ends MMA's brief life as a public company.

The investigative reporter I conjure finally shows up in March 1993, by which time the Desnick Eye Center has twenty-five locations. The reporter is Sam Donaldson of ABC's *Prime Time Live* instead of *Sixty Minutes*. "We begin tonight with the story of a so-called 'big cutter,' Dr. James Desnick," Donaldson begins his on-air report on June 10, 1993. "[W]e turned up evidence that he may also be a big charger, doing unnecessary cataract surgery for the money." (OpenJurist website, 1994. 5) Medicare takes no action on the media event. In 2015, an Internet and telephone search finds no listings for Desnick Eye Center.

I see Dr. Desnick's story as a cautionary parable of underestimating the ingrained philosophical obstacles to expanding a medically based business. Many investors want to believe that consolidating fragmented businesses is the path to higher profits, but MMA's tale illustrates the manifold philosophical and operating fishhooks that can derail such business-school dreams. Not to be overlooked is the possibility, yea probability, that many persons, animated by Dr. Desnick's $9.5 million pay in 1987 and overlooking his $700,000 salary as MMA's head, sought to pluck the golden goose with investment banking fees, severance charges, high prices to buy eye centers outside Chicago, and so on. Whatever the cause, MMA's brief effort to create the first publicly traded corporation dedicated exclusively to eye care is history.

A HOME FOR HAMILTON

Soon after setting up C&D, we come into contact with Sefton Stallard, a nationally known mortgage banker whose Hamilton Investment Trust of Elizabeth, New Jersey, is in debt doo-doo. After an initial $25 million offering in July 1971, Hamilton grows rapidly into a much larger REIT until, by 1978, it holds an $81 mortgage portfolio subject to a highly leveraged $54 million debt. Its mortgages are 26 percent nonearning, and 39 percent of assets are foreclosed properties.

Realty Stock Review sizes up Hamilton's position in September 1982 when its market value is $11.8 million in these words: "Steadily reducing debt and liquidating assets, then down to $25 million; Repaid $2.6 million to banks from 1978 to 1982 and expects to repay rest soon. Most condo end loans being sold and is refinancing apartments to boost cash; Seeks partner." Those final two words flash like neon.

Hamilton's trustees comprise a blue ribbon panel of New Jersey notables, including the presidents of Mutual Benefit Life Company, Jersey Mortgage Company, Union Dime Savings Bank, Public Service Electric & Gas Company, Drexel University, and chairman of the Port of New York Authority. This board moves very deliberately to work out of this hole. Somewhere along the line, Hamilton is contacted by the Johnstown organization, a private apartment and office manager. Talks proceed slowly because Johnstown is really a group of interrelated entities, and that corporate tangle must be simplified.

When C&D is finally retained by Hamilton in late 1982 to render a fairness opinion on merging the two, we hop a late-evening plane to Atlanta, bunk in the only rooms available in a motel undergoing substantial renovation, and spend two or three days at Johnstown's headquarters in a business park just inside Atlanta's north perimeter highway.

Johnstown manages 204 apartment projects with 48,300 dwelling units plus 3.4 million square feet of offices, mainly across the Southeast, using a sophisticated proprietary computer monitoring system to make sure the properties operate profitably. I am overwhelmed at the depth of their day-to-day tracking of rents, traffic, and signed leases, the detail far exceeding anything I had witnessed before.

After deeper investigation of Johnstown's management corps and after eliminating some conflicts inherent within its organization, we determine to issue the fairness opinion in late 1982 in a transaction creating Johnstown American Companies as the new entity. The new Johnstown American lists on the American Stock Exchange (symbol JAC) in February 1983, and its 6.75 million shares enjoy good reception from investors pushing market cap to $65 million by March 1986.

"The undersigned rendered a fairness opinion to the Trustees of Hamilton in this transaction which resulted in formation of Johnstown American Companies," says our March 1983 tombstone ad.

The JAC acquisition brings us into contact with John Lie-Nielsen, Johnstown's exuberant CEO, who leads his staff in singing the company fight song every morning.

A year later, JAC retains C&D to provide a valuation for Johnstown's acquisition of two more companies in Lie-Nielsen's orbit, Marshall Homes and Johnstown Mortgage Co. There are no major issues in this deal, and we sign off in January 1984.

"The undersigned advised the independent Trustees of Johnstown American Companies in this transaction and rendered a Fairness Opinion to them," our January 1984 tombstone recounts.

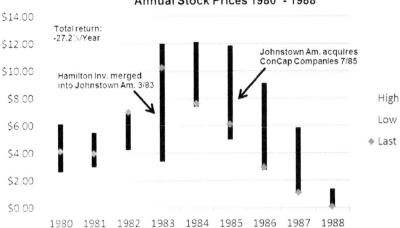

Exhibit 22.3: Hamilton/Johnstown Amer. (A: JAc)
Annual Stock Prices 1980 - 1988

In July 1985, JAC acquires the assets and management business of Consolidated Capital Companies, or ConCap, a syndicator based in Emeryville, California, whose sponsored REITs and partnerships own the majority of JAC's managed properties. The acquisition includes seven publicly registered but nontraded REITs managed by ConCap.

Those management contracts should be a profitable asset, but the ConCap trusts are already weighed down by bad assets when the acquisition takes place, and this acquisition strains JAC's resources. C&D does *not* opine on this acquisition.

"JAC has hit an air-pocket since acquiring the major West Coast syndicator ConCap," *Realty Stock Review* tells investors in February 1987 as the magnitude of this misstep surfaces. By that time, JAC stock is down by two-thirds, from a high of $12 in February 1985 to $3.63.

JAC reports its first loss, of $1.15 a share, for its August 1987 fiscal year, the result of falling ConCap revenue plus other ConCap losses, and JAC suspends its dividend. "JAC remains one of the bigger losers in realty stocks," we report in December 1987, "falling 60% this year atop a 49% drop last year."

In February 1988, Southmark, the always eager buyer, cuts a deal to buy JAC for $7 million—a pittance for a company once valued at about $125 million. Four business days after announcing the deal, Southmark omits its common dividend to "preserve capital."

"We are removing both Southmark and Johnstown American from Portfolio Selector until the situation clarifies," we advise subscribers on February 12, 1988, "even though it means a loss for investors who bought previously and even though we may be selling at the bottom and missing some recovery in these two depressed stocks."

Southmark Corporation, the Dallas-based real estate conglomerate that turns out to be one of the great failures of the 1980s (chapter 19, "The Reit Catchers"), completes its acquisition of JAC in December 1988.

A month later, in January 1989, Southmark directors sever ties with Gene E. Phillips, Southmark's CEO, and management of the seven ConCap REITs passes to Phillips (see chapter 19—The Reit Catchers).

To me, these unlovely ConCap pariahs of the REIT industry already kill one company and the deal sounds more like Southmark directors are trying desperately to save their company from Johnstown American's sorry fate.

They fail. Johnstown American loses 27 percent a year between its 1982 acquisition of Hamilton and its December 1988 acquisition by Southmark. The short lesson here is that when the hole keeps getting deeper, stop digging. The larger take-away is that both JAC and Southmark err in trying to rescue ConCap as the tax-shelter syndication business becomes obsolete under multiple federal clamp-downs in the mid-1980s (chapter 19, "The Reit Catchers").

THE ABSORPTION OF WESTERN

Almost from the beginning, Bob and I are intrigued by prospects of doing something—advising, taking over, anything—with Western Mortgage Investors, a tiny mortgage REIT based in Boston. Very early in our partnership, in February 1982, we buy 53,000 WMI shares or a 5.3 percent stake in this $5 million market value trust and use the block as leverage with management.

One of the oldest mortgage trusts, Western was founded in 1964 by Bill Blackfield, a former president of the National Association of Home Builders (NAHB), whom I know from my *House & Home* days. Over the years, it grows slowly, confining itself initially to FHA-insured fixed-rate housing loans. But as the mortgage REIT craze advances, it ventures into more aggressive lending fields. Now, in 1981, it is on the path toward becoming an involuntary property REIT like many of its compatriots.

The situation and some of its properties catch the eye of Landon Clay, a legendary Boston investor who is both heart and soul of Eaton Vance Corporation, one of the largest mutual fund complexes in the land. Landon seems infatuated with the potentials of real estate and sets out to acquire Western.

Over the months of 1982, he keeps acquiring WMI shares until by year-end he controls 30 percent of WMI shares and presses the trust to enter real estate management and development under a new name, WMI Equities. Ink on the new name is barely dry in March 1983 before Clay presses to merge WMI into Eaton Vance so he can install Western as the real estate arm of Eaton Vance.

Western hires C&D to advise its trustees and vet the terms of any deal. After a great deal of back-and-forth, in which we meet directly with Clay on two occasions—he is polite but unshakable in his demands—terms for an agreement are reached.

"Only one directorship to an industry," Clay repeats several times, which we take to mean he is determined that WMI will be his single real estate industry bet. After finally convincing Clay to improve the terms of his first proposal, we deem the transaction fair and WMI is absorbed into Eaton Vance in September 1983.

"The undersigned acted as financial adviser to WMI's Trustees, assisted in negotiations improving the terms of the transaction, and rendered a fairness opinion to the Trustees of WMI," recites our tombstone ad.

BREAKOUT FOR UDR

During the late 1970s, I grow friendly with John McCann, head of a very small Richmond, Virginia, trust named Old Dominion REIT. Old Dominion is so small that I omit it from both my 1970s books, *America's Newest Billionaires* in 1971 and *New Opportunities in Realty Trusts* in 1978.

When I first meet McCann, he is virtually the trust's only employee but has already carved out an important niche as a renovator and upgrading specialist of moderate-income apartments.

Trustees make a couple of aborted expansion efforts, and so Old Dominion remains locked into apartments and industrial properties, all in its home state of Virginia.

Realty Stock Review's first look at Old Dominion in March 1981 offers no opinion but describes the $5.6 million market value trust as "assets are all Virginia, half apartments targeted toward the middle apartment markets. In 1980 trust floated $3 million debentures to repay $2.3 million balloon mortgage. Sale gains also provide funds for reinvestment."

McCann is not content to run a tiny trust and shares his visions of growth sugar plums for Old Dominion REIT. In my reading, I run across an even smaller trust, Piedmont REIT, based in Charlotte, North Carolina, and contact Piedmont to ask if they will meet with McCann.

Remember, if you don't ask, you don't get.

Piedmont managers at Ruddick Corporation, Piedmont's manager, are interested because running a small trust is burdensome to Piedmont's managers, who own and run the much larger Harris-Teeter Supermarkets chain.

At the initial meeting on September 1, 1982, in Charlotte, North Carolina, Herman McManaway, Piedmont's principal, is openly scornful of Old Dominion's small market value, now grown to $12.8 million with the stock price up 11 percent from the initial *RSR* listing.

"You have no liquidity in your stock," he taunts McCann.

"I can show you more liquidity than you think," parries McCann.

I fly back to New York convinced the deal is dead.

But McCann is single-minded in pursuing his goal of a larger trust, and he and I keep going back to Piedmont until McManaway agrees to more serious talks.

Eventually Piedmont agrees to merge into Old Dominion for 106,000 shares worth just over $1 million. But talks hit a snag when McCann balks at including a Florence, South Carolina, shopping center in the deal. McManaway is adamant that Old Dominion must take everything; he wants out completely.

"Will you give me a right of assignment at closing?" McCann asks in desperation.

"Sure," says McManaway after a long pause.

Again, you don't get if you don't ask.

This highly unusual concession gives McCann the right to market this property during pendency of the deal and lets him substitute a new buyer at closing. McCann promptly puts the asset out to the commercial brokerage network and has a strong buyer under contract within weeks.

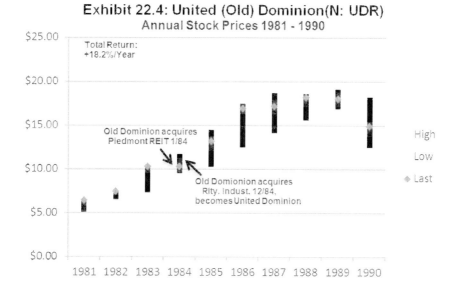

Exhibit 22.4: United (Old) Dominion(N: UDR)
Annual Stock Prices 1981 - 1990

The deal closes in January 1984, and C&D tells the world in this tombstone ad: "The undersigned initiated this transaction and represented Old Dominion REIT."

The ad is pure gold in the M&A world.

Before the year 1984 is out, McCann engineers the acquisition of a similar-sized Richmond entity, Realty Industries, for 2.5 million new shares valued at $27.5 million and the combined REIT becomes United Dominion REIT. Market value leaps to $47 million.

With deftly timed sales of $23 million of 9 percent convertibles in July 1985 and 1.5 million shares at $15.25 in December 1986 to raise $23 million, McCann keeps UDR's cash flow and dividends per share rising at a 7.5 percent annual clip through the first five years after that breakout Piedmont acquisition. United Dominion returns 18 percent annually to shareholders from 1981 through the recession year of 1989, fancy stepping for any REIT for any environment.

The trust adopts the name UDR Inc. in 2007, and in 2015, the little

REIT that thought it could operates as a national apartment player, owning interests in 51,293 apartment units with an $8.2 billion market value.

Fancy stepping for a REIT launched into the big time by that one small deal.

John McCann and I remain friends, and representing NAREIT, he presents me the REIT Industry Leadership Award in May 1996. He leaves UDR in 2001 to develop apartments and a new town mixed-use community at Williamsburg, Virginia.

TEXAS IN A TIME OF TRAVAIL

In the spring of 1986, we are invited by the Landsing Group to visit their Menlo Park, California offices and discuss issuing a fairness opinion on the merger of two REITs sponsored and managed by Landsing. Organized in 1972, Landsing is the vehicle for two Stanford MBA grads, Gary Barr and Grayson Saunders, to inject some new and creative ideas into the real estate world. By 1975, they give life to the first SEC-registered nontraded finite-life REIT, meaning assets will be liquidated in approximately ten years and proceeds returned to shareholders.

Gary Barr is the inside man, skilled in handling operations and all the legal issues that arise from a diversified real estate practice. He develops a number of computer applications that enhance Landsing's underwriting of property investments and local real estate trends.

Grayson Saunders, the outside man, is the consummate salesman, sophisticated and polished in presentations. Grayson cranks up a sizable marketing effort that ultimately sells over $600 million of REIT shares and real estate limited partnership interests throughout the country. His marketing efforts bring him into contact with thought leaders across the spectrum, and Grayson eventually is elected a director of the Pension Real Estate Association and a governor of the National Association of Real Estate Investment Trusts. (He eventually leaves Landsing in 1988 to become director of real estate investments for Ameritech Corporation, one of the seven "Baby Bells" created by the split-up of American Telephone & Telegraph in the mid-1980s. At Ameritech, he manages a $1.5 billion real estate portfolio.)

During the first half of the 1980s, Landsing and dozens of other real estate syndicators raise about $100 billion through the sale of limited partnership units to many thousands of investors. Syndicators seek to leverage the money they raise by borrowing two to four times their equity, so that this huge surge of equity capital into real estate results in an influx of from $400 to $500 billion into real estate.

Unlike many of its competitors, Landsing also focuses on setting up real estate investment trusts and becomes among the earliest advocates of finite-life REITs designed to liquidate after a specified number of years.

The honey drawing these investors was the ability to write off real estate losses against ordinary income under the IRS code of that day. "Gimme shelter," is the watchphrase for investors who seek out the purveyors of high write-off syndicates. Very rarely do investors seek details of the properties into which their money is poured.

The atom bomb drops October 22, 1986, when Congress enacts the Tax Reform Act of 1986, effectively outlawing the ability of non-real estate professionals to use passive losses from tax shelters to offset their regular income. The tax-shelter business halts almost immediately, and syndicators are now left with the massive task of filling the offices, shopping centers, and apartments they finance.

In the second half of the 1980s, this gives rise to forests of see-through office buildings (offices with no tenants) in virtually every American city. Hundreds of commercial properties are foreclosed in one of the worst real estate recessions since World War II.

Against this backdrop of mounting real estate distress, our assignment in June 1986 is to value the assets of two equity REITs, First

Western Income and Second Western Income Realty Trusts. To protect from just such distress, Landsing concentrates investments west of the Mississippi River in diversified portfolios, including offices, shopping centers, and apartments. This strategy dictates concentrating holdings in the hottest real estate markets of that day, namely the Southwest and specifically Texas.

It does not help that Congress's death knell for syndicators arrives just as the US oil industry grapples with its worst slump in decades. That June of 1986, oil prices plunge briefly below ten dollars per barrel, and the drilling rig count—a measure of industry health—is the lowest in years. Those stats strike a dagger into the heart of oil country.

Our first stop is the trust's largest investment, a downtown Oklahoma City office building where we find occupancies in the 80 percent range and asking rents falling fast. We travel with Charles Bailey, a real estate appraiser, who collects rent and occupancy data in a thorough and dispassionate way.

Then we set off by rented car for Amarillo, Texas, about 210 miles to the south, for a look at properties in the distressed oil patch. Arriving in Amarillo about 4:00 p.m., we visit a 120-unit apartment complex and ask the rental agent, a young woman, for data on the property.

"What is your occupancy?" asks Bailey.

"One hundred percent rented for apartments available for rent," she replies.

"How many apartments is that?" persists Bailey.

"Ninety-three," she says.

"But my information is that the project has 120 units," says Bailey.

"That's right," she says evenly. "We have twenty-seven apartments not rentable."

The searing Texas sun chars the roofs atop large swaths of the two-story project, and leaks during any rain kill any chance of renting these units. Worse, with nearly 25 percent of the units uninhabitable, the project has no way of generating enough excess cash flow after mortgage payments to repair the cracked roofs.

The rental agent copes with this dire strait by using every penny of available cash to patch enough roofs to make units livable again. The afternoon we arrive, she drains petty cash to send the maintenance superintendent to buy one more five-gallon drum of tar to give her one more apartment to rent.

The super, an ingenious man, has rigged Rube Goldbergian plastic funnels inside leaky apartments so that rainwater flows into one of those empty five-gallon cans and does not ruin carpets or furnishings. The woman is a tigress, using every trick at her command to save enough money for that long-awaited new roof.

In all my years of touring real estate projects, I never witness anything remotely resembling such ingenuity to keep a project going.

That night, we dine at the Big Texan on Route 66, renowned since its opening in 1960 for its standing offer: if you can eat a thirty-six-ounce steak with all the trimmings in one hour, it's free. Otherwise, the cost is thirty-six dollars. (Inflation boosts the offer to a seventy-two-ounce steak for seventy-two dollars, says the restaurant's website.) A showcase inside the entry displays statistics carefully culled over many years: about 15 percent get the free dinner.

That evening, I order and eat rattlesnake for the one and only time in my life. Never again: my rattler is desiccated, bony, and totally devoid of real nutrition. During our stay, one customer orders the thirty-six-ouncer. In little over an hour, he is being helped to the door by his female companion. (Over a decade later, I introduce our fat one-hundred-page-plus presentation book as "our thirty-six-ounce steak" to a pension selection committee at Texas A&M University. Unknown to me, the committee chair is a one-time Big Texan eater, and we are hired.)

The next morning, it's off for Lubbock, a sunbaked town about one hundred miles south and home of Texas Tech University. The trust owns a handsome three-story apartment complex marketed to university students, meaning units are very full nine months of the year but languish during the hot summer. The manager tries to reach nonstudents, but the property is struggling. Still, the roofs do not leak and the project generates some free cash.

Information garnered, we set off across the flat plains of West Texas for Midland, another 110 miles south and capital of an early 1980s drilling and building boom. We arrive in Midland in midafternoon, minus a speeding fine and a less-than-sterling attitude toward Texas justice. The trust owns a never-occupied shopping center in Midland, an oil-boom mistake.

This whirly-gig appraisal tour lets us establish values for the two trusts, and in due course, we issue our fairness opinion. That sad Texas tour resonates today as exhibit A in the case for investment diversification.

XPNSVQT

That same summer of 1986, Landsing employs us to find a merger partner for one of its stand-alone REITs, recalled as Western Properties Fund. Western has very little value left in its property holdings, which I do not recall specifically, so we start by listing all companies who might be buyers of low-grade properties. The list includes North America Savings and Loan Association of Santa Ana, California, an S&L started, run, and wholly owned by an Orange County dentist turned S&L tycoon, Duayne D. Christensen.

Doc Christensen, as everyone calls him, is a prosperous dentist who begins making personal real estate investments in the 1970s. As his reputation as a savvy investor grows, he begins offering investment seminars to other dentists and doctors.

In 1982, he seeks and receives permission to found North America

S&L, of which he is sole owner. At about the same time, he meets Mrs. Janet Faye McKinzie, then starting out as a local real estate broker, who becomes his companion and administrative assistant while also heading a separate real estate company (Christensen is divorced).

Christensen's North America S&L eschews home mortgage loans, the bread-and-butter of most S&Ls, and from inception North America focuses on buying, selling, and developing real estate.

But we know none of this when we arrive at North America's office at the end of a hot Wednesday, July 22, 1986.

We arrive after 4:30 p.m. and park in the building's parking garage, which is almost empty since most employees have already gone home. Near our parking spot is a remarkable Rolls-Royce Corniche, a $165,000 luxury car at the time. It sports a mysterious vanity license plate: "XPNSVQT." Now insider-chic license plates are legion in California. O. J. Simpson's murdered wife's car sports this plate: "L84AD8," being interpreted as "Late for a date." One gets desensitized to trying to penetrate the meaning of California plates. So we pass by.

Doc Christensen's office is on the highest floor of a four- or five-story building. After announcing our presence and waiting a few minutes, the woman behind the secretary's desk pushes a button, and double walnut doors swing open to admit us to Doc Christensen's office: a full 1,500-square-feet aerie walnut-paneled on all walls *and the ceiling*—the only paneled ceiling I have ever seen, before or since. Altogether, it is among the most lavish offices in my experience—and that covers a lot of territory. We explain our mission and describe the properties held by Western. Doc Christensen's interest flags after a few minutes. The meeting ends relatively quickly, and we exit through those double walnut doors, down the elevator, and back to the parking garage to confront again that magnificent Rolls-Royce Corniche.

Bob, ever the afficionado of high-end automobiles, can't restrain his curiosity.

"What," he wonders, "do those scrambled letters mean on that license plate?"

By now, I've figured out the puzzle.

"Sound out the letters," I say. "Ex-pen-sive Q-T or cutie. The Corniche is an expensive cutie."

And off we go.

But, as mid-twentieth-century newscaster Paul Harvey always said, there is always the rest of the story.

Less than six months later, on Friday, January 16, 1987, at about 6:30 a.m. in the morning, Doc Christensen dies when his 1985 Jaguar "missed a curve while driving northbound at 70 to 75 m.p.h. on the Corona del Mar Freeway. His car traveled 400 feet down the center divider before smashing into an abutment at the Bristol Street overpass," reports the *Los Angeles Times*. He was fifty-seven.

Christensen reportedly works through the preceding night to fashion a plan to satisfy S&L regulators and forestall a takeover of North America. His death ends whatever actions he might have taken, and later that day, California S&L regulators seize North America, later charging insolvency and fraud.

Doc's death is eventually ruled an accident, even though he buys a ten-million-dollar life insurance policy only three days before his death, naming Mrs. McKinzie sole beneficiary.

In the probe that follows, the *Los Angeles Times* and other news media report that investigators charge that Mrs. McKinzie, the woman who, in our minds, opens those imposing double walnut doors for us, is involved in a complex fraud with Doc Christensen to loot the S&L's assets. In particular, they cite the case of a twenty-unit condominium project near Lake Tahoe; Christensen buys it for $3.6 million through a real estate investment trust he controls and then sells an option to North America to buy the property for $3 million. Later, he causes North America to acquire the property for $14.7 million. The property goes on North America's books at $17.7 million (purchase price plus option price), inflating the S&L's net worth.

North America then sells the property to two investors for $20.5 million, financed with an $18.4 million loan from North America. Mrs. McKinzie receives a $1 million commission on this transaction. When the investors default in 1986, the repossessed property is again sold for $30 million, eventually ending up in a company headed by Mrs. McKinzie's father. Investigators charge that Mrs. McKinzie's company, Plaza Group, receives $1.7 million in "advance commissions" during two weeks in May 1986.

Mrs. McKinzie, investigators allege, buys that $165,000 Rolls-Royce Corniche for herself with those proceeds—hence an *expensive cutie*. (Press reports at the time give her license plate as "XTACT," meaning "Ecstasy," but Bob and I always assume—rightly or wrongly—that the Corniche is related in some way to Doc Christensen.) Mrs. McKinzie buys a less expensive Rolls-Royce model for Doc, say press reports.

After a trial in July 1990, Mrs. McKinzie, at age forty-one, is convicted and sentenced to twenty years for fraud; it is the second longest prison term meted out in the S&L scandals of the 1980s until that time.

The $10 million life insurance policy is voided.

* * *

During the C&D decade of the 1980s, Bob and I travel far and wide in pursuit of clients, visiting California often and crossing the Atlantic to London to meet potential clients, to Brussels to court a real count, and from Zurich, Switzerland to Monaco by motorcar with our wives, again in pursuit of clients.

The four stock charts incorporated into this chapter attempt to grade Campbell & Dillmeier's work as investment bankers. Unhappily, I cannot trace the outcome of our other deals.

Our two big winners succeed because their CEO strategies work. Clyde Engle's soak-up-the-stock plan at Sunstates produces big gains for shareholders who stay the course, and United Dominion Realty CEO John McCann's single-minded focus on solid growth creates a long-term powerhouse.

Our two big losers stem from CEO missteps and poor execution, events investment bankers cannot foresee or prevent. British Land of America's leaders never overcome a very mediocre property portfolio, and the handoff to Medical Management of America falters on poor selection of acquisitions, while Johnstown American cannot recover from exuberant CEO John Lie-Nielsen's fatal choice to acquire Consolidated Capital Companies.

After 1990, Bob must spend more time on the family glass business as his father's involvement diminishes.

Campbell & Dillmeier ceases business in the early 1990s as effortlessly as it began.

"Campbell & Dillmeier" survives in 2015 only in the alumni rolls of academically demanding St. Michael's College in the Burlington, Vermont, suburb of Colchester. All of Bob and Peggy Dillmeier's children graduate from St. Mike's in the 1980s and 1990s, and Bob serves on the board of trustees for a few years. Our granddaughter Grace Campbell receives her St. Michael's diploma in 2007.

C&D does not always achieve its lofty goals. Read on for two bitter failures.

Chapter 23
THE SURPRISES

George Weinstein, from whom we learn about British Land's desire to enter the United States, tells Dillmeier and me one day in spring 1982 that financial circles say that the sponsor of another suffering REIT, Heitman Mortgage Investors of Chicago, wants out of the REIT business and Heitman Chairman and CEO Norman Perlmutter is looking for a deal to present to his fellow trustees. Perlmutter is a towering industry figure, sparking parent Heitman Financial Services' growth into the largest full-service real estate company of its time and a pioneer in the real estate asset management business.

But Heitman Mortgage presents a huge challenge. Heitman, in March 1982, swaps $11 million in assets to repay all bank debt, shrinking assets to $24 million from a peak $229 million. The swap leaves only $23.6 million assets to repay $17.2 million of convertible debentures that require $1.7 million sinking fund payments each year beginning December 31, 1982. Debentures are convertible into common at $14.70 a share, but with Heitman's common shares trading at thirty-eight cents in over-the-counter markets, conversion is academic.

Realty Stock Review, in June 1982, calls shares "an option on a potential merger or acquisition."

One Heitman effort to find new management fails in March 1982, and Weinstein believes that a partnership of his Weinstein Associates with Campbell & Dillmeier might win a nod from Heitman's leaders.

We fly to Chicago on July 29, 1982, and meet with Heitman officials. Our gathering that July day is slightly surreal, as no more than eight persons, our group of four plus three Heitman Mortgage officers, rattle around in a boardroom built to seat twenty.

We propose buying from the trust $100,000 of 9 percent Senior Convertible Notes due August 31, 1983, plus 800,000 warrants, exercisable at $1 per share, for one cent a warrant or $8,000. It is a very thin equity deal, but Heitman is running out of options. After much back-and-forth, we reach an amicable business deal to change the trust's name, move headquarters to Milwaukee, and attempt to deal with the imminent sinking fund payment.

After some discussion, the Heitman contingent accepts and the lawyers begin to draft legal documents.

Within weeks, the deal, structured to require only approval from Heitman's current trustees, closes on August 31, 1982, and we assume management of Heitman. We promptly rename the trust Regency Investors after the Regency Hotel in Manhattan where Weinstein normally stays. I am named chairman, Bob becomes president and chief operating officer, George acts as secretary, and a Milwaukee friend named Dick Kite becomes treasurer.

Voila, the "Campbell group" has taken over a broken-down mortgage REIT with a chance to make a name (and possibly some money) if we can restructure the looming debt problem.

Bob sets about working the assets but quickly finds the two largest mortgages, two-thirds of assets, are complex and difficult to restore to health, a condition not uncommon among mortgage trusts of that day. Two land parcels, another 23 percent of assets, aren't earning income.

At the 424-room Hotel Le Concorde in Quebec City, Canada,

Regency holds a 53 percent participation in a $22 million, 10-percent-interest mortgage, whose interest is payable only to the extent cash flow permits. With the local economy very sour, Regency is getting only 4.4 percent cash interest versus the 10 percent stated rate. Bob Dillmeier investigates and reports that management fees to Loews Hotels, the manager controlled by billionaires Robert and Laurence Tisch of Manhattan, cause much of the shortfall. No easy way to boost yield exists.

At a 356,000-square foot shopping center in Adrian, Michigan, Regency holds a 30.5 percent participation in a $9.46 million mortgage. The mortgage carries a 7 percent coupon, but the trust guarantees a 10 percent return to the bank owning the other 69.5 percent, meaning "the trust receives virtually no interest income with regard to its participation."

Worse, the center's owner "stopped making any payments with regard to the mortgage loan in June 1982, claiming that the money was needed to fund approximately $400,000 of repairs to the mall," says our 1982 annual report to shareholders.

Dillmeier says roofs leak so badly at one anchor store that the manager deploys buckets about the store when it rains to limit merchandise damage and keep shoppers dry. We fear this major tenant will depart, and the mortgage squeeze puts the trust in default on the underlying loan to a Chicago bank.

Thus squeezed, we sue to put the center's owner into foreclosure, to which the owner, like most pressured owners, responds by filing bankruptcy for the owning entity.

This leads to a long court battle that is never resolved on our watch.

But Regency's biggest problem is that it now has only $15.7 million in net assets after $5.9 million loss reserves to repay those $17.2 million of 7.5 percent subordinated convertible debentures.

We seek to contact bond holders, but our efforts turn up dry holes because owners of debentures are not required to disclose their holdings, as are stockholders under the 13-D filing law (chapters 18 to 20).

In December 1982, we as management offer to exchange a package of one hundred shares for each $1,000 bond plus new non-interest-bearing debentures at par for the outstanding debentures as the only way out for bondholders.

The offer flops, and less than 5 percent of holders accept.

OUT OF THE SHADOWS

As the swap offer's failure becomes apparent in January 1983, Manhattan attorney Marvin Olshan of the Park Avenue firm Olshan Grundman & Frome arrives in our offices and advises that the bulk of the debentures are owned by unnamed "persons who do not sit on boards."

His message is the rudest of rude surprises.

He says the only deal that will fly is a "realistic" exchange offer giving control to designees of these large holders.

In follow-up discussions, we learn that Olshan represents bond brokers Drexel Burnham Lambert and Neuberger & Berman, owners of 10.4 and 8.5 percent of bonds respectively.

We have no choice but to begin discussing Olshan's demands and begin crafting a new bond exchange offer suitable to these major holders.

Upon further inquiry, it turns out that a 24 percent block of debentures is owned by Executive Life Insurance of Los Angeles, then a high-flying insurance company and well-known Drexel client.

Combined with the Drexel and Neuberger blocks, the Executive Life block means 43 percent of Regency's bonds are held by Olshan's group and Regency is now clearly a satellite within Drexel Burnham's junk-bond trading and client universe.

At that time, Drexel's Beverly Hills, California, high-yield bond-trading operation is run by Michael and Lowell Milken, brothers who essentially become the public face of brokerage firm Drexel Burnham

Lambert. A brilliant scholar, Michael, while earning his MBA degree at Wharton School at the University of Pennsylvania in Philadelphia, becomes heavily influenced by a credit study of the 1930s concluding that non-investment-grade bonds offer risk-adjusted returns exceeding those of investment-grade bonds.

Through Wharton contacts, Michael Milken lands a summer job in 1969 at Drexel Harriman Ripley, one of Philadelphia's oldest investment banks. After graduation, he joins Drexel, by then known as Drexel Firestone, as director of low-grade bond research, a job carrying a small amount of trading capital. When Drexel merges with Burnham & Company in 1973 to form Drexel Burnham and Company, Milken persuades Tubby Burnham, his new boss and also a Wharton alumnus, to set up a high-yield bond-trading department.

When Milken's operation earns an astounding 100 percent return on investment, the Milkens in 1978 move the trading operation to Los Angeles, first in Century City and later at 9560 Wilshire Boulevard near the Beverly Wilshire Hotel in Beverly Hills. Sitting at an elevated X-shaped desk above his trading floor, Michael Milken shouts orders during the trading day to a dedicated corps of bond traders and investment bankers.

Milken's vision soon extends far beyond the trading floor as he and his colleagues embrace the proposition that junk bonds, Wall Street's shorthand for non-investment-grade bonds, can provide readily accessible capital for younger, faster-growing but non-investment-grade companies. Southmark Corporation, a real estate shooting star of the 1980s turned dark star, is an early and frequent customer of Milken's money machine (chapter 19, "The Reit Catchers").

Working extraordinary hours, Milken, by the 1980s, is able to raise undreamed sums for his clients. The roster of Milken clients of the early 1980s runs from MCI Communications, then a smallish provider of long-distance telephone services, to Ted Turner's upstart Turner Broadcasting to casino operator and real estate entrepreneur Steve Wynn and to dozens of smaller and midsized companies looking for start-up or expansion capital.

Milken is credited with financing numerous Las Vegas companies, such as MGM Mirage, Mandalay Resorts, Park Place, and Harrah's Entertainment. During most of the 1980s, Milken's operations dominate the underwriting and trading of high-yield junk bonds.

SEC investigators begin looking into Milken's operations as early as 1979, but nothing comes of their inquiries until arbitrageur and hedge fund manager Ivan Boesky (chapter 18, "The Reit Chasers") pleads guilty to securities fraud in 1986 and reportedly implicates Milken in several illegal transactions.

Fred Joseph, a contributor to my *America's Newest Billionaires* fifteen years earlier and now Drexel president, continues to insist that nothing is amiss until December 20, 1988, when Drexel lawyers find suspicious trading in a private partnership set up to let members of Milken's team make their own investments.

Trading in the partnership raises the very serious possibility that Drexel has broken its fiduciary obligations to its clients. A day later, Drexel pleads *nolo contendere* (no contest) to six counts of stock parking and stock manipulation and agrees that Milken must leave the firm if he is indicted.

Michael Milken is indeed indicted on ninety-eight counts of racketeering and fraud in March 1989 and pleads guilty to six securities and reporting felonies on April 24, 1990. As part of his plea, Milken agrees to pay $200 million in fines and disgorge $400 million for shareholders allegedly hurt by his actions.

Attorney General Richard Thornburgh, through US Attorney Rudolph Giuliani, threatens to indict Lowell Milken, an attorney for

Drexel, for racketeering, but this threat is later dropped. As a result, Michael Milken serves twenty-two months in prison, beginning in March 1991. He subsequently becomes a nationally recognized philanthropist and funder of pioneering cancer research, tracing to his diagnosis of prostate cancer in January 1993.

But in January 1983, all this constitutes an unknown future. All we know is that the Milken brothers are kings of the junk bond world, they are Olshan's client, and we have no choice but to negotiate with Olshan's clients.

INVITE TO THE PREDATOR'S BALL

Once we agree to go forward with an exchange offer suitable to the Olshan group and the exchange offer is made official in late spring 1983, an acquaintance in Milken's Los Angeles office—the same Drexel office that supplied *Realty Trust Review* with REIT bond quotes all during the 1970s—invites me to attend Drexel's high-yield bond conference in Beverly Hills in June 1983.

Hopping a plane, I stay at a hotel on Century Boulevard and attend the conference being held that year at the Beverly Wilshire Hotel. Attendance exceeds two thousand, and the meetings are crammed with Milken acolytes from around the world. At that conference, I witness Milken in action at his famed X-shaped desk, more by accident than any special invitation.

Author Connie Bruck bases her 1988 best seller *The Predator's Ball* on Milken's annual high-yield bond conclaves.

The second Regency bond offer—675 common shares per $1,000 bond plus a new debenture secured by all Regency's assets but paying no interest until 1986—finally is completed in summer 1983. Completion gives voting control to bondholders. I serve for a year on Regency's transition board of trustees, now chaired by Olshan. I leave the Regency board after one year.

Thirty-two years later, that Regency ambush surprise still stings.

My only balm is that Regency repurchases the Campbell group debentures at par, returning our bait money. We are money good and receive salaries for our management services to boot. Not so bad after all.

From my one visit to the Predator's Ball, I bring home a cup emblazoned "I Survived The Drexel 1983 High Yield And Convertible Bond Conference."

Unfortunately, the conference sponsors neglect to fire-harden the cup's legend, likely due to time pressures, and the words soon degrade when the cup is washed with detergent. It sits, faded letters and all, on my desk today. See photo section.

Sic transit gloria! Always know who sits behind the curtain.

THE LOSING WINNER

In November 1983, we are visited by an Irishman named John Murphy, a handsome fellow with a yard-wide grin and an answer for everything. He tells of modest success with a company named Dublin and London Developments and now wants to seek fame and fortune in the United States. He brings the backing of two Irish brothers, Paddy and Alister McGuckian, dairy farmers whose privately owned Masstock Corp. was a sophisticated multinational agribusiness operating in the United Kingdom, eastern Europe, Saudi Arabia and Africa,

Within a few months, Murphy presents the idea of taking over management of Central Mortgage & Realty Trust, another broken mortgage REIT based in Minneapolis. We negotiate for a time with Hugh Klein, Central's principal, and reach agreement on this deal: the trust will pay to then-current shareholders a $6.2 million dividend, or $8.00 per share, being substantially all gains on property sales. After the dividend, the trust will sell 600,000 new shares to an investor group consisting of the McGuckians and Campbell & Dillmeier. We agree to pay fifty-two cents a share, a 37 percent premium over the thirty-eight-cent book value, for the new shares, enough shares to give us 44 percent control of the 1.375 million shares outstanding post-closing.

When the papers arrive, we learn that our partners are investing via a couple of Channel Island companies, well known tax efficient locales in the United Kingdom compatible with the multinational Masstock. Bob Dillmeier shakes his head and says he wants out. Since we agree early on to give each partner full disclosure, this seems fair.

Undeterred, Irene and I put up $62,400 to buy 120,000 shares of the renamed Central Realty Investors (CRI) stock at fifty-two cents a share in October 1984. Ultimately, our stake in this company rises to 130,000 shares, all held in my SEP-IRA pension plan. I am installed as chairman and with the board, which includes several prominent real estate professionals, sets about trying to resuscitate CRI. Market value never exceeds $1 million, and the shares never sell for much over a seventy-five-cents bid, precluding raising significant new capital.

Over the years, Central Realty Investors (CRI), as we rename it, never is able to acquire sufficient earning assets to prevent losses and proves an investment Waterloo over the longer term. Along the way, we acquire an even smaller REIT based in Phoenix, but its industrial properties have roof problems and so are sold off one by one to build cash and limit capital expenditures.

We never can grow staff to critical mass, and Murphy, with all his charm and his creative mind, becomes a one-man band searching for home-run deals with a limited chance of success.

Then in 1994, against all odds, Murphy pulls together a fully financed $80 million deal to acquire Major Realty, owner of a large Orlando tract now home to Universal Studios theme park. But the acquisition fails because of a counter offer by an insider shareholder, gravely disappointing all concerned. Worse, Central loses its due diligence and legal expenses. It is the big fish that got away. Today it stands as the landmark deal that would have culminated a decade's labors and justified my work with Central.

After this, the McGuckian brothers invest another $60,000 in Central in late 1994 to cover operating expenses while a new deal is sought.

In the meantime, Central stock spirals down and eventually is delisted from NASDAQ. John Murphy, his confidence broken by the failure of the Major Realty deal and inability to close another acquisition, resigns as president in October 1995. Feeling that Central's failure taints his future in the United States, Murphy sets sail for Europe.

In June 1996, one of the remaining directors writes me saying the McGuckians would respond to "any reasonable offer ... that might be particularly advantageous to you."

Without an offer, he says, "I will resign occasioning, I believe, the demise of C.R.I."

By then, I have sold my 130,000 CRI shares for a penny to establish a tax loss and there is no reason to respond.

That CRI stock sale marks the saddest surprise and largest single loss of my investment life.

Murphy and I continue to correspond by e-mail, and he eventually settles in a small town in rural France and starts a profitable business repositioning and selling bar properties. During the 2008–09 financial crisis, he makes a good play in undervalued bank stocks.

He suffers a heart attack in 2010 and e-mails that "the regime of meds that keep the life source pumping do have considerable side effects, thus I had to adapt to a different way of life because of a different level of energy ... The adaptation has slowed me down but it also left me more time and inclination to pursue more literary interests." We still correspond, and I still hope to visit John in France at some future time.

End of Central, end of story. Moral: Listen to your partners.

Chapter 24
THE CLIENTS

"Why do you sell your market research and advice for a song [our highest annual subscription was $164 in 1980] instead of using it for your own use in the market?" an investor friend asks during the late 1970s.

It becomes a haunting question as we enter the 1980s.

Publishing investment advisory services is demanding physically and of time and resources. During the 1970s, we literally publish our way out of perdition by pumping about 6,900 pages out of our tiny office (chapter 17, "The Lemonade"). The effort leaves scant time to mull trends and context or to envision a bigger picture for clients.

Ruminating on the 1970s, I view my first decade like running madly in a squirrel cage. Renewal rates for *Realty Trust/Stock Review*, our best periodical service, are never much over 50 percent. That demands constant trolling for new subscribers. Subscriber acquisition costs, measured as the amount needed for newspaper advertising and promotional mailing, become significant. If the average subscriber lasts only a year or so, periodical publishing saddles Audit with high front-end costs without matching rewards, namely higher gross profit margins.

As we turn the calendar into the 1980s, Irene and I vow to try to work smarter, not harder. The enormous output of printed material in the 1970s, whether measured in pages or words, is enervating. Moreover, I commute to Manhattan for nearly two decades, spending between one to two hours daily at each end of the trek locked in bus or train, and this begins to wear on me physically as I mark my fiftieth birthday right after New Year's Day 1980.

Stock taking is in order, and here's how I size up the choices for the 1980s.

PERIODICAL PUBLISHING

Equity REITs escape the direst consequences of the 1970s crash and indeed begin an unprecedented bull market run from that December 1974 low lasting thirteen years. But I cannot count on the bull market's longevity in 1980, and besides, the REIT market is tiny—market capitalization is only about $1.75 billion for only seventy-one REITs. To me, in 1980, pouring more resources into periodical publishing seems very chancy, at best. Better merge *Realty Trust Review* with our other print services to create one combined service for core subscribers and search elsewhere for profits. We do this, and our first combined service appears in January 1981. Renamed *Realty Stock Review*, it covers sixty-seven remaining qualified REITs (market value: $2.47 billion by then) along with 114 homebuilders, land developers, former REITs, and mortgage and diversified companies (market value: $6.8 billion).

INVESTMENT MANAGEMENT

As an investment adviser registered with the SEC, Audit, from inception, has full legal authority to manage money for unrelated clients but uses this power only for a brief time in 1973 and 1974, just in time to catch a big bear market. We are told by other money managers that investment clients tend to stay on board for several years, making client turnover the polar opposite to our publishing experience. The front-end costs of tooling up to acquire and service investors are significant, but the effort seems worth the cost. Moreover, potential margins for money management are much higher than the thin slice of profits we realize in publishing. Each $1 million in assets under management (AUM) can generate from $5,000 to $10,000 revenue at estimated management fees ranging from 0.5 to 1.0 percent of AUM. That sum equals thirty to sixty subscriptions at the then-going rate of $164 yearly.

The major negative is that no one on our staff has direct experience with a money management firm. I spin this in my mind as a positive by telling myself we will not be tainted by the bad habits of others.

So I take a deep breath, figure that my personal stock-picking experience will carry the day, and decide to go for the money management brass ring!

By end of the 1970s, my thinking turns strongly toward the equity REITs, which mount a dramatic 117 percent climb from the December 1974 bear-market low, more than doubling the 57 percent rise of the S&P 500 in the same span. When the higher dividend income for REITs is added, equity REITs are clear winners in the performance derby. This superior performance over five years is the basis for my thesis that smart investors should consider hiring Audit, the only independent REIT adviser standing, as their investment manager for REITs.

To signal the change in corporate direction, we change Audit's name from Audit Investment Research, which signifies third-party research to investors, to Audit Investments, implying that investing client assets is our primary business. I can never prove that this name change makes any difference—many people just wanted to deal with Ken Campbell—but the new name is like donning a spanking new suit, guaranteed to spruce up your outlook on life and business. Somehow, it works.

The prospect of working closely with both institutional and individual investors excites me as we enter a new decade. Looking back from 2015 on this transition, it's clear I should have spent a lot more time and energy romancing institutional investors and let individual investors go elsewhere. But that is the lesson of experience. Detroit Red Wings

Coach Mike Babcock is quoted as saying, "There's something about experience … In life, when you don't have it, you think it's overrated. When you have it, it's obviously very, very important."

At that time, I did not yet have enough experience working with money management clients to recognize the difference, and so I expend a fair amount of time during the 1980s chasing individual investors. Much later, I learn that individual investors are much like *RTR* subscribers— fickle and much more likely to jump ship than institutional clients. But institutions want to set up long-term relationships with managers who are also larger and equally well capitalized. I am a minnow likely to be swallowed by the whales.

THE SENATOR CALLS

Imagine my surprise when the phone rings in my office one day in October 1980 and Senator Lloyd Bentsen of Texas is on the line with a pregnant question: would Ken Campbell and Audit manage a blind investment account for him?

Would we?

Of course, of course!

The senator likes to invest in homebuilding and other housing stocks, but his position as chairman of the Senate's Housing and Urban Renewal Committee creates an insuperable conflict, preventing him from investing on his own. So somehow—and I never learn details—he tags me as the greatest housing guru around and wants me to manage a blind account. The blind discretionary account—meaning I as manager possess full authority to select the stocks and number of shares to be bought or sold—would assure the world that Senator Bentsen has no control over the identities of the housing stocks owned in the account.

Well, the offer is bittersweet because it sets back my dreams of attracting investors in equity REITs, because it means my older past in housing still has power in the marketplace. But a money manager needs money to manage, and Audit clearly needs assets to begin establishing a track record as a manager. And here is Senator Bentsen, bolt from the blue, offering to put assets in my care.

I accept, and in short order, an investment contract is signed and an account opened. Again *voila*, Audit is a bona fide money manager with a very prominent client.

The only negative is that the Senator won't let me use his name in any promotional material or share his name with other potential clients.

That arrangement continues for one and a half years, with Audit duly buying and selling homebuilding stocks in the account and sending quarterly reports to his administrative assistant. Every so often, Senator Bentsen rings me up to chat about conditions in housing, sometimes sending chatty letters commenting on the market. He invites me several times to stop in and chat when in Washington, but in all the years of management, the occasion never presents itself.

What a terrible omission. I shoot myself in a vital spot—my pocketbook.

When the account is terminated in April 1982, I have never met the man. His termination letter says, "I would certainly be pleased to recommend you to any of my friends." I take this as salve to ease the termination sting.

My exact track record in managing the account is lost in the mists, but I am really proud that I return more money to the senator than his initial stake during a chaotic market cycle when the Dow-Jones Industrials falls 11.0 percent and the Standard & Poor's 500 Index shrinks 12.2 percent.

From the senator's chair, those market readings may simply persuade him that 1982 is a poor time to be long common stocks.

In 1988, Democratic presidential candidate Michael Dukakis picks Senator Bentsen as his vice presidential running mate, giving me occasion to try to revive the relationship. But my letter goes unanswered. Vice presidential candidates certainly have more important things on their minds. Thus ends my unusual intersection with Senator Bentsen, who dies in May 2006.

A REAL FOUNDATION

Along the way, I meet a broker at Loeb Rhoades named Peter Tcherepnine. Peter is of Russian extraction and seems to know many investors who emigrated from Europe to the United States.

In October 1981, Peter tells me about the Ludwig Vogelstein Foundation, a small foundation he has run across whose idea of investment is to keep their money in a bank checking account. Peter suggests, and I concur, that we propose moving this account under Audit's management, with Loeb as the named broker, and apply the higher dividends of REITs to pay the foundation's modest operating costs, estimated at about $2,000 to $3,000 a quarter, giving the foundation the benefit of any resulting capital gains. The foundation works through a part-time executive director, and its board is headed by a Manhattan attorney, who perennially seems too busy to meet with us.

Thus it is that on November 9, 1981, Audit assumes management of the Foundation assets of $806,348. *Voila*, Audit acquires its first true institutional account. But because I am managing all Foundation assets, I develop a diversified portfolio with a heavy tilt of about 70 percent toward REITs. In the ensuing years, the account grows by 19 percent to $960,073 at the end of 1986 after providing nearly $657,000 in grants and operating costs to the foundation. Without those withdrawals, the foundation account would stand at a little over $1.6 million.

The year 1987 marks the notorious flash crash of late October when the market drops over 20 percent in a single day. Real estate securities "fall about two-thirds of the market's 22.3% decline," I report to Vogelstein trustees, "but cash flow and dividends for nearly all security holdings remain unimpaired and prospects remain bright for further cash flow gains."

The account ends 1987 at $725,408 value after making $188,000 distributions for operating expenses, our largest annual withdrawal. I am not sure trustees understand the large withdrawals but seem blocked from making personal contact.

The account rallies 16.35 percent in 1988, besting both the S&P 500 and Dow-Jones Industrials, and withdrawals fall to $108,500, ending the year with $735,000 market value.

In early April 1989, we receive a short note from the Foundation indicating without further explanation that the account is being transferred from Shearson (which has acquired Loeb Rhoades) to another broker. To this day, I regret never being able to meet personally with the foundation's chairman to tell our investment story in person.

We record a 14.9 percent annual total return for the seven full years of management, a bit behind the S&P 500 return of 17.0 percent. But we return $953,450 in cash to the foundation for grants and operating costs, or about 118 percent of the amount initially entrusted to us. Again, I am proud of our work for the foundation.

INDIVIDUALS IN THE MIX

During the Vogelstein Foundation years, other subscribers to *Realty Stock Review* pick up the change in emphasis and inquire about managing accounts in the early and mid-1980s. The most interesting is a Boston businessman who, in November 1986, places a portion of his assets, initially $293,000, into our hands with instructions to invest through an account he establishes at Fidelity Investments. Within a year, the account grows to $517,000 from a combination of additional funds and appreciation, and two years later, the account stands at $676,000. I am very excited about prospects for the account, but unfortunately, I never meet this important client because of scheduling conflicts. In October

1993, the account's manager/adviser notifies us that holdings are being trimmed to six stocks to "simplify" the account. The account is closed as of December 31, 1993, with a $761,000 balance.

A fairly well known Wall Street operative provides a $200,000 account on January 1, 1984, also domiciled at a third brokerage firm. I meet him during a REIT analysts' meeting, and he seems interested in the sector. But he soon proves elusive to contact, and I begin to suspect he is using our information to trade in larger quantities away from the account. We part ways on March 31, 1988, after seventeen quarters.

A Southern California doctor comes on board in August 1985 with a $100,000 account domiciled at first with State Street Bank & Trust of Boston. When State Street's fees prove onerous for this small account, it moves to Fidelity. The doctor and I talk fairly often by phone, but his schedule is jammed and I never meet him personally. No money is added to the account over the years, and it grows to $160,000 during six and a half years of management before being closed as of December 31, 1991.

A real estate man from Richmond, Virginia, opens a $200,000 account on October 1, 1985, to be domiciled with a Richmond brokerage firm. I am never able to meet him, and the account is closed as of March 31, 1988, with a value of about $212,000 during the late 1980s real estate recession. I suspect he needs the funds for other purposes.

A gentleman from Oregon opens a family trust account for about $250,000 in June 1978; this account remains open for almost exactly one year and then is closed for reasons never made apparent. The account rises a very small amount, although real estate stocks are in a down market at the time.

These experiences sour me on managing accounts for individuals on several scores: First, each individual gives slightly different investment instructions, preventing me from ever developing anything approaching a single portfolio strategy. Second, since management begins at different times, no two accounts ever hold the same percentages of the same securities, hence results vary widely. Third, and terribly important, nearly all clients insist that I trade through friendly or "designated" brokerage firms, making it impossible to issue a single order for a single stock and be assured all clients are getting the same execution price. And finally there is inherent conflict with advice given to subscribers that no amount of advance disclosure can overcome.

Yes, the management fees outstrip those for subscription services, and yes the clients stay in the fold much longer than typical subscribers, but given the generally unsatisfactory conditions listed above, I come to the end of the 1980s determined to shed money management for individuals.

One bright spot gleams through after all these years. I never fail to return to a client more money than he or she entrusts to my care initially. That stands as true success in my book.

THE WORLD BANK

In early summer 1984, George Alvarez-Correa and Hilda Ochoa-Brillembourg, staffers of the Staff Retirement Plan (SRP) for the World Bank (officially the International Bank for Reconstruction and Development, or IBRD) begin meeting with me in Audit's Manhattan offices at 230 Park Avenue.

Hilda and George are researching the feasibility of expanding SRP's real estate investments into publicly traded real estate securities and search me out because George, in a previous life as controller of a REIT, Mortgage Investors of Washington, is aware of our REIT research in *Realty Stock Review.*

We assemble in Audit's conference room furnished for just such occasions, commodious enough to hold ten or twelve persons, not flashy but replete with an impressive rosewood conference table. Hilda Ochoa remembers the setting in these words: "By the way, I do not remember a large conference room. I remember a small office with a metal desk, which we found most convincing and appropriate for a start-up. We were never impressed; to the contrary, we would have been very unimpressed and even turned off with lavish office space. It would not have boded well for a startup. But we were very impressed with your knowledge of the REIT industry."

After a couple of meetings, at which they ask for an enormous quantity of information and opinions about REITs, it dawns on me that they are looking for an investment manager and at the second or third meeting, I blurt: "Look, rather than have me educate you, why don't you just let Audit Investments manage an account for IBRD?" My files show that in June 1984, I proposed that Audit manage an account for the World Bank, and I believe this proposal followed my brash comment.

Reviewing my impulsive and annoying comment afterward--I am irked at the time spent—I fear my temper may have come across as rude and thereby blown this important opportunity.

Unknown to me, by this point in the talks, Hilda and George have decided to recommend a ten-million-dollar commitment to REITs and Audit's June 1984 proposal becomes the basis for more talks.

Hilda Ochoa in 2015 recalls the encounter in these words:

"My recollection of the events, which I have confirmed with George, is different. We recall that we had been engaging you as a consultant for a while and given the wealth of information you did have on REITs, we decided to experiment with you as an active manager of REITS, for which there were none that we knew of at the time.

"For that reason, we asked you to put together a portfolio management proposal to induce you to think, to put down in writing and verify that you would have a robust methodology for making investment decisions in a segment of the market you knew well.

"You reacted with enormous delight. For us it was not a unique or isolated undertaking. We had already embarked in a very successful program of 'incubating' new strategies and 'farm-team' managers in segments of the market where we felt those managers would enjoy a competitive advantage.

"Being faithful to George's and my own recollection, the life and business lesson to be derived from this successful undertaking is that in life it pays to be responsive to client or potential client needs and queries and be generous with information (without revealing trade secrets). Over the course of my personal and professional life I have found that if you are creative, intelligent and knowledgeable, you should be generous with those good willing people who seek your advice. It does not pay off all the time (nothing does) but over time it gives you one of the greatest joys we can aspire to: contributing to human knowledge and development, including your own.

"And the positive life lessons I would derive from the experience would be just as valuable but different from the one to which you refer, namely 'If you do not ask, you do not get.' The ask-and-get lesson, while also true, should perhaps be reserved for marital proposals or discounts on overvalued merchandise."

Finally, George Alvarez calls in late July 1984 to say that, *voila*, IBRD wants to take me up on my challenge and will forward their standard investment management contract within a few days.

That is all—no grilling by investment consultants, no forwarding of reams of performance data, no agonizing wait for committee approval. My shortcut experience is polar opposite to the rigorous and lengthy process by which all US institutional investors, including the World Bank, vet prospective managers today before tendering a contract. Audit is hired by a short and sweet process bespeaking the simpler world of the mid-1980s.

The IBRD investment contract arrives within days, and I review it with our lawyer Howard G. "Gerry" Seitz. The major issue is whether the 0.5 percent annual advisory fee on average assets offered by the World Bank—fixed by bank fiat and nonnegotiable—is fair to our individual clients, who are paying a higher fee for smaller accounts. Moreover, the World Bank insists upon monthly reporting of performance versus the quarterly reporting norm for individual accounts. The issue is resolved by distinguishing between the wider range of investment policy mandates potentially possible for individual accounts and their smaller account size, a distinction incorporated into our SEC filings. Once the fee issue is resolved, Audit agrees on August 18, 1984, to manage a modest World Bank Account, which soon grows as the bank adds funds over time.

Much later, I learn that George and Hilda made the rounds of many peers and the bank's selection of Audit made a lot of competitors unhappy. The experience validates my first rule of business, not unique and repeated many times by others: *If you don't ask, you don't get!*

In a competitive environment, one must never be too proud or satisfied to forget to ask for the business. This extends to ordinary conduct. If you want a new job opening in your company, ask.

Or if you want to marry that lovely young woman you're dating, the woman who shuns marriage so she can pursue her academic dreams, who seems genuinely unimpressed with you, just ask. I did, and she said, "Yes." That was sixty-four shining years ago.

George Alvarez-Correa and Hilda Ochoa-Brillembourg depart the World Bank in November 1987 to start Strategic Investment Partners, an investment manager and consultant in Arlington, Virginia.

The World Bank's patina helps establish Audit as an institutional money manager during those embryonic years when REIT securities are struggling for market recognition and managers of REIT securities labor in obscurity. Other institutions learn through the industry grapevine of the arrangement, even though our client agreement dictates confidentiality in our relationship and prohibits our mentioning or advertising any aspect of the relationship, including amounts managed, performance, and fees. Thus the World Bank account's origins in 1984 give Audit and me the distinction of having the longest institutional money management record among REIT managers.

By the time we combine Audit with Radnor Advisors to form Campbell-Radnor Advisors (CRA) in 1992 and 1993, the account is by far our largest. When I join Ritson Ferguson and Jarrett Kling to form CRA, the institutional track record built since 1984 is arguably the most important single asset of Audit. A superseding contract is executed January 1, 1994, with Campbell-Radnor Advisors, the new corporate entity.

So never forget: if you don't ask, you don't get.

There's one caution to the World Bank story. The bank ends its association with CRA, Audit's successor, nineteen years later in late 2003, by which time the account has grown considerably. Termination reasons are never clear.

All good things must come to an end. The longevity of the World Bank account proves the logic of moving Audit into money management.

CLIENT TAKEAWAYS

The seven individual accounts attracted during the 1980s stay an average of eighteen quarters under management, or an average three and a half years. This certainly surpasses the high turnover of our periodical advisory services, but revenues from individual clients never exceed 3 percent of annual revenues, clearly far short of amounts needed to sustain a strong marketing effort. Operational difficulties further militate against the effort.

Institutional accounts, such as the World Bank's, are truly the prize because the potentially larger asset base and longer relationships far outweigh the smaller management fee. Institutions are by definition passive pools of money that must be invested in some corner of the securities markets to maintain return and growth. The World Bank is just one of literally thousands of institutions whose assets must remain committed to the market. These institutions are managed by some level of bureaucracy—trustees or some corporate structure—assisted by squads of pension-fund advisers, whose job is to direct the bureaucrats to the best market sectors and asset classes for investment. The bureaucratic structure of pension funds requires an equally stratified firm for the management job. Hence large institutions gravitate toward large managers.

My goal for the 1990s is to help build a larger and more successful management company.

Chapter 25
THE PARTNERS

As the calendar turns to 1990, I determine to exit investment newsletter publishing. Investment publishing lets me display my wares before the eyes of thousands of investors and get my name out there for all to see. Now it's time to move on.

I've published *Realty Trust/Stock Review, Housing & Realty Investor* and other services for over two decades, writing and editing four investment letters a month, mostly eight pages in length, for two decades. It totals over one thousand weekly issues and seven thousand pages.

The physical grind of publishing exacts a steep toll. I am tired, burned out, used up.

I am not giving up on REITs, just publishing.

The path of least resistance is to try expanding the money management business, building on the World Bank institutional account. But I vow to keep other doors open, especially in investment banking where demand for work keeps me busy.

In early 1990, I have no idea that choosing between these two paths will take four years.

Two main reasons militate against continuing in publishing. *First,* newsletter publishing is a low-margin business whose volatility and cyclicality does not generate consistent profits but requires carrying a heavy overhead burden. I survey Audit's financial performance for the 1980s and see a company locked in a $300,000-a-year revenue range save for an upward and unsustainable blip in 1988 (exhibit 25.1). At root, my investment banking activities under the Campbell & Dillmeier aegis seek to compensate for those persistent low margins. The low and inconsistent margins reflect the small audience for our main product, never much over one thousand subscribers. True, *Realty Stock Review* commands industry influence and respect far beyond its size, giving me outsized psychic income. But the low margins and extra risk are outsized, too.

Exhibit 25.1: Audit Investments Inc.
Annual Revenues -- 1980 - 1989 -- Th. $

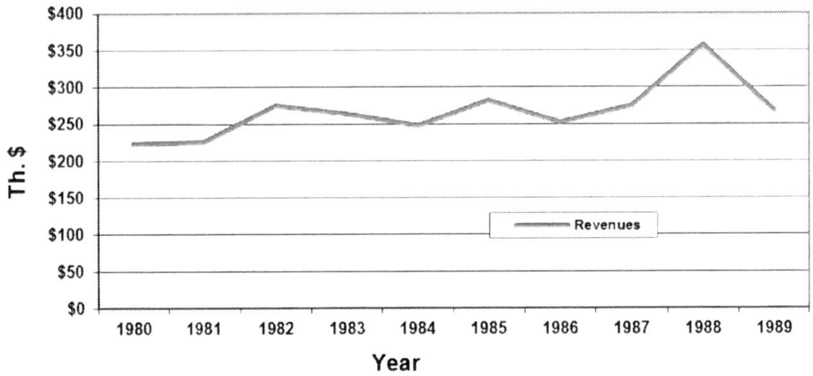

Worse, I cannot foresee—mistakenly it turns out—any big surge in readers because the REIT market remains tiny at $11.7 billion at the end of 1989 even after a few notable stock offerings in the mid-1980s.

THE MIRACLE WORKER

The first notable stock offer of the 1980s comes from Houston, where a summer 1985 break in oil prices below ten dollars a barrel is like castor oil to the Texas economy. In Houston, Stanford Alexander hopes against long odds to bring his small but growing shopping center company, Weingarten Realty Investors (WRI), public as a REIT. No significant REIT has cracked the IPO barrier since the 1970s, but soft-spoken Alexander presses his story tirelessly.

The WRI roadshow runs into a market reeling from recent failure of five S&Ls with $7 billion assets and punishing any realty entity showing signs of distress. But Alexander persists, and on August 16, 1985, Weingarten raises $50.7 million by selling 2.6 million common shares at $19.50 to the public. *RSR* ranks shares "B" initially because its 6.6 million square feet of shopping centers is 90 percent occupied in a soggy market, debt is conservative, and it pays an 8 percent dividend.

Weingarten becomes a darling for stock analysts because its simple story resonates on Main Street as well as Wall Street. WRI centers are anchored by best-in-class grocers who sell everyday necessities to everyday buyers every day. Weingarten earnings take off, and so does its stock price.

After the offering, I buy 13,000 shares for my one institutional client, and by the end of 1989, WRI shares trade at $31.63 a share, up 62 percent from the IPO price despite a nasty real estate recession. WRI stock is my largest single holding from 1985 through 1990. Happy client, happy manager.

THE HOCKEY STICK

The second notable offering arrives via a byzantine chain of events. One day in summer 1985, I am invited to a meeting in the offices of Goldman Sachs. It turns out I am an audience of one asked to critique a proposal, concocted by some clever Goldman investment bankers, to sell a slice of Rockefeller Center to the public as Rockefeller Center Properties, Incorporated (RCP). David Rockefeller, former head of Chase Manhattan Bank, and the Rockefeller family wish to extract a significant portion of the property's value, all well and good except for one tiny detail: The property isn't worth the asking price right now.

To bridge that yawning value chasm, Goldman's bankers propose an exceedingly complex deal. RCP will generate $1.1 billion in cash by selling to the public $600 million worth of common shares, then the largest equity offering in Wall Street history, plus $500 million in an exotic cocktail of two convertible debentures. Rockefeller Center Properties, Inc., the new REIT, in turn will lend the $1.1 billion to two partnerships, Rockefeller Center Properties and RCP Associates, which own most of Rockefeller Center in midtown Manhattan. Rents at the venerable 6.2-million-square-foot midtown office complex, built between 1931 and 1940, are nothing to shout about.

But low-rent leases on 42 percent of the space expire in 1994, and the Goldman men keep pointing to projections showing an upward-tilting "hockey stick" rent spike nine years out in 1994, when the center should reap a rent bonanza. At that point, RCP will be covering its interest costs and the convertibles should be nicely "in the money." The SEC lets RCP bolster the hockey stick projections by including estimates of Manhattan office occupancies and rents in the prospectus, ending a long SEC ban on forward projections in company offerings. My takeaway: the Goldman-Rockefeller tandem carries a lot of weight in high places.

At the end of that Goldman meeting, I am skeptical of the deal's dizzying complexity and its bet on that hockey stick rent bump. But *RSR*'s research finds Manhattan office rents rising by about 9 percent annually over the last fifteen years, so the projected 6 percent inflation assumption seems in line.

David Rockefeller puts himself on the line at road show lunches to vouch for the deal. An eager investing public places big orders, ecstatic that the Rockefeller family is selling its crown jewel to the public and putting its imprimatur on revival of the equity REIT format.

Thus encouraged, underwriters boost deal size by $200 million to $1.3 billion, divided $750 million common equity and $550 million convertibles. The historic offering is oversubscribed and, less than a month after Weingarten's ice-breaking offer, Rockefeller Center Properties Inc.

(NYSE: RCP) begins NYSE trading September 13, 1985, giving REITs a brief and much-needed shot in the arm.

From my early 1990 perspective, RCP shares are dull, ending 1989 up only 3 percent at $20.63 versus a $20 offering price and yielding 9.1 percent. I dodge the RCP bullet and never buy the shares for my clients. (Manhattan office rents never make that hockey stick bend, and RCP ultimately seeks Chapter XI bankruptcy protection in May 1995. Rockefeller Center ultimately winds up in the arms of privately owned Tishman Speyer.)

Market follow-through to these two widely watched successes is tepid, enabling a few smaller equity REITs to sell stock in the afterglow but the well quickly runs dry, partly because a grinding real estate recession begins eighteen months later in early 1987. In 1988, only one equity REIT, $200 million Koger Properties, is able to come public. Wall Street still is able to sell about a half-dozen smaller mortgage REITs in 1988—shades of the 1970s—as investors thirst for yield.

The next year is worse as not a single equity REIT passes muster with REIT buyers in 1989, causing me to view the REIT landscape as exceedingly bleak when I contemplate the future in early 1990. Ultimately, 1990 repeats 1989 with a blank in the equity REIT IPO column.

I miss 1980s seedlings planted for the REIT Revolution:

In Indianapolis, mall mogul Melvin Simon took MSA Realty Corp. public in March 1984 with a $25 million stock offering. But this non-REIT never caught fire with investors and ended the 1980s at $77 million market value. Its successor, Simon Property Group (SPG), under tutelage of Mel's son David Simon, in 2015 is the world's largest REIT with $59.4 billion equity market value.

In New Jersey, Steven Roth and his Interstate Properties won a 1980 proxy contest to control struggling discounter Vornado Inc., a $248 million entity by 1989. From this base Roth ultimately created the powerhouse Vornado Realty Trust (VNO), valued in 2015 at $18.6 billion.

In Los Angeles, B. Wayne Hughes began merging nearly two dozen small limited partnerships into an entity that became the 2015 self-storage colossus, $43.2 billion Public Storage Inc. (PSA).

In Toledo, OH, Bruce Thompson in 1985 merged several local realty funds into tiny Health Care REIT, valued at $87 million by 1989. By 2015 the resulting Welltower, Inc. has grown to $23 billion. And in Los Angeles, Kenneth Roath founded Health Care Property Investors, taking it public in May 1985 and worth $285 million by 1989. In 2015 it is known as $17 billion HCP, Inc.

Bottom line, I mistakenly judge the REIT market won't produce a cure for low publishing margins.

The *second* point on my decision list is rapidly changing technology that likely will require significant new investment in equipment to deliver our periodicals. The fax machine arrives in the mid-1980s and facilitates our move in April 1986 from Manhattan, our base for sixteen years at 230 Park Avenue, to a new office on Summit Avenue in Montvale, New Jersey, about three miles from our home. Multiple faxes to subscribers are a newsletter delivery option, but I pass because I cannot guarantee that individual subscribers own fax machines.

Worse, our connection to a reliable printer begins breaking down even before the move. The owner of Fermaprint, our printer for many years, sells and retires to Florida, leaving us with a new owner far less interested in serving newsletters. Alternate printers fizzle and jack up the price.

We try producing the letters on a large color copier, but the machine overheats easily, leading to missed mailing deadlines and angst all about.

During my travels, I had seen small printing presses and decide to give them a try to internalize production and end the headaches of third-party printers. We locate a used press in New Brunswick, New Jersey, and after backbreaking labor, install this six-hundred-pound monster in our Montvale office. But it is even more finicky than the copier, makes an enormous din during operation, and in general is no solution.

In golfing lingo, I've hit the ball from the sand trap into the lake.

But Michael Houston, one of our writer analysts, takes a liking to the machine and in time begins to tame its intricacies.

So I plan a double exit.

In March 1990, I agree to sell *Realty Stock Review* and our other publications, plus the printing press, to Michael, effective June 30, 1990.

The offer appeals to his entrepreneurial spirit because he wants to set up shop on his own.

The strike price is $25,000 but since Michael is short of cash, I agree to take back a note. Michael fears he cannot handle the entire operation on his own, so I agree, very reluctantly, to assist in writing the service for one year, for a fee of course.

It's a double unforced error for me.

TAKE YOUR BEST SHOT

At almost exactly the same time, Tony Gumbiner of Hallwood Group Incorporated, whom we met in chapter 19, "The Reit Catchers," is trying to combine—or roll-up, in the language of the day—eight separate limited partnerships sponsored by Equitec Financial Group Incorporated, a major partnership sponsor of the time. Hallwood announces an agreement to attempt the roll-up in October 1989, and by spring 1990, lawyers file a draft proxy with the SEC. The roll-up will create a new entity named Hallwood Realty Partners LP, a publicly traded master limited partnership with about $535 million assets to be listed on the American Stock Exchange.

I and many other followers of the industry want access to the draft proxy, but Gumbiner exercises an SEC rule to keep the document "quiet" until the SEC signs off and the final document is ready for circulation to Equitec limited partners.

I meet with Gumbiner on Wednesday, May 2, 1990, at his Manhattan office to make a case for access. As the publication with the largest circulation among professional realty stock investors, *Realty Stock Review* is ideally situated to examine the intricacies of the deal. At the time, the allocation of units among constituent partnerships in roll-ups is hotly contested and frequently the target of lawsuits by plaintiff lawyers.

After a great deal of back-and-forth, Gumbiner assents to making the draft available to me with one condition: I cannot publish anything until the proxy becomes final. Knowing that winning approval of the deal may be difficult, his parting words to me are:

"Take your best shot."

When the document arrives a few days later, I find that about 78 percent of the assets by appraised value are offices with 90 percent average occupancy, numbers that excite me because no office company of size operates in the public sphere at the time.

Better, three office towers in Baltimore and around Washington DC with slightly over one million square feet account for about 28 percent of the value. After hopping into my car one day, I am able to visit these three properties, talk with tenants and area brokers, and satisfy myself that there are no major fishhooks evident despite Equitec's overall cash flow problems. The hardiest assets remain with the Hallwood master limited partnership, or MLP, since Equitec recently disposes of several problem properties.

Just before 5:00 p.m. on Friday, June 29, 1990, I receive word that the SEC has cleared the prospectus for distribution to limited partners. It is also the last business day before I am to close my sale of *RSR* to Michael Houston.

On Monday, July 2, 1990, I publish *RTR's* article under the headline,

"Hallwood Realty Partners L.P.: First Rescue Rollup Proposed." It is my last *RSR* issue.

"The Hallwood Realty proposal marks the first time a real estate syndicator has agreed to turn over administrative control and property supervision to a new general partner," *RSR* reports. "The new HRP would be managed by a subsidiary of Hallwood Group Incorporated, a company specializing in rescue financing mainly in real estate, energy and financial industries … The proposal holds the prospect of providing stock market liquidity to limited partnership unit holders which heretofore have had very limited trading markets."

My concluding paragraph:

> "If we are correct that fresh and interesting faces will revive the languishing realty stock market, then HRP has potential for becoming a major player in this new ball game for national real estate stocks. While HRP's concentration in offices may be perceived as a negative, we think HRP's higher quality urban offices should be among market leaders during the recovery certain to follow today's credit-induced cutbacks in new building. Hallwood's willingness to commit to lower G&A [general and administrative expenses] and property management expenses gives HRP a chance to shine where it counts most, in the leasing and stock markets. And Hallwood's intent to pass on benefits of a leaner, more economical management to unit-holders in tangible distributions should be a refreshing change for Equitec investors."

Within a few days, a Hallwood official calls to ask for permission for

Hallwood to distribute copies of the letter to Equitec limited partners. I agree, because I own rights to that July 2 issue and, mindful of the potential for litigation, set a price of one dollar per copy. A rival sniffs that we have set a new high for sale of reprints.

Ultimately, we and Michael Houston deliver about 110,000 to 115,000 copies for mailing to the limited partners.

The lawsuits and subpoenas soon follow, and Audit is named as a defendant for alleged biased reporting. There is nothing to do except stick it out and wait for the court's ruling, our lawyer advises. In 1993, the court rules that we acted in good faith and dismisses Audit from the suit. Hallwood finally agrees in 1994 to pay ten million dollars to limited partners for misconduct attributed to Equitec, the previous limited partner.

Hallwood Realty Partners remains in public markets for nearly fifteen years, weathering lawsuits alleging misconduct by its general partner and two unsolicited low-ball bids from activist investors eager to capture the values hidden in its units.

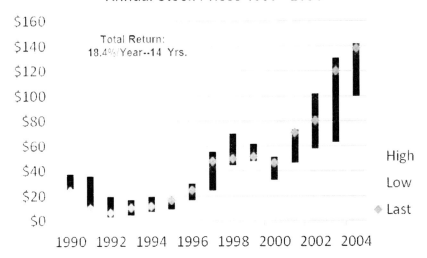

Exhibit 25.2: Hallwood Realty Part. (A:HRY)
Annual Stock Prices 1990 - 2004

HRP finally is sold in 2004 for $137.91 a unit, returning 18.4 percent a year to patient investors, nearly 6.5 percent a year better than the 12.0 percent annual return posted by the Standard & Poor's 500 over those same years.

The buyer, HRPT Properties Trust, itself succumbs in 2014 to another activist investor looking for hidden values and is now named Equity Commonwealth (NYSE: EQC).

TWO DRY HOLES

After the June 1990 *RSR* sale, I continue to write the bulk of *RSR* during the second half of 1990 under my continuing contract with Houston, forcing me to make numerous trips into Manhattan to attend analyst meetings and gather information to tend the World Bank and other managed portfolios. Our Summit Avenue lease ends in April 1991, and we move office furniture and files into an office suite attached to our home at 16 Glenwood Road, Upper Saddle River, New Jersey. I keep up a regular schedule, walking "to the office" about 8:30 a.m. and returning "home" at day's end. I bill the office as "Suite 100," and while some days are lonely, my windows afford spectacular views of surrounding woods and for the first time, I can truly savor the changing seasons.

The June 1990 sale cuts nearly 50 percent from revenue for our now tinier company, and Irene and I struggle during 1991 with our lowest income since 1969. But we see growth ahead for our single business line of investment management.

In summer 1991, the Evangelical Lutheran Church in America (ELCA) issues a request for proposal (RFP) to manage ten million dollars in real estate securities. Since I attended a Lutheran college, I respond with a forty-page proposal that contains all the firepower I can muster.

As I drop the missive into the postal slot, I hear a voice whisper, "*Deus vult.*" This strange visitation startles me because I have no idea

what the words mean. Is this the voice of God affirming money management as a new life direction? Or did I imagine the words?

Some weeks later, after intensive research—no Google then—I learn
this to be Pope Urban II's exhortation to nobles assembled at Clermont,
France, in July 1095 to begin the first Crusade to recapture Jerusalem:
"*Deus vult*"—God wills it.

But this strange event is no short-term magic amulet. My schedule
precludes meeting with ELCA staff when it interviews several competitors in Manhattan, and I travel to Minneapolis on November 7, 1991,
to press my case.

Another competitor wins the account, to my great disappointment.
Deep down, I know my track record doesn't measure up.

You don't get every time you ask, divine intervention or no.

But I have a backup to jump-start institutional money management:
Grayson Saunders.

The former marketing partner for now-disbanded Landsing
Corporation and the man who assigned Bob Dillmeier and me to roam
through oil-parched Texas and to see Doc Christensen in Anaheim,
California (chapter 22, "The Bankers"), Grayson Saunders has moved on
to head pension investments at Ameritech Corporation, one of the Baby
Bells created by the 1980s breakup of American Telephone & Telegraph.
Figuring Saunders is likely predisposed toward realty securities, I wangle
an appointment to meet him in Chicago in early January 1992 and present much of the ELCA case for selecting Audit to manage an account.

Unhappily, Saunders engages a consultant to advise him on the
realty sector and the consultant is thoroughly negative.

No sale!

These two dry holes convince me that Audit Investments and Ken
Campbell, as a stand-alone manager, will never win major institutional
accounts, *deus vult* notwithstanding.

I need the equivalent of the Rock, solid institutional pillars behind me to be competitive in the hectic market for REIT shares quickly emerging.

RESURRECTION DAY

For while I am courting ELCA and Ameritech, New Plan Realty Trust, a shopping center REIT founded in 1960, becomes the first equity REIT to surpass $1 billion in equity market cap at the end of 1991. *RSR*, for which I still write, carries the news to investors under this headline: "Market Strategy: More Super REITs Emerge to Lead Market."

"Behind New Plan come 35 other Super REITs with over $100 million market value," *RSR* says. "A decade ago only four REITs topped the $100 million hurdle. Seen in this longer term perspective, the emergence of Super REITs marks a sea change in investor perceptions."

Analysts press New Plan CEO Bill Newman on his prospects for acquiring Kimco Corporation, a well-known but reportedly troubled Long Island shopping center company, which I encountered briefly in 1969 (see chapter 8, "The Chase"). "We've looked at it carefully, but it's too far gone," Newman confides to me in a quick aside.

But at Kimco's Long Island headquarters, Kimco cofounder Milton Cooper is far from the grave. In fact, Cooper is talking with Richard Saltzman, head real estate investment banker at Merrill Lynch. It's a time when many real estate cognoscenti figure that for many realty companies, the decision is "Go broke or go public." Cooper and Saltzman devise an ingenious plan derived from past bank rescues. They will split Kimco into two companies: a "good bank," owning 124 healthy shopping centers containing 14.3 million square feet of rentable space, and a "bad bank" holding 45 unprofitable centers, most occupied by Hills Department Stores, then in bankruptcy. In the proposed stock offering, "good bank" Kimco will get an option to buy the "bad bank" assets if and when they become profitable.

Kimco agrees to limit debt leverage to 50 percent of total assets, a key pledge pushed by Saltzman in getting Merrill to underwrite the deal and winning support from stock investors fearing the proclivity of realty developers to leverage their assets to the moon.

In November 1991, Kimco sells 6.4 million shares to the public at $20 a share, and Milt Cooper—who never knew he was "dead" in Bill Newman's eyes—is alive and liquid. I buy shares at the $20.00 offer price for my one institutional client and reap a 7.5 percent price gain by year-end 1991. In 1992, I add another two thousand shares, paying $25.375 per share. KIM closes 1992 at $31.00 a share, and I can report a 55 percent gain on original shares to my client.

Again, happy client, happy manager.

The "Lazarus" Kimco, to which *RSR* did not assign a rating at the time of the offering, goes on to post rising earnings for ten years running, handsomely rewarding shareholders who figure that Kimco's option on "bad-bank" assets was a one-way bet they could scarcely lose.

The successful Kimco stock offering revives the REIT Revolution, for good.

BANKING ON BANKING

While scouting for new investment management clients, I also am being asked to advise various entities about their investment banking needs, a carryover from the heyday of Campbell & Dillmeier. These assignments add fee income and start building revenue back to pre-*RSR* sale days.

In September 1991, CleveTrust Realty Investors asks C&D to advise on raising new capital. After an unhappy experience selling and then repurchasing shares from a British pension plan (see chapter 20, "The Biggest Winners"), CleveTrust needs new capital to grow. I meet with management and trustees through spring 1992 but am never able to offer any definitive help; Bob Dillmeier's schedule precludes his involvement.

In February 1992, investment banker Bart Gurewitz of Los Angeles brokerage firm Wedbush Securities calls to inquire how I would feel about a REIT that owns only properties in Alaska. I'm intrigued because only one tiny REIT has ever owned a single property there, and agree to meet Gurewitz on a subsequent trip to Los Angeles.

Gurewitz is courting the owners of Carr-Gottstein Properties, who are considering what to do with several supermarkets and other Anchorage properties left after selling their related Carr-Gottstein Supermarkets to their employees. Bart and I make two trips to Anchorage during 1992, but nothing materializes. Bob Dillmeier again is not involved. But Barnard "Barney" Gottstein, one of the two principals, places some money under my management, a big plus.

In September 1992, Commonwealth Equity Trust, a small Sacramento-based equity trust, asks if Campbell & Dillmeier will render a fairness opinion on a planned transaction. Bob and I inspect property in Sacramento and San Francisco in September and October 1992 and, after reviewing property appraisals, issue an opinion that the transaction is "fair." It marks the last time Bob Dillmeier and I work together as investment bankers, effectively ending Campbell & Dillmeier's run.

THE PHONE CALL

One summer day, either in 1991 or 1992 (the date is uncertain), comes a phone call from a man calling himself Ritson Ferguson. At first, I think the name is a put-on, but a few days later, a real person shows up at my bucolic office and I learn that Ritson is an old and proud family name.

Ritson is ramrod straight, his military bearing befitting his US Air Force service as a computer expert in the Pentagon. Later, I learn his father is a retired air force general. He also has a master's degree in business from the prestigious Wharton School at University of Pennsylvania. Best of all, he is young—thirty-three, almost exactly the age of my younger son—whereas I am sixty-two.

He has convinced partners of his employer, Radnor Advisors, a real estate consulting and direct property management firm outside Philadelphia, to explore creating a presence in the evolving public real estate securities business. He inquires about the newsletter, but I tell him I have already sold it to concentrate upon managing money.

He invites me to meet his associates, Jarrett "Jerry" Kling and Dick Layman, in Radnor on Friday, September 11, 1992, and I accept. At first, I mistake that first conversation as an invitation to join an investment banking venture, and we exchange a couple of visits between my New Jersey spot and his Radnor, Pennsylvania office, about a two-hour drive away, on this topic.

Several important facts surface during those talks. Ritson is a dedicated Episcopalian with deep convictions and moral rectitude, and his partner Jerry Kling is an impressive marketer of financial products. He's also a scratch golfer whose affability and connections let him golf with some of America's business leaders. Better, Jerry is not quite fifty, almost exactly between our ages, an important fact to me because I believe a partnership among persons of varying ages can create a durable entity.

The big negative is my experience that three-cornered partnerships are tricky because any two partners can gang up on the third, creating the possibility for dissension. The positive is that the partnership is joined by Dick Layman, Radnor's real estate director, who brings one of the most fertile real estate structuring minds to the table and provides balance as a fourth partner.

While we talk, Detroit shopping center developer Alfred Taubman, then sixty-seven and creator of unique high-end malls festooned with modern art, seeks a way to take his Taubman Centers Incorporated public without disturbing institutional partnerships he's fashioned with General Motors Pension Trusts.

Alfred Taubman turns to his sons Robert and William and his company's brain trust and, along with others, they come up with a totally new legal device they call the Umbrella Partnership, dubbed an UPREIT, to slice through this legal Gordian knot. At a couple of conferences, I am regaled by mind-numbing legalese explaining why UPREITs should work for Taubman and others with the same issues. The essence of their case is this: under partnership law, different partners can and frequently do have differing cost bases for their partnership stakes.

Taubman's proposition is simple: convert an existing partnership between Taubman and the GM trusts into an umbrella partnership owned partly by public shareholders (33 percent interest), the GM trusts (44 percent), and Taubman family and management (23 percent).

The preliminary or red herring prospectus in the fall of 1992 has Street analysts, including me, shaking their heads because nothing like this has ever been done before. I and other money managers question the inherent conflicts of interest built into UPREITs, and I discuss the deal with Ritson and his Radnor colleagues at a November 1992 session.

"I'm still trying to get my mind around the concept," one peer manager tells me.

At a New York luncheon to explain the offering, Chairman Al Taubman, who towers nine inches above my five-feet-six-inch frame, waves a cigar in my face and says this is simply the way big-time real estate must be financed in the future because no single company has enough capital to buy major properties. Some are not convinced, but I figure the real estate is super good, with malls generating industry-leading sales over $300 a square foot, and buy three thousand shares of Taubman (NYSE: TCO) at the $11 offer price on November 20, 1992. Taubman raises $295 million in the offer.

By year-end, TCO stock has risen a modest 5.7 percent to $11.625 a share, and our clients are happy again. TCO has initial growing pains at its Short Hills, New Jersey, mall but management, led by Al's son Bobby Taubman, ultimately proves the virtue of the UPREIT structure as a viable way to let property owners with differing costs and objectives invest in the same public vehicle.

The world of real estate securities is never the same after Taubman's successful offering and that UPREIT format plus Kimco's pledge to limit leverage paves the way for the modern REIT industry. Looking through the structure to the quality of underlying assets proves the touchstone to investor gains in the complex deals that follow.

MARKETING THE PARTNERSHIP

The Taubman success excites me and the Radnor group about prospects for real estate securities, and we finally agree on December 22, 1992, to form a new joint venture to manage securities accounts. Knowing the difficulty of attracting clients, I project money management assets totaling $25 million at the end of year 1 (1993) and $50 million by the end of year 2 (1994). Those estimates turn out close to the mark.

At that point, we see enormous growth potential in equity REITs because, while market cap has been growing at 10 percent yearly, total industry market cap remains a still-tiny $15.9 billion at 1992's end when we seal our deal.

We begin marketing like mad to institutional investors during 1993. Marketing management services is an art; it's not as simple as selling lawnmowers or widgets, because potential customers are both everywhere and nowhere, many times not readily apparent and not always willing to invite you to hear your sales pitch. Our goal is to make a formal presentation to a pension or trust committee, generally advised by a hired pension plan consultant, empowered to invest the entity's money to maximize returns and limit risks.

Since real estate securities are then emerging as a new and unproven asset class for many entities, we must overcome skepticism to real estate in general and its performance while establishing our bona fides as qualified managers.

Early in 1993, we set about developing a brochure to introduce ourselves and our services, involving many phone conversations and faxes between my office in New Jersey and the Radnor, Pennsylvania, office where Ferguson and Kling, base. After much agonizing over each word, we decide to bill ourselves in a new brochure as "Real Estate Investment Managers for the 1990s" emphasizing these main points:

- Securitization Creates Historic Real Estate Investment Opportunities
- The Advantages of Real Estate Securities
- An Investment Team for the 1990s and Beyond

"To strengthen Campbell's proven real estate securities management capabilities, he has joined forces with Radnor Advisors Inc., the principals of which have managed direct investments in real estate on behalf of institutional and individual investors for over 20 years. Radnor has been involved in over $2 billion of real estate investments and financings throughout the US," that brochure reads.

Gradually we refine our presentations, shaped by storylines flowing from the back-and-forth between Ritson and me, stressing these four points:

- We are the most experienced team in the business led by our chairman's thirty years in real estate advisory work.
- We have deep institutional resources.
- We follow a proven and disciplined investment process.
- We have a strong audited track record.

During 1993, we carry this message to as many investment groups as will listen.

In the meantime, on Wall Street, investors cannot buy enough

REIT stocks. REITs flip from pariahs to "flavor of the day" within weeks. Underwriters suddenly can sell almost anything so long as the word *REIT* is attached. NAREIT tallies forty-five initial public offerings (IPOs)—nearly one a week—during 1993 with investors forking over an astounding $8.5 billion for new REIT stocks.

Three other major mall giants join Taubman in launching IPOs and account for nearly 20 percent of 1993's new money. Martin Bucksbaum returns to the market with his *second* mall company named General Growth Properties, raising $363 million in April; Frank Pasquerilla's Crown American Realty Trust tops that with a $423 million offer in May; and Mel Simon's Simon Property Group bests them all by selling $840 million of new stock in December.

REIT industry market value more than doubles to $32.2 billion by the end of 1993.

The year 1994 continues the beat as forty new REITs pluck $6.7 billion from public markets. Thus a startling ninety-five real estate companies raise $15.2 billion over two years, more than tripling the REIT industry's size and stature with investors.

All this frenzied activity boosts our marketing efforts, and a Manhattan insurance company awards us a ten-million-dollar mandate in October 1993. Combined with Audit's $13.5 million assets under management (AUM), we are near enough to our initial target of $25 million to make the enterprise nearly cash-flow positive.

I notify my World Bank client contact in November 1993 that we have formed Campbell-Radnor Advisors (CRA) to combine the securities management expertise of Audit with the direct property experience of Radnor Advisors, currently managing about $500 million of direct property investments.

The new venture gives me the strong institutional pillars I've long desired.

During a bitter snowstorm on New Year's Eve 1993, I load my office furniture and files onto a rented truck and, with help of a friend's strong son, plant them in the early hours of the New Year in a vacant Radnor Advisors office.

There is no turning back, and on my sixty-fourth birthday, January 2, 1994, CRA officially opens for business.

FINDING A NEW SPONSOR

But during the early months of 1994, the market for specialists in REIT securities changes dramatically as several competitors form ties with firms advising pension plans on their direct real estate holdings. These larger firms already have established ties to pension plan staffs and consultants and are looking for ways to access securities management.

During fall 1994, we are visited by staffers from one or two direct property firms who "just stop by while in the neighborhood." Reading industry press and tea leaves convinces us that young boutique firms like ours need to be aligned with one of these large national firms instead of regionally focused firms, such as Radnor.

When Ritson broaches our need to build ties to a larger firm to Radnor's managing partner Dan Quinn at a Friday afternoon meeting, Quinn retorts testily: "Tell me where you want to sit on Monday morning."

Shocked, Ritson, Jerry, and I meet the following morning over breakfast and decide we must act quickly to find a new sponsor. The recent calls from several larger realty advisors leave us confident another connection won't be difficult to arrange.

Quinn agrees to give us time for a search and appoints Dick Layman as his negotiator to arrange the terms of the split-up. This puts Layman on the other side of the table and as he is no longer a member of our partnership, reduces the number of partners to three.

We begin meeting with potential substitute sponsors and within about sixty days decide to align with Jones Lang Wooten Realty Advisors, led by four former Citibank realty executives who've formed their own direct property advisory practice with backing from the British property firm of Jones Lang Wooten.

We're attracted by the similar management styles and close working relationships of the JLW partners, traits that mirror the evolving way in which we run our business. A deal is struck, and the four JLW partners—John Weisz, Steve Furnary, Charlie Grossman, and Frank Sullivan—individually buy a stake in our firm in March 1995.

In September 1995, we win our first significant new pension account, a $50 million award by a state pension fund bringing year-end 1995 assets under management (AUM) to just under $100 million.

The New Year 1996 brings spring victories in two other state pension competitions and vaults year-end 1996 AUM to $568 million. At the end of 1996, we open our first mutual fund, now named Voya Real Estate Fund, and I am asked to buy the initial shares. Putting on my big-money hat, I write a check on New Year's Eve 1996 to buy ten shares at $10 each, or $100 total. Over the next seven years, through 2003, I put a healthy sum from my paycheck into the fund, good markets or bad, and these purchases plus bonuses along the way mount until I am the largest individual share owner. My dollar-cost averaging of purchases plus the fund's strong performance makes the fund an absolute money machine over the years, perhaps my best single investment ever. "Eat your own cooking" works the best.

NAREIT's president Mark Decker calls early in 1996 and informs me that NAREIT is awarding me the NAREIT Industry Achievement Award for the year, a high honor. In May 1996, my Radnor and New York colleagues join me in Washington to watch me receive the award from NAREIT representative John McCann, the United Dominion

CEO who played an important role in my first completed merger (chapter 22, "The Bankers").

"There's a motto chiseled in stone on Pennsylvania Avenue that says: 'The Past Is Prologue,' I say. "Washington cabbies joke that it means, 'You ain't seen nothing yet.' That's the way it has been for the thirty-five years I've been privileged to be around REITs, and that's the shape of the future. You ain't seen nothing yet. Thank you and God bless you all."

Fast-forward to November 2013 because client confidentiality restricts what I can say about those intervening years. My partner Ritson Ferguson, our firm's CEO since I stood aside in 2001, is tapped to receive the same award. Under Ritson's tutelage, the firm has grown to ninety strong with offices around the globe and tending twenty-two billion dollars placed under our care by investors worldwide.

The only catch is that the presentation is to be made in San Francisco, not Washington.

Keeping my plans secret, I arrange with Stephen Wechsler to reserve a seat at the awards table, hop a plane, and surprise Ritson as he is honored.

Congratulations, Partner. You've earned it.

Chapter 26
THAT RAT HOLE

Dinner at Beaumont Retirement Community, where Irene and I now reside, is a gracious affair, unhurried to allow residents ample time to explore their life experiences and enthusiasms. Leisurely dining is a prized perk of retirement, although I am among the relatively few residents who still ply the workaday world.

Most residents dine in one of our seven dining rooms in The Mansion, a century-old Main Line turreted stone landmark. Most dining venues feature white linen tablecloths and personalized table service replicating an upscale restaurant. Tonight we are dining with neighbors in the Green Room, named for the greenery surrounding its white marble fireplace.

As our entrees arrive, the conversation turns to inflation.

"I remember the two-cent stamp right after World War II," the wife of our neighbor states firmly. "Now it's forty-nine cents. Isn't inflation way higher than what they tell us?"

"I remember the five-cent subway fare," I retort. "That was when I came to New York City in 1961. Now it's about $2.50."

Turns out we both are wrong.

The two-cent stamp ended July 6, 1932, according to *Wikipedia*, replaced by the three-cent stamp, which held sway all the way through July 1958 before climbing to four cents.

And the nickel subway fare ended in 1948 and rose to fifteen cents by the time I arrived in Manhattan in 1961.

Both our memories are fallible.

While the specifics are awry, we are both right directionally. First-class postage of forty-nine cents currently is 12.3 times the rate in 1960 when John F. Kennedy was elected president, and the $2.50 subway fare is 16.7 times the 1960 tariff.

In contrast, the official inflation index is up 8.1 times since January 1960.

"What is inflation anyway?" persists the woman.

"Inflation is generally seen as a rise in general prices," I say. "But that probably is too simple. We were taught in business school that inflation is the price level measured against a nation's constant basket of goods and services. Prices rise when too much money is chasing too few goods. So you have to think in terms of 'nominal' prices—the price you pay today—and 'inflation-adjusted' prices when thinking about that postage stamp or subway ride of yesteryear."

"Does inflation hurt us or help us?" the woman asks.

"It depends upon who you are," say I. "If you are young and getting rapid pay increases, inflation helps because your take-home pay probably increases faster than your purchases. If you are older and living on a pension or fixed income, you are likely hurt because the prices of the goods and services you buy rise faster than your income. In this sense, inflation amounts to a vast transfer of wealth from savers to nonsavers."

"How do you measure inflation?" continues the woman.

"The Federal Bureau of Labor Statistics prices a market basket of goods and services in all major cities once a month and produces a consumer price index (CPI) representing price changes for the food, clothing, and shelter that people buy. Over the years, some people claim the federal government is changing CPI components and calculations to reduce the reported inflation rate. Not so incidentally, this also reduces the federal budget deficit by holding down growth in Social Security payments, which are tied to the official inflation rate. So the purchasing power of assets owned by us oldsters is ravaged slowly and imperceptibly.

"Inflation also helps the federal government by letting it pay back its eighteen-trillion-dollar debt—a stack of hundred-dollar bills 1,221 miles high—in cheaper dollars. A successful Manhattan office developer once told me, 'My secret is that I borrow in big dollars and pay back in small dollars.' That same principle also works for the government.

"Net net, the Feds benefit by getting to pay in cheaper dollars all the debt and Social Security and the other promises they've made to us. It's win-win for the Feds, regardless of whether Democrats or Republicans are in power."

"Could this be true?" the woman inquires, fully engaged now because she is well beyond retirement age.

"Anything is possible," I retort. "I've read several academic articles recently questioning whether the CPI accurately measures inflation. They argue that if you price oil in various currencies, the US dollar shows far more inflation than the Euro or other currencies over the longer term. We need to look much more skeptically at whether the numbers emanating from the federal stat mill are truly accurate."

"What does all that mean? How can you use that in investing?" the woman's husband interjects.

"For me, it means I never buy a bond or fixed-income security," I reply. "To me, bonds are certificates of confiscation because the purchasing power of a bond's face value, the money you get back when a bond matures, will inevitably diminish. At 2 percent inflation—the Federal Reserve Board's official inflation target in 2015--a $1,000 bond will buy only $906 worth of goods and services in five years and only $820 worth of goods in ten years. If inflation rises to just 3 percent, that $1,000 bond buys only $858 and $737 worth of goods in five and ten years.

"I have never bought a bond, except when I managed my mother's money and needed high income to pay her bills. Only about one-third of the four billion dollars in mortgage securities sold in the 1920s survived the Great Depression of the 1930s [see appendix I, "Run-Up to the REIT Revolution"]. The last time I invested in a mortgage REIT for clients was in 1987 or 1988, and the results were so unpleasant I have never gone that path again. There is no such thing as 'match funding' in mortgage REITs, in my mind, and you can be blindsided so quickly by sudden rate changes that the posted high dividend yields become an illusion. The history books say that equity ownership is the only way to real estate investment success."

"No bonds in a portfolio," the husband recoils in mock horror. "Where did you get that crazy idea?"

"That's right; I invest entirely in equities," I fire back, "and believe that most financial planning advice to increase bond holdings as you get older is akin to malpractice. The rule of adding more bonds as we age originated in a time of low inflation and stable currency.

"That world is gone, period! Inflation averaged 5.2 percent annually from 1970 through 1999, and while it's fallen considerably the last few years, averaging 2.37 percent since 2000, it's still a threat in most people's minds.

"Also we are all living longer and if we put larger portions of assets in bonds, we almost surely will come up short at some time."

"What would you advise then?" the husband counters.

"My experience leads me to three cardinal rules for equity investing: First, *diversify*. Never put all your eggs into one basket, not one stock, not one industry, not one country, and certainly not with one investment entity or broker. A useful guide is to limit holdings in any one security to

5 percent of the total portfolio, implying a portfolio of twenty individual securities. Some investors may feel comfortable with fifteen or ten securities. Mutual funds and other portfolio-type holdings obviously count for more than one in this calculus.

"Here's how Irene and I do it without owning individual stocks or bonds and divvying our liquid assets in this fashion: Eighteen percent is in full-risk real estate, both domestic and global mutual funds, because that's the industry I know best and its results tend to follow the broad economy very closely.

"Thirteen percent goes into a real estate long/short fund, or hedge fund if you prefer, managed to take the dips out of real estate cycles and provide moderate long-term appreciation. Nearly half, or 46 percent, is invested in assets benchmarked to the Standard & Poor's 500 Index, a broad measure of US stocks with strong presences in global markets. We put 20 percent in an annuity backed by a major US insurance company. And 3 percent goes into an infrastructure mutual fund focusing on energy and transportation, because cash-strapped and leveraged governments around the world increasingly must depend upon the private sector to fund these sinews of our civilization."

"That's our diversification," chimes in Irene. "Your diversification may be different, but diversity is the cornerstone."

"I can't believe you don't own individual stocks," the wife exclaims. "I never heard of such a thing."

"Our second rule is *think asset classes and portfolio exposure, not individual stocks*. Every one of the funds mentioned above is available to the public, and they have been carefully chosen to provide exposure to economic areas with defined growth—meaning I expect them to beat inflation.

"I favor a carefully selected menu of professionally managed mutual funds or exchange traded mutual funds (ETFs) because both are portfolios and not individual stocks. And our third rule is *to be unemotional and self-disciplined.* Make changes slowly, no more frequently than quarterly, and then only after considering whether an alternative investment will perform as you desire. I learned this lesson by painful experience in the spring of 2008 when I transferred some assets from a domestic real estate fund into a global real estate fund, thinking global real estate would outperform the US assets. The move failed to give any diversification protection because everything was real estate, which now trades in a global market with only modest variations between most national markets, especially in down markets.

"That failure teaches me that the only useful transfer would have been into cash or Treasury securities—yes, those dreaded fixed-income securities. Such transfers can make sense, but don't panic at market bottoms. A useful guide is that if the market is so high that it makes the front page of the *New York Times*, lighten up or consider taking some profits. If a market bottom makes page 1 of the *Times*, buy. Invest without emotion, and don't panic in downturns."

"But don't you have an advantage of size?" inquires the husband. "You have more money [under management], and thus you can buy inside deals that the individual investor never sees."

"It often is the reverse," I respond. "A number of academic studies show that individual investors can do very well and even beat the market in securities that are too small for an institutional investor, such as our company. Most institutional investors do not want to own more than 5 percent of a company's stock, although some managers may go up to 10 percent on occasion. That's just simple diversification—rule one—and forces the manager to spread his clients' funds into a larger portfolio of stocks.

"Warren Buffett, generally regarded as the canniest and most successful investor of this day, commands a portfolio so large that he cannot consider an investment under five billion dollars. That limits where he can put his money. In contrast, the investor with a fifty-thousand-dollar portfolio can choose from many thousands of potential investments. Size is not a meaningful constraint to successful investing."

"Why are you so fond of real estate securities?" inquires the wife.

"Real estate is the classic store of value since the Egyptians built the pyramids and the Mesopotamians built Babylon," I respond. "Real estate is a hard asset, easily visible and not portable, so its condition may be easily observed by an outsider. You can't hide it, and you can't forge it.

"In today's world, residential real estate constitutes our living environment and commercial real estate becomes the spine of our financial society. Buildings may succumb to wear and tear over the longer term, but most last longer than an individual's lifetime.

"A building's technology—plumbing and heating systems, electricity delivery, and the like—can and generally are upgraded to meet changing standards. The Internet can create virtual reality in almost every part of our everyday life except the buildings in which we live and work."

"But commercial buildings are so large, can their securities really be traded by people like us?" asks the husband.

"Right after the Civil War, real estate professionals began trying to find ways to trade real estate, especially very large commercial buildings. The New York Real Estate Securities Exchange was organized in 1929 primarily to trade commercial mortgages and constitutes the most ambitious effort toward that goal. But the Great Depression killed this pioneering effort [see appendix I].

"Then along came the real estate investment trust, or REIT, over three decades later, and becomes my rat hole—the new and untested idea that became a globe-changing force by a serendipitous chain of events. That rat hole connected sprawling markets, in stocks and real estate, and defined and dominated my professional and personal life since 1961."

"How boring," scoffs my female dinner companion. "How can you stand doing the same thing over and over?"

"Watching that rat hole, never a darkened or quiet stage, was relatively simple when I got my assignment in 1961, with NYSE volume averaging 3.3 million shares a day and REITs a gleam in real estate's eye. Today the Rat Hole seethes with action every minute of every day with events new, scheduled, or unexpected, at home and abroad, headlines and storylines, all marching onto traders' computer screens faster than they can be read or digested. Today 130-plus million REIT shares worth three to four billion dollars cross the US tape on an average day. 'Keep up, keep up,' they exhort, 'or you will fall behind.'

"These basics—the recurring drama playing out from my rat hole—never change the interplay between the twin players occupying that rat hole, the stock markets and real estate markets. That constant motion, constant action, keeps me engaged."

"It all sounds so rush-rush that I wonder if a person getting on in years like me can keep up with it all," the husband interjects.

"There are two constants that any investor of any age must understand: the rapidity of change and the role of future projections. Changes may unfold rapidly, as when a governmental agency approves or denies a needed permit or approval (think governmental approval of plans to erect a major complex like reconstruction of the World Trade Center). Or they may play out over many years as when Manhattan's office market slowly unraveled over the decade of the Great Depression [see appendix I].

"The common but often unacknowledged element is time, that inexorable but uncontrollable fourth dimension. Investors in both stocks and real estate need to understand more fully the extent to which both industries live in the future.

"The earnings, dividends, cash flows, and balance sheets of every REIT stock traded on every exchange are modeled in highly complex computerized spreadsheets by up to four dozen Wall Street analysts. Every quarterly report is analyzed in detail for any squiggles from those models and earnings estimates generated for one, two, three, and more quarters and years into the future. Billions of dollars in stock change hands every day based on these projections.

"And thanks to a 1995 law, the majority of publicly traded companies may now provide earnings 'guidance' to investors, in effect dropping the veil a bit on the numbers management sees every day and making every investor's job easier.

"Similarly, commercial real estate properties are bought and sold every day based on projections of the cash flow each building will produce over the next three, five, or ten years. That cash flow is discounted to present value and a sale price estimated based on a projected capitalization rate, or expected rate of return [see Appendix V, "Real Estate Glossary"].

"This underscores the reality that both stock and real estate markets rely on estimates of events transpiring in the future. Generations of real estate and stock pros have taken their turns at predicting the future, but I have never met nor read about one who succeeded consistently enough to merit trust over the longer term.

"So we who are older have time and perspective on our side. I am attracted to Warren Buffett's approach. He tries to envision what a company or real estate portfolio will look like in ten years. Buffett's tack results in dozens of profitable acquisitions and investments over the years. Think Coca-Cola, Gillette, and many others, contributing to an extraordinary investment record. Try it, and you'll find out envisioning a company ten years from today isn't as easy as you might expect."

By now, we have lingered over dessert and a second cup of coffee or tea. The waitstaff is busily clearing tables and readying the Green Room for next day's diners, subtly reminding us that we are the last diners in the room.

"None of these ideas are profound or unique," I say. "I started in the library and went on to business school in my thirties. There is no shame and a lot of pride in the do-it-yourself path to market knowledge, whether in real estate or stocks. Time is money. Finally, don't lose faith in the power of REITs to produce sturdy investment returns over the longer term.

"In September 1999, near the bottom of a grueling market decline that left REIT shares down about 30 percent over nearly two years, I penned a poem extolling the virtues of REITs and their power to generate cash dividends for shareholders. The *Wall Street Journal* subsequently picked up the verse under a headline, 'Delicate REIT, How Thou Drive Me Nuts.' (Martinez, 2000.) The verse remains as true today as when it was written, when REIT stocks were being abandoned wholesale by investors panting to buy dot-com striplings with zero earnings but limitless hype."

INVESTMENT 101

Ask not what this stock will earn
In some distant yearly turn;

Think not of prices spiraling high
Toward some misty, capital-gains sky.

But rather inquire, I pray:
What dividend does this stock pay

In cash, dependable,
Eminently spendable

Cash? That stock with sturdy yield
Holds value unconcealed.

And if a REIT stock, better yet:
It owns nonvirtual properties to vet.

And that is why I've watched my rat hole these many years.
And why you should find your rat hole to watch.

Appendix I
RUN-UP TO THE REIT REVOLUTION: THE UNTIMELY LIFE AND DEATH OF THE NEW YORK REAL ESTATE SECURITIES EXCHANGE

A frail and mysterious document passes into my hands during the 1970s. It is titled simply:

Securities Admitted to Trading

on

REAL ESTATE SECURITIES EXCHANGE
·INC·

It is dated July 12, 1930, only seven months after I arrive on this planet!

Until the moment this document arrives, the New York Real Estate Securities Exchange is terra incognita to me, a shocking revelation because by then I have spent nearly two decades reporting and writing about the inner workings of real estate and homebuilding as reflected in the stock market.

That shock morphs into a mystery and a challenge: to unravel the story underlying the NYRESE, or *The List*, as I come to tag my unexpected time traveler.

The mystery screed arrives courtesy of Andy Davis, my attorney at the time, who turns up the enigmatic pages while cleaning his firm's files. Andy ventures, very tentatively, that the exchange had been a tiny corner of the New York Stock Exchange where traders quietly and infrequently trade mortgage bonds.

Knowing my interest in all things real estate, he presses the document into my hands. It is either me or the round file.

But I can never verify Andy's hunch, and several efforts to solve the mystery quickly hit dead ends. So the document, all of six nine-by-twelve-inch pages folded in half to create a thin twenty-four-page booklet, unmarked but yellowed by age, migrates from Andy Davis's file cabinet into my care. Intending to pursue the mystery at a later time, I tuck it into a special file.

"SAVE," in large red letters, reads the file tab.

Every so often, I rescue this mysterious visitor from sequestration and read through its unfamiliar contents to glean some understanding of the story behind this unexpected visitor. What, indeed, is this document telling the world?

In the 1980s, I attempt to pick up the trail via some desultory inquiries using newspaper microfilm and library stacks, the best research tools of that day. That painfully time-consuming and laborious attempt produces such pitiful results that I soon abandon it with the mystery unsolved. Back into the file goes my visitor from the 1930s.

But today, research files are digitized, and four decades after the time traveler's arrival, investigative digging in the digital stacks—allowing inspection of nearly fifteen thousand entries in the electronic files of the *New York Times* from the 1920s and 1930s and Google tracks to locate vintage documents and books—now brings to light most facts bearing on my mystery text. Sample entry:

| | MATURITY AND | |
ISSUES	INTEREST RATES	SYMBOLS
*The Alden 225 Central Park West, N.Y.C. 1st Mtge. Serial Gold Bond Ctfs., 6s (S. W. Straus & Co.)	1928–1941 … J & J	ALD … … 28–41

* The issue is legal investment for trust funds in the State of New York.

A simple Google search reveals that the Alden remains in business today and is described in these words, attributed to Carol E. Levy of Carol E. Levy Real Estate:

> The Alden was designed as an apartment hotel by the renowned architect Emery Roth, and opened by Bing and Bing in 1926–1927. The magnificent 15-story building was built in 1925 and converted into a cooperative in 1984. The Alden boasts a spectacular lobby with 24 hour doormen and concierge, beautiful roof deck, garage and bicycle room. The 310 (approximately) apartments range in size from studios up to five bedrooms in residences that have been combined. Located on the prime corner of Central Park West and 82nd Street, the gracious layouts, high beamed ceilings, Central Park views and prewar details make the exquisite Alden a highly sought-after address!

Completed during a time when a wave of apartment towers marched northward on the west side of Manhattan's Central Park, the Alden's apartments fill quickly in the second half of the 1920s. The rent: seventy-five dollars monthly.

To finance construction, the Alden's developers sell 6 percent first mortgage gold bond certificates, most likely in one-thousand-dollar denominations, in an offering underwritten by S. W. Straus & Co., the most active purveyor of mortgage bonds in the 1920s. These original three million dollars of bonds trade under the symbol ALD and are due from 1928 through 1941, with repayment of individual bonds most likely based upon a lottery by bond serial numbers. Perhaps best of all, the Alden's backers offer to pay interest in gold coin, a powerful inducement to buyers in the days before the United States chucks the gold standard.

Dipping into the files of the *New York Times* reveals that the Alden's bonds hit trouble by July 1932, when they trade at fourteen cents on the dollar and become involved in reorganization hearings later that year.

In 2015, owners of the Alden's apartments clearly benefit from endemic housing inflation in the Big Apple. StreetEasy, a realty website, reports a two-bedroom, two-bath unit in contract for $2,595,000 in April 2015 and a three-bedroom, three-bath apartment listed for $3,450,000. Sales or listings for smaller studio or one-bedroom apartments range from $349,000 to $699,000. When they can be found, Alden rentals are quoted at $2,350 and up per month for studios.

But what of office towers? Think Grand Central Terminal! For 1920s real estate developers, the terminal is Main-and-Main and the Holy Grail all wrapped into one single location, ground zero for commuter rail and subway lines, bus and taxi routes, and a two-level street network funneling thousands of autos daily past its doors.

Grand Central's prime location sparks a midtown office building boom in the late 1920s, bringing six million square feet of offices to market and ultimately sparking a race to the sky. But timing is everything for new office towers, palpably true as the Grand Central market explodes in the late 1920s and developers jockey to sign up enough tenants to reach stabilization in leasing—i.e., the point where rents cover all operating and financing costs. Once a building stabilizes, the landlord-owner must lease only a small fraction, say 10 to 20 percent, as leases roll annually.

Here's how two striking Grand Central office towers, at opposite ends of the 1920s financing scale, fare in the race for tenants.

Lincoln Building sits diagonally across Forty-Second Street from Grand Central at 60 E. 42nd Street. The Lincoln doesn't join the Grand Central office party until its unveiling in May 1928 with a press release saying the fifty-two-story, 915,000-square-feet tower is "believed to be the largest office building in the world," according to *the New York Times* (press releases outsizing predecessors seem built into developer genes). The Lincoln controls a strategic site, formerly occupied by Lincoln storage warehouse, on the south side of Forty-Second with three entrances from both Forty-First and Forty-Second Streets and Madison Avenue.

The Lincoln appears on page 6 of The List, under "FEES," its entry reading:

Lincoln Building, N.Y.C.
60 E. 42nd Street
1st Mtge. S.F. Gold Loan 5-1/2s
(Chase Securities Corp.)

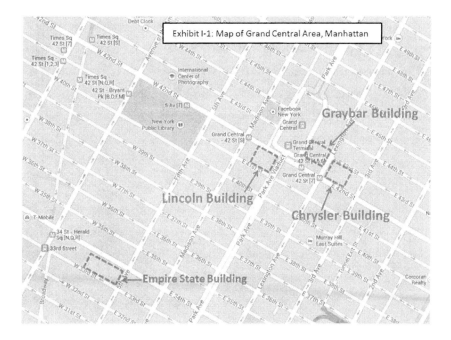

Exhibit I-1: Map of Grand Central Area, Manhattan

The Lincoln's owner, Lincoln Forty-Second Street Corporation, is an amalgam of tested and savvy developers: John H. Carpenter, a well-known real estate dealer of the day; Dwight P. Robinson & Co., Inc., an active building and management company; and J.E.R. Carpenter, John's brother, one of the building's architects. All three have worked together before on high-end apartment and co-op apartment buildings on upper Fifth and Park Avenues.

They advertise their project to prospective investors as a "fifty-two story office building of the most modern fireproof construction … which will tower approximately 640 feet above the 42nd Street level and be one of the tallest and most imposing structures in the city." Early major tenants attracted to the Lincoln include Air Reduction Company, at about 7 percent of the space; Franklin Railway Supply, at about 4 percent of space; and The Uptown Club, occupying the twenty-sixth and twenty-seventh floors.

A banking syndicate led by Chase Securities Corporation aggressively finances the Lincoln in May 1928, selling sixteen million dollars' of first mortgage 5.5 percent sinking fund gold loans due in twenty-five years (1953). But sponsors also sell $5.5 million twenty-year 6.5 percent sinking fund gold debentures. This $21.5 million public bond financing is followed by $1 million of 6.0 percent sinking fund purchase money notes, due in 1935; $3.5 million 7.0 percent preferred stock; and 600,000 shares of common stock. Whew!

Financing thus totals $26.6 million, or about 105.5 percent of the asserted $25.2 million total building cost and 103 percent of the appraised value of $25.9 million. Both ratios are easily computed from the Lincoln's offering ads. Double whew! The Lincoln thus becomes a poster child for the overlending excesses of the 1920s.

Little wonder that the Lincoln is among the first Manhattan office towers to feel Depression pain, seeking receivership March 20, 1932, little more than two years after opening its doors on March 1, 1930. At that point, the *Times* reports the enterprise has assets of $31,405 against $21.3 million debt obligations (the three bond issues) and total liabilities of $25 million. On July 1, 1933, the Lincoln is sold at foreclosure auction to the first mortgage bondholder's committee for $4.75 million, or 18 percent of that $26.6 million financing only five years earlier.

(In November 2002, the Malkin family interests acquire full management control and rename the tower One Grand Central Place; on October 2, 2013, the building becomes part of the Empire State Realty Trust REIT (ESRT) initial public offering. The owners spend about $32 million to reposition the building and upgrade its $49.40 average rents, reflecting a much sounder financial footing. The Lincoln is now back in public markets.)

The Chrysler Building is a distinguished member of The List, nestling on page 14 under "LEASEHOLDS." The entry reads:

Chrysler Building, N.Y.C.

ES Lexington Ave., 42nd to 43rd Streets

1st Mtge. Leasehold 6-1/2% S.F.G. Bonds

(S.W. Straus & Co.)

Exhibit 1-2: Tombstone ad for Chrysler Building
mortgage bonds.
Source: *The New York Times*

The Chrysler Building strides into public view in October 1928, six months after the Lincoln's unveiling. At 1.195 million square feet, or 30 percent larger than the Lincoln, and sited at Lexington Avenue and East Forty-Second Street, the Chrysler Building is the behemoth of this midtown splurge with a premier site only a stone's throw from Grand Central.

"There is an excellent demand for well-planned office space in this section of the city," opines the bond's advertisement offering $7.5 million of mortgage bonds to finance Chrysler's undertaking. The $7.5 million first mortgage leasehold 6 percent sinking fund gold bonds, issued in October 1928, are floated through S. W. Straus & Co., the leading bond underwriter and distributor of that day. The $7.5 million financing, due to mature in 1948, is modest at less than half the $18 million estimated total cost, with the difference being a good equity chunk from Walter P. Chrysler, chairman of the nation's third largest automaker, Chrysler Corporation, who stamps his name on the tower.

His Chrysler Building is initially planned to tower seventy-seven stories above Lexington Avenue. By its September 1928 groundbreaking, the Chrysler is locked into a feverish race for title of world's tallest building with a tower in the downtown financial district at Forty Wall Street being built for the Bank of Manhattan Trust Co. by Wall Street investment banker George Ohrstrom.

Ohrstrom hires H. Craig Severance as his architect. He happens to be the former partner of William Van Alen, the architect Chrysler chooses to give cachet to the landmark building he has in mind. To ensure that the Chrysler bests Severance's building's height, Van Alen obtains permission to erect a 125-foot spire atop the Chrysler, secretly fabricates this spire in four sections inside the under-construction building, and hoists it into position at a dramatic last moment. Thus emerges a distinctive art deco building that remains a fixture of Manhattan's East Side skyline for the intervening eight decades.

Van Alen's inspired spire not only pushes Chrysler Building's peak to a then-world-record 1,046 feet above street level, well above the 927 feet notched by Ohrstrom's Forty Wall Street in April 1930, but also bequeaths an unmistakable permanent addition to New York's nighttime skyline. The spire, or crown, consists of seven overlapping arches formed from triangles, creating a distinctive cascade of light by night. By day, the spire's gleaming stainless steel evokes the pristine look of a new auto (Chrysler, of course).

When the Chrysler opens its doors in May 1930, it immediately becomes the skyscraper king in New York City, the United States, and the world.

In a tip of his hat to his patron, Van Alen decorates the building with gargoyles replicating radiator caps from the 1929 model Chrysler, and at one point, a band of hubcaps morphs into an ornamental frieze. Most of the building is essentially handcrafted and individualistic. Each elevator is distinctive in design, and the lobby dazzles with unique marble cladding and stunning original murals.

Reaching stabilization is essential in this 1920s free-for-all because new towers are announced almost weekly.

Surprise! Chrysler (the man) is able to arrange for Chrysler Corporation (the company he chairs) to occupy space in the building under lease as its New York headquarters until the mid-1950s. To avoid any conflict between the owner (Chrysler, the man) and the tenant (Chrysler, the company), Chrysler Corporation never holds an equity interest in this trophy structure.

That long-term corporate lease imparts stability to the building's finances during the maelstrom of the Great Depression, since Chrysler Corporation loses money in only one year (1932) during the 1930s, even though unit production falls 50 percent from 1929 to a 1932 nadir. Chrysler leases a significant part of the building's 1.195 million square feet of rentable offices, including an auto showroom on the first floor where Chrysler Corporation displays its new models annually to great fanfare.

This lets Chrysler announce the building is cash-flow positive at 65 percent occupancy a few weeks after the May 27, 1930, opening. Name tenants attracted to the prestige building include Carrier Corporation, Crucible Steel Company of America, Texas Company on floors 15 through 19; Time Incorporated on floors 50 and 51; Walter Chrysler's personal offices on floors 58 and 59; and the glamorous Cloud Club on the top three floors, 66 through 68.

With this stable financial footing, the Chrysler bonds never trade below 30 percent of par during the Depression's darkest hours, versus single-digit quotes for many competitors and bankruptcy for the Lincoln Building. They are called at 103 percent of par in April 1937, making the bonds an excellent investment.

(Today the Chrysler is owned and operated by Tishman Speyer, a major New York realty concern, and is valued at one billion dollars or more.)

The competing Empire State Building, on Thirty-Fourth Street and Fifth Avenue, comes to market a year after the Chrysler, by which time the office market is essentially kaput and half its space lingers vacant for a decade. The Metropolitan Life Assurance Company finances it with a $27.5 million loan, which is reworked in 1937 but never goes into foreclosure.

INSIDE THE LIST

My takeaway: deciphering the details behind even three entries in The List requires laborious research, but the fact that these properties are valued in 2015 at between twenty-five and fifty times the original cost underscores how inflation's march, even when broken by the rocky 1930s, invisibly benefits commercial property owners over long time spans.

Ah, but The List is packed with 270 such listings, each with an inside story. And could a collection of 270 such stories conceivably be of interest to anyone except the building's owners or occupiers? I judge not.

Initially, I merely categorize the goodies filling The List's pages and count 238 fixed-rate mortgages, or seven-eighths of all securities lodged in The List. The eighteen and a half pages devoted to mortgage bonds breaks down at 165 first mortgage bonds secured by properties built on land owned in fee, 53 first mortgages on buildings erected on leased land, and 20 junior mortgages or debentures.

A look at property locations makes clear The List's organizers hoped to create a better mousetrap, attracting listings from real estate mortgages and stocks across the land, but New York City dominates mortgage listings with over three-fourths, or 182 of 238 mortgages, registered. Other major cities are lightly represented: Chicago chips in fifteen mortgages, and Philadelphia sends ten, with Detroit, Boston, and California represented by smaller numbers.

A skimpy STOCK section covering scarcely over one page bespeaks the NYRESE's focus on mortgages. The List contains only twenty common stock listings by nineteen companies, five preferred stocks, and seven units of both common and preferred.

Mortgage title and trust companies, nearly all based in New York City or environs, dominate stock listings with twelve of twenty common stocks. S. W. Straus & Co., the ubiquitous realty mortgage underwriter, lists its common, as do one garage operator, two companies owning individual buildings, and three builder/developers. Fred F. French Company lists combined common and preferred stock units owning seven buildings, including the French Building at 551 Fifth Avenue at Forty-Fifth Street.

S. W. Straus & Company is far and away the leading underwriter of mortgages on The List with sixty issues, or over 25 percent of mortgages. About seventy bond houses populate The List, the most significant after Straus being P. W. Chapman & Company, fifteen issues; Prudence Company, Inc., fourteen; Halsey, Stuart, & Company, twelve issues; New York Title & Mortgage Company, ten; and Hayden Stone & Company, seven issues. Only New York Title survives today. Among present-day investment banking houses, only Goldman, Sachs, & Company, which underwrote an issue for Saks Realty Corporation, and Merrill, Lynch, &

Company, underwriter of mortgages for Merchants National Properties, Inc., make The List.

AN ERA OF ANYTHING GOES

The List opens a window into a long-dead, and rightfully so, world of anything-goes 1920s commercial mortgage financing, a world so stacked against the customer that one major NYRESE goal is to simply give an even chance to the clerks and shopkeepers and elderly who bought prodigious amounts of mortgage bonds to receive generous, above-market interest yields.

Explore The List's provenance with me. We begin in the world of Jay Gatsby and his shadowy underworld contacts, an era of bathtub gin and speakeasies, of Nathan Detroit and "the oldest established permanent floating crap game," a shining time of endless partying for flappers and hustlers alike, a carefree time of the Charleston and "Ja Da Ja Da Jing Jing Jing," when all tuned to the beckoning roar of a stock market arcing ever higher, coining new millionaires daily (or so everyone assumes), in a salubrious land of ever faster growth and prosperity, marching onward and upward without pause.

Skyscrapers sprout like daisies in Manhattan and many other cities, reaching for the skies as if to fill boundless demand from tenants eager for only the biggest and the best, the latest and greatest. "More office buildings taller than 70 meters [about 230 feet or 20 stories] were constructed in New York between 1922 and 1931 than in any other ten-year period before or since," write William N. Goetzmann and Frank Newman in a 2010 copyrighted National Bureau of Economic Research working paper *Securitization in the 1920s*. "These 235 buildings represented more than an architectural movement; they were largely the manifestation of a widespread financial phenomenon."

WILD WEST FINANCE

A goodly number of these skyscrapers are financed in a fast and furious, watch-your-back financial market that today reads like a financial Wild West tale. Simon W. Straus, a Chicago investment banker who took over his father's business in 1886 and migrated to New York in 1915, originates the mortgage bond in March 1909 when his S. W. Straus & Company sells bonds secured by the income from a completed commercial property. The idea catches on, and bond houses around the nation emulate the idea after World War I.

The Straus firm remains king of the field by relentlessly extoling the virtues of the "Straus Plan" or "Straus Bonds," boasting its staff of "experts which in knowledge, judgment, numbers and technical skill is alone in the field," and repeating its slogan, "44 YEARS WITHOUT A LOSS TO ANY INVESTOR" on thousands of plain display newspaper ads. (The number of years changes annually dating from the firm's founding.) Straus sticks to first mortgages until 1924, when the organization has grown to one thousand persons in fifty cities and demands more products. In 1924, Straus begins peddling second mortgages—christening them "general mortgages"—and construction loans, products that ultimately bring down the business after it has sold an estimated one billion dollars in mortgage bonds.

The mortgage bond business is enormously profitable, with buyers paying commissions of 10 percent or more split between the salesman and the bond house. The system works something like this. The developers or backers of a proposed new building line up a bond underwriter from among a coterie of bond houses populating Wall Street and ask them to sell mortgage bonds to finance the enterprise. Once an underwriter signs on, the project is announced to the press amid great fanfare; tenants for the new building are secured in about only half the new office towers, meaning many buildings and their bonds are "on spec"—a fact often overlooked by bond salesmen. These mortgage bonds, plus preferred and common stocks secured by these towers, become a handy way of raising more money than conservative insurance company un-derwriters are often willing to okay.

Exhibit 1-3: S.W. Straus & Co. ad of 1924.
Source: *The New York Times*

Goetzmann and Newman, in their copyrighted study, describe the symbiotic relationship between developers and the 1920s bond houses, who "generally served simultaneously as originators, underwriters and distributors. Building companies can depend on the bond house to identify willing buyers of real estate bonds, purchase all of the bonds not sold to the public, and act as dealers between the building company and the public to facilitate bond issuance. Performing these three functions proves incredibly lucrative in an optimistic real estate market."

But troubles are already brewing. Some bond houses—the exact number is unknown—commingle net proceeds from issues with their general bank accounts, doling out funds to developers as needed but also paying interest, required amortization, and property taxes on buildings already financed from prior bond sales. If a building falls behind in interest or amortization, the bond house dips into its general funds to make payments to investors, who are thus blissfully unaware that anything is wrong. "Independent" trustees looking out for bondholders are often subsidiaries of the bond house. With such tight control of the money, building a multiyear track record of never losing money for investors seems, in retrospect, a no-brainer.

Today we might call this a Ponzi scheme.

The investor who seeks to sell his bond also faces troubles. Once issued, these real estate securities are subsequently traded in an opaque over-the-counter secondary market where brokers seek to attract buyers by listing their wares, prices, and interest yields in newspaper ads. Bid and asked spreads, if revealed at all, are often dauntingly wide, piling on hidden but even more unseemly costs. The true status of any single building is difficult to determine, sketchy and couched in arcane accounting lingo when found, and almost always behind the times. Property valuations and appraisals are frequently cited in broker literature, but their validity is viewed as suspect at best.

These pernicious practices inside bond houses start surfacing in July 1926, when Pennsylvania's secretary of banking seeks to suspend the license of G. L. Miller & Company, Inc., then the third largest bond underwriter with twenty offices in the East, charging Miller with paying the interest and sinking fund charges for bond issues in default. Citing data showing nearly 20 percent of Miller-issued bonds in default, Pennsylvania charges Miller with "dual deception in concealing from investors that the borrower corporations could not and did not meet interest and sinking fund obligations; [and] in inflating the assets of borrower corporations in default to make it appear they were well able to meet their obligations," as reported in the *New York Times*.

One month later, in August 1926, G. L. Miller & Company collapses because it could not meet a $50,000 payment to a client. Receivership follows in September "as a result of their practice of pooling the proceeds of the sale of their bond issues and of freezing their assets in unsalable bonds," according to a deputy state attorney general.

"What had driven Miller over the edge," relates James Grant in his book *Money of the Mind*, "was its failure to meet a deadline to pay one of its investment-banking clients. The proceeds of the bond sale had not, as the investors might have assumed, been immediately turned over to the borrower. They had been lumped in with the Miller general accounts."

The ensuing investigation by New York Attorney General Albert Ottinger leads Ottinger early in 1927 to enact new rules to end some of the worst practices unearthed by his Miller investigation. Bond houses must segregate proceeds of bond sales for uncompleted buildings for the benefit of the buildings; borrower payments for interest, amortization, and taxes also must be segregated; bondholders are to receive "reasonable notice" of defaults; and bond houses must disclose and may not conceal "any material fact that will affect the value of the bond," according to the *Times*.

Each sounds reasonable today, but Ottinger's edicts send lawyers into a frantic search for loopholes, because of course no one wants to remove the punchbowl. As one result, S. W. Straus & Company drops its claim of "XX YEARS WITHOUT A LOSS TO ANY INVESTOR." Otherwise the party must—and did—go on.

The mortgage bond business is a bonanza for bond houses and developers alike. Lake Forest (Illinois) College business professor Ernest A. Johnson reports in his 1936 study "The Record of Long-Term Real Estate Securities," published in *The Journal of Land and Public Utility Economics*, that mortgage bond issuers raised $4.1 billion from 1919 to 1931. "Offerings were considerably over half a billion dollars in 1927 and reached $683.7 million in the following year," Johnson finds. "In 1925, 1926 and 1928 real estate flotations exceeded those for railroads." Johnson analyzes 1,090 offerings over $1 million in his study, suggesting that well over 2,000 mortgage bond issues found their way into the hands of investors, mostly individuals searching for the average 6 percent yield putatively paid on these issues.

REALIZING THE DREAM

Such overt excesses invariably generate equal and opposite reactions. During those years of the Great Delusion, and perhaps under the spell of the Delusion, powerful real estate promoters, under aegis of the Realty Board of New York, strive to bring reality to their powerful dream: *Make illiquid real estate liquid and easily tradable. Achieve the eternal alchemy of real estate by giving real estate a securities wrapper—mortgage or bond or stock—and let those wrappers trade like other commodities. And, oh yes, make facts about the underlying real estate readily available to traders.*

Make real estate just like corn and wheat, railroads and steel mills, airplane and auto companies. Let investors share in the rewards—and risks—of putting their money into real estate, just as easily as they could take a view on stocks and bonds by buying and selling on the Big Board. And make it honest; give the little guy a fair shake.

Just make commercial real estate tradable like any other industry! The dream is not new and is pockmarked with notable failures of the past.

That animating dream, that visceral urge of property men in New York City and elsewhere, first catches public notice on September 13, 1883, when "A number of prominent real estate agents, brokers and auctioneers met … to take steps to organize a Real Estate Exchange," according to the *New York Times*. "Our plan now is to create an Exchange similar to the Stock or Produce Exchange … Our idea is to bring together all persons who are interested in the transfer and improvement of property."

John Jacob Astor and many fellow real estate luminaries soon step up to buy stock in the new enterprise, named the Real Estate Exchange and Auction Room (Limited), and by the end of 1884, the exchange buys the Wall Street property at Numbers 59, 61, 63, and 65 Liberty Street for $421,000 and hires an architect for another $112,000 to construct there a grand eighty-seven-by-forty-three-foot exchange room standing thirty-three feet high.

The exchange flourishes, with auctioneers presiding over the sale of whole properties, until mid-1892 when a bitter dispute over commissions erupts, impelling about two-thirds of the auctioneers to form a competing New York Real Estate Salesroom at 111 Broadway. "The trouble with the Liberty Street Exchange is that it has grown to be a very close and powerful corporation, and proposes to do just what it pleases ..." the *Times* quotes dissidents. By June 1900, the split drains so much power from the Real Estate Exchange and Auction Room that it sells its Liberty Street quarters for $580,000 and disbands.

The Salesroom continues to be actively used by auctioneers, mainly for legal auctions, for another decade before activity tails off after 1910 and it disappears altogether from the *Times* purview in 1921. Before its demise, a committee of the Real Estate Board of New York in 1903 takes up the cudgel for tradable real estate, but after several meetings, World War I intervenes and the effort is abandoned.

Thus ends the first large-scale attempt to make real estate tradable. But the dream remains alive.

As the Great Delusion of the 1920s sets in, a new generation of real estate operatives in New York City reclaims the dream of harnessing liquidity to enhance the supply of capital to build even grander cathedrals of commerce to adorn the island of Manhattan.

Their blueprint: recast real estate in the image of the glamorous new companies creating the sinews of an emerging industrial society, companies making steel and automobiles and radios, companies flying airplanes and running railroads, all dominating popular dreams as their shares trade effortlessly on the Big Board and enabling them to raise all the capital they need to create a new-age urban America.

Making real estate tradable, they reason, is the gateway for raising immense amounts of new capital because market liquidity lets investors effortlessly realign their holdings as conditions change. Without trading, an investor stands locked into his or her investment sans the capability to change as economic winds shift.

The thought of making commercial real estate tradable becomes a shimmering, powerful compulsion for these men, united under the banner of the Real Estate Board of New York (REBNY).

RUN-UP TO START-UP

On November 18, 1928, REBNY president Peter Grimm announces that REBNY will form "an exchange for the sale of real estate securities exclusively." "The formation of the Exchange is regarded in real estate circles as the most progressive step in the development of the profession since the establishment of the Real Estate Board in 1896," comments the *New York Times*. The tentative name is the Real Estate Board of New York Exchange, Inc.

"It will save the investing public millions of dollars a year by discouraging offerings of real estate securities issued on over-appraised, dishonest valuations," a high New York State official says in a letter to Peter Grimm. "It will establish the difference between investment and speculation as applying to real estate securities."

Exhibit I-4: Cyrus C. Miller, President New York
Real Estate Securities Exchange
Source: *The New York Times*

A twenty-one-man board of governors is empaneled—women rarely rise above secretary in those days—and seven committees, comprising forty-nine men, go to work. Ideas are shared and debated, personal prerogatives set aside for higher goals, hours and days consumed over and beyond the daily rigors of business, all to achieve the common goal of making real estate tradable.

For president of their shining new enterprise, the backers turn to Cyrus Chace Miller, a square-jawed, sixty-one-year-old blunt-talking Manhattan lawyer who lives in the Bronx, where he serves one term as borough president on a Fusion ticket to clean up a "mess" there. Miller commutes daily by taxi from his Bronx home to his Manhattan office well into his eighties, saying tartly, "If you want to get buried quick, retire." Miller is equally blunt in describing the need for reform in real estate finance in a March 1930 magazine article in *Annals of the American Academy of Political and Social Science.*

> One might state without exaggeration that no other
> industry could suffer the waste from inexperienced

ownership, speculative and costly building, poor architecture, neglect, diversion of revenues, injurious neighborhood buildings, and other causes too numerous to
mention, and still survive.

In Cyrus Miller, the real estate mavens have found their Mr. Clean
to sell their ideas to a skeptical public.

The exchange planners grapple with the mechanics of trading mortgage bonds, an innovation first introduced in 1909 by S. W. Straus &
Company, as we have seen, instruments that effectively slice multi-
million-dollar mortgages into $1,000 or $500 bonds but are ill-suited
for resale after their initial purchase. They ponder the mechanics of
disseminating information about a property's operations and rental performance after the initial bond sale, the ongoing value of the property,
and cutting through the sheer complexity of real estate customs that
repel small individual investors. Their overriding goal is to ensure that
interest coupons attached to each bond are paid on time and in full so
bond holders receive their agreed-upon interest.

They do all this under the shadow of the 1926 failure of the G. L.
Miller bond house (unrelated to Cyrus Miller), amply demonstrating
that New York state laws bequeath enormous latitude for hanky-panky
to bond houses and bond trustees, and the resulting reforms mandated
by Attorney General Ottinger.

The urgency driving organization of the NYRESE may, perhaps,
contain an element of trying to stave off tougher governmental regulations and oversight. Evidence on this point is circumstantial and not
entirely convincing, however.

Working through the months of 1929, the New York real estate
men finally agree on many details: create a truly national real estate
exchange, modeled after the New York Stock Exchange, to trade both

mortgages on individual buildings and the stocks of companies owning one or more buildings.

Bylaws are drafted and a final name chosen: New York Real Estate Securities Exchange, Inc. (NYRESE). Conceived as national in scope, the exchange is geared to trade securities from every city in the land just as the NYSE attracts listings from companies all across the country and around the world.

All during 1929, they proudly trumpet their creation in numerous newspaper articles in the *New York Times* as the first dedicated central marketplace for real estate securities in US history, a place where mortgage bonds and debentures, common and preferred stocks, all representing fractional interests in real properties, can trade regularly, reliably, and openly.

Methodically, patiently, exchange planners shape their dream into concrete form, a trading floor modeled after the Big Board, where individual investors can buy and sell stakes in real estate in all its forms, from "safe" first mortgages to "riskier" common stocks. They hope their proud creation, the New York Real Estate Securities Exchange and author of The List, will increase the flow of investor money into real estate while elevating real estate's low esteem among the populace.

THE MUSIC STOPS

Around Labor Day of 1929, the stock market peaks at 381.17 on the Dow-Jones Industrials and begins running out of money as lenders balk at staking margin buyers chasing ever-ascending stock prices.

The market turns ugly in mid-October, and the break everyone remembers comes Monday, October 28, 1929, when the Dow-Jones Industrials plunge a sickening 12.8 percent, from 298.97 to a 260.64 close. Volume rises to 9.2 million shares, modest compared to the record 12.9 million shares the previous Thursday, October 24. Everyone sleeps, hoping for the best.

But Tuesday sees another jarring 11.7 percent cut in market values, the DJI closing at 230.07, for a shocking 68.90 point, or 23.0 percent, plunge in two historic days. Volume soars to a record 16.4 million shares.

Stocks recover 44.44 points the following two days, or nearly two-thirds of the drop, but then resume their downward arc, closing November 13 at 198.69, down 100 points, or 33.5 percent, in little over two weeks. The bull is dead.

At first, disbelief reigns. There is widespread resistance to accepting the "bloodless verdict" of the marketplace. The market crash is only a blip, a momentary pause, many hope. NYRESE's opening day is postponed from October 1, 1929, until December 16, 1929, for "technical reasons." After the traumatic 23 percent stock market plunge of October 28–29, exchange backers check their signals and stick to the December 16, 1929, launch.

Powerful dreams die hard.

As surely as the 1920s slide into the 1930s, America enters a churning decade of diminished expectations, of austerity and darker dreams, of making do with whatever happens to be at hand, of altered and sometimes tragically truncated lives, of bread lines and soup kitchens, of armies of shaken men trooping the streets in search of gainful employment, of homes and commercial buildings foreclosed and companies bankrupted, of debts compromised and interest unpaid.

The economy gets really bad really fast. By 1933's end, nearly 44 percent of urban homes are in default or foreclosure and nearly 25 percent of the labor force is jobless.

My dad feeds four hungry mouths by working a succession of patchwork jobs, including a stint in Wildwood coal mine north of Pittsburgh; he quits because the coal dust nearly kills him. Finally in 1936, he catches on as a brakeman for the Bessemer & Lake Erie Railroad, where he stays over thirty-five years before retiring.

People survive those parlous times on guts and grit!

I recall my old *Columbus Citizen* colleague Perry Morison's story of how his family survived two successive pay cuts of 10 percent each during the Depression. Then came the third cut.

"But that third 5% pay cut was a ball-buster. I don't know how we made it. But we did."

Thus the Great Delusion slides ineluctably into the Great Depression.

Alas, the dream of NYRESE's visionaries becomes reality on the cusp of the Great Depression, when business, especially for any property that happens to be highly leveraged, begins deteriorating from bad to worse to dismal.

The mystery of The List is solved, the dreams of its authors defined.

With the dream identified, we need to know more, much more, about why the dream failed in the 1930s. The timing of The List on the cusp of the longest and deepest economic depression in US history provides a perfect laboratory to examine boots-on-the-ground property-level insights too often buried in macro studies. These questions cry out for answers.

For real estate securities markets and the NYRESE, this second look ultimately leads to realization of the dream in altered form—the real estate investment trust, or REIT.

But that is another story.

First, we must understand the dream's demise.

THE NIGHTMARE

The exchange tests this proposition: "If you build it, will they come."

The New York Real Estate Securities Exchange finally opens for business Monday, December 16, 1929, after a ten-month publicity buildup, one postponed opening date, and the tumult of over five hundred of New York's property elite trooping two blocks from a lionizing lunch at the Biltmore Hotel on Forty-Third Street to the Exchange's new digs at the

Real Estate Board of New York building at 12 East Forty-First Street, essentially across Fifth Avenue from the New York City Public Library. The opening bell rings at 3:00 that afternoon on a trading floor modeled after the Big Board with six trading posts and a telephone bank to report sale prices promptly, according to reports in the *New York Times*.

The central question for NYRESE backers is how investors will accept this new toy.

Ten bonds are traded that first day, all being 7 percent second mortgage bonds secured by the Real Estate Board Building due 1946 under REB symbol. (Traders typically refer to bonds by the name followed by the coupon and maturity date. Hence these bonds are the Real Estate Board 7s of '46.) Prices fluctuate between 98 and 97-1/8 of par. Trading lasts thirty minutes before the realty men turn to other duties, says the *Times*.

In the thirteen trading days before New Year's Eve, 104 bonds change hands—an average of eight bonds daily—and a tiny fraction of the approximately $175 million to $200 million principal amount of bonds of sixty-nine issuers initially listed on the exchange. Those initial listings include sixty-seven mortgage bond issues secured by properties, all in Manhattan, plus two corporate bond issuers, signaling that the exchange is betting its future on the fixed-income market. No common stocks are listed initially, and hence none are traded.

Prices hold firm during the first two weeks of trading, with all issues pricing between 94 and 99 save for three issues: 165 Broadway 5-1/2s of 1951 change hands at 88-1/2, Graybar Building 5s of 1946 price at 89, and Savoy-Plaza Hotel 6s of 1945 trade at 92-7/8. Bonds of seventeen separate issuers turn over those first two weeks, according to quotations appearing in the *Times*.

The Dow-Jones Industrials steady after the late October sell-off, closing at 245.88 on the exchange's first trading day, up a soothing 6.9

percent from the October 30 sell-off low but down 35.5 percent from its September 3 high. The DJI is little changed by year-end, closing at 248.48, still down 34.8 percent from that peak but above the panic bottom.

The relatively light initial turnover seems not to faze the exchange's backers. "While its early weeks have been very gratifying to its sponsors, it [the exchange] is having the experiences which it anticipated," writes NYRESE president Cyrus Miller. Sponsors continue to admit more issues into the exchange fold, bulking up the list by July 1930 to the 238 mortgages and 20 equity issues contained in my thin list.

But the light initial volume also serves as an early caution light. Perhaps, just perhaps, the need for liquidity by bondholders is not nearly as acute as anticipated.

Backers have two major goals: *create liquidity for current and future bond and stock holders, and improve listing standards and investor access to information.*

Liquidity becomes the number-one focus in the long run-up to the exchange's launch for several reasons.

"Mortgage investments have always lacked one of the elements which make an ideal investment," says Nathan S. Jonas, board chairman of Manufacturers Trust Company in a letter quoted in the *Times*. "That element is marketability, the ability to dispose of a security quickly and at a moderate cost."

"Real estate securities have been frozen," Exchange president Miller avers in extolling liquidity's benefits to individual investors, saying on one occasion, "When an investor prepares to lay out his money in an investment, he wants to feel that the securities are adequately backed. He wants to be able to sell them whenever he decides to and be able to reinvest under similarly good conditions. He wants to be able to borrow money on the securities if the occasion arises."

Miller is also forthright about the benefits bond houses may reap from enhanced liquidity, telling the *New York Times* in an August 1929 interview, "The mortgage bond issuing houses are today faced with the tremendous selling problem of distributing their bonds to a public which realizes the frozen condition the money will be in after it is invested.

"It is felt by the sponsors of the exchange that because of the knowledge the public will have that the securities are liquid that many issuance houses will list their securities so that they may be able to sell them with less resistance."

MORTGAGE BOND FATIGUE

By the time the exchange arrives, US investors already buy nearly $3.5 billion of mortgage bonds in the ten years following the end of World War I—and $2.6 billion, or about 75 percent, floods the market in the four years between 1925 and 1928. The pipeline for new bonds is still pumping away but is having indigestion as the buying public is chock-full.

Consider the likely exchange whenever customers' men from bond houses pitch a new issue to previous customers.

"Is this a better investment than the one you sold me last year? If so, can I sell my older bond and put the money into this new one?" Or …

"The bond you sold me two years ago hasn't paid me the interest it owes, and I can't get any information on what is happening at the property. Can you get me out of this dog at a decent price so I can put my money into something better?"

In either case, the customer's man will almost certainly inquire if his bond house can take the older bond back at a discount to keep the customer happy.

No matter how these encounters go, the customer's man isn't likely to get a commission unless the older issue can be sold, often with the bond house taking the older bond into inventory at a concessionary price. Such conversations always wind up confronting that age-old question: "Sell? To whom?"

Given the stringent listing standards applying to the sixty-nine initial exchange listees, current distress or default can be ruled out as a reason holders do not rush to sell in those fading days of 1929. Why, then, the lack of volume?

One reason may be the lack of dealers holding an inventory of readily salable bonds. The Big Board, after which the exchange is modeled, provides smooth markets because designated specialists are willing to buy or sell stock from their inventory in a continuous auction market. But in all descriptions of the exchange, similar specialists are never mentioned. Rather, the exchange emphasizes that broker members will complete trades on their own, relying upon inventory held in the bond houses for merchandise.

A second reason for anemic volume may lie in investor uncertainty over current and future values. The *New York Times* stories leading up to the exchange's opening contain an undercurrent of anxiety; the phrase "need to stabilize mortgage bond trading" appears several times, and exchange sponsors in late November decide to go ahead with the December opening after "careful consideration … of every factor in the situation that has recently developed," a euphemistic allusion to widespread fear, uncertainty, and consternation following the 23 percent stock market drop of October 28 and 29.

And if fear and uncertainty fill the air, what wise investor will yield to panic and sell, giving up reliable income at the same time?

Hence trading volume is almost certain to be light on the fledgling exchange. Economic realities have essentially checkmated months and years of careful planning.

That leaves the exchange facing a potential financial bind. Each of its 191 initial members pony up $5,000 to join the exchange and also pledge to pay $300 a year in dues (a $1,000 initiation fee is waived for the first 500 members). That gives the exchange over $1 million to cover first-year operating costs. But income is pinched because commissions are set low, at "not less than $2 per $1,000 par value" per bond, and from three cents to thirty cents per share depending on price for common stocks. That first half-month of trading generates $208 in bond commissions and a nominal amount from other merchandise, such as common stocks and mortgage participation certificates, forerunners of today's CMOs and CMBS (collateralized mortgage obligations and commercial mortgage-backed securities). The handle is not nearly enough to pay all the clerks, floor reporters, phone operators, and other employees required to tend the exchange's six trading posts.

Initially, the exchange hopes to open for business five hours each trading day, from 10:00 a.m. to 3:00 p.m., but given the tortuous pace with which the listing committee clears issues, the exchange at its onset endeavors to open for trading for only one hour daily, from 11:00 a.m. to noon on weekdays.

The shortened hours and tiny volume thus imperil the exchange's business model.

Perhaps, though, volume will pick up in 1930 when more issues are listed.

By all accounts, the listing committee, headed by Robert Dowling, performs a meticulous job of poring through reams of documentation submitted by sponsors of prospective listees, appraising properties via REBNY members when any whiff of watered valuation appears, and making careful reference checks into backgrounds and business practices of issuer sponsors. Withal, the committee diligently hews to the line that its listing decisions are not recommendations to buy or sell any mortgage bond.

ACTION PICKUP IN 1930

Trading does indeed pick up a bit in 1930, peaking at 16.2 bonds per day in October but averaging 11 bonds per day for the 157 trading days, or 52 percent, of all days I am able to track through *New York Times* daily trading reports. Fifty bonds change hands on November 6, the year's busiest day. Listings of additional common and preferred stocks and mortgage participation certificates (shares in income from a pool of mortgages) help overall turnover, but volume remains so light that the one-hour trading day remains in force.

Prices for the most part cling in the 80s and 90s, with the popular Real Estate Board Building 7s of '46 pricing at 93-1/8 at year-end, off only 4-1/2 for the year-plus since that opening day trade. Some specific issues take gas: Merchants National Properties 6s of '48 trade at 48 in mid-December and the Fifth Avenue and 29th Street Building 6s of '48 change hands at 75.

But generally firm prices during 1930 seem to validate the strength of real estate investments, given that the Dow-Jones Industrials lose 33.8 percent for the year 1930, ending at 164.58 after a spring rally dies at a 294.07 peak on April 17.

BIG DROPS IN 1931

Alas, hopes for a stronger 1931 fade as the months advance. In the spring, anonymous *New York Times* reporters crafting daily activity articles roll through *Roget's Thesaurus* for new words to describe the market's lassitude:

"One of the dullest weeks," on May 7, 1931

"Doldrums" on May 8

"Dullness" on May 13

The monotony is broken when a block of thirty-five bonds secured by a W. Thirty-Eighth Street building trade on June 2. "One of the largest blocks of bonds changing hands ... was sold yesterday at less than two-fifths of the par value [38]," reports the *Times*. But this activity burst is followed by more slack trading:

"Dull and reactionary," on June 6

"Activity ceased entirely yesterday," on June 11

"Continued lethargic," on June 16

"Trading lagged," on June 25

In July 1931, large point changes, mostly down, begin showing up on trades. A single 6-1/2 of '45 bond of Fifth and 28ᵗʰ Realty Corporation trades at 55 percent of par on July 28, down 34 percent from the previous trade. One Dodge Building 6-1/2 of '43 bond changes hands at 45 percent of par on July 21, down 30 percent. During July and August, at least six other issues cross the tape off from 8 to 16 percent of par.

A few bonds buck the trend: 15 Lincoln Building 5-1/4s of '53 tick up 6.25 to 58.75 percent on July 13, but by October 19, this bond brings only 38.25 percent, down 20.5 percent from mid-July. Pennsylvania Building 6s of '39 advance 9.25 percent to 65 on July 17, but by November's end, these bonds are quoted at 30 percent bid, 93 percent asked.

That impossible 63-point spread between bid and ask prices is one of the widest quotations in the exchange's history and bespeaks the yawning gap between buyer and seller expectations. A month later, the 30 percent bid has vanished, leaving some hopeful bondholder hanging out with a "93 percent ask" quote, hoping someone will come along and buy his or her bond.

By year-end 1931, quotes are posted for fifty-two bonds. Ten bonds have both bid and ask quotes at an average spread of 23.5 percent of par, with a high spread of 68 percent of par (15 percent bid, 83 percent ask). Seven bonds register bids-only at an average 38.75 percent of par, while thirty-five bonds show ask-only quotes at an average 68.5 percent. The wide spreads between bid-ask quotes on less than 20 percent of issues are buyer/seller negotiations or "workouts" in bond market parlance and underscore the illiquidity in the exchange's market as it looks forward to 1932.

December 1931 closes with a puny 1.44 average bond sales per day. For the year, volume slumps 55 percent on a daily basis to 4.8 bonds a day.

Not that equity markets are doing much better. The Dow-Jones Industrials close out 1931 at 77.90, down a wrenching 52.7 percent for the year.

NEW LEADER IN 1932

Unfortunately, the presidential election year of 1932 turns out just as bad, if not worse, by some measures. Volume on the exchange falls to a meager 1.9 bonds a day, and prices fall further, with investors clearly favoring office properties over hotels. Office property Lincoln Building 5-1/2s of '53, which end 1931 on a trade of 30 percent of par, are quoted at 20 percent bid, 25 percent ask a year later. In the hotel sector, Savoy-Plaza 6s of '45 fall from 26 percent of par at end of 1931 to 7.5 percent by end of 1932, after The Savoy files for bankruptcy protection. (By 1962, the magnificent Savoy is razed to make way for the General Motors Building at Fifty-Ninth Street and Fifth Avenue.)

In equity markets, the Dow-Jones Industrials fall "only" 23.1 percent, ending the year 1932 at 59.93 but up 45 percent from the recession low 41.22 touched on July 8.

By year-end 1932, hopes run high that newly elected President Franklin Roosevelt can shape a path to prosperity. A wave of optimism sweeps through the exchange after President Roosevelt is sworn into office in March 1933 and declares, "… the only thing we have to fear is fear itself."

Bond volume spikes to twenty bonds a day in April 1933, sparking a sharp rally in beaten-down bonds.

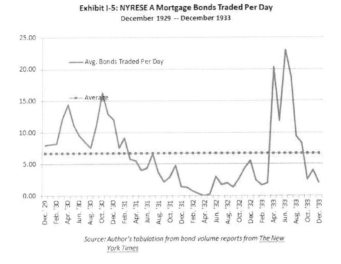

Exhibit I-5: NYRESE A Mortgage Bonds Traded Per Day
December 1929 -- December 1933

Source: Author's tabulation from bond volume reports from *The New York Times*

Lincoln Building 5-1/2s, which changed hands at 25.5 percent of par in mid-April, trade up 68 percent to 43 percent by July 23.

Chrysler Building 6s of '48 trade at 53 percent of par that same day, up 40 percent from 37.75 percent on April 20.

Even the downtrodden Savoy-Plaza 6s of '45 catch the updraft, rising 41 percent from 11 percent of par to 15.5 percent in the same span. Diehard followers of the exchange make some handsome profits, especially because this trio of bonds still pays interest.

But the volume rally tails off after July and torpid trading again sets in. The Lincoln Building bonds drop back 5 percent by year-end as prices weaken.

By December 1933, only two bonds are trading daily and the exchange seems back at square one. Fewer and fewer daily or weekly trading reports make their way into the pages of the *Times*, and the trail grows cold afterward. The exchange's price reports largely omit net changes from previous sale prices, likely because the declines are so chilling to investors.

Exhibit I-5 traces average daily trading volume rising handily from the exchange's inception through the end of 1930, when investors still hold hope of economic recovery. Volume then falls off the cliff in 1931 and 1932. The election of President Roosevelt in 1932 and his ascent to office in March 1933 touches off a massive volume spike that lets discerning traders cash outsized gains on bonds of properties still paying interest. But this volume and price rally peters out by year-end 1933, leaving the exchange back where it started.

OFFICES OUTPERFORM HOTELS

Using daily and weekly activity reports gleaned from the pages of the *New York Times*, I reconstruct price trends for bonds of two major property types during the first four years of the exchange's life, ending in 1933. These price profiles are benchmarked against the Dow-Jones Industrials indexed to December 31, 1929, to enable readers to compare how mortgage bonds of these property types fared against the Dow.

Exhibit I-6, covering office property bonds, demonstrates that mortgage bonds provided price returns slightly better on average than those of the Dow, with significant differences. Both the Chrysler and Graybar Buildings, which never defaulted and whose bonds eventually are repaid at par, outperform the Dow handily. The Equitable Building, the largest in the Wall Street downtown area, and Lincoln Building, across from Grand Central Terminal in midtown, are both loaded with debt that proves unsustainable, causing their bonds to trail the Dow. It appears that enough property-level information seeps out to let investors catch the differences and price bonds accordingly on the exchange.

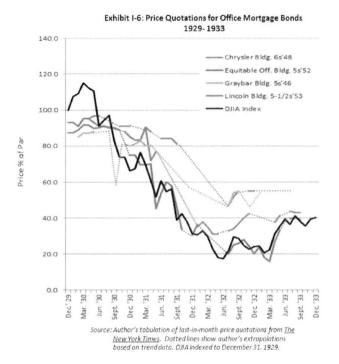

Exhibit I-6: Price Quotations for Office Mortgage Bonds
1929- 1933

Source: Author's tabulation of last-in-month price quotations from *The New York Times*. Dotted lines show author's extrapolations based on trend data. DJIA indexed to December 31, 1929.

Exhibit I-7 tells the story of a quite different asset class, hotels. Since hotels rent their rooms night by night, they remain supersensitive to changing economic conditions. Two upscale hotels, Hotel Pierre and Sherry-Netherland, both fronting on Fifth Avenue between Fifty-Ninth and Sixty-First Streets, seek to hedge those risks by giving over a significant number of rooms to apartment renters, becoming apartment hotels. The third hotel, Savoy-Plaza, between Fifty-Eighth and Fifty-Ninth Streets, is more exposed to the economy. All three hotels go through bankruptcy and receivership. Bonds of both Savoy-Plaza and Sherry-Netherland trail the DJI by wide margins, while Hotel Pierre enters reorganization so soon after its October 1930 construction that no definitive bond pricing is available.

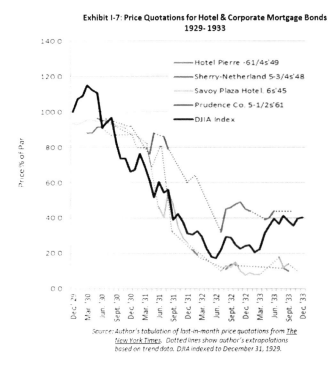

Exhibit I-7: Price Quotations for Hotel & Corporate Mortgage Bonds
1929- 1933

Source: Author's tabulation of last-in-month price quotations from *The New York Times*. Dotted lines show author's extrapolations based on trend data. DJIA indexed to December 31, 1929.

Exhibit I-7 also compares the corporate bonds of the Prudence Company, one of the leading bond houses of the 1920s and 1930s, with hotels and the Dow. Surprisingly, the Prudence bonds outperform both hotels and the Dow, likely because Prudence Company's more diversified revenue base gives it the stability to outperform any single property.

This gives rise to the most important insight of all: securities of a portfolio will almost invariably outperform single-property securities.

NASTY AFTERMATH

S. W. Straus & Company, king of the bond house hill and a principal Prudence competitor, becomes embroiled in several nasty bond disputes early in 1932 and enters receivership in March 1933. In its five decades in business, the firm sells about $1 billion of mortgage bonds, earning approximately a 10 percent commission or $100 million, which it splits with about two hundred salespersons. Unfortunately, Simon W. Straus, the firm's founder, dies in September 1930, leaving the grief of unwinding the firm to his brother, Samuel J. T. Straus.

The Straus firm's undoing proves to be its 1924 decision to begin selling second and third mortgage bonds, whose claims stood behind those of first mortgage holders. Selling these bonds under the euphemism of "general mortgages" to buyers who think they are buying first mortgage bonds provokes a flood of fraud claims when the bonds begin defaulting in the 1930s. Samuel Straus maintains the firm has spent nearly $15 million paying interest and taxes on bonds it issued but cannot cope with the tide of $360 million defaulted bonds held by eighty thousand bondholders.

After a lengthy investigation, a court referee in 1935 upholds fraud claims in 410 of 1,402 complaints. "A very large number of the claimants are women. Among them are teachers, nurses, waitresses, domestics and housewives—in the main persons inexperienced in business matters," according to the September 7, 1935, *New York Times*. The Straus firm's rise and fall is a parable of a company's need to hew to ageless financing standards even when competitors are grabbing business by following paths that "are different this time."

But the Straus firm is hardly the only casualty. Researcher Ernest A. Johnson, a business professor at Lake Forest (Illinois) College, whom we met earlier in this segment, in his landmark 1936 study zeroes in on investor experiences with $2.68 billion mortgage bonds from 1919 to 1931 in 1,090 offerings of over $1 million and finds: "Slightly more than one-eighth of the issues have been called, one-eighth have been paid at maturity, about one-eighth are outstanding and have met the required payments, and slightly less than five-eighths have failed in some degree to meet the contract terms.

"The fortunate holders of securities offered in 1919 realized practically 100 cents on the dollar," Johnson concludes, "but buyers of securities issued in subsequent years suffered considerably. Except for 1922, the recoverable value declined consistently year by year until it reached a low of 37.6 cents per dollar for the issues of 1928 … On the entire 1,090 issues investors could have realized about 50 cents on the dollar."

AN AUTOPSY REPORT

The Exchange clings to life for eight years after it essentially disappears from the visible record. The Securities and Exchange Commission becomes its boss and regulator with passage of the Securities Exchange Act of 1934, and the NYRESE cooperates with the SEC in every way, seeking approval for new listings, mainly of the income bonds that appear on the scene as a result of reorganizations for many originally listed bonds.

In June 1941, the SEC approves withdrawal of the NYRESE's registration as a national securities exchange. The 102 remaining members vote to close shop, the *New York Times* reports, "without a contrary vote."

Today, the NYRESE is consigned to the dustbin of history, little remembered, a forgotten relic of an age when conventional wisdom holds that trading mortgages on individual properties is the way to achieve the burning dream of making real estate tradable.

When queried about the exchange's history, the Real Estate Board of New York and patron of the exchange points to a paragraph in its 1996 annual report saying,

> "In the mid-1930s, economic recovery shimmered in the distance like a mirage. In a burst of premature optimism, REBNY thought the time was fast approaching when real estate could be traded as an equity like stocks or bonds … Plans to open such an exchange devoted solely to trading real estate-related securities had been announced with great fanfare in November of 1928. With investor

confidence shaken by the Depression, however, the plan could not be implemented … In the 1970s, 1980s and 1990s, real-estate investment trusts would have mixed success as vehicles for providing financing when more conventional lenders were out of the market."

We have exhumed the exchange and the autopsy reads as follows:

The exchange springs to life with exquisitely bad timing, just after the peak of the mortgage bond frenzy of the Great Delusion and a roaring bull market in stocks.

The exchange fosters transparency and factual disclosure to investors at a time when the valuations supporting real estate securities are widely suspect, thus becoming the forerunner of the full disclosure standards of today's securities markets.

The exchange demonstrates that fully informed buyers and sellers can agree upon the value of real estate securities using the bid/ask market system during a time of great duress, even though most listed mortgage bond issues are too small to attract widespread trading attention.

Finally, the exchange stands as a noble experiment in making real estate tradable, but it cannot withstand the economic juggernaut of the Great Depression.

Time marches on, memories fade, and dreams become mutable.

Less than twenty years after the exchange is shuttered in June 1941, Congress gives rise to a new dream to make real estate tradable, the real estate investment trust or REIT. Some early practitioners in this new REIT world extract lessons from the table-setting experience of the exchange. They play their parts, all just as excitedly and exciting as the men who gave life to the dreams of the New York Real Estate Securities Exchange.

The exchange enters at the most unfortunate time in a century. It exits not because its backers execute their dream poorly or duplicitously, but because history comes crashing down upon it.

The exchange's sad denouement recounts how that dream faded, slowly became a nightmare, and is now largely forgotten.

RIP, NYRESE.
Your labors prepared the way for the REIT Revolution.

This monograph contains excerpts from The New York Times, articles dated July 9, 1926, © 1926; November 19, 1928, © 1928; August 4, 1929, September 8, 1929, October 6, 1929, and November 21, 1929, all © 1929 The New York Times. All rights reserved. Used by permission and protected by the Copyright Laws of the United States. The printing, copying, redistribution, or retransmission of the Content without express written permission is prohibited.

* * *

APPENDIX II
K.D. CAMPBELL STOCK TRADING
August 1964 -- July 1969
See Chapter 7 for discussion

Name	Symbol	Shares	Type	Purchases or Short Sales Date	Price	Cost	Shares	Sales or Short Covers Date	Price	Proceeds	Net G/L	% G/L
Citizen Life	N/A	10.0	L	8/7/64	$40.00	$409	10	3/11/65	$28.38	$277	($132)	(32.3%)
Insurance Secs.	N/A	10.0	L	8/7/64	$24.38	$250	10	3/11/65	$17.50	$169	($81)	(32.4%)
Mid-Cont. Teleph	N/A	10.0	L	8/7/64	$28.63	$286	10	3/18/65	$24.88	$242	($44)	(15.4%)
Genl. Bronze	GLZ	25.0	L	3/18/65	$30.25	$1,211	40	4/12/65 A	$36.25	$1,430	$219	18.1%
Magnavox	MAG	34.0	L	4/14/65	$42.63	$1,469	34	6/9/65	$39.00	$1,307	($162)	(11.0%)
N.Mex.&Az. Land	NZ	45.0	S	7/2/65	$25.00	$1,106	45 Cvr.	6/10/65	$22.38	$1,022	$85	7.6%
Control Data	CDA	50.0	S	7/8/65	$35.50	$1,749	50 Cvr	7/7/65	$39.25	$1,987	($238)	(13.6%)
McKesson-Robbi	MCK	25.0	L	7/13/65	$45.88	$1,163	14	7/28/65 B	$40.38	$1,093	($70)	(6.0%)
Collins Radio	CRI	50.0	L	9/23/65	$43.00	$2,177	50	11/23/65	$48.25	$2,382	$206	9.5%
McKesson-Robbi	MCK	25.0	S	11/24/65	$42.88	$1,055	25 Cvr	7/23/65	$44.38	$1,125	($71)	(6.7%)
Western Equities	WE	100.0	L	11/26/65	$26.88	$2,720	100	12/3/65	$31.75	$3,139	$419	15.4%
Fairchild Camera	FCI	22.0	L	12/7/65	$144.25	$3,206	22	3/2/66	$190.75	$4,163	$956	29.8%
Valley Metal Proc	VMP	100.0	L	3/7/66	$47.75	$4,818	100	4/22/66	$43.00	$4,255	($562)	(11.7%)
Northwest Airline	NWA	18.0	L	5/6/66	$211.25	$3,830	36	10/24/66	$87.88	$3,129	($701)	(18.3%)
Control Data	CDA	100.0	S	11/4/66	$26.13	$2,578	100 Cvr	10/27/66	$27.38	$2,770	($192)	(7.4%)
Lab for Electroni	LFE	100.0	L	11/17/66	$19.81	$1,981	100	1/3/67	$19.13	$1,913	($69)	(3.5%)
Ling-Temco-Vou	LTV	20.0	L	1/18/67	$97.58	$1,952	20	3/1/67	$120.00	$2,400	$448	23.0%
Basic Inc.	N/A	80.0	L	3/9/67	$22.32	$1,785	80	5/25/67	$18.63	$1,490	($295)	(16.5%)
Ling-Temco-Vou	LTV	37.5	L	4/13/67	$84.94	$3,185	38	8/19/67	$137.06	$5,140	$1,955	61.4%
Data Processing	N/A	20.0	L	6/2/67	$72.47	$1,449	20	7/11/67	$83.50	$1,670	$221	15.2%
XTRA Inc.	XTR	20.0	L	7/17/67	$98.66	$1,973	20	8/22/67	$90.00	$1,800	($173)	(8.8%)
Roberts Co.	N/A	105.0	L	8/18/67	$17.15	$1,801	100	9/16/68 C	$20.90	$2,195	$394	21.9%
Fedders Corp.	FJQ	120.0	L	8/24/67	$24.06	$2,887	120	4/10/68 D	$53.70	$6,444	$3,557	123.2%
Christiana Oil	CST	100.0	L	10/3/67	$4.37	$437	100	12/12/67	$4.75	$475	$38	8.8%
Christiana Oil	CST	200.0	L	10/3/67	$4.39	$878	200	7/25/68	$5.94	$1,188	$309	35.2%
Atlantic Co.	ATC	30.0	L	1/10/68	$26.63	$812	25	7/29/68 E	$31.63	$917	$105	13.0%
Consol. Leasing	CLC	300.0	L	4/25/68	$12.48	$3,745	300	2/3/69 F	$21.00	$6,300	$2,555	68.2%
Kenton Corp.	KTN	50.0	L	7/29/68	$26.59	$1,329	50	1/2/69	$67.88	$3,394	$2,064	155.3%
First Mtg.In. Wts.	FMG/w	320.0	L	9/16/68	$10.98	$3,515	320	12/12/68 G	$13.30	$4,255	$740	21.1%
Federated Mtg.In	FDM	100.0	L	11/6/68	$14.23	$1,423	100	1/2/69	$16.13	$1,613	$190	13.3%
Monarch Indus.	N/A	100.0	L	12/12/68	$24.08	$2,408	100	10/20/69	$16.25	$1,625	($783)	(32.5%)
Key Co.	KC	50.0	L	7/23/69	$15.38	$769	50	9/16/69	$12.13	$606	($163)	(21.2%)
TOTALS				Average	$43.45	$60,356		Average	$45.41	$71,914	$10,727	17.8%
				Median	$40.00			Median	$39.00			

	Number	Summary of Trading Results by Year of Purchase	S&P 500	Proceeds	Net G/L	% G/L
1964 Trades	3	$945	13.0%	$688	($257)	(27.2%)
1965 Trades	9	$15,857	9.1%	$17,649	$1,344	8.5%
1966 Trades	4	$13,207	(13.1%)	$12,067	($1,524)	(11.5%)
1967 Trades	9	$16,347	20.1%	$22,801	$6,454	39.5%
1968 Trades	6	$13,231	7.7%	$18,103	$4,872	36.8%
1969 Trades	1	$769	(11.4%)	$606	($163)	(21.2%)
	32	$60,356		$71,914	$10,727	17.8%

Notes: A--GLZ: Plus 15 shs. Bought 3/11/65 at $28.88. B--MCK: 11 shs. Sold 8/3/5 at $49.00. C--Roberts: Sold 5 shs. 1/29/68.

D--FJQ: Sold 30 shs. at $49.38 on 9/16/68 and 40 shs. at $48,13 on 10/28/68. E--ATC: Sold 5 shs. At $25.25 2/2/68.

F--CLC. Sold 100 shs. on 2/3/69 and 200 shs. on 3/7/69. G--FMG/wts: Sold 150 wts. at $12.50 12/20/68.

L = Long; S = short Sale. Dollars rounded except trade prices. Commissions included in cost basis.

Source: Author's records.

APPENDIX III
BLOCK HOLDINGS IN REIT SHARES
August 1978 and November 1983
See Chapters 18 to 20 for discussion

Trust	Sh. Out (Th.)	Buyer (s)	Report Date	Sh. Owned (Th.)	% of Total	Mkt. Value (Th. $)
		Listings of August 11, 1978				
Atlanta National RE	1,273	Reed Rubin, Lee Balter et al	4/4/1978	213.1	16.7%	$1,066
Builders Inv. Gr.	2,929	Morse D. Van Horn et al	6/30/1978	191.3	6.5%	$478
Citizens Growth	811	Brent D. Baird et al	4/10/1978	150.0	18.5%	$563
Fidelco Growth	1,580	Asset Management Co.	2/14/1978	67.0	4.2%	$184
Fidelco Growth	1,580	Wm. R. Wister Jr. et al	4/28/1978	99.0	6.3%	$272
Hospital Mtg. Gr.	1,178	Transco Realty Trust	4/28/1978	183.4	15.6%	$1,880
Kentucky Property	1,100	Brent D. Baird et al	4/3/1978	170.8	15.5%	$427
Lincoln Mtg. Inv.	1,155	Ted Nelson, Dan. Montano et al	3/31/1978	108.4	9.4%	$258
Lincoln Mtg. Inv.	1,155	Morse F. Van Horn et al	7/6/1978	74.4	6.4%	$177
Maryland Realty	760	Federated Reinsurance Corp.	4/5/1978	143.0	18.8%	$536
Midland Mtg. Inv.	2,382	E. Peter Horrman Jr.	28,685	313.5	13.2%	$627
Miller (Hen.S.)	560	James Jackson et al	5/5/1978	63.8	11.4%	$862
Pennsylvania REIT	1,516	DeRance, Inc., Milwaukee	7/10/1978	95.9	6.3%	$1,486
Texas First Mtg.	1,055	Brent D. Baird et al	4/14/1978	76.7	7.3%	$278
Transco Realty Tr.	476	Lee Gray	4/13/1978	92.0	19.3%	$276
U.S. Bancorp R&M	840	Merritt W. Truax	2/27/1978	56.1	6.7%	$715
TOTALS 8/11/78				16		$10,085
		Listings of November 18, 1983				
American Century	4,739	John H. Roberts Jr.	9/6/1983	2,471.8	52.2%	$37,077
American Equity	2,497	Life Investor Insur/Dev Co	8/26/1983	639.1	25.6%	$9,427
American Pacific	6,221	John E. Wertin/TNPC INC	10/25/1983	2,951.5	47.4%	$14,758
American Realty	2,220	Southmark Corp	6/30/1983	808.2	36.4%	$5,051
American Realty	3,506	Southmark Corp	6/30/1983	2,093.9	59.7%	$13,087
Anret Inc	4,578	Lee Balter/Reed Rubin	10/5/1983	966.2	21.1%	$4,106
Arlen Realty	29,396	Arthur Cohen/Arthur Levin	6/1/1983	6,978.3	23.7%	$6,560
Atlantic Metro	33,355	M&G Investment Mgmt. Ltd.	2/14/1983	3,770.4	11.3%	$5,203
Atlantic Metro	33,355	Britannia Group	2/14/1983	1,885.2	5.7%	$2,602
Atlantic Metro	33,355	Lombard Place Securities	2/14/1983	2,820.6	8.5%	$3,892
Atlantic Metro	33,355	Hallwood Holdings B.V.	6/8/1983	3,901.6	11.7%	$5,384
Bay Financial	3,142	Paragon/Brad Dryer III	6/30/1983	522.7	16.6%	$8,363
Bay Financial	3,142	Morgan Guaranty Trustee	6/30/1983	254.9	8.1%	$4,078
Bay Financial	3,142	Citibank - Trustee	6/30/1983	212.2	6.8%	$3,395
Bayswater Realty	868	Carl Icahn/Icahn Acq. Grp.	9/23/1983	715.2	82.4%	$10,728
BRT Realty	4,515	Gould Investors Trust	8/26/1983	3,362.2	74.5%	$12,205
Central Mtg.	775	Warren Buffett et al	3/11/1983	47.5	6.1%	$380
Central Mtg.	775	Peregrine Investments et al	3/11/1983	260.6	33.6%	$2,085
Charan Inds	6,091	Charles P. Ryan Family	8/31/1983	4,852.7	79.7%	$15,771
Citizens Growth	648	Eastover Corp/B. Baird	3/31/1983	280.5	43.3%	$3,787
CleveTrust Rlty	2,822	Merchant Navy Offcr Pension	12/28/1982	847.2	30.0%	$12,395
CMT Investment b	2,330	Deltec Panamerica S.A.	6/14/1983	1,160.3	49.8%	$5,511
Commonwealth Rlt	1,468	Country & New Town Props	6/27/1983	980.3	66.8%	$8,333
Commonwealth Fin	4,103	De Rance Inc	10/21/1983	232.4	5.7%	$2,238
Del-Val Financial	3,105	RW&K Rlty/Kenrich et al	4/7/1983	652.0	21.0%	$9,291
DMG Inc.	7,378	Equity Group Holdings	8/1/1983	1,830.8	24.8%	$8,019
Dominion M&R	3,272	Southmark Corp	9/27/1983	2,165.0	66.2%	$9,743
Eastgroup Prop	2,872	Eastover Corp/Citzn Growth	7/20/1982	1,000.0	34.8%	$33,000
Eastgroup Prop	2,967	Kemper Financial Services	2/3/1982	413.9	14.0%	$13,659

APPENDIX III
BLOCK HOLDINGS IN REIT SHARES
August 1978 and November 1983
See Chapters 18 to 20 for discussion

Trust	Sh. Out (Th.)	Buyer (s)	Report Date	Sh. Owned (Th.)	% of Total	Mkt. Value (Th. $)
Eastover Corp	1,326	American Securities Corp	3/31/1983	115.9	8.7%	$2,984
Eastover Corp	1,326	LeLand Speed	3/31/1983	228.7	17.2%	$5,889
Eastover Corp	1,326	Brent Baird et al	3/31/1983	150.1	11.3%	$3,865
Eastpark Realty	908	Parkway Co/Eastgroup Props	5/4/1983	604.9	66.6%	$9,074
Federal Realty	5,757	Siam Lrd. (BVI)/Cofintab BV	8/22/1983	828.7	14.4%	$14,709
FGI Investors	2,314	Lend lease (AUS)/US Lend LS	10/21/1983	1,400.0	60.5%	$7,532
First Carolina	1,133	Harris Associates	9/8/1983	56.3	5.0%	$873
First Carolina	1,133	Brent Baird et al	2/22/1983	430.6	38.0%	$6,674
First City Prop	3,695	Belzberg Brothers	5/13/1983	5,997.1	69.0%	$83,240
First Union	10,572	Merchant Navy Offcr Pension	1/1/1983	926.2	8.8%	$21,886
Florida Cos	13,369	Fairfield communities	11/4/1983	3,778.3	28.3%	$13,942
Florida Gulf	1,993	Thos Kempner/P Loeb/J Lester	7/1/1983	149.3	7.5%	$1,866
Florida Gulf	2,055	Benj Elec Eng Profit Share	11/8/1983	402.0	19.6%	$5,025
FMI Financial	12,922	Richard W. Larson	4/28/1983	760.0	5.9%	$5,890
FMI Financial	25,287	American Financial Corp	11/8/1983	14,262.2	56.4%	$110,532
Fraser Mtg.	1,038	Richard D. Green	10/13/1983	129.2	12.4%	$743
Fraser Mtg.	1,038	Fraser Mtg. Co/Profit Shr	8/1/1983	276.2	26.6%	$1,583
General Growth	7,557	Kemper Financial Services	12/1/1982	678.6	9.0%	$14,251
General Growth	7,827	Sun Life Ins. (Kaufman & Brd)	9/23/1983	691.5	8.8%	$14,522
General Growth	7,557	Bucksbaum Family & Trusts	9/2/1983	1,341.9	17.8%	$28,180
Gould Investors	1,278	Marshall Rose et al	10/14/1983	79.0	6.2%	$1,768
Gould Investors	1,278	De Rance Inc	3/10/1983	75.3	5.9%	$1,685
Gould Investors	1,278	Gould Family	1/14/1983	367.9	28.8%	$8,234
Gould Investors	1,278	Arthur Hurland	1/14/1983	88.0	6.9%	$1,969
Growth Realty	3,081	British Land Co Plc	9/30/1983	1,113.8	36.2%	$4,455
Growth Realty	7,903	British Land Co Plc	9/30/1983	5,961.7	75.4%	$23,847
Great American M&	7,385	Equity Holdings (Zell)	10/27/1983	4,449.9	60.3%	$71,198
Great American M&	9,885	Continental Illinois Bank	7/6/1983	2,813.0	28.5%	$45,008
Health Care FD	1,639	De Rance/First Wilshire Sec	12/31/1982	174.6	10.7%	$2,816
HMG Prop Inv	1,224	Maurice & Barry Halperin	8/8/1983	110.4	9.0%	$2,002
HMG Prop Inv	1,224	Transco Realty Trust	10/17/1983	496.6	40.6%	$9,003
Homac Inc	2,027	Gilbert B Silverman	11/16/1983	143.6	7.1%	$503
Homac Inc	2,027	Gould Investors Trust et al	10/28/1983	347.0	17.1%	$1,215
Homac Inc	2,027	James T Barnes Jr.	11/16/1983	172.9	8.5%	$541
Homac Inc	2,027	Kenneth Neal	11/16/1983	191.4	9.4%	$670
Hotel Investors	2,640	Morgan Guaranty Trustee	11/5/1982	433.4	16.4%	$10,293
Hotel Investors	2,640	De Rance Inc	3/10/1983	213.2	8.1%	$5,064
Hotel Investors	2,640	US Steel & Carnegie Pension	11/5/1982	217.3	8.2%	$5,161
Hotel Investors	2,640	Harris Associates Inc.	7/5/1983	134.1	5.1%	$3,185
Indiana Fincial	1,154	Wisc REIT/Tech LSG/C Engle	10/19/1983	506.3	43.9%	$2,091
Indiana Fincial	1,154	Norman K Brown	9/23/1983	78.6	6.8%	$325
Institutional	38,088	Hees Internationa Corp	8/10/1983	4,000.0	10.5%	$3,760
Institutional	38,088	Unicorp Canada (Mann)	9/23/1983	4,020.3	10.6%	$3,779
IRT Property Co	2,363	First Williams Sec Mgmt	12/31/1982	146.2	6.2%	$2,924
IRT Property Co	2,363	Citibank N.A.	12/31/1982	213.2	9.0%	$4,264
Lifetime Com	5,310	Dunspaugh-Dalton Foundation	1/18/1983	274.0	5.2%	$1,850
Lifetime Com	5,310	Marine Midland Bank	1/18/1983	472.7	8.9%	$3,191

APPENDIX III
BLOCK HOLDINGS IN REIT SHARES
August 1978 and November 1983
See Chapters 18 to 20 for discussion

Trust	Sh. Out (Th.)	Buyer (s)	Report Date	Sh. Owned (Th.)	% of Total	Mkt. Value (Th. $)
Maryland Realty	1,786	Federated Dev Co et al	6/7/1983	815.3	45.6%	$3,873
Maryland Realty	1,786	Kozmetsky Group	2/12/1982	354.1	19.8%	$1,682
Mission West	1,750	Byron Webb Jr./Webb Co	1/31/1983	94.8	5.4%	$711
Mission West	1,749	Intermark Inc	5/24/1983	630.8	36.1%	$5,759
Mission West	1,750	Shamrock Assoc/Cinerama Inc	8/8/1983	223.3	12.8%	$1,675
MIW Inv Wash	3,786	Gim Campagne Group	6/13/1983	1,984.7	52.4%	$11,670
MIW Inv Wash	5,036	Gim Campagne Group	6/13/1983	3,234.7	64.2%	$19,020
Mortgage Growth	4,171	US Steel & Carnegie Pension	4/28/1983	176.9	4.2%	$2,676
Mortgage Growth	4,171	John Hancock Insurance Co	4/28/1983	225.7	5.4%	$3,415
Mortgage Growth	4,171	General Electric Pension	4/28/1983	404.7	9.7%	$6,123
Mutual REIT	1,453	John V Winfield	10/27/1983	100.0	6.9%	$950
National Mtg	3,707	Eastover/Parkway/Baird	9/6/1983	1,050.4	28.3%	$2,763
New Plan Rlty	8,820	Merchant Navy Offcr Pension	2/18/1983	2,607.2	29.6%	$29,670
New Plan Rlty	8,820	Newman Family	1/10/1983	1,927.9	21.9%	$21,940
Novus Propty	1,850	Southmark Corp	9/15/1983	1,114.0	60.2%	$15,596
Old Dominion	1,509	David Allen Beach	8/31/1983	81.6	5.4%	$734
Old Dominion	1,509	Charles Rotgin Jr.	4/1/1983	163.6	10.8%	$1,472
Old Dominion	1,509	Eric Heiner	4/1/1983	151.1	10.0%	$1,360
Parkway Co	1,375	Eastover Corp et al	9/19/1983	561.4	40.8%	$9,403
Pearce Urstadt	710	PM&G Holding/Chas Urstadt	12/10/1982	524.2	73.8%	$3,145
Penn REIT	2,342	De Rance Inc	5/20/1983	169.1	7.2%	$3,847
Penn REIT	2,342	Sylvan Cohen	5/20/1983	220.5	9.4%	$5,016
Penn REIT	2,342	Marvin Orleans	5/20/1983	150.0	6.4%	$3,413
Pres Rlty-B	2,737	Empire of Carolina (Halperin)	7/5/1983	146.5	5.4%	$1,062
Pres Rlty-B	2,737	Officers & Directors	4/1/1983	236.8	8.7%	$1,717
Presdntl RL-A	479	E Shapiro/J Shapiro/Viertel	4/1/1983	200.5	41.9%	$1,905
Presdntl RL-A	479	Jack Harry Stewart	6/27/1983	62.1	13.0%	$590
Prop Inv Colo	2,028	J F Barton Contrctng et al	3/14/1983	1,358.0	67.0%	$10,864
Property Cap	4,212	US Steel & Carnegie Pension	10/1/1982	260.0	6.2%	$9,035
Property Cap	4,212	Pres & Fellows Harvard Col	12/3/1982	622.2	14.8%	$21,621
Property Capitl	4,212	Morgan Guaranty Trust	10/1/1982	456.3	10.8%	$15,856
Property Capitl	4,212	First Pacific Advisors	10/1/1982	190.3	4.5%	$6,613
Property Tr Am	3,582	James A Cardwell et al	3/24/1983	212.1	5.9%	$2,757
Rampac	3,192	British Natl Coal Bd. Pens	9/29/1983	333.8	10.5%	$11,516
RE Invstmt Prop	959	Edward L Miller et al	10/10/1983	63.0	6.6%	$929
Realamerica	3,600	Banque Scandinave en Suisse	4/21/1983	187.5	5.2%	$774
Realamerica	3,600	Niwin Corp N.V. et al	4/21/1983	750.0	20.8%	$3,098
Realamerica	3,850	Gaetan Carnot	4/21/1983	477.2	12.4%	$1,971
Realamerica	3,788	Arthur D Emil	4/21/1983	314.7	8.3%	$1,300
Realty Inds	800	Sam Kornblau	2/18/1983	412.2	51.5%	$7,523
Realty Refund	1,377	Alfred Lerner	3/18/1983	76.3	5.5%	$906
REIT Amer Inc	2,665	Sun Life/Kaufman & Broad	8/26/1983	498.0	18.7%	$15,438
REIT Amer Inc	2,665	Unicorp American Corp	10/14/1983	1,390.6	52.2%	$43,109
Saul (BF) RE	6,026	Saul Co/Columbia Securits	7/15/1983	2,534.8	42.1%	$34,854
Saul (BF) RE	6,144	Harris Associates	9/8/1983	491.5	8.0%	$6,758
Saul (BF) RE	6,896	State Farm Insurance	11/12/1982	1,257.2	18.2%	$17,287
Security Cap	6,575	Smith Barney RE Corp	11/10/1982	923.1	14.0%	$10,154
So Atlantic	2,706	Aries Hill/Brent Baird	5/13/1983	179.3	6.6%	$472

APPENDIX III
BLOCK HOLDINGS IN REIT SHARES
August 1978 and November 1983
See Chapters 18 to 20 for discussion

Trust	Sh. Out (Th.)	Buyer (s)	Report Date	Sh. Owned (Th.)	% of Total	Mkt. Value (Th. $)
So Atlantic	2,706	M G Roberts/A H Gordon	12/31/1982	200.9	7.4%	$528
Southmark Corp	29,221	Phillips/Friedman/May Trust	5/31/1983	8,040.5	27.5%	$88,446
Sunstates Corp	2,192	Joe R Love	6/30/1983	144.0	6.6%	$1,044
Sunstates Corp	2,192	C. Kendrick/Finacial Grp	3/22/1983	119.1	5.4%	$863
Sunstates Corp	2,192	C Engle/Treco et al	9/1/1983	538.7	24.6%	$3,906
Thackeray Corp	5,107	Odyssey Ptnrs (14155 Corp)	7/26/1983	1,477.5	23.9%	$9,604
Thackeray Corp	5,107	Peter Sharp (Greystone Prp)	7/26/1983	1,500.0	29.4%	$9,750
Tierco Group	2,101	Gellert Family (Windcrest)	3/21/1983	802.9	38.2%	$4,015
Tierco Group	2,101	Herbert Lang	3/21/1983	158.2	7.5%	$791
Towermarc	1,074	Morgens/Waterfall/Freehold	6/21/1983	476.4	44.4%	$3,573
Transamer Rly	2,862	Transamerica Corp	5/5/1983	1,127.4	39.4%	$14,374
Treco Inc	5,556	Wisconsin REIT/C Engle	10/19/1983	2,334.5	42.0%	$7,307
Tri-South Inv	6,716	Deltec Panamerica S.A.	11/9/1983	2,334.5	34.8%	$14,310
Triton Group	39,409	J B Fuqua	11/2/1983	2,000.0	5.1%	$2,760
Triton Group	43,092	Chase Manhattan Bank	11/2/1983	4,627.8	10.7%	$6,386
Triton Group	51,676	Fuqua Industries	11/2/1983	12,581.6	24.3%	$17,363
Umet Props	6,587	Lombard Place Securities	2/23/1983	976.7	14.8%	$3,790
Umet Props	6,587	Perpetual Storage Inc	2/23/1983	251.7	3.8%	$977
Umet Props	6,587	Hallwood Holdings	2/23/1983	722.5	11.0%	$2,803
Unicorp Amer	3,067	Unicorp Canada Corp	6/15/1983	1,750.0	57.1%	$39,165
US Equity & Mtg	1,083	Marilyn Loesch/R Loesch	12/17/1982	168.3	15.5%	$926
USP REIT	2,500	Ralph Strangis et al	10/28/1983	322.7	12.9%	$2,743
USP REIT	2,500	Life Investors Inc	3/11/1983	849.6	34.0%	$7,222
Vyquest Inc	1,885	George M Jaffin	2/1/1983	151.6	8.0%	$1,971
Vyquest Inc	1,885	Malcolm H Weiner	2/1/1983	127.0	6.7%	$1,651
Vyquest Inc	1,885	Brian D Vesley	2/1/1983	110.1	5.8%	$1,431
Washington Corp	2,344	David C Brown Jr	4/18/1983	150.4	6.4%	$451
Washington Cp	2,344	David Kinney et al	4/18/1983	400.0	17.1%	$1,200
Washington Cp	2,344	D F Antonelli	4/18/1983	503.0	21.5%	$1,509
Washington Cp	2,544	William Demas	4/18/1983	404.7	15.9%	$1,214
Wisconsin REIT	1,553	De Rance Inc	2/28/1983	104.1	6.7%	$494
Wisconsin REIT	1,553	Hickory Furn/Tec Eqmpt/Engle	8/30/1983	757.9	48.8%	$3,600
TOTALS 11/18/83				156		$1,484,378

Source: *Realty Trust Review*, August 11, 1978; *Realty Stock Review*, November 18, 1983.

Appendix IV
REITS THROUGH THE YEARS

Appendix IV seeks to provide historical context on how the 2015 US REIT industry reached its present scope of nearly $1 trillion in market value in the United States and well above that figure globally. To do this, Appendix IV tracks market capitalization of major REITs and former REITs at five widely separated but meaningful dates to give a wide-angle snapshot of players in my rat hole.

- *August 1971* is the deadline for *America's Newest Billionaires*, the first book devoted exclusively to this nascent industry, when 86 percent of a $4.4 billion industry market cap was in fifty-two short-term mortgage trusts and only 14 percent in thirty-nine equity trusts with only $598 million market value.
- Fast-forward to *June 1978*; following the 1974 market crash and with *New Opportunities in Realty Trusts* ready for the printers, REIT market value is halved to $2.1 billion. Equity REITs have grown to one-third of the pie while mortgage REITs are down to 32 percent.
- By *June 1990*, my last regular *RSR*, market cap is up to $11.1 billion, equity REITs command 70 percent of market value, and the stage is set for the "modern" REIT industry to emerge.

- By *December 2002*, the "modern" REIT era has pushed total capitalization to $162 billion with equity REITs representing 95.6 percent of the total while mortgage types have only 4.4 percent.
- By *December 2014* industry market cap stands at $907 billion with equity REITs at 93 percent.
- Also in *December 2014* the largest non-US REITs and operating companies count another $1.25 trillion market value around the globe, showing how the US REIT concept has spread to nearly three dozen nations. REITs are clearly here to stay.

Appendix V
GLOSSARY OF REAL ESTATE SECURITIES TERMS

accretion. Amount by which a new investment adds to a company's current return on its investment portfolio. For example, a new investment returning 8.0 percent will be accretive to a portfolio returning 7 percent currently, while a 6 percent investment will dilute or reduce overall portfolio return. See also *dilution*.

ADR or average daily room rate. Measure of revenue for hotel REITs, being average daily room rate received for all rooms rented in a day.

AFFO or adjusted funds from operations. Measure of a REIT's ability to generate free cash from operations. AFFO is calculated by adding to FFO (which see) any amortized financing costs, then subtracting the following items: (1) straight-lined rents (see also straight-line), and (2) a normalized level of recurring (a.k.a., nonincremental) capital expenditures necessary to maintain a REIT's portfolio and revenue stream. These expenditures include leasing commissions and tenant improvements paid to lease a space, both capitalized and then amortized over the lease term.

anchor tenant. Large national or regional retailer, which typically is the primary draw for a retail venue. Department stores usually anchor regional malls while grocers or so-called "big box" users generally anchor community and power centers. See also *big box* stores and *category killers*

area measurements. The most common measurements used in real estate are:

SF or square foot. Unit of area measuring twelve inches on each side in the United States; square feet are used as a primary measure of computing annual rent in the United States.

SM or square meter. Unit of area measuring one meter square (approximately thirty-nine inches) in countries using the metric system; approximates ten square feet in area.

tsubo—Unit of area used in Japan, approximating 35.6 square feet and 3.3 square meters, based on the area of a tsubo mat.

ATM or at-the-market stock issuance. Procedure under which exchange-listed companies may raise new capital by selling newly issued shares through a designated broker-dealer into the secondary trading market in limited quantity.

bankruptcy code. Bankruptcy laws of the United States under which troubled businesses may avail themselves of certain protections. The sections most commonly used by publicly traded companies are:

Chapter VII. This section is used by businesses to liquidate when they are so deeply in debt they cannot repay creditors in a timely fashion.

Chapter XI. This section gives a company court protection from creditors while it seeks to reorganize operations and work out a settlement with creditors, ultimately restoring the company to sound operations.

big box stores. Large-volume retailers usually anchoring a retail venue. Big box users include food store and drugstores, discount department stores, and stores specializing in pet care, athletic goods, office products, and other categories (sometimes called "category killers"). See also *anchor tenant*.

blind pool. An offering of securities that does not disclose to investors the specific assets to be purchased with offering proceeds. Blind pools are distinguished from offerings in which use of proceeds is fully disclosed or specified in advance of pricing.

BPS or basis points. One one-hundredth of a percent, a term used to refer to interest rates, bond yields, total returns, and other measures requiring precise measurement.

C&D loans. Short-term mortgage loans that finance construction and development of real estate.

CAD or cash available for distribution. Cash available for distribution measures company or REIT cash flow after all obligations, including dividends, are paid. Hence this free cash flow indicates the entity's financial health and helps determine the safety of a REIT's dividend. See also *FAD*.

CAGR or compound annual growth rate. Annual rate at which a variable increases or grows over multiple periods, usually years. CAGR is sometimes expressed as "annual growth rate" or "growth rate."

CAM or common area maintenance charge. Tenant's pro rata share of total expenses for upkeep of common areas for a mall or other large property.

cap ex or capital expenditures. Money used to acquire or improve capital assets. Cap ex spending is found in a company's flow of funds statement under GAAP accounting.

cap rate or capitalization rate. Initial return an investor will receive by buying a property or portfolio at a given price. The capitalization rate is computed by dividing the property's net operating income (NOI) by its purchase price. Low cap rates bespeak prime properties while high cap rates generally indicate higher returns and greater perceived risk.

capital stack. Total company capitalization, usually referring to where a particular security stands relative to other invested funds. See also *company capitalization.*

cash-on-cash return. This metric captures cash return on actual cash invested and equals net operating income (NOI) less interest expense divided by cash invested in a property.

catalyst. An event or trend, either positive or negative, presumed to set a company apart from its peers and lead to stock market performance exceeding its peer group.

category killer. Specialty store that dominates its product category. Big box users include food stores and drugstores, discount department stores, and stores specializing in pet care, athletic goods, office products, and other categories. See also *anchor tenant.*

company capitalization and market capitalization. Company capitalization is the total amount of funds invested in a company stated at historic cost, including senior and subordinated debt, preferred stock, and common shareholder's equity. Market capitalization values each component at current market prices.

correlation. Statistic measuring the extent to which one set of data or events is correlated with or related to a second set. Correlations are stated on a logarithmic scale and correlations of 0.81 (i.e., 0.9 squared) or higher are generally regarded as showing strong relationships.

cost of capital. Cost of capital is the cost to a company or REIT of raising capital in the form of common or preferred equity or debt. The cost of equity capital generally is the total return expected by investors from both dividends and change in stock prices. The cost of debt capital is the interest expense on the debt incurred. See also *WACC* or weighted *average cost of capital.*

current value. Estimate of the current market price at which a property or portfolio of properties would sell to a willing buyer. Current value almost always will vary from the property or company net depreciated value under historic cost accounting in the United States. For many countries outside the United States, International Financial Reporting Standards (IFRS) require non-US owners to report current value periodically.

depreciation. Noncash charge to income intended to estimate the reduction in a real property's value from ordinary wear and tear. For tax purposes, depreciation charges let a building's owner recover its cost over a long period of years, currently thirty-nine years for nonresidential real property and 27.5 years for rental residential property.

debt-to-EBITDA ratio. Ratio of total company debt to EBITDA, or a measure of a company's ability to generate funds to cover required debt payments. Ratios below 5.0-to-1 are considered nonthreatening, while ratios above 7.5-to-1 are considered high. See *EBITDA*.

dilution. Measure of whether a shareholder's pro rata interest in a company is reduced by company events. Company sales of stock below net asset value (NAV) or current value and investment in nonaccretive properties dilute a shareholder's return. See also *accretion*.

dividend yield. The yield an investor receives from a stock investment calculated by dividing the annualized dividend by current stock price.

EBITDA. Earnings before interest, taxes, depreciation, and amortization; a measure of a company's ability to generate cash flow from operations before financing costs.

equity market capitalization (or cap). Market value of all outstanding common stock of a company or REIT and, where applicable, including operating partnership (OP) units. See also *UPREIT*.

equity REIT. A REIT primarily owning equity interests in income producing commercial properties, such as apartments, shopping centers, enclosed malls, and office and industrial properties; sometimes called a *property REIT*.

FAD or funds available for distribution—Essentially the same as CAD, which see.

FASB or Financial Accounting Standards Board. Official governing body for accounting principles in the United States, under authority of the SEC.

FFO or funds from operations. A supplemental and most widely accepted measure of earnings for a REIT. FFO equals net income (as computed in accordance with GAAP) before gains or losses from property sales and extraordinary losses, plus real estate depreciation and, where applicable, a REIT's pro rata share of FFO from unconsolidated joint ventures, less dividends paid on any outstanding preferred stock. FFO computed in accord with NAREIT guidelines has been approved by the SEC as an accepted *alternative measure* of income and therefore may be stated on a per-share basis.

FINRA or Financial Industry Regulatory Authority, Inc. FINRA is a nongovernmental private corporation serving as a self-regulatory organization overseeing member brokerage firms of the New York Stock Exchange and other exchanges. FINRA oversees trading in equities, corporate bonds, securities futures, and options. FINRA succeeded to the operations of the National Association of Securities Dealers (NASD) in 2007.

fully diluted earnings—Earnings or FFO stated on a per share basis, reflecting exercise of all convertible securities, options, and other share equivalents.

GAAP or Generally Accepted Accounting Principles. A system of accounting for financial results of a company based upon historic cost of assets and liabilities. GAAP principles are administered by the Financial Accounting Standards Board under authority from the SEC and are required for publicly traded companies in the United States.

gateway cities. Term generally referring to New York, Washington, San Francisco, and Los Angeles as major entry points for foreign visitors.

Boston, Chicago, Miami, and Seattle are sometimes included in this definition.

GLA or gross leasable area. Square feet available for rent in a building.

gross absorption. Measure of the total square feet leased over a specified period of time with no consideration given to space vacated during the same period, typically referring to the same geographic area. See also *net absorption.*

ground lease. Legal structure under which a landowner leases land beneath an income-producing property to a land tenant. The land tenant is responsible for building construction and all improvements.

guidance or earnings guidance. Public estimate of future earnings or FFO per share provided by company management for a quarter or year in the future. Earnings guidance made under defined conditions is generally protected from lawsuits by the Private Securities Litigation Act of 1995 and related regulations. SEC Regulation Fair Disclosure, or Reg. FD, adopted in August 2000 requires public companies to disclose material public information to all investors at the same time.

IFRS or International Financial Reporting Standards. System of accounting for company results and financial position based upon current value of assets and liabilities. IFRS is used mainly in the United Kingdom, Eurozone, Canada, Australia, Hong Kong, and Singapore.

in-line stores. Nonanchor retail tenants at a mall or shopping center, sometimes called "small shop" tenants. In-line tenants typically provide the majority of rental revenues for regional malls and shopping centers. See *anchor tenant.*

IPO or initial public offering. An offering by which a previously private company sells its shares or other securities to public investors for trading in the public market. The company then becomes obligated to make certain periodic financial disclosures to investors by filing required forms with the SEC. See *SEC forms.*

leverage. Relative amount of debt in a company's capitalization, generally expressed as the percentage of debt in total capitalization. For REITs, debt leverage percentages of 40 percent or lower are generally regarded as conservative. See also *company capitalization* and *debt-to-EBITDA ratio.*

M&A or mergers and acquisitions. Mergers between two public companies and acquisitions of private companies or properties are two avenues for REIT growth. These data are usually combined into a category called *transaction volume.*

major property types. Term generally referring to three property groups: office and industrial; retail, including shopping centers and regional malls; and apartments or multifamily residential. See appendix IV for the proportion of equity and mortgage REITs within the REIT industry as of December 31, 2014.

MLP or master limited partnership. Large partnerships whose ownership units trade in public markets. MLPs pay no corporate level taxes, which are borne by unitholders (i.e., "shareholders") on a pro rata basis at their individual tax rate. MLPs must generate 90 percent of income from qualified sources, such as real estate or natural resources, but are not required to pay any fixed percentage of income as dividends (as contrasted with REITs, which must pay 90 percent of income to shareholders).

match funding. The objective of funding investments with debt or equity maturities matching the expected life of the investment. The match funding concept usually applies to both equity and debt issuance made at the closing of a transaction.

mortgage REIT. A REIT primarily owning mortgages on residential or commercial properties. Mortgage REITs of the 1970s primarily made and held construction and land development loans, an asset class not now found in public markets. Mortgage REITs in 2015 primarily hold pools of residential or commercial mortgages.

NAREIF, or **National Association of Real Estate Investment Funds.** Predecessor to NAREIT.

NAREIT or National Association of Real Estate Investment Trusts. The trade organization acting as the worldwide representative voice for REITs and publicly traded real estate companies with an interest in US real estate and capital markets. The successor to the National Association of Real Estate Investment Funds, NAREIT members comprise REITs and other businesses that own, operate, and finance income-producing real estate and firms or individuals who advise, study, and service these businesses. NAREIT maintains public relations and research programs providing current industry statistics and information to the public and represents the REIT industry before Congress and federal agencies.

net absorption. Square feet leased in a specific geographic area over a fixed period of time after deducting space vacated in the same area during the same period. See also *gross* absorption.

NAV or net asset value. An estimate of the current market value of a company or REIT assets, including but not limited to its properties, less all of a company's liabilities and obligations stated at market value. NAV is usually stated on a per-share basis.

NOI or net operating income. Property owner's rental revenues from a property or group of properties less all property operating expenses, including taxes and insurance. NOI ignores real estate depreciation and amortization expenses as well as interest on loans incurred to finance the property.

NoCal. Northern California, particularly the San Francisco and San Jose areas.

NoVa. Northern Virginia around Washington DC.

NOL or net operating loss. A company sustains a net operating loss (NOL) whenever its tax-deductible operating expenses exceed revenues. The US Internal Revenue code permits companies, under certain conditions, to use these NOLs to offset income from either past or future years. NOLs are distinguished from capital losses. See IRS Publications 536 and 542 for additional details.

NTRs or nontraded REITs. REITs whose shares are sold to investors with the up-front understanding that shares will not be listed on any securities exchange for secondary or after-market trading. Investors are implicitly asked to hold NTRs for lengthy periods, typically seven to ten years. The NTR sponsor typically is expected to arrange a *liquidity event* at the end of this anticipated holding period.

occupancy percentage. Percentage of a building's leasable area (GLA) leased to tenants in occupancy.

OP unit or operating partnership unit. Units of limited partnership interest in the operating partnership managed by a REIT. OP Units may usually be redeemed for cash or converted one-for-one into common shares. See UPREIT.

offerings. An offering of securities by a company, or the issuer, and registered with the SEC. Offerings may be made to the public under rules established by the SEC or may be made privately to investors qualified by income and size under exemptions from SEC rules. Main offering types:

> **initial.** The first public offering by a previously private company.
> **follow-on.** Any offering of new or additional equity securities *after* a company's initial offering.
> **secondary.** An offering by the holder of previously registered and outstanding shares. Secondary offerings do not increase the number of company shares outstanding.

prospectus. A document containing all facts relative to the company making a securities offering required by the SEC to be delivered to an investor at the time of purchase. The prospectus for an initial public offering (IPO, which see) may run several hundred pages, while seasoned companies with longer histories of SEC filings may deliver much shorter documents.

proxy. Official document by which companies seek shareholder approval for election of directors and other corporate actions at regular or special shareholder meetings. See also SEC Form 14-A or definitive proxy materials.

Real Estate Investment Trust Act of 1960. The federal law authorizing REITs. The law was enacted to permit small investors to pool their investments in a real estate investment entity to obtain the benefits of direct ownership while also diversifying risks and obtaining professional management.

red herring. The preliminary prospectus for a securities offering circulated before shares may be sold to give potential investors details of the offering, so-called because of its red-letter legend advising investors the prospectus is not yet final.

REIT or real estate investment trust. Corporation or business trust that combines the capital of many investors to acquire or provide financing for all forms of real estate. Over the years, REITs specializing in equity ownership or income-producing properties (equity REITs) have come to dominate the industry while REITs investing in mortgages (mortgage REITs) hold a much smaller share of investment assets. A REIT is generally not required to pay corporate income tax if it distributes at least 90 percent of its REIT taxable income to shareholders each year.

REVPAR or revenues per available room. For hotel REITs, a measure of room revenues derived from the rental of sleeping rooms at the hotel divided by rooms available for rent.

same-store comparisons. Comparisons of property operating results based upon the same set of assets in both periods being compared.

SEC or Securities and Exchange Commission. Official federal agency charged with overseeing and regulating the securities markets and industry.

SEC forms. These forms are required to be filed with the SEC by public companies and their contents become public upon filing. Principal SEC forms are:

> **Form 10-K.** Annual report covering a company's business, activities, and financial results; a basic document covering all company operations.
>
> **Form 10-Q.** Quarterly report containing quarterly financial results and statements.
>
> **Form 8-K.** Report required within four business days after a material event occurs.
>
> **Form 13-D.** Report required within ten days after an investor acquires over 5 percent of a public company's stock or when holders of 5 percent or greater decrease their investment below 5 percent.
>
> **Form 14-A or Definitive Proxy Materials.** Material circulated to public company shareholders seeking their vote at an annual or special shareholders' meeting.

secondary stock offering. The public offering of equity or debt securities by a company subsequent to the company's initial public offering (IPO), which see. Secondary offerings are sometimes referred to as "follow-on" offerings.

senior securities. Any debt or preferred security whose claim to company assets stands ahead of common shareholders' equity.

SoCal—Southern California, from Los Angeles to San Diego.

stabilized property. Property whose initial lease-up is deemed complete twelve months after completion or after a certain occupancy threshold is reached.

straight-line rent. The requirement under GAAP accounting that REITs and other companies owning income-producing real estate "straight line" the rents they receive by reporting as income the average annual rent to be received over the life of a lease instead of actual cash received in any period. Investors add or subtract from GAAP rents to arrive at actual cash rents received. See also *depreciation*.

synergies. Expected benefits arising from a merger or property acquisition due to perceived superior operating skills or cost savings.

TIs or tenant improvements. Capital improvements the landlord must make to a new tenant's space, like specifically reconfiguring a floor plan. TIs are tenant-specific, and charges are considered to be nonrecurring, most frequently seen with office, retail and industrial tenants.

tenant recoveries. Reimbursements made by tenants to landlords for certain expenses, typically property taxes, insurance, and other property operating expenses. See also *CAM*.

total return. Return a shareholder receives from both dividends and price change in a given period, usually one year.

triple net lease. Lease stipulating that the tenant, not the landlord, is responsible for all costs, including maintenance, utilities, taxes, insurance, and other expenses. Net leases are usually longer in term and protect against inflation by including contractual rate step-ups based on either a stated contractual rate or an index such as the Consumer Price Index

(CPI) over the life of the lease. Allocation of capital improvement costs, such as roofs and parking lots, is negotiable.

UPREIT or umbrella partnership REIT. Legal structure in which shareholders own interests in an operating partnership, which owns and controls a property portfolio through its role as general partner. UPREITs were introduced in 1992, and a high proportion of subsequent REIT public offerings have utilized the UPREIT structure. The structure lets property owners transfer their properties to the umbrella operating partnership in exchange for operating partnership (or OP) units exchangeable for REIT shares. Such transactions allow property owners to defer any tax liability until their units are sold. UPREITs typically offer to redeem these OP units for cash or exchange them for REIT shares, hence the number of OP units outstanding is included in share counts for computing fully diluted earnings per share.

WACC or weighted average cost of capital. Weighted average cost of company or REIT capital raised from all sources, including debt, preferred stock, and common equity. See also *cost of capital* and *company capitalization*.

Appendix VI
IN CELEBRATION AND MEMORIAM

INDIVIDUALS MENTIONED IN THIS WORK WITH KNOWN DATES OF DEATH

Name	Organization/Title	Died	Age
Applegate, Gladys F.	Irene's mother	10/22/2003	95
Applegate, Harry E.	Irene's father	5/12/1968	62
Applegate, John Wesley	Irene's grandfather	12/23/1953	86
Campbell, Ira Pressley	Ken's father	11/30/1991	84
Campbell, Isaac Pressley	Ken's grandfather	10/30/1934	76
Campbell, Lyle E.	Ken's cousin; same birth date	9/10/2010	80
Campbell, Madge F.	Ken's mother	8/7/1999	89
Campbell, Marjorie Ruth	Ken's sister	2/8/1936	1
Clynes, Patricia M.	Ken's cousin in NJ	1/30/2002	83
Clynes, Richard W.	Husband of Ken's cousin	8/6/2001	84
Miller, Abbie McNees	Ken's grandmother	4/1/1950	85
Miller, Chester G.	Ken's uncle	11/7/1958	70
Schmidt, Elizabeth L.	Ken's sister	1/7/2014	72

COLLEAGUES

Aley, Jonathan	*House & Home*, Assoc. Ed.	9/9/1974	49
Birkner, Edward C.	*House & Home*, Assoc. Ed.	7/15/2004	84
Breckenfeld, Gurney	*House & Home*, Asst. Man. Ed.	7/27/1995	75

Brooks, A. Charles	Dev. Cmte. Gr. Cols, Asst. Dir.	5/13/1982	57
Chasteney, Robert	*House & Home*, Man. Ed.	6/7/1997	90
Curtis (Hunt), Charlotte	*Columbus Citizen / NY Times*	4/17/1987	58
Elia, Charles J.	*Cols. Citizen / Wall St. Jnl.*	3/9/1997	72
Franken, Harry	*Columbus Citizen,* Reporter	9/26/2003	79
Gallagher, James Paul	*House & Home*, Assoc. Ed.	9/15/2013	94
Goldman, Arthur Swarm	*House & Home*, Marketing	12/17/1989	83
Goldsmith, John F.	*House & Home*, Asst. Man. Ed.	10/14/2010	92
Grossman, Charles	JLW/Clarion partner	8/18/2007	63
Huntoon, Maxwell C. Jr.	*House & Home*, Assoc. Ed.	9/8/2011	88
Keller, Jack	*Columbus Citizen*, Man. Ed.	6/3/1978	66
Kreisman, Faye	Audit Investments, Res.	3/14/2001	76
Manning, Ralph "Rip"	*Columbus Citizen*, Asst. CE.	5/1/1964	67
Morison, Perry	*Columbus Citizen*, Reporter	4/10/1962	67
Mott, Robert F.	Dev. Cmte. Gr. Cols, Ex. Dir.	6/9/2007	85
Murray, Robert W. Jr.	*House & Home*, Assoc. Ed.	NA	NA
O'Neill, Richard W.	*House & Home*, Editor	11/24/1980	55
Portman, Maurice "Maury"	*Columbus Citizen*, Reporter	7/1/2003	89
Prentice, Pierrepont I.	*House & Home*, Ed. & Pub.	2/1/1989	89
Rochon, Edwin W. "Ned"	*House & Home*, Assoc. Ed.	5/6/1998	80
Solas, Bernard	Audit Investments, Res. Dir.	7/23/2013	81
Wagner, Walter F. Jr.	*House & Home*, Asst. Man. Ed	7/6/1985	58
Weaver, Don	*Columbus Citizen*, Editor	9/26/1991	89
Weisz, John	JLW/Clarion partner	9/11/2005	60
White, Jan V.	*House & Home*, Art Dir.	12/30/2014	86

OTHERS ENCOUNTERED ALONG THE WAY

Ablah, George J.	Blue Hill Office Buyer	10/27/2014	85
Bellemore, Douglas H.	NYU Grad School, Prof.	5/23/1993	83
Belzberg, William	First City Props., Principal	4/30/2014	82
Bentsen, Sen. Lloyd	Senator, TX; Audit Client	5/24/2006	85
Berra, Lawrence (Yogi)	NY Yankees catcher	9/22/2015	90
Boisi, James O.	Morgan Guar.; Pace U. Lecturer	8/21/2013	94

Bourneuf, Henri J.	REIT of Amer., Pres.	12/5/1987	76
Brilof, Abraham J.	CCNY, Acctg. Prof.; Barron's	12/12/2013	96
Bucksbaum, Martin	Genl. Growth Pr., Founder	7/10/1995	74
Cingolani, Armand R. Jr.	Butler H.S., Debate team	10/25/2004	75
Cohen, Sylvan M.	Pennsylvania REIT, Founder	9/8/2001	87
Courshon, Arthur H.	First Mtg. Inv., Founder	1/6/2006	84
Disney, Roy O.	Walt Disney Prod., CEO	12/20/1971	78
Dell, George F.	Capital Univ., English Prof.	7/18/1992	90
Elfers, Robert	Longtime friend	5/16/2009	88
Felixson, Robert J.	Growth Realty, CEO	1/12/2011	90
Foote, Donald F.	Amer. Central, CEO	6/20/1998	68
Fraser, Charles E.	Palmas del Mar, Developer	12/17/2002	73
Fuqua, John Brooks	REIT Income Fund, Buyer	4/5/2006	87
Futterman, Robert A.	Syndicator, NYC	11/11/1961	33
Galbreath, Daniel	Pittsburgh Pirates	9/3/1995	67
Galbreath, John W.	Pittsburgh Pirates, Owner	7/20/1988	90
Gardiner, John H.	Backer of REIT legislation	4/14/1983	67
Gionfriddo, Albert F.	New York Yankees, Player	3/14/2003	81
Joseph, Frederick H.	Drexel Burnham, Pres.	11/27/2009	72
Kahn, B. Franklin	Washington REIT, Founder	3/8/2007	82
Kassuba, Walter Judd	Apartment builder, 1970s	11/13/2011	77
Keidel, Albert Jr.	Rouse Company, CFO	5/4/2003	91
Lazarus, Charles Y.	Lazarus Store, Pres.	5/14/2007	93
Lowen, Rev. deForest	Emmanuel Baptist, Pastor	11/1/2001	91
Lund, Joseph W.	Backer of REIT legislation	3/13/1982	75
Lurie, Robert H.	Sam Zell partner	6/20/1990	48
Marcus, Bruce W.	Author, Marketing expert	12/1/2014	89
Melis, F. Kenneth	New York Securities, Prin.	10/5/1986	69
Miller, Cyrus C.	NY Rl. Est. Sec. Exch., Pres.	1/21/1956	89
Miller, E. Lawrence	Bradley Real Est., CEO	2/07/1996	53
Miller, Harvey R.	Weil, Gotshal, Attorney	4/27/2015	82
Mintz, Jack Isadore	Store owner, Butler, PA	2/17/1957	46
Mintz, Mary	Store owner, Butler, PA	12/6/1993	78

Montgomery, Allene	Butler H.S., Debate coach	9/22/1999	93
Norris, Roderick G.	Butler H.S., Debate team	11/30/2014	85
Patman, Wright	Congressman, TX	3/7/1976	82
Pasquerilla, Frank J.	Crown American, Founder	4/21/1999	72
Proxmire, William	Senator, WI; Banking cmte.	12/15/2005	90
Rainwater, Richard	Bass Bros. Investment mgr.	9/27/15	71
Randall, B. Carter	Wall Street Week, Panelist	12/21/1999	73
Rukeyser, Louis R.	Wall Street Week, Founder	5/2/2006	73
Salinger, Pierre E. G.	*House & Home*, Assoc. Ed.	10/16/2004	79
Schooler, Lee W.	Disney interviewer; Friend	12/21/1971	62
Schooler, Paul	Capital Univ., Roommate	7/9/1991	63
Scribner, David	REIT Income Fund, Director	11/3/1974	67
Sensenbrenner, Maynard	City of Columbus, Mayor	8/2/1991	88
Simon, Melvin	Simon Property Gr., Founder	9/17/2009	82
Smerling, Saul A.	Standard & Poor's Corp.	5/9/1991	76
Smith, Harrison W. Jr.	Annex. Attorney, Columbus	8/2/2009	83
Sonnenblick, Jack. E.	No. Amer. REIT, Founder	4/10/2015	91
Taubman, A. Alfred	Taubman Ctrs., Founder	4/17/2015	91
Theopold, Philip H.	Backer of REIT Legislation	2/14/1989	86
Thompson, Bruce G.	Health Care REIT founder	11/24/2005	76
Thompson, Stephen G.	*Architectural Forum*, Ass. Ed.	2/10/1973	60
Viner, Arthur W.	Inv. Central Mgt., Founder	6/19/2014	92
Weaver, Robert C.	HUD Secretary	7/19/1997	89
Wein, Lawrence A.	Attorney, Realty syndications	12/10/1988	83
Weinstein, George	Weinstein Assoc., Chair	11/18/2000	76
Weyeneth, Eugene E.	*House & Home*, Publisher	7/3/2009	93
Wagner, Edward F.	Nationwide Ins., Exec.	2/19/1993	85
Wilson, Robert W.	Hedge fund operator	12/23/2013	87
Wolfe, Preston	*Columbus Dispatch*, Pres.	5/7/1996	90
Zeckendorf, William	Webb & Knapp, CEO	9/30/1976	71

NA = Not Available.

BIBLIOGRAPHY
(Citations exclude quotations from Audit's
periodical investment services)

PREFACE

Herman, Jerry, "Hello, Dolly!" an American musical first produced on Broadway by David Merrick in 1964; quoted by Wikipedia, the free encyclopedia, Synopsis, Act II.

CHAPTER 3—THE PREP

"Aly Khan Here to Inspect Horses," the *Columbus Citizen*, August 23, 1952.

"Bexley City Hall Behind Schedule," the *Columbus Citizen*, May 26, 1951.

"Half-Hourly Contests Popular," the *Columbus Citizen*, August 25, 1951.

"Sentence Commuted by Lausche 12 Hours After Amerman Dies," the *Columbus Citizen*, November 16, 1951.

Campbell, Kenneth, "Capt. Eddie's Visit Cut Short by Crash," the *Columbus Citizen*, October 19, 1953.

Campbell, Kenneth, "Condemned Man Still Denies Guilt," the *Columbus Citizen*, November, 1953.

Campbell, Kenneth, "Flying Parson Back From Korea," the *Columbus Citizen*, June 12, 1951.

Campbell, Kenneth, "Pilot Protected Lives on Ground," the *Columbus Citizen*, August 14, 1954.

Campbell, Kenneth, "Price Chislers [c.q.] Face Fight, Official Says," the *Columbus Citizen*, June 8, 1951.

Campbell, Kenneth, "They Meet the Unknown," the *Columbus Citizen*, July 15, 1951.

Campbell, Kenneth, "Vallees 'Live Out of a Suitcase,'" the *Columbus Citizen*, December 12, 1951.

Campbell, Kenneth, "Worthington Boy Wins Derby," the *Columbus Citizen*, July 20, 1953.

John, Gospel of, Chapter 18:38, quoting Pontius Pilate while interrogating Jesus.

Walpole, Horace, coined "serendipity" in a 1754 letter referring to a Persian fairy tale, *The Three Princes of Serendip*; cited in Webster's Seventh New Collegiate Dictionary, G. & C. Merriman Co., Springfield, MA: 1965.

CHAPTER 4—THE BEAT

"Check Names on Challenged Sharon Petitions," the *Columbus Citizen*, September 29, 1954.

Campbell, Kenneth, "Annexation Poses Truro School Puzzle," the *Columbus Citizen*, March 27, 1954.

Campbell, Kenneth, "Evict Figure Called High," the *Columbus Citizen*, December 20, 1956.

Campbell, Kenneth, "He Proposed and She Said Yes—Only It Was Over 60 Years Later," the *Columbus Citizen*, January 7, 1954.

Campbell, Kenneth, "Map Accuracy Enters Annexation Struggle," the *Columbus Citizen*, June 6, 1954.

Campbell, Kenneth, "Mayor Takes Annexation Fight Direct to Township," the *Columbus Citizen*, April 14, 1954.

Campbell, Kenneth, "Says Annexation Means Prosperity," the *Columbus Citizen*, March 25, 1954.

Deeds, Betty Garrett, "Jack Sensenbrenner, A Straw Hat and Spizzerinctum," *Short North Gazette*, April, 2003.

Development Committee for Greater Columbus, "D-Day For Goodale," Annual Report, May, 1959.

Development Committee for Greater Columbus, "Relocation Housing Committee Report," Annual Report, May, 1958.

Sullivan, Katherine, "70 Families Face Bleak Christmas," the *Columbus Citizen*, December 13, 1956.

Woods, Jim, "Harrison W. Smith Jr., lawyer who helped guide Columbus' growth, dies at 83," the *Columbus Dispatch*, August 3, 2009.

CHAPTER 5—THE MARCH

Note: This chapter is drawn from unpublished letters cited below:

Alexander, Roy, Letter to Kenneth Campbell: June 12, 1959.

Breckenfeld, Gurney, Letter to Kenneth Campbell: January 18, 1961.

Campbell, Kenneth, Addendum to Application of Kenneth D. Campbell: A Fresh
    Perspective on the Record, January 9, 1961:

Campbell, Kenneth, Letters to Gurney Breckenfeld, *House & Home* Magazine:
    October 19, 1960; November 17, 1960; December 7, 1960; December
    12, 1960; December 20, 1960.

Campbell, Kenneth, Letters to John Titman, Time Inc. personnel: June 25, 1960;
    October 19, 1960; December 7, 1960.

Campbell, Kenneth, Letter to Steve Thompson, *Architectural Forum*: December
    7, 1960.

Campbell, Kenneth, Query replies to Lilley at Time Inc. correspondent desk re
    urbanization in Columbus, Ohio: November 29, 1956; January 14, 1957.

Campbell, Kenneth, TIME WORDS, compilation of unusual words used in *Time*
    Magazine from August 25, 1958 to May 18, 1959.

Titman, John, Letters to Kenneth Campbell: March 28, 1958; June 29, 1960;
    December 2, 1960.

Williamson, Ben, Letter to Kenneth Campbell: March 30, 1958.

CHAPTER 6—THE BREAK

"Prospects Fade for Syndicates," the *New York Times*, November 17, 1963.

"Transcript of Blough's News Conference on Price Increases by United States
    Steel," the *New York Times*, April 13, 1962.

Barron, James, "Robert C. Weaver, 89, First Black Cabinet Member, Dies," the
    New York Times, July 19, 1997.

Braestrup, Peter, "President Urges Vast Housing Aid to Combat Slump," the *New
    York Times*, March 10, 1961.

Carroll, Wallace, "Steel: A 72-Hour drama With an All-Star Cast," the *New York
    Times*, April 23, 1962.

Executive Order 11063, "Housing and Urban Development – Equal opportunity
    in housing," Executive Offices, the White House, November 20, 1962.

House & Home Magazine, "Round two: will the anti-bias order slow housing?"
    April 1963.

Thomas, Dana L., *Lords of the Land*, page 271, quoting William Zeckendorf; G.P.
    Putnam's Sons, New York: 1977.

Zeckendorf, William, with McCreary, Edward, *Zeckendorf: The Autobiography of William Zeckendorf*, pages 205, 214, 215, 220; Holt, Rinehart and Winston, New York; 1970.

CHAPTER 10—THE BOOK

Campbell, Kenneth, Editor and Principal Author, *The Real Estate Trusts: America's Newest Billionaires*: Audit Investment Research, Inc., New York: 1971.

Harman, William, Presentation to New York University class on REITs, edited transcript included in *The Real Estate Trusts: America's Newest Billionaires*: pages 239-247: Audit Investment Research, Inc., New York: 1971.

Joseph, Frederick, Presentation to New York University class on REITs, edited transcript included in *The Real Estate Trusts: America's Newest Billionaires*, pages 97-103: Audit Investment Research, Inc., New York: 1971.

Keidel, Albert R. Jr., Presentation of economics of Willowbrook Shopping Center, Wayne, NJ, to New York University class on REITs, edited transcript included in *The Real Estate Trusts: America's Newest Billionaires*: pages 22-26: Audit Investment Research, Inc., New York: 1971.

Oppenheimer, Martin J., Presentation to New York University class on REITs, edited transcript included in *The Real Estate Trusts: America's Newest Billionaires*: pages 163-164: Audit Investment Research, Inc., New York: 1971.

Rose, Cornelius C. Jr.,, Presentation to New York University class on REITs, edited transcript included in *The Real Estate Trusts: America's Newest Billionaires*: pages 106-115: Audit Investment Research, Inc., New York: 1971.

Taub, Merrill, Presentation to New York University class on REITs, edited transcript included in *The Real Estate Trusts: America's Newest Billionaires*: pages 156-161: Audit Investment Research, Inc., New York: 1971.

CHAPTER 12-THE MODS

Cole, Robert J., "U.S. Says Stirling Homex Reported Phantom Sales," the *New York Times*, July 3, 1975.

Laubasch, Arnold H., "Homex Fraud Trial of Five Under Way," the *New York Times*, December 24, 1976.

Laubasch, Arnold H., "Prison Sentences Pronounced for 4 at Stirling Homex," the *New York Times*, March 12, 1977.

"U.S. Jury Indicts 2 on Payoff Charges to 7 Union Officials," the *New York Times*, December 12, 1974.

CHAPTER 13—THE SELL

Abele, John J., "Continental Mortgage Sees Dip," the *New York Times*, November 18, 1971.

Abele, John J., "Real Estate Trusts Mauled by Bears," the *New York Times*, November 21, 1971.

Abele, John J., "Realty Trusts Split on Outlook," the *New York Times*, November 19, 1971.

Meyer, Priscilla S., "Major REIT Shakeout Looming," the *Wall Street Journal*, January 21, 1974.

Paine, Webber, Jackson & Curtis, Inc., Paine Webber Index, "Relative Price Information, pages 3 and 4," New York: Undated.

CHAPTER 14-THE GIFT

Campbell, Kenneth D., "Statement of Kenneth D. Campbell, President, Audit Investment Research, Inc., New York, to Committee on Banking, Housing and Urban Affairs, United States Senate," May 27, 1976.

CHAPTER 15—THE SEMINAR

Cohen, Sylvan M., as president of the National Association of Real Estate Investment Trusts, Letter to Director of Administration, Financial Accounting Standards Board, urging further study of the AICPA Statement of Position on accounting for receivables, June 30, 1975.

Lantier, Brian F., "Seminar Presentation and Answers to Questions," pages E-1 to E-13, *REIT's: What's Ahead*, transcript of seminar held June 6, 1975: Audit Investment Research, Inc., New York: 1975.

Miller, Harvey R., "Seminar Presentation, Answers to Questions and Associated Papers," pages C-1 to C-48, *REIT's: What's Ahead*, transcript of seminar held June 6, 1975: Audit Investment Research, Inc., New York: 1975.

Sonnenblick, Jack E., "Seminar Presentation and Answers to Questions," pages D-1 to D-12, *REIT's: What's Ahead*, transcript of seminar held June 6, 1975: Audit Investment Research, Inc., New York: 1975.

CHAPTER 16—THE INQUIRY

"Housing: Crunch Becomes Crush," Transcript of Appearance of Kenneth D. Campbell, President, Audit Investment Research, Inc.; Wall $treet Week #430, Maryland Center for Public Broadcasting, Baltimore, Maryland; February 21, 1975.

CHAPTER 17—THE LEMONADE

Astrology Insight website, "The Goat December 22 to January 20," Capricorn Page.

New Opportunities in Realty Trusts, Audit Investment Research, Inc., 296 pages, New York: 1978.

REITs, Their Banks and Bondholders, Audit Investment Research, Inc., 188 pages, New York: 1977.

CHAPTER 19—THE REIT CATCHERS

Batson, R. Neal, "Final Report of Examiner Neal Batson – Southmark Corporation--The Examiner's Perspective on How it Happened," July 15, 1990.

"Southmark Sues Milken Over Junk Bond Deals," Associated Press, July 13, 1991.

Starkman, Dean, "Real Estate Magnate Gene Phillips Draws Investor Ire for Dealings," the *Wall Street Journal*, February 16, 2001.

CHAPTER 20—THE BIGGEST WINNERS

Goldberger, Paul, "Settling the Suburban Frontier," the *New York Times*, December 31, 1995.

Zell, Sam, "The Grave Dancer," *Real Estate Review*, published by Warren, Gorham and Lamont: Vol. 5, No. 4, Winter: 1976.

CHAPTER 21—THE VALUE SEEKER

Wechsler, Steven A., "Letter to NAREIT Corporate Members Re: Earnings Guidance and Funds From Operations (FFO)," Washington, D.C.: September 24, 2014.

CHAPTER 22—THE BANKERS

"Agency Confirms Making Charges Against S&L Owner," the *Los Angeles Times*, January 22, 1987.

British Land of America ("BLA") and Medical Management of America ("MMA"), combined Proxy Statement and Prospectus for the transfer by BLA of all its real estate assets…other than BLA's interests in 90 Broad Street and 315 Park Avenue South, New York, New York, to MMA, and the payment by BLA of $4,653,000, subject to adjustment…for 4,500,000 newly issued shares of Common Stock…of MMA…: Dated August 26, 1988, for Special Meeting of Stockholders of BLA to be held September 22, 1988.

Desnick, Dr. James H., Unpublished email to Kenneth Campbell, July 8, 2015.

Granelli, James S. and Jane Applegate, "Fraud Inquiry Into Failed Santa Ana S&L Under Way," the *Los Angeles Times*, January 29, 1987.

Granelli, James S. and Mark Landsbaum, "Secrets Come to Light: Dead Banker's Past Reveals a Troubled Man," the *Los Angeles Times*, February 1, 1987.

Granelli, James S., "U.S. Regulators Sue Janet McKinzie in Collapse of S&L: FSLIC Accuses Her and Late Owner of Illegal Self-Dealing," the *Los Angeles Times*, February 12, 1987.

Medical Management of America, "Annual Report on Form 10-K Pursuant to Section 13 or 15(d) of the Securities Exchange Act of 1934, for the Fiscal Year Ended October 31, 1988.

Medical Management of America, "Annual Report on Form 10-K Pursuant to Section 13 or 15(d) of the Securities Exchange Act of 1934, for the Fiscal Year Ended October 31, 1989.

Medical Management of America, "Annual Report on Form 10-K Pursuant to Section 13 or 15(d) of the Securities Exchange Act of 1934, for the Fiscal Year Ended October 31, 1990.

Medical Management of America, Annual Report 1989.

OpenJurist website by Bailey & Galyen, Attorneys; summary of *J.H Desnick, M.D. Eye Services, Limited, et al, v. American Broadcasting Companies Incorporated*, Argued November 1, 1994 before United States Court of Appeals, Seventh District, Posner Chief Judge; Decided January 10, 1995.

Perez, Ray, "S&L Owner Didn't Commit Suicide, Associate Thinks," the *Los Angeles Times*, January 18, 1987.

Stevenson, Richard W., "Untangling a Savings Failure," the *New York Times*, June 30, 1988.

Woodyard, Chris, "4 Sentenced in Santa Ana S&L Failure," the *Los Angeles Times*, August 18, 1990.

CHAPTER 23—THE SURPRISES

Murphy, John, Unpublished emails to Kenneth Campbell, April 2, 2015; May 25, 2015.

CHAPTER 24—THE CLIENTS

Miller, Rusty, "Red Wings take 3-0 series lead," quoting Detroit Red Wings Coach Mike Babcock, Associated Press, April 22, 2009.

Ochoa-Brillembourg, Hilda, Unpublished email to Kenneth Campbell, dated July 30, 2015.

CHAPTER 26—THAT RAT HOLE

Martinez, Barbara, "Delicate REIT, How Thou Drive Me Nuts," the *Wall Street Journal*, February 9, 2000.

APPENDIX I—RUN-UP TO THE REIT REVOLUTION

"$958,878 Awarded Straus Investors on Fraud Claims," the *New York Times*, September 7, 1935.

"2 Magazines Lease in Chrysler Tower," the *New York Times*, September 5, 1931.

"52,000 Sq. Ft. in 42nd St. Leased to Rail Group," the *New York Times*, March 22, 1930.

"A Real Estate Exchange," the *New York Times*, September 13, 1883.

"Another Real estate Exchange—Organized by Men Who Have Left the Old Association," the *New York Times*, May 8, 1892.

"Asks More Reform in Realty Bonds," the *New York Times*, February 8, 1927.

"Asks New Receiver of S.W. Straus & Co.," the *New York Times*, March 22, 1933.

"Bankers Approve Realty Exchange," the *New York Times*, August 25,1929.

"Big Office Building Bonds are Offered," the *New York Times*, May 23, 1928.

"C. C. Miller Dies; Bronx Ex-Leader," the *New York Times*, January 23, 1956.

"Chrysler Building is on a Paying Basis," the *New York Times*, June 15, 1930.

"Chrysler Building Lease," the *New York Times*, October 30, 1929.

"Committees Named for Realty Exchange," the *New York Times*, February 23, 1930.

"Economists Praise Realty Exchange," the *New York Times*, September 1, 1929.

"Exchange Drops Registry," the *New York Times*, June 6, 1941.

"Exchange to Draw Short-Term Funds," the *New York Times*, September 8, 1929.

"Exchange to Sell Realty Securities," the *New York Times*, November 19, 1928.

"Explains Aim of Realty Exchange," the *New York Times*, February 3, 1929.

"Explains Attack on G. L. Miller & Co.," the *New York Times*, July 9, 1926.

"Large Lease Closed in Chrysler Building," the *New York Times*, May 27, 1932.

"Large Space Rented in Lincoln Building," the *New York Times*, May 11, 1930.

"Lifts Receivership of S.W. Straus & Co," the *New York Times*, October 22, 1932.

"Lincoln Building Brings $4,750,000," the *New York Times*, July 12, 1933.

"Mahoney Estate Auction," the *New York Times*, November 13, 1921.

"Mortgage Inquiry Opens Here Today," the *New York Times*, September 25, 1934.

"New Market for Real Estate Securities," the *New York Times*, March 17, 1929.

"Quits as Receiver of S.W. Straus & Co.," the *New York Times*, March 20, 1933.

"Realty Exchange Names Members," the *New York Times*, August 18, 1929.

"Realty Exchange Opening," the *New York Times*, November 21, 1929.

"Realty Exchange Opens for Trading," the *New York Times*, December 17,1929.

"Realty Exchange Opens Tomorrow," the *New York Times*, December 15, 1929.

"Realty Exchange Ready to Open Soon," the *New York Times*, February 5, 1929.

"Realty Exchange to Benefit Public," the *New York Times*, October 6, 1929.

"Realty Exchange Will Open Oct. 1," the *New York Times*, August 4, 1929.

"Realty Exchange Will Open Soon," the *New York Times*, December 2, 1928.

"Realty Men Launch Securities Market," the *New York Times*, August 1, 1929.

"Realty Securities," daily and/or weekly reports of NYRESE trading: May 7, 1931; May 8, 1931; May 9, 1931; May 13, 1931; June 3, 1931; June 6, 1931; June 11, 1931; June 16, 1931; June 25, 1931.

"Receiver is Named for G.L. Miller & Co. in Default on Loan," the *New York Times*, September 4, 1926.

"Rent in Chrysler Building," the *New York Times*, March 4, 1930.

"Rents Three Floors in Lincoln Building," the *New York Times*, April 18, 1930.

"Rivalry for Height is Seen as Ended," the *New York Times*, May 2, 1931.

"S.W. Straus & Co. Accepts Receiver," the *New York Times*, March 3, 1933.

"S.W. Straus & Co. Deny Bondholder Charges; Continental Bank Hits Rumor About Control," the *New York Times*, July 28, 1932.

"S.W. Straus & Co. Put Into a Receivership," the *New York Times*, October 8, 1932.

"S.W. Straus Dead; Banker Long Ill," the *New York Times*, September 8, 1930.

"Securities Exchange Marks New Era for Real Estate," the *New York Times*, December 8, 1929.

"Skyscraper Owner Asks Receivership," the *New York Times*, March 20, 1932.

"State to Broaden Mortgage Inquiry," the *New York Times*, September 5, 1935.

"Stock Financing Seen Aid to Realty," the *New York Times*, August 6, 1929.

"Straus & Co.'s Fall Detailed in Court," the *New York Times*, March 22, 1935.

"To Commence Work on Lincoln Building," the *New York Times*, June 3, 1928.

"Wide Scope for Realty Exchange," the *New York Times*, February 10, 1929.

"Will Watch Value of Realty Stocks," the *New York Times*, August 11, 1929.

Alden, The, website. Property description May 2015, attributed to Carol E. Levy of Carol E. Levy Real Estate.

Byrt, Frank, 2010, National Bureau of Economic Research, separate one-page digest of *Securitization in the 1920s* by Goetzmann, William N. and Newman, Frank; "The Digest is not copyrighted and may be reproduced freely with appropriate attribution of source."

Goetzmann,William N. and Newman, Frank, *"Securitization in the 1920s,"* Working Paper 15650, National Bureau of Economic Research; 2010.

Grant, James, *Money of the Mind*, Farrar Straus Gioux, New York: 1992.

Johnson, Ernest A., 1936. *The Record of Long-Term Real Estate Securities, The Journal of Land & Public Utility Economics*, University of Wisconsin Press, Vol. 12, No. 1: February 1936, pages 44-48.

Miller, Cyrus C., 1930. *"An Organized Real Estate Securities Exchange,"* Annals of the American Academy of Political and Social Science, Vol. 148, Part 1: March 1930: pages 26-32:

Real Estate Board of New York (REBNY), Annual Report 1996.

StreetEasy, website, recent property transactions at The Alden "Copyright 2015 StreetEasy. All rights reserved."

INDEX

CPSIA information can be obtained at www.ICGtesting.com
Printed in the USA
BVOW02*1451290116

434497BV00001B/1/P

9 781480 823143